VIDEO NIGHT in KATHMANDU

ALFRED A. KNOPF

NEW YORK

1988

Pico Iyer

VIDEO NIGHT in KATHMANDU

AND OTHER REPORTS FROM THE NOT-SO-FAR-EAST

To my mother and father,

Guides, guardians and friends

THIS IS A BORZOI BOOK

PUBLISHED BY ALFRED A. KNOPF, INC.

Library of Congress Cataloging-in-Publication Data
Iyer, Pico.
    Video night in Kathmandu.
    1. Asia – Description and travel – 1951-
2. East and West.   3. Iyer, Pico – Journeys – Asia.
I. Title.
DS10.I87   1988   950'.42   88-2781
ISBN 0-394-55027-7

Manufactured in the United States of America
First Edition

CONTENTS

LOVE MATCH   3

BALI: On Prospero's Isle   29

TIBET: The Underground Overland Invasion   59

NEPAL: The Quest Becomes a Trek   77

CHINA: The Door Swings Both Ways   103

THE PHILIPPINES: Born in the U.S.A.   151

BURMA: The Raj Is Dead! Long Live the Raj!   195

HONG KONG: The Empire's New Clothes   221

INDIA: Hollywood in the Fifties   241

THAILAND: Love in a Duty-free Zone   287

JAPAN: Perfect Strangers   317

The Empire Strikes Back   357

Acknowledgments   375

VIDEO NIGHT in KATHMANDU

Wind in the west,
fallen leaves
gathering in the east.

> *— Buson*

All tourist people are my bread and butter. So I
need to help everything as I could. If I do not
help them, they will never forgive me because I
fully understand their love or sincerity. I don't
have enough money, but I need to pay their
gratitude at one day.

> *— The credo of Maung-Maung,*
> *trishaw driver,*
> *chalked up on a blackboard inside*
> *his hut in Mandalay*

Love Match

R AMBO HAD conquered Asia. In China, a million people raced to see *First Blood* within ten days of its Beijing opening, and black marketeers were hawking tickets at seven times the official price. In India, five separate remakes of the American hit went instantly into production, one of them recasting the macho superman as a sari-clad woman. In Thailand, fifteen-foot cutouts of the avenging demon towered over the lobbies of some of the ten Bangkok cinemas in which the movie was playing, training their machine guns on all who passed. And in Indonesia, the Rambo Amusement Arcade was going great guns, while vendors along the streets offered posters of no one but the nation's three leading deities: President Suharto, Siva and Stallone.

As I crisscrossed Asia in the fall of 1985, every cinema that I visited for ten straight weeks featured a Stallone extravaganza. In Chengdu, I heard John Rambo mumble his *First Blood* truisms in sullen, machine-gun Mandarin and saw the audience break into tut-tuts of headshaking admiration as our hero kerpowed seven cops in a single scene. In Jogjakarta, I went to *Rambo* on the same night as the *Ramayana* (though the modern divinity was watched by hosts of young couples, stately ladies in sarongs and bright-eyed little scamps, many of whom had paid the equivalent of two months' salary for their seats, while, on the other side of town, the replaying of the ancient myth remained virtually unvisited). Just five days later, I took an overnight bus across Java, and, soon enough, the video screen next to the driver crackled into life and there—who else?—was the Italian Stallion, reasserting his Dionysian beliefs against Apollo Creed. As the final credits began to roll, my neighbor, a soldier just returned from putting down rebels in the jungles of East Timor, sat back with a satisfied sigh. "That," he pronounced aptly, "was very fantastic."

Silencing soldiers, toppling systems, conquering millions and making money fist over fist across the continent, Rambo was unrivaled as the most powerful force in Asia that autumn. "No man, no law, no woman can stop him," gasped the ads in the Bangkok papers. "Everyone Is Applauding Screen's Most Invincible Hero," agreed one of the three ads on a single page of India's respected *Statesman*. "The Second Greatest U.S. Box Office Hit in History," roared the marquee in faraway Sabah. "I think he's very beautiful," cooed a twenty-three-year-old Chinese girl to a foreign reporter. "So vigorous and so graceful. Is he married?"

Rambo had also, I knew, shattered box-office records everywhere from Beirut to San Salvador. But there seemed a particular justice in his capturing of Asian hearts and minds. For Rambo's great mission, after all, was to reverse the course of history and, single-fisted, to redress America's military losses in the theaters of Asia. And in a way, of course, the movie's revisionism had done exactly that, succeeding where the American army had failed, and winning over an entire continent. Some of the appeal of the blockhead-buster lay, no doubt, in its presentation of a kung fu spectacular more professional than the local efforts and more polished than the competing displays of Norris and Bronson. Some might just have reflected the after-tremors of its earthshaking reception in the States. But whatever the cause of the drama's success, the effect was undeniable: millions of Asians were taking as their role model an All-American mercenary. When William Broyles returned to his old battlegrounds in Vietnam in 1984, he found the locals jiving along to "Born in the U.S.A.," Bruce Springsteen's anthem for the disenfranchised Vietnam vet, and greeting him with cries of "America Number One!" "America," concluded Broyles, "is going to be much more difficult to defeat in this battle than we were in the others. Our clothes, our language, our movies and our music—our way of life—are far more powerful than our bombs."

The prospect of witnessing that low-intensity conflict was one of the impulses that took me first to Asia. Over the course of two years, I spent a total of seven months crisscrossing the continent on four separate trips, mostly in order to see its sights, but also in order to visit the front lines of this cultural campaign. I was interested to find out how America's pop-cultural imperialism spread through the world's most ancient civilizations. I wanted to see what kind of resistance had been put up against the Coca-Colonizing forces and what kind of counter-strategies were planned. And I hoped to discover which Americas got through to the other side of the world, and which got lost in translation.

This contest for cultural sovereignty was nothing new, of course. Colonel Sanders and General Motors had first set up base camps across the global village years ago, and America's Ambassador-at-Large throughout the world had long been the retired World War I flying ace Snoopy. Fifteen years before the first American troops showed up, Norman Lewis described families in Saigon listening respectfully to a local rendition of "When Irish Eyes Are Smiling." And fully a quarter century ago, Arthur Koestler had stated as a given that the world was moving toward "a uniform, mechanized, stereotyped culture," a mass culture that struck him as a form of mass suicide. The syllogism was old enough now to be almost an axiom: pop culture ruled the world, and America ruled pop culture. Thus America ruled the waves— or at the very least, the airwaves.

In recent years, however, the takeover had radically intensified and rapidly accelerated. For one thing, satellites were now beaming images of America across the globe faster than a speeding bullet; the explosion of video had sent history spinning like the wheels of an overturned bicycle. For another, as the world grew smaller and ever smaller, so too did its props: not only had distances in time and space been shrunk, but the latest weapons of cultural warfare—videos, cassettes and computer disks—were far more portable than the big screens and heavy instruments of a decade before. They could be smuggled through border checkpoints, under barbed-wire fences and into distant homes as easily, almost, as a whim. In the cultural campaign, the equivalent of germ warfare had replaced that of heavy-tank assaults.

Suddenly, then, America could be found uncensored in even the world's most closed societies, intact in even its most distant corners. Peasants in China or the Soviet Union could now enjoy images of swimming pools, shopping malls and the other star-spangled pleasures of the Affluent Society inside their own living rooms; remote villagers in rural Burma could now applaud Rambo's larger-than-life heroics only days after they hit the screens of Wisconsin; and the Little House on the Prairie was now a part of the neighborhood in 108 countries around the world.

More important, the video revolution was bringing home the power of the Pax Americana home with greater allure and immediacy than even the most cunning propaganda. Already, the ruling mullahs in Iran were fretting that their capital's newly formed clandestine Michael Jackson clubs could easily turn into revolutionary cells. And I once heard one of Washington's most senior foreign policy veterans privately maintain that the single issue that most exercised the Soviets was not the nuclear arms race, or the war of espionage, or Afghanistan or Nicaragua or Cuba, or even the rising confidence of China, but simply the resistless penetration of video.

In 1985, another influence was also carrying American dollars and dreams to every corner of the world with more force and more urgency than ever before: people. Tourists were the great foot soldiers of the new invasion; tourists, in a sense, were the terrorists of cultural expansionism, what Sartre once called "the cool invaders." Scarcely forty years ago, most of the world's secret places were known only to adventurers, soldiers, missionaries and a few enterprising traders; in recent years, however, the secrets were open, and so too was the world—anyone with a credit card could become a lay colonialist. Nepal, which had never seen a tourist until 1955, now welcomed 200,000 foreign visitors each year; China, which had rigidly closed its doors for decades, had 11,000 tourists a day clambering along the Great Wall by 1985. The road to Mandalay and even the road to Xanadu were crowded now with Westerners—men in search of women, dreamers in search of enlightenment, traders in search of riches. In 1985, many Asians considered the single great import from the West, after Rambo, to be AIDS.

Not all the incoming forces, of course, were American. Mick Jagger was as much the poet laureate of the modern world as Michael Jackson, and Sophie Marceau vied with Phoebe Cates as the poster queen of Southeast Asia. If Springsteen turned out to be my unexpected traveling companion across the continent, so too did the British group Dire Straits: their latest album greeted me in a tiny inn in Hiroshima, then blasted my eardrums from a car in Beijing, then wafted over me in the soft tropical night of a Balinese guesthouse, then serenaded me once more in the Kathmandu home of a local Lothario. And the back roads of Asia were far more crowded with Canadians and Germans and Australians than with Americans. But still, when it came to movies and TV, the United States remained the Great Communicator. And if pop culture was, in effect, just a shorthand for all that was young and modern and rich and free, it was also a virtual synonym for America.

Everywhere, in fact, dreams of pleasure and profit were stamped "Made in America." Cities from San Salvador to Singapore turned themselves into bright imitations of Californian, not Parisian or Liverpudlian, suburbs; Garfield, not Tintin, had become the alter ego of millions of Germans and Japanese; and it was not the yen or the Deutschemark that had become the universal currency, but the dollar, even—no, especially—in the Communist bloc. The hymn of the East Side, as well as the West, was still "I Want to Live in America."

This kind of influence was not by any means stronger or more pervasive in Asia than elsewhere in the developing world. Yet of all the fronts on which the battle was being waged, Asia seemed to be the fiercest and most complex. Asia, after all, had been the site of the world's most vexed and various colonial struggles, and Asia was also the theater for most of America's recent military confrontations. Asia was also increasingly mounting a formidable counterattack upon the long-unquestioned economic domination of the West, and Asia now included three out of four of all the world's souls. Asia, above all, seemed home to most of history's oldest and subtlest cultures. How, I wondered, would proud, traditionalist societies founded on a sense of family and community respond to the Fighting Machine's grunting individualism and back-to-basics primitivism? How would developing nations deal with refugees from affluence, voluntary dropouts from the Promised Land? And what would decorous Buddhists make of the crucifix-swinging Madonna?

Asia also appealed to me because it was unmatched in its heterogeneity; in China, Japan and India alone, the continent had three great traditions as deep as they were diverse. Texts read us as much as we do them, and in the different ways that different cultures responded to forces from the West, I hoped to see something of their different characters and priorities.

Rambo again proved illustrative. In China, the very showing of the film had advertised a new cultural openness to the West, even as the black-market chicanery it set off betrayed some of the less happy foreign influences streaming in through the open door; ideologically, the movie served both as political propaganda (confirming the Chinese in their belief that the Vietnamese were devious swine) and as a subject for earnest self-criticism, dialectically worked out in the letter columns of the *China Daily.* In India, the movie had been seized upon by the quick-witted moguls of the world's largest film industry and swiftly redesigned to fit the mythic contours of Indian formula fantasy; yet its heroic success had also set off bouts of typical Indian philosophizing—even a newspaper ad couched its come-on in a kind of marveling rumination: "No sex, no romance, no lady character, yet constantly patronized by Male and Female. The RAMBO syndrome."

In the Philippines, the movie had passed, like so much American cultural debris, into the very language and mythology of the country, blurring even further the country's always uncertain division between politics and show biz: onetime Defense Minister Juan Ponce Enrile was wont to represent himself, on posters and in threats, as a kind of homegrown Rambo. And in Vietnam, to complete the circle, this latest version of the war had, inevitably, become an instrument of propaganda: the Vietnamese accused Ronald Reagan of trying to "Ramboize" the youth of

America, hardly mentioning the more unsettling fact that Rambo was "Reaganizing" the youth of all the world.

AS I DRIFTED out of the theater where I had seen *Rambo*, and into the warm Indonesian night, only one line from the movie really stayed with me. The hero's boss, Colonel Trautman, had been discussing the maverick naked ape with the heartless Washington bureaucrat Murdock. "What you choose to call hell," he had said of his explosive charge, "he calls home." However inadvertently, that sentence suggested many of the other ideas that first sent me East: that home has nothing to do with hearth, and everything to do with a state of mind; that one man's home may be his compatriot's exile; that home is, finally, not the physical place, but the role and the self we choose to occupy.

I went to Asia, then, not only to see Asia, but also to see America, from a different vantage point and with new eyes. I left one kind of home to find another: to discover what resided in me and where I resided most fully, and so to better appreciate—in both senses of the word—the home I had left. The point was made best by one great traveler who saw the world without ever leaving home, and, indeed, created a home that was a world within—Thoreau: "Our journeying is a great-circle sailing."

To travel across the globe simply to locate the facilities of the place one has quit would, of course, be an elaborate exercise in perversity. Only those who travel for business, and nothing more, would really wish to ask the questions addressed by Anne Tyler's Accidental Tourist: "What restaurants in Tokyo offered Sweet 'n Low? Did Amsterdam have a McDonald's? Did Mexico City have a Taco Bell? Did any place in Rome serve Chef Boyardee ravioli? Other travelers hoped to discover distinctive local wines; Macon's readers searched for pasteurized and homogenized milk." Pasteurized and homogenized cultures are not what take us abroad. Yet, at the same time, many a traveler knows that the Temple of the Golden Arches and the Palace of the Burger King never seem so appealing as when one is searching for a regular meal in the back streets of Kyoto. And Father *Time* never seems so authoritative, or so agreeably familiar, as when one is yearning for news in the mountains of Tibet.

If the great horror of traveling is that the foreign can come to seem drearily familiar, the happy surprise of traveling is that the familiar can come to seem wondrously exotic. Abroad, we are not ourselves; and as the normal and the novel are transposed, the very things that we might shun at home are touched with the glamour of the exotic. I had never seen, or wished to see, a Burt Reynolds movie until I found myself stuck in a miserable guesthouse in Bandar Sari Begawan; I had never been to a Dunkin' Donuts parlor until I decided to treat myself after a hard day's work in Bangkok. I enjoyed my first ever Yorkie bar in Surabaya (and my second there too, a few minutes later). And my first experience of the Emmy Awards came in the darkened lobby of a run-down hotel in Singapore, where the ceremonies were annotated, with beery profanities, by a gang of tattooed European and Australian sailors who broke off from their lusty commentary only when a French or Filipina trollop drifted barefoot through the room and out into the monsoony night.

While I was in Asia, I made ritual pilgrimages to the Taj Mahal, Pagan and Borobudur; I climbed live volcanoes in the dead of the Javanese night and rode elephants through the jungles of Nepal. I spent nights in an Indonesian hut, where my roommates consisted of two pack rats, a lizard and a family-size cockroach, and other nights in a Mogul palace on a lake, where I sat for hours on the marbled roof, watching the silver of moon on water. In Bali, I witnessed a rare and sumptuous cremation, and in Kyoto, I saw the unearthly Daimonji Festival, when all the town is lit with lanterns to guide departed spirits home. None of this, however, is recorded in the pages that follow, partly because all of it has gone on, and will go on, one hopes, for centuries, and partly because such familiar marvels may be better described by travelers more observant than myself.

More than such postcard wonders, however, what interested me were the brand-new kinds of exotica thrown up by our synthetic age, the novel cultural hybrids peculiar to the tag end of the twentieth century. "Travel itself," observes Paul Fussell in *Abroad*, "even the most commonplace, is an implicit quest for anomaly," and the most remarkable anomalies in the global village today are surely those created by willy-nilly collisions and collusions between East and West: the local bands in socialist Burma that play note-perfect versions of the Doors' "L.A. Woman," in Burmese; the American tenpin bowling alley that is the latest nighttime hot spot in Beijing; the Baskin-Robbins imitation in Hiroshima that sells "vegetable" ice cream in such flavors as mugwort, soy milk, sweet potato and "marron"; or the bespectacled transvestite in Singapore who, when asked to name the best restaurant in a town justly celebrated for its unique combination of Chinese, Indian and Malaysian delicacies, answers, without a moment's hesitation, "Denny's."

I wanted also, while I was in Asia, to see how America was regarded and reconstituted abroad, to measure the country by the shadow it casts. Much of the world, inevitably, looks to its richest industrial nation for promiscuous images of power and affluence; abroad, as at home, the land of Chuck Bronson and Harold Robbins will always command a greater following than that of Emerson and Terrence Malick. Often, in fact, the America one sees around the globe seems as loud and crass and overweight as the caricatured American tourist. And just as celebrities pander to the images they foster, acting out our dreams of what they ought to be, so America often caters to the world's image of America, cranking out slick and inexpensive products made almost exclusively for foreign consumption—in Jogjakarta, the cinema that was not showing *Rambo* offered *The Earthling*, with Ricky Schroder and William Holden, and *Dead and Buried*, starring Melody Anderson and James Farentino.

Yet America also projects a more promising and more hopeful image around the world, as a culture of success stories and of the youthful excesses that may accompany them. Lee Iacocca's memoirs are devoured far more eagerly from Rio to Riyadh than those of Akio Morita or Giovanni Agnelli, and George Washington is a folk hero in many Asian classrooms in a way that George III will never be. The most popular contemporary American writer in the very different markets of France and West Germany is Charles Bukowski, the disheveled boho laureate of booze and broads in low-life L.A. In the world's collective popular imagination, America the Beautiful stands next to America the Technicolor Dreamcoast.

This division in itself is hardly unique: every culture casts conflicting images before the world. We associate India with desperate poverty and maharajah opulence, Britain with punks and patricians. But in the case of America, subject of so many daydreams and ideals, so intensely felt and so eagerly pursued, the contradictions are even more pronounced: for not only is the country's political power enormous, but it is matched—and sometimes opposed—by its cultural influence. When Reagan speaks, the world listens; yet Springsteen is shouting the opposite message in the other ear. While Congress sends money to the contras, the global village tunes in to Jackson Browne.

And if the image of America is perplexingly double-edged, the responses it provokes in many parts of the globe are appropriately fork-tongued: with one breath, they shout, "Yankee Go Home," and with the next, "America Number One!" "In the Third World," writes Michael Howard, "anti-Americanism is almost a *lingua franca.*" Yet in the Third World, a hunger for American culture is almost taken for granted, and "making it" often means nothing more than making it to the Land of the Free. The Communist guerrillas in the Philippines fight capitalism while wearing UCLA T-shirts. The Sandinista leaders in Nicaragua wage war against "U.S. Imperialism" while watching prime-time American TV on private satellite dishes. And many whites in South Africa cling to apartheid, yet cannot get enough of Bill Cosby, Eddie Murphy and Mr. T.

All these contradictions are further exacerbated by one simple but inevitable fact: the disproportion between America's formidable power around the globe and the much more modest presence of individual Americans abroad. "We think of the United States," writes Octavio Paz, on behalf of all Latin Americans, "simultaneously, and without contradiction, as Goliath, Polyphemus and Pantagruel." Yet that daunting weight falls upon the shoulders of the small and decidedly unmythic traveler, tourist or expatriate. Around the world, S. J. Perelman noted, the American occupies "the curious dual role of skinflint and sucker, the usurer bent on exacting his pound of flesh and the hapless pigeon whose poke was a challenge to any smart grifter." The incongruity applies equally, of course, to the Russians abroad, as it did to the Englishman, the Chinese and all the other imperialists of the past. But in the case of America, at once so ubiquitous and so many-headed throughout the world, the schizophrenia seems especially charged. If Bruce Springsteen is not Reagan, still less is that backpacking social worker from Tacoma. Again and again in my travels, I had been asked, by Greeks, Nicaraguans and Moroccans, how the American government could be such a ruthless a bully, while the American people seemed so friendly, good-natured and warm. I went to Asia in part to find out.

II

To mention, however faintly, the West's cultural assault on the East is, inevitably, to draw dangerously close to the fashionable belief that the First World is corrupting the Third. And to accept that AIDS and Rambo are the two great "Western" exports of 1985 is to encourage some all too easy conclusions: that the West's main contributions to the rest of the world are sex and violence, a cureless disease and a killer cure; that America is exporting nothing but a literal kind of infection and a bloody sort of indoctrination. In place of physical imperialism, we often assert a kind of sentimental colonialism that would replace Rambo myths with Sambo myths and conclude that because the First World feels guilty, the Third World must be innocent— what Pascal Bruckner refers to as "compassion as contempt."

This, however, I find simplistic—both because corruption often says most about those who detect it and because the developing world may often have good reason to assent in its own transformation.

This is not to deny that the First World has indeed inflicted much damage on the Third, especially through the inhuman calculations of geopolitics. If power corrupts, superpowers are super-corrupting, and the past decade alone has seen each of the major powers destroy a self-contained Asian culture by dragging it into the cross fire of the Real World: Tibet was invaded for strategic reasons by the Chinese, and now the dreamed-of Shangri-La is almost lost forever; Afghanistan was overrun by Soviet tanks, and now the Michauds' photographic record of its fugitive beauties must be subtitled, with appropriate melancholy, "Paradise Lost"; Cambodia, once so gentle a land that cyclo drivers were said to tip their passengers, fell into the sights of Washington and is now just a land of corpses.

On an individual level too, Western tourists invariably visit destruction on the places they visit, descending in droves on some "authentic Eastern village" until only two things are certain: it is neither Eastern nor authentic. Each passing season (and each passing tourist) brings new developments to the forgotten places of the world—and in a never-never land, every development is a change for the worse. In search of a lovely simplicity, Westerners saddle the East with complexities; in search of peace, they bring agitation. As soon as Arcadia is seen as a potential commodity, amenities spring up on every side to meet outsiders' needs, and paradise is not so much lost as remaindered. In Asia alone, Bali, Tahiti, Sri Lanka and Nepal have already been so taken over by Paradise stores, Paradise hotels and Paradise cafés that they sometimes seem less like utopias than packaged imitations of utopia; Ladakh, Tibet and Ko Samui may one day follow. No man, they say, is an island; in the age of international travel, not even an island can remain an island for long.

Like every tourist, moreover, I found myself spreading corruption even as I decried it. In northern Thailand, I joined a friend in giving hill tribesmen tutorials in the songs of Sam Cooke until a young Thai girl was breaking the silence of the jungle with a piercing refrain of "She was sixteen, too young to love, and I was too young to know." In China, I gave a local boy eager for some English-language reading matter a copy of the only novel I had on hand—Gore Vidal's strenuously perverse *Duluth*. And in a faraway hill station in Burma, a group of cheery black marketeers treated me to tea and I, in return, taught them the words "lesbian" and "skin flicks," with which they seemed much pleased.

Yet that in itself betrays some of the paradoxes that haunt our talk of corruption. For often, the denizens of the place we call paradise long for nothing so much as news of that "real paradise" across the seas—the concrete metropolis of skyscrapers and burger joints. And often what we call corruption, they might be inclined to call progress or profit. As tourists, we have reason to hope that the quaint anachronism we have discovered will always remain "unspoiled," as fixed as a museum piece for our inspection. It is perilous, however, to assume that its inhabitants will long for the same. Indeed, a kind of imperial arrogance underlies the very assumption that the people of the developing world should be happier without the TVs and motorbikes that we find so indispensable ourselves. If money does not buy happiness, neither does poverty.

In other ways too, our laments for lost paradises may really have much more to do with our own state of mind than with the state of the place whose decline we mourn. Whenever we recall the places we have seen, we tend to observe them in the late afternoon glow of nostalgia, after memory, the mind's great cosmetician, has softened out rough edges, smoothed out imperfections and removed the whole to a lovely abstract distance. Just as a good man, once dead, is remembered as a saint, so a pleasant place, once quit, is recalled as a utopia. Nothing is ever what it used to be.

IF THE FIRST World is not invariably corrupting the Third, we are sometimes apt to leap to the opposite conclusion: that the Third World, in fact, is hustling the First. As tourists, moreover, we are so bombarded with importunities from a variety of locals —girls who live off their bodies and touts who live off their wits, merchants who use friendship to lure us into their stores and "students" who attach themselves to us in order to improve their English—that we begin to regard ourselves as beleaguered innocents and those we meet as shameless predators.

To do so, however, is to ignore the great asymmetry that governs every meeting between tourist and local: that we are there by choice and they largely by circumstance; that we are traveling in the spirit of pleasure, adventure and romance, while they are mired in the more urgent business of trying to survive; and that we, often courted by the government, enjoy a kind of unofficial diplomatic immunity, which gives us all the perks of authority and none of the perils of responsibility, while they must stake their hopes on every potential transaction.

Descending upon native lands quite literally from the heavens, *dei ex machinae* from an alien world of affluence, we understandably strike many locals in much the same way that movie stars strike us. And just as some of us are wont to accost a celebrity glimpsed by chance at a restaurant, so many people in developing countries may be tempted to do anything and everything possible to come into contact with the free-moving visitors from abroad and their world of distant glamour. They have nothing to lose in approaching a foreigner—at worst, they will merely be insulted or pushed away. And they have everything to gain: a memory, a conversation, an old copy of *Paris Match*, perhaps even a friendship or a job opportunity. Every foreigner is a messenger from a world of dreams.

"Do you know Beverly Hills?" I was once asked by a young Burmese boy who had just spent nine months in jail for trying to escape his closed motherland. "Do you know Hollywood? Las Vegas? The Potomac, I think, is very famous. Am I right? Detroit, Michigan, is where they make cars. Ford. General Motors. Chevrolet. Do you know Howard Hughes? There are many Jewish people in New York. Am I right? And also at *Time* magazine? Am I right?" Tell us about life behind the scenes, we ask the star, and which is the best place in the whole wide world, and what is Liz Taylor really like.

The touts that accost us are nearly always, to be sure, worldly pragmatists. But they are also, in many cases, wistful dreamers, whose hopes are not so different from the ones our culture encourages: to slough off straitened circumstances and set up a new life and a new self abroad, underwritten by hard work and dedication. American dreams are strongest in the hearts of those who have seen America only in their dreams.

I first met Maung-Maung as I stumbled off a sixteen-hour third-class overnight train from Rangoon to Mandalay. He was standing outside the station, waiting to pick up tourists; a scrawny fellow in his late twenties, with a sailor's cap, a beard, a torn white shirt above his *longyi* and an open, rough-hewn face—a typical tout, in short. Beside him stood his bicycle trishaw. On one side was painted the legend "My Life"; on the other, "B.Sc. (Maths)."

We haggled for a few minutes. Then Maung-Maung smilingly persuaded me to part with a somewhat inflated fare—twenty cents—for the trip across town, and together we began cruising through the wide, sunny boulevards of the city of kings. As we set off, we began to exchange the usual questions—age, place of birth, marital status and education—and before long we found that our answers often jibed. Soon, indeed, the conversation was proceeding swimmingly. A little while into our talk, my driver, while carefully steering his trishaw with one hand, sank the other into his pocket and handed back to me a piece of jade. I admired it dutifully, then extended it back in his direction. "No," he said. "This is present."

Where, I instantly wondered, was the catch—was he framing me, or bribing me, or cunningly putting me in his debt? What was the small print? What did he want?

"I want you," said Maung-Maung, "to have something so you can always remember me. Also, so you can always have happy memories of Mandalay." I did not know how to respond. "You see," he went on, "if I love other people, they will love me. It is like Newton's law, or Archimedes."

This was not what I had expected. "I think," he added, "it is always good to apply physics to life."

That I did not doubt. But still I was somewhat taken aback. "Did you study physics at school?"

"No, I study physics in college. You see, I am graduate from University of Mandalay—B.Sc. Mathematics." He waved with pride at the inscription on the side of his trishaw.

"And you completed all your studies?"

"Yes. B.Sc. Mathematics."

"Then why are you working in this kind of job?"

"Other jobs are difficult. You see, here in Burma, a teacher earns only two hundred fifty kyats [$30] in a month. Managing director has only one thousand kyats [$125]. Even President makes only four thousand kyats [$500]. For me, I do not make much money. But in this job, I can meet tourist and improve my English. Experience, I believe, is the best teacher."

"But surely you could earn much more just by driving a horse cart?"

"I am Buddhist," Maung-Maung reminded me gently, as he went pedaling calmly through the streets. "I do not want to inflict harm on any living creature. If I hit horse in this life, in next life I come back as horse."

"So"—I was still skeptical—"you live off tourists instead?"

"Yes," he said, turning around to give me a smile. My irony, it seems, was wasted. "Until two years ago, in my village in Shan States, I had never seen a tourist."

"Never?"

"Only in movies." Again he smiled back at me.

I was still trying to puzzle out why a university graduate would be content with such a humble job when Maung-Maung, as he pedaled, reached into the basket perched in front of his handlebars and pulled out a thick leather book. Looking ahead as he steered, he handed it back to me to read. Reluctantly, I opened it, bracing myself for porno postcards or other illicit souvenirs. Inside, however, was nothing but a series of black-and-white snapshots. Every one of them had been painstakingly annotated in English: "My Headmaster," "My Monk," "My Brothers and Sisters," "My Friend's Girlfriend." And his own girlfriend? "I had picture before. But after she broke my heart, and fall in love with other people, I tear it out."

At the very back of his book, in textbook English, Maung-Maung had carefully inscribed the principles by which he lived.

1) Abstain from violence.
2) Abstain from illicit sexual intercourse.
3) Abstain from intoxicants of all kinds.
4) Always be helpful.
5) Always be kind.

"It must be hard," I said dryly, "to stick to all these rules."

"Yes. It is not always easy," he confessed. "But I must try. If people ask me for food, my monk tell me, I must always give them money. But if they want money for playing cards, I must give them no help. My monk also explain I must always give forgiveness—even to people who hurt me. If you put air into volleyball and throw it against wall, it bounces back. But if you do not put in air, what happens? It collapses against wall."

Faith, in short, was its own vindication.

I was now beginning to suspect that I would find no more engaging guide to Mandalay than Maung-Maung, so I asked him if he would agree to show me around. "Yes, thank you very much. But first, please, I would like you to see my home."

Ah, I thought, here comes the setup. Once I'm in his house, far from the center of a city I don't know, he will drop a drug in my tea or pull out a knife or even bring in a few accomplices. I will find out too late that his friendliness is only a means to an end.

Maung-Maung did nothing to dispel these suspicions as he pedaled the trishaw off the main street and we began to pass through dirty alleyways, down narrow lanes of run-down shacks. At last we pulled up before a hut, fronted with weeds. Smiling proudly, he got off and asked me to enter.

There was not much to see inside his tiny room. There was a cot, on which sat a young man, his head buried in his hands.

There was another cot, on which Maung-Maung invited me to sit as he introduced me to his roommate. The only other piece of furniture was a blackboard in a corner on which my host had written out the statement reproduced in the epigraph to this book, expressing his lifelong pledge to be of service to tourists.

I sat down, not sure what was meant to happen next. For a few minutes, we made desultory conversation. His home, Maung-Maung explained, cost 30 kyats ($4) a month. This other man was also a university graduate, but he had no job: every night, he got drunk. Then, after a few moments of reflection, my host reached down to the floor next to his bed and picked up what I took to be his two most valuable belongings.

Solemnly, he handed the first of them to me. It was a sociology textbook from Australia. Its title was *Life in Modern America*. Then, as gently as if it were his Bible, Maung-Maung passed across the other volume, a dusty old English-Burmese dictionary, its yellowed pages falling from their covers. "Every night," he explained, "after I am finished on trishaw, I come here and read this. Also, every word I do not know I look up." Inside the front cover, he had copied out a few specimen sentences. *If you do this, you may end up in jail. My heart is lacerated by what you said. What a lark.*

I was touched by his show of trust. But I also felt as uncertain as an actor walking through a play he hasn't read. Perhaps, I said a little uneasily, we should go now, so we can be sure of seeing all the sights of Mandalay before sundown. "Do not worry," Maung-Maung assured me with a quiet smile, "we will see everything. I know how long the trip will take. But first, please, I would like you to see this."

Reaching under his bed, he pulled out what was clearly his most precious treasure of all. With a mixture of shyness and pride, he handed over a thick black notebook. I looked at the cover for markings and, finding none, opened it up. Inside, placed in alphabetical order, was every single letter he had ever received from a foreign visitor. Every one was meticulously dated and annotated; many were accompanied by handwritten testimonials or reminiscences from the tourists Maung-Maung had met. On some pages, he had affixed wrinkled passport photos of his foreign visitors by which he could remember them.

Toward the end of the book, Maung-Maung had composed a

two-page essay, laboriously inscribed in neat and grammatical English, called "Guide to Jewelry." It was followed by two further monographs, "For You" and "For the Tourists." In them, Maung-Maung warned visitors against "twisty characters," explained something of the history and beauty of Mandalay and told his readers not to trust him until he had proved worthy of their trust.

Made quiet by this labor of love, I looked up. "This must have taken you a long time to write."

"Yes," he replied with a bashful smile. "I have to look many times at dictionary. But it is my pleasure to help tourists."

I went back to flipping through the book. At the very end of the volume, carefully copied out, was a final four-page essay, entitled "My Life."

He had grown up, Maung-Maung wrote, in a small village, the eldest of ten children. His mother had never learned to read, and feeling that her disability made her "blind," she was determined that her children go to school. It was not easy, because his father was a farmer and earned only 300 kyats a month. Still, Maung-Maung, as the eldest, was able to complete his education at the local school.

When he finished, he told his parents that he wanted to go to university. Sorrowfully, they told him that they could not afford it—they had given him all they had for his schooling. He knew that was true, but still he was set on continuing his studies. "I have hand. I have head. I have legs," he told them. "I wish to stand on my own legs." With that, he left his village and went to Mandalay. Deeply wounded by his desertion, his parents did not speak to him for a year.

In Mandalay, Maung-Maung's narrative continued, he had begun to finance his studies by digging holes—he got 4 kyats for every hole. Then he got a job cleaning clothes. Then he went to a monastery and washed dishes and clothes in exchange for board and lodging. Finally, he took a night job as a trishaw driver.

When they heard of that, his parents were shocked. "They think I go with prostitutes. Everyone looks down on trishaw driver. Also other trishaw drivers hate me because I am a student. I do not want to quarrel with them. But I do not like it when they say dirty things or go with prostitutes." Nevertheless, after graduation Maung-Maung decided to pay 7 kyats a day to

rent a trishaw full-time. Sometimes, he wrote, he made less than
1 kyat a day, and many nights he slept in his vehicle in the hope of
catching the first tourists of the day. He was a poor man, he went
on, but he made more money than his father. Most important, he
made many friends. And through riding his trishaw he had
begun to learn English.

His dream, Maung-Maung's essay concluded, was to buy his
own trishaw. But that cost four hundred dollars. And his greatest
dream was, one day, to get a "Further Certificate" in mathematics. He had already planned the details of that far-off moment
when he could invite his parents to his graduation. "I must hire
taxi. I must buy English suit. I must pay for my parents to come
to Mandalay. I know that it is expensive, but I want to express
my gratitude to my parents. They are my lovers."

When I finished the essay, Maung-Maung smiled back his
gratitude, and gave me a tour of the city as he had promised.

THE AMERICAN EMPIRE in the East: that was my grand theme
as I set forth. But as soon as I left the realm of abstract labels and
generalized forces, and came down to individuals—to myself,
Maung-Maung and many others like him—the easy contrasts
began to grow confused. If cultures are only individuals writ
large, as Salman Rushdie and Gabriel García Márquez have
suggested, individuals are small cultures in themselves. Everyone is familiar with the slogan of Kipling's "Oh, East is East, and
West is West, and never the twain shall meet." But few recall that
the lines that conclude the refrain, just a few syllables later,
exclaim, "But there is neither East nor West, border, nor breed,
nor birth, / When two strong men stand face to face, though
they come from the ends of the earth!"

On a grand collective level, the encounters between East and
West might well be interpreted as a battle; but on the human
level, the meeting more closely resembled a mating dance (even
Rambo, while waging war against the Vietnamese, had fallen in
love with a Vietnamese girl). Whenever a Westerner meets an
Easterner, each is to some extent confronted with the unknown.
And the unknown is at once an enticement and a challenge; it
awakens in us both the lover and the would-be conqueror. When
Westerner meets Easterner, therefore, each finds himself often
drawn to the other, yet mystified; each projects his romantic

hopes on the stranger, as well as his designs; and each pursues both his illusions and his vested interests with a curious mix of innocence and calculation that shifts with every step.

Everywhere I went in Asia, I came upon variations on this same uncertain pattern: in the streets of China, where locals half woo, half recoil from Westerners whose ways remain alien but whose goods are now irresistible; in the country-and-western bars of Manila, where former conqueror and former conquest slow-dance cheek to cheek with an affection, and a guilt, born of longtime familiarity; in the high places of the Himalayas, where affluent Westerners eager to slough off their riches in order to find religion meet local wise men so poor that they have made of riches a religion; and, most vividly of all, in the darkened bars of Bangkok, where a Western man and a Thai girl exchange shy questions and tentative glances, neither knowing whether either is after love or something else. Sometimes, the romance seemed like a blind date, sometimes like a passionate attachment; sometimes like a back-street coupling, sometimes like the rhyme of kindred spirits. Always, though, it made any talk of winners and losers irrelevant.

Usually, too, the cross-cultural affairs developed with all the contradictory twists and turns of any romance in which opposites attract and then retract and then don't know exactly where they stand. The Westerner is drawn to the tradition of the Easterner, and almost covets his knowledge of suffering, but what attracts the Easterner to the West is exactly the opposite—his future, and his freedom from all hardship. After a while, each starts to become more like the other, and somewhat less like the person the other seeks. The New Yorker disappoints the locals by turning into a barefoot ascetic dressed in bangles and beads, while the Nepali peasant frustrates his foreign supplicants by turning out to be a traveling salesman in Levi's and Madonna T-shirt. Soon, neither is quite the person he was, or the one the other wanted. The upshot is confusion. "You cannot have pineapple for breakfast," a Thai waitress once admonished me. "Why?" I asked. "What do *you* have for breakfast?" "Hot dog."

It is never hard, in such skewed exchanges, to find silliness and self-delusion. "Everybody thought that everybody else was ridiculously exotic," writes Gita Mehta of East-West relations in *Karma Cola*, "and everybody got it wrong." Yet Mehta's cold-eyed perspective does justice to only one aspect of this encounter. For the rest, I prefer to listen to her wise and very different compatriot, R. K. Narayan, whose typical tale "God and the Cobbler" describes a chance meeting in a crowded Indian street between a Western hippie and a village cobbler. Each, absurdly, takes the other to be a god. Yet the beauty of their folly is that each, lifted by the other's faith, surprises himself, and us, by somehow rising to the challenge and proving worthy of the trust he has mistakenly inspired: each, taken out of himself, becomes, not a god perhaps, but something better than a dupe or fraud. Faith becomes its own vindication. And at the story's end, each leaves the other with a kind of benediction, the more valuable because untypical.

Every trip we take deposits us at the same forking of the paths: it can be a shortcut to alienation—removed from our home and distanced from our immediate surroundings, we can afford to be contemptuous of both; or it can be a voyage into renewal, as, leaving our selves and pasts at home and traveling light, we recover our innocence abroad. Abroad, we are all Titanias, so bedazzled by strangeness that we comically mistake asses for beauties; but away from home, we can also be Mirandas, so new to the world that our blind faith can become a kind of higher sight. "After living in Asia," John Krich quotes an old hand as saying, "you trust nobody, but you believe everything." At the same time, as Edmond Taylor wrote, Asia is "the school of doubt in which one learns faith in man." If every journey makes us wiser about the world, it also returns us to a sort of childhood. In alien parts, we speak more simply, in our own or some other language, move more freely, unencumbered by the histories that we carry around at home, and look more excitedly, with eyes of wonder. And if every trip worth taking is both a tragedy and a comedy, rich with melodrama and farce, it is also, at its heart, a love story. The romance with the foreign must certainly be leavened with a spirit of keen and unillusioned realism; but it must also be observed with a measure of faith.

III

Let me add, finally, a few words of explanation about what I did while traveling, and what I have tried to do while writing. I make no claim to be authoritative about the places I visited. Quite the opposite, in fact. I spent no more than a few weeks in each country, I speak not a word of any of their languages and I have never formally studied any Asian culture. Nor did I try— except in India and Japan—to consult local experts (a job best left to other experts). Punditry comes expensively enough at home; abroad, it was well beyond my reach. Entire books have been written on even the smallest of my themes, and if I had even tried to keep up with all the literature that comes out every week on China or the Philippines or Japan, I would never have found the time to write a paragraph myself.

Instead, I let myself be led by circumstance. Serendipity was my tour guide, assisted by caprice. Instead of seeking out information, I let it find me. I did not bend my plans to look for examples of the Western presence, or to bolster any argument. I simply read those books or articles that chanced to come my way and listened to the rickshaw drivers, strangers and fellow travelers I happened to meet on the road. Most of my intelligence, in fact, came from the kind of locals that a tourist is likely to meet—touts and tarts and black marketeers, cabbies, storekeepers and hotel workers. Such characters are hardly typical of their countries; but they are, in many ways, representative of the side of the country that the visitor sees.

What results, then, is just a casual traveler's casual observations, a series of first impressions and second thoughts loosely arranged around a few broad ideas. The only special qualification I can bring to my subject, perhaps, is a boyhood that schooled me in expatriation. For more than a decade while I was growing up, I spent eight months a year at boarding school in England and four months at home in California—in an Indian household. As a British subject, an American resident and an Indian citizen, I quickly became accustomed to cross-cultural anomalies and the mixed feelings of exile. Nowhere was home, and everywhere. Thus, for example, when I was seventeen, I spent a long summer traveling around India, returned to England in the autumn for a final term at school, devoted my winter to working as a busboy in a Mexican restaurant in Southern California and then spent the spring traveling by bus with a school friend from San Diego through Central America and across Colombia, Ecuador and Peru to Bolivia, before hopping back to

Miami through Brazil, Suriname and the West Indies, and Grey-
hounding back to the West Coast. Once home, I started up the
cycle again. A little later, I spent two summers careering around
Europe writing guidebooks on France, Greece, Italy and Britain,
and from there I embarked upon a four-year stint of writing on
World Affairs for *Time*. I do not know whether such experiences
sharpened my instincts for traveling, but I hope that they taught
me a little about how much to trust, and when to doubt, first
impressions.

THE READER WILL notice too that this book is patterned less
like a conventional travel diary than a series of essays. Each
chapter, moreover, is structured to reflect not a physical but a
mental itinerary—it follows, that is, not the chronological
sequence of my movements so much as the twists and turns of
my thoughts as I tried to make sense of the places I saw. Occasionally, of course—as when I visited a country just once—the
two coincide. But in most cases, I revisited a place in different
seasons and different moods—sometimes as many as six times
—and spaced out my trips in order to give both the countries and
myself a chance to change. In addition to my experiences, I
therefore include all the other factors that guide one's feelings
for a place—one's expectations before arriving, one's thoughts
while leaving and, most important, one's reflections in all those
stray hours at home when a place comes back from afar and one
tries and tries to puzzle it out. The final destination of any
journey is not, after all, the last item on the agenda, but rather
some understanding, however simple or provisional, of what
one has seen.

To some extent, of course, this treatment forgoes some of the
jolts and intensities and pangs of one's experiences. I acknowledge that loss, and feel it. In trying to sight-read a place as if it
were a text, one can easily fall into pretension, as well as pre-
sumption, and in recollecting it in tranquillity, one can dampen
or even distort one's essential feelings: a reader might not guess
from the following pages that the country of my dreams is still
Japan.

Yet it seemed to me that the vivid day-to-day account of a
journey through Asia, with all its momentary impulses, emotions and excitements, had already been written, and rather well.

Readers who wish to savor adventures in the hidden East, recorded with a worldly shrewdness that makes their moments of surrender all the more affecting, can turn to Peter Fleming or Norman Lewis or Robert Byron; those who want a clever and quick-witted jaunt through the Asia of the seventies will find few better companions than Paul Theroux or John Krich; those who seek sensitive and passionate guides to embattled areas of the spirit can visit Ladakh with Andrew Harvey, or Tibet with John Avedon; and those who like to watch the irresistible triumph of sensibility over substance are hereby advised to return, and return again, to S. J. Perelman's incomparable *Westward Ha!*.

I, however, have tried to take a slightly different tack; rather than showing how one personality acts in different places, I have sought to show how different places act on one personality. For just as we are different people with a mother, a lover, a teacher, a priest, a salesman and a beggar, so we are to some extent assigned different roles by the countries we visit. This may in part be the result of personal circumstance: in one country I found myself an American journalist, in another a former British schoolboy, in yet another a homecoming Indian relative and in a fourth a plain tourist. It may also have to do with the place's circumstances: in all of Tibet, I found only a handful of locals who could speak English, while in India, there are tens of millions of fluent and loquacious locals more than eager to have their say. But it is also true that places to some extent remake us, recast us in their own images, and the selves they awaken may tell us as much about them as about ourselves. "To survive a war," as Rambo says in a rather different context, "you've got to become a war." Thus in Thailand, though a teetotaler, I spent most of my evenings in bars, and in Tibet, though not a Buddhist, I devoted all my days to the quiet of mountaintop lamaseries. In Japan, where a foreigner seems always to be an outsider, I found myself turning slightly Japanese—aloof, efficient and lyrical; while in the Philippines, where every visitor is a participant whether he likes it or not, I tended to become as earnest and unguarded as the people I met.

Logistically too, I tried to stay protean. Those Grand Tourists who follow what might be called the Hiltercontinental circuit, allowing themselves to be whisked from one air-conditioned coach to the next and transported from four-star Hyatt to five-star Hyatt, are likely to experience little of the foreign world they have allegedly come to observe; yet the low-budget traveler who would rather sleep on a bench and eat stale grass than pay 50 cents for the bourgeois comforts of an inn imposes on himself a different kind of tunnel vision. For my part, I tried to commute between the two worlds, slumming it in style as I moved between hovel and hotel. In Thailand, I spent a few nights at the $150-a-night Oriental Hotel, said to be the finest such palace in the world, and a few other nights on the floor of lightless huts in the animist villages of the north (though mostly I stayed in a modest $10-a-night apartment building somewhere between the two); in Tokyo, I sampled both a Holiday Inn and the cheapest *minshuku* in the city, an inn with cells so tiny that it was impossible for me to stand up inside my "room" and possible to enter only by crawling headfirst through a screen door. Likewise, taxi alternated with bullock cart, Amex café with filthy roadside stall. Burma I circumnavigated once by plane, and once by army truck, horse-drawn cart and third-class train. And nearly everywhere, I traveled alone, in order to give myself the space to think and the chance to meet strangers.

The chapters that follow fall into three rough groups, progressively more complex. The first four are all fairly simple and straightforward discussions of the most basic kinds of meeting between East and West along the tourist trail, and the different forms they take in two places relatively new to the trade (Tibet and China) and two old pros (Bali and Nepal). The next three chapters explore in a little more detail some of the forms of Empire still to be found in the East: the legacy of American cultural colonialism in the Philippines; faded remnants of British rule, curiously preserved in isolationist Burma; and, in Hong Kong, the first outlines of the multinational empire that seems likely to rule the generic world of tomorrow. The final three chapters, the longest and most complicated, try to look more deeply into some of the East's deepest cultures—India, Thailand and Japan—by examining one specific aspect of the way they adopt, and adapt to, Western influences, and make them distinctively their own.

At times, I am sure, ignorance has conspired with wistfulness to make me blind to the obvious and receptive to the specious.

When first I went to Bali, for example, I was so transported by its luxuriant sense of magic that I took the mosquito coils placed each night in my room for sticks of holy incense, and mistook the smell of clove cigarettes for the scent of some exotic flower. Though I was disabused of both illusions when I returned to the island the following year, many other such misconceptions doubtless remain. Still, mistakes can, in their way, be as revealing as epiphanies, and even a wrong impression may say as much about a place as a right one. If Bali had not been so full of real magic, my false assumptions would, no doubt, have been very different. And wide eyes are, if nothing else, quite open.

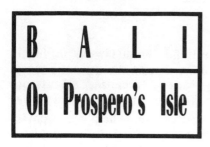

BALI
On Prospero's Isle

I HAD COME
into town the previous afternoon watching video reruns of
Dance Fever on the local bus. As I wandered around, looking for
a place to stay, I had noted down the names of a few of the stores:
the Hey Shop. The Hello Shop. Easy Rider Travel Service. T.G.I.
Friday restaurant. And after checking into a modest guesthouse
where Vivaldi was pumping out of an enormous ghetto blaster, I
had gone out in search of a meal. I ran across a pizzeria, a sushi
bar, a steak house, a Swiss restaurant and a slew of stylish
Mexican cafés. Eventually, however, I wound up at T.J.'s, a
hyper-chic fern bar, where long-legged young blondes in tropical
T-shirts were sitting on wicker chairs and sipping tall cocktails.
Reggae music floated through the place as a pretty waitress
brought me my corn chips and salsa.

After dinner, I had made my way to a nearby café for a
cappuccino. Next to the cash register were enough stacks of old
copies of *Cosmo*, *Newsweek* and the London Sunday *Times* to
fill six doctors' waiting rooms. Behind the counter was a

backgammon set for customers and a homemade library of faded paperbacks—Erica Jong, Ken Follett, Alexandra Penney. From Casablanca, the showy, two-story singles bar across the street, Bruce Springsteen was belting out "Dancing in the Dark." Hungry-eyed girls in tiny skirts were cruising the place in pairs, while muscular guys with gold medallions dangling across their bronzed chests perched on the balcony, drinking beer.

After an unquiet sleep, I had woken up and walked around the three or four square blocks of the town. Most of the stores seemed to be trendy boutiques, across whose windows were splashed New Wave Japanese T-shirts and pretty sundresses in *Miami Vice* turquoise and pink. Surfaris. Tropical Climax. Cherry. Mariko. *An American Werewolf in London* was playing at the local cinema. The Narnia. Frenchy. Pancho's. The Pub. A few Men at Work songs were pouring out of cassette stores opened to the street, only to be drowned out by the roar of Suzukis erratically ridden by local boys in leopardskin shirts. Fatty. The Beer Garden. Depot Viva. The Duck Nuts. "Marijuana and hashish," whispered one man to me. "Hashish and cocaine," muttered his friend. Joe's. Lenny. Jerry. Elly's. Elice's. I walked back to my guesthouse—Van Morrison had now replaced Vivaldi on the system—and a couple of the boys there invited me to sit down over some guacamole and give them my opinion of Michael Landon and John McEnroe.

I was, of course, in Bali, the Elysian isle famous for its otherworldly exoticism, its cultural integrity, its natural grace.

SAY BALI, AND two things come to mind: tourism and paradise. Both are inalienable features of the island, and also incompatible. For as fast as paradises seduce tourists, tourists reduce paradises. Such are the unerring laws of physics: what goes up must come down; for every action there is an equal and opposite reaction. Hardly has a last paradise been discovered than everyone converges on it so fast that it quickly becomes a paradise lost.

Nowhere, however, had this struggle been so protracted or intense as in Bali, most pestered and most paradisiacal of islands. The first Westerners ever to land here, Dutch sailors in 1597, announced their discovery of Eden, and two of them decided never to leave. By 1619, Balinese girls were already fetching 150 florins in the slave markets of Réunion and by 1847, the first tract in the fertile field of Baliology was already being brought into print. And for more than half a century now, Bali had been perhaps the world's best-kept idyll and its worst-kept secret: a race of charmed spirits still danced in its temples, and a crush of foreigners kept pushing their way in for a view. Tourism hung around Bali like chains around a mermaid.

The animist Hindus who grace the island regard all of life as a battle between the spirits of light and darkness, and nearly every native dance plays out this unending elemental struggle in the form of a celebration or an exorcism. But Bali had also become the world's most popular stage for a subtler battle, and a less ethereal dance—between the colonizing impulse of the West and the resistant cultural heritage of the East. Like Prospero's isle, Bali was a kind of paradise crowded with wood nymphs and cave-hidden spirits. Like Prospero's isle, it was governed by a race of noblemen, artisans and priests that had been chased into exile across the seas. And like Prospero's isle, it was now being threatened by a new mob of aliens, who found themselves charmed by its virgin goddesses, made sleep-heavy by its unearthly music. Bali had thus become the magical setting on which the two forces were deciding destinies larger than their own: could Ariel, airy spirit and agent of the gods, disarm Antonio, worldly and usurping Duke of Milan, before it was too late?

Like Prospero's isle too, Bali offered all the amenities of Eden. Its regally graceful people dwelt in a lush Rousseauesque garden of snakes and tropical flowers. Young girls, careless of their loveliness, bathed in running streams, wore scarlet hibiscus in their hair and silken sarongs around their supple bodies; the soft-eyed local men seemed likewise gods of good health, dazzling smiles offsetting the flowers they tucked behind their ears. In Bali, even old women were slender creatures who moved with a dancer's easy grace. There was no friction in this land of song and dance, and nothing unlovely: children, taken to be angels of purity descended from the heavens, were never scolded or spanked, crime was unknown and even cremations were opulent festivals of joy. Nature had been charmed by Art. Everything was at peace.

In Bali, indeed, life itself, and everything in it, was taken to be sacrament and dance. The Balinese traditionally had no particular conception of "art," since every villager wove or danced or painted as a matter of course; every house, moreover, had its own shrine, and every village had three temples, open to the heavens and wrapped in white and golden sashes. Every day, as I arose, bare-shouldered women in sumptuous silks were sashaying through the early morning sunlight, stately and unhurried, piles of fruit on their heads to be placed as offerings before the gods. And every night, in village courtyards, radiant little girls, in gorgeous gold brocades, white blossoms garlanding the hair that fell to their waists, swayed together out of the darkness, their eyes rolling, twisting their hands like sorcerers, moving as one to the gongs and cymbals of the spellbinding gamelan. Like Prospero's isle, Bali was "full of noises, sounds and sweet airs . . . a thousand twangling instruments."

And the beauty, and the curse, of Bali was that a piece of this paradise was available to everyone who entered. For $2 a night, I was given my own thatched hut in a tropical courtyard scented with flowers and fruit. Each sunny morning, as I sat on my veranda, a smiling young girl brought me bowls of mangoes and tea, and placed scarlet bougainvillaeas on the gargoyle above my lintel. Two minutes away was the palm-fringed beach of my fantasies; an hour's drive, and I was climbing active volcanoes set among verdant terraces of rice. Along the sleepy village lanes, garden restaurants served tropical drinks and magic mushrooms, while a hundred stores offered giddy T-shirts, sixties paintings and cassettes galore. And all around were dances, silken ceremonies and, in a place scarcely bigger than Delaware, as many as 30,000 temples.

Thus the paradox remained: Bali was heaven, and hell was other people. Tourism had become the island's principal detraction. And the specter of commercialism shadowed every visitor from his first step to his last: one might debate the issue or demean it, but one could not ignore it. Sightseers were inclined not to say that Bali was beautiful or terrible, only that it had been raped or was still intact. " 'Isn't Bali spoiled?' is invariably the question that greets the returned traveler . . . meaning, is the island overrun by tourists?" wrote Miguel Covarrubias. He had written that in 1937. "This nation of artists is faced with a Western invasion, and I cannot stand idly by and watch its destruction," wrote André Roosevelt, in his introduction to a book on Bali, entitled (what else?) *The Last Paradise.* He had written that in 1930.

And after fifty years of such anxieties, Bali had, inevitably, become a paradise traduced by many tourists, the place that sophisticates hated to love: many of my British friends would rather have vacationed in Calais or Hull than submit to what they regarded as the traveler's ultimate cliché. Even those who adored the island found it more and more trying. For if it is the first vanity, and goal, of every traveler to come upon his own private pocket of perfection, it is his second vanity, and goal, to shut the door behind him. Paradise is a deserted island or a solitary glade. Bali, however, was a common paradise, a collective find and, as such, an insult to the imagination. For years, the island had swarmed with crowds desperate to get away from the crowds. "The thing I hate about Bali," an American in Hong Kong told me, "is that everyone on the island is American or Australian, but every one of them is ignoring all the others and pretending that he's the only foreigner who's discovered the place."

Yet still Bali remained unavoidable and irresistible. And what distinguished it most from its rivals for the Pyrrhic distinction of the world's loveliest paradise island—what set it apart from Mustique or Ios or even Tahiti—was the variety of its enticements. Bali had something for everyone. Some people traveled to pamper themselves, some to enjoy themselves, some to improve themselves; all of them came to Bali. And all of them, whether sun worshipper, antique collector or truth seeker, were guaranteed absolute satisfaction. For though the Indonesian government had wisely stuck by the Dutch policy of "Bali for the Balinese" and permitted tourists only in the eastern half of the island—the west remained virtually impenetrable—there was still a wealth of guidebook riches to be found here: pamphlet-perfect surf and sand for the beach bum; five-star resorts for the sybarite; myths and rituals in abundance for the culture vulture.

Through a miracle of convenience, moreover, the separate needs of the separate species of *Homo touristicus* were satisfied in three separate areas, located within a twenty-mile radius of one another. Along the western side of the super-developed southern peninsula was Kuta Beach, once a major rest stop for hippie gypsies on their way from Kathmandu to Cuzco, and now primarily a holiday camp for Australian surfers and their blondes; on the other side of the peninsula—ten miles, and a thousand worlds, away—was Sanur Beach, a strip of concrete, luxury hotels set along the sea, the Waikiki or Cannes of the East, where the international set came out to play; and at the apex of the compact triangle, set in the heart of Bali's magical middle kingdom, was the hillside village of Ubud, where trendy visitors came to study the native culture and foreign artists set up home and shop.

Even more conveniently, tourism in Bali was remarkably seg-regated. No self-respecting self-styled student of the local culture would ever be caught dead inside the discos and juice bars of Kuta, while few of the musclemen on the beach had time for the festivals and galleries of Ubud; both groups scorned the Sanur life they could not afford, and the Sanur settlers looked down on the basic conditions of Kuta and Ubud, which they found uncomfortably close to those of the Balinese they so admired. And everyone, in all three areas, shunned Denpasar, the noisy, traffic-choked town at the middle of the triangle, which had the unenviable task of underwriting the pleasures of Eden with practical facilities.

Thus Ferdinand and Antonio and Gonzalo all drifted around the enchanted island, each in his own private dream, each largely unaware of the others' proximity, all watched only by their invisible hosts.

II

Bali's most famous tourist community—cursed and coveted around the world—was Kuta. Fifteen years ago, the quiet fishing village had been the cheap utopia of bohemians in quest of rural hangouts and vegetable highs; watching a psychedelic sunset at Kuta was said to be almost as good as seeing Jerry Garcia at the Fillmore West or conversing with Buddha on a Himalayan mountaintop. And fifteen years ago, there had been only two restaurants in the area. The first hotel in Kuta had opened only in 1959; by now, however, the area was pockmarked with more than three hundred *losmens*, or guesthouses. Bali, in fact, had become for Australians what Greece is for many Europeans, the Bahamas for New Yorkers and Hawaii for those in the Far West—the most convenient paradise island on their doorsteps. Every day brought planeloads of pleasure-loving Aussies streaming into Kuta, fresh from the streets of Perth or Darwin.

And a kind of Darwinian devolution had, so it seemed, been the result. For most of these visitors were not, as a rule, the kind of visitor whose pleasures were subtle or understated: they were mostly straight-ahead, no-nonsense blokes, bikers and surfers and bruisers and boozers who were rough and ready for fun. All they wanted were some basic good times—great waves, cheap beer, pretty girls. Thus Kuta had become their raucous home from home, a boisterous playground for piss-ups and pick-ups and rave-ups. Sure, Prospero's isle might be full of angels and artists, but it also had room for some drunken Stephanos and Trinculos.

So "Captain Good Vibes" stickers had been spattered across many of the village surfaces, and Perth badges attached to many a local breast. Koalas and kangaroos peered out of shirts and shelves, and around the tiny desk in my guesthouse, the Lasi Erawati, the number of surfing decals totaled 170. The most popular T-shirt in town said "No, I don't want a F——ing Bemo/Postcard/Massage/Jiggy Jig."

A glossy photo in my five-year-old guidebook cited Doggies restaurant as an "Antique setting: the only place with a Disco." By now, however, Doggies itself was an antique, since almost every place had a disco. And one local bar offered "Aussie-style steaks," another "special Aussie H'Burger with the lot." One sign promised "Suci's Aussie Breakfast" and another "Waltzing Maltilda Sarongs." "Real Cheese and Vegemite Sandwich Eating Competitions" were held at Casablanca, and "Bintang Beer and Coke Drinking Contests" at Madé's Tavern. The drinks in the pubs were called, at their most delicate, "Bali Kiss" and "Love Potion" and "Dirty Mother." And the second most popular T-shirt in town announced "Bloody Good Tucker: Kuta, Bali."

Kuta, then, had all the rowdiness, and all the unacknowledged sadness, of every beachfront holiday camp jam-packed with people looking around for the good time they had promised themselves; it had all the skin-peeling bustle of Cape Cod in the summer, say, or Corfu, or Cancún. In Kuta, red-faced couples held hands, touched sunburned knees under the table, asked the waiter to take pictures of them in their tans, lost themselves in long kisses on the streets. This was fun time, the visitors said, and the first thing to do was break all the rules—native customs or no. Get drunk. Get high. Get laid. This was such stuff as dreams are made on.

In its most exalted state, Bali had long been renowned as a place for falling in love. A local boy who wished to capture the heart of a maiden would traditionally turn to witchery, collecting from a shaman a moon coin or an amulet or a love potion compounded of the saliva of a snake and the tears of a child. Another might stare all night into the flame of a coconut lamp on which he had imprinted the image of his beloved. Even casual visitors to the island often found themselves entranced here, caught in one of those Shakespearean zones of magic in which young romantics lose their heads, and later their hearts, and stumble, by the light of an uncertain moon, into the presence of a divinity. I first got wind of this when an English friend of mine visited Bali for a brief vacation, and fell, almost instantly, into the arms of a German, with whom she enjoyed a fantasy week of love in thatched cottages and postcard sunsets on the beach. I myself met a shining Pre-Raphaelite from Munich who seemed to be moving under a similar spell, and came back each year in memory of her first and finest boy friend, a gentle Indonesian. And almost every foreign writer on the island, from Hickman Powell to Jacques Chegaray, had, sooner or later, found himself playing Ferdinand to some enchanted nine-year-old Miranda, recording his worship in flowery prose and sunstruck diction. On my very first night in Bali, as I watched the sun drop into the sea, an Indonesian girl came up, and sat down beside me, and said, not glibly, but with an eerie, penetrating intensity, "I had a dream last night. I found two flowers and put one of them in my hair. That flower was you."

Most of the midsummer night's dreams in Kuta, however, were a good deal more down-to-earth. Every evening, the place looked like Duval Street in Key West on a Saturday night, or Santa Barbara's lower State. For as soon as the sun went down, all the beautiful people came out of the woodwork to trawl—beefy men with sunglasses propped up in their hair, freshly turned blondes in halter tops and miniskirts. Here, it seemed, was the poor man's Club Med. In one café, a tall sandy-haired guy was zeroing in on an English girl just off the bus, and telling her that he was an artist who lived in the hills; she might find it interesting to look at his canvases. In the snackbar of my *losmen*, two good-looking rogues just released from a British public school were agreeing to meet up with a pair of *jeunes filles* from Paris. Inside Madé's Warung (today's special: French pâté), a bearded hipster was saying to a girl from Santa Cruz, "You stay in Kuta? You know, if ever you have any problems, I've got a bungalow . . ."

And though Balinese girls still had about them a faint air of *noli me tangere*, the local boys were fully welcomed into the Bacchanalian roundelay. In Sex Pistols T-shirts and Mohawk cuts they whizzed through the narrow streets on unmuffled motorbikes. At Wayan's Tavern, a leather-jacketed local biker slouched up to the bar with one Australian mama on each arm, while a curly-haired Italian girl in a *Vogue* T-shirt sauntered off into the night with a cigarette in one hand and a Balinese boy in the other. Along one dusty Kuta lane, a small space had even been set up for longhairs to strum listless guitars under posters of Mick Jagger and share their smokes (for a price) with foreigners, the whole crowd of them looking red-eyed and vaguely poleaxed. The third most popular T-shirt in Kuta said "Bullshit. I had a ball in Bali."

IF FOREIGN VISITORS had turned Kuta into a free-for-all Aussie singles bar, they had turned Sanur into a luxury retirement home. In Kuta, the guesthouses were bandaged with surfing decals; in Sanur, the shops in the sunny hotel arcades were decorated only with the reassuring blue-and-white badges of American Express. In Kuta, it was the locals who sported T-shirts that said "Maui" and "California"; in Sanur, it was the tourists.

Once famous for its priests and demons, Sanur had been among the first of Bali's areas to be colonized: both Margaret Mead and the German painter Walter Spies had lived here once upon a time. These days, however, the most famous sojourners in Sanur were Mick Jagger and Magic Johnson. Sanur, in fact, had been turned into one of those super-costly super-resorts where guests could get away from it all—Bali included. It was one of those pieces of exotic property where tourists could close their eyes to the world, and pretend that they, or it, no longer existed. The prototype of all the sky-scraping pleasure palaces was the ten-story Bali Beach Hotel, set a ten-minute walk from the main road, down a sweeping, beautifully landscaped driveway. In its quiet green gardens, *Hausfrauen* lay on deck chairs, copies of *Stern* and *Der Spiegel* protecting their faces from the sun.

One bright morning, I spent several hours trespassing on the hotel's private beach, lost in a transcendent stillness. There was not a single vendor as far as the eye could see. Not even a single surfer. No bathers in the beautiful, surfless blue. Nothing, in fact. Just two thatched umbrellas, the ocean and me. Sanur was one of those yawning resorts by the side of the sea where nobody actually enters the water because the hotel swimming pool is a few yards closer.

Naturally, the hotels in Sanur did consent to make a few concessions to their surroundings. The staff wore sarongs, sugarcane juice was served at the poolside bar, statues of tutelary deities were set among the trees. But the Bali Beach Hotel had the quiet discretion of a well-trained servant; it took pains not to intrude on its master's daydreams. And it took every precaution to ensure that he wouldn't miss home. "A holiday in Sanur," said an Australian travel brochure, "allows the freedom to sample the various styles of cuisine and freedom developed in response to the demands of international tourism." Customers, in other words, were given the luxury of imagining themselves in Jamaica, the Costa Smeralda or Cap d'Antibes: discos, nightclubs, twenty-four-hour coffee shops were as de rigueur in the super-structures of Sanur as the lizards and mosquitoes that came free of charge with every room in Kuta. Sanur was the place for people who wished to travel 6,000 miles in order to lie down, take dips in a pool and enjoy a good burger any time of day or night.

Best of all, the Sanur-toriums ensured that their guests need never leave their premises. The Bali Beach Hotel provided a tenpin bowling alley, three swimming pools, a mini golf course and a regular eighteen-hole course (even though the village already boasted a course set inside a volcano that had been named one of the top fifty courses in the world). It also had two stages for the performance of nightly dances so that guests need not leave the grounds in search of native culture; the native culture would come in search of them. The hotel also went out of its way to sympathize with the needs of the Balinese; its Cultural Department still organized tours around the grounds for awe-struck local villagers.

THOSE WHO WERE set on finding "the real Bali," however, forsook the beaches of both Kuta and Sanur and flocked together off the beaten track to Ubud. Here hotels were set among the rice paddies, and restaurants built atop dreamy lotus ponds. Ubud had a Frank Lloyd Wright house, and shops with names like Tantra, Arjuna, Yoga and Nirvana. In Kuta, the used-book stores were stocked with Harold Robbins and John Jakes; in Ubud, they were bursting with Huxley, Wilde, Castaneda and Anaïs Nin. And the visitors in the Ubud streets were chipper sexagenarians, Pan-like boys with headbands around their black curls, well-preserved Century City executives in sarongs with pretty young companions by their side and French women in their late thirties in search of something exotic. Ubud was one beautifully designed gift shop with wind chimes all around.

Ubud was also the capital of the so-called Theater State, Bali's government of, for and by the imagination. For years it had been the haunt of Bali's artists from abroad and at home; the Dutch painters Hans Snell and Arie Smit had put down their roots in this tropical Big Sur many years ago and, more recently, the place had attracted such contemporary heroes of the arts as Iggy Pop and David Bowie (not to mention, as the ad for one hotel eccentrically boasted, Koo Stark). Electricity had come to Ubud only in 1975, but, within a decade, the place had filled up with artists' cooperatives run by craftsmen from Switzerland and New Age settlers from Seattle. Ubud was the place where students of Bali came to learn the gamelan or master the steps of the *legong* dance or acquire some other precious talent that would go down well back home in Marin.

The minute I arrived in Ubud and got off my *bemo* (the small pickup truck that serves as Bali's only form of public transportation), I was greeted by a radiant little charmer who offered to sell me some sarongs. Her name, she said, was Madé Sri, she was ten years old and her school had finished for the day. My name was what, and where did I come from? I told her, and we talked some more and then, chattering brightly as she went, she led me off to the Lotus Café.

I walked inside the large wooden hut to find Wyndham Hills music on the system, elegantly framed prints about the walls. Outside the main building was a garden the size of a football field, with a temple next door and a lotus pond at its center. Above the pond was an open sunlit pavilion just big enough for a single low wooden table. I went out to the pavilion and reclined on some of its pillows, and moments later, a beautiful damsel brought me a sky-blue pot of strong Earl Grey tea and some orange poppy-seed cake on homemade crockery the color of the sea. I lay back, opened my copy of *Ada* and thought I had landed in aesthete's heaven.

Yet as I stayed longer in Ubud, I found that it was sometimes hard to smell the frangipani, so strong was the perfume of artiness. One of the village's main landmarks, for example, was the gaudy palace erected by the Spanish artist Antonio Blanco in honor of the great Spanish artist Antonio Blanco. One day, I walked up to its front gate and pressed a bell. After a few moments, an aged Balinese gardener opened the door. As soon as I paid the admission fee, he informed me, I could walk all around the house, inspect the paintings and savor the poems of Antonio Blanco. If I were very lucky, I might even enjoy a meeting with the Artist.

Paying up, I made my way to the two rooms that contained Blanco's artwork. The vast majority of the canvases represented Balinese girls dancing or Balinese girls nude; some showed Balinese girls dancing in the nude. Yet these, I gathered, were as nothing next to Blanco's greatest creation—the life of an artist he had fashioned with his Balinese dancer wife. This was brought home by the poems that had been placed between the paintings, lovingly handwritten and dated by the artist. The verses, written in English splintered by design or necessity (it was impossible to tell), were mostly a Dali-rious collage of sixties buzzwords, cries of artistic defiance and *épater le bourgeois* belches. Their theme was best summarized by the one in which Blanco declared that anyone who met him could bask in "my warmth and serenity" and drink in "the ambience of MY GOODNESS."

The popular response to these surprising effusions was ecstatic. "You need ask no questions—the answers are all there," wrote one visitor in the guest book. "To laugh, to cry, to live," was the compact assessment of another typical Ubudite. "The two people here have created together a most delicious feast of exotic, tender, beautiful, pensive, meaningful, reminiscent morsels," reported an American lady. "Yum."

A German had been moved to exclaim, "Love is life and life is spirit," and an even more Delphic fellow to cry, "No arts, no views, no position, no subject, no zoo . . . only the world we all create." But my favorite appraisal was the considered opinion of the savant who declared, simply, "Ubud, ses cheesecakes et ses plages."

None of this, however, prepared me for my audience with the Great Man. As I walked into the third of his galleries and began looking around, I noticed, suddenly, that He was there—an elfin figure in a beret, perched on a wooden chair with an aphorism on his lips, and a cigarette too. I began basking in his warmth and serenity. He began quoting prices.

Before he could start talking discounts, I tried to deflect him. "Ubud must have changed a lot in the twenty years that you've lived here."

"Ah yes." He sighed extravagantly and showed me his profile. "But I . . . I am a romantic. I think only of the old Bali. It lives in my heart. I"—he paused—"I am a dreamer."

Silence.

I drank in the ambience of HIS GOODNESS.

"And what," he began absently, to break the extended silence, "do you do?"

"I write."

"Ah." He paused approvingly. "It takes an artist of real genius to create a cavalcade, to create a story of many generations. It takes a great risk to create such a cavalcade. Many fear such a challenge. But I, I am reading a novel now—it was made into a movie, I think—by just such an artist." I held my breath. "His name"—he paused—"is Sidney Sheldon."

AND AS EACH of the three tourist havens had grown more bloated, each of them in time had spawned a kind of shadow self, an annex-town that had materialized by its side to cater to the overflow. As Kuta became overcrowded, the surplus had spilled over into Legian, one mile to the north. By the time I strolled through the once quiet village, there was little to be seen except a fledgling Kuta. Norm's, Don and Donna, Diane, Ed's and Ned's ("An Aussie Type of Pub"). The Bali Waltzing Matilda, Koala Blue, Surfer's Paradise. Next to Bali Aussie was the New Bali (serving "Aussie and Chinese food"). For its grand opening, the place promised cockfights and all-you-can-eat orgies.

So too, as every last inch of Sanur had been claimed by a receiving line of thirty hotels strung along the coast, the government had decided to create a new high-rise resort a little farther south, called Nusa Dua. In 1985, at least eleven new hotels were being built in the man-made settlement, and by now there were 4,525 guest rooms in Nusa Dua, offering what one travel brochure called "an oceanfront setting in an exclusive atmosphere." Nearly all of them were stocked with convention facilities and conventional facilities—squash courts, health clubs, equipment for wind surfing and, of course, theaters for the presentation of local culture. For a touch of imported romance, there were even horse-drawn buggies on hand.

And as Ubud had become every traveler's favorite place for avoiding every other traveler, more and more people, so it seemed, had decided to hang out in other funky towns such as Jogjakarta, in neighboring Java. Like Ubud, Jogja was still soft and accommodating enough to entice the kind of traveling party rarely seen in Southeast Asia: serious-looking Dutch or German couples reading translated editions of George Eliot, ethereal girls in peasant skirts traveling by themselves with flowers in their hair, whole families that had taken to the road. Murni's, a landmark in Ubud, served up "Authentic American Upper Elk Valley Hamburgers," "chili con carne a la Albuquerque" and "the best chocolate chip cookies east of San Francisco." It also sold postcards, vases, exquisite books. But Lovina, a typical joint in Jogja, went one step further: it had 400 items on its menu (the *spécialité de la maison* was, *bien sûr*, guacamole), as well as filtered coffee; it provided free maps, English-language newspapers and a small library of European paperbacks that could be bought or traded; it posted notices on which Australian girls reported missing boyfriends; and, on its wall, it gave pride of place to a sign that exhorted: "Kefir Rehabilitates Your Health! Please, Drink Kefir every day and you will be healthy!"

At five in the morning, as light flowed into my Jogja *losmen*, a German girl sat at the breakfast table poring over Jung's *Memories, Dreams, Reflections*.

III

Yet even as each of the resorts had stretched and stretched to accommodate the crowds, still the tourists kept swarming in, scattering north and south and east and converging like mosquitoes on one unvisited corner after another. And even though many a visitor treated Bali with the regretful solicitude one might extend to a lovely girl on the brink of adolescence—at once purified by her presence and somewhat terrified by her future—each year found new towns in eastern Bali popping up like insect bites. In 1984, the new haven of solitude was Lovina, the thinking man's Kuta-Legian on the northern coast; in 1985, it was Candi Dasa, to the east, another place previously unmarked on the map, which had doubled the number of its *losmens* in just six months and began to report its first cases of thieving. One quiet place after another became a Quiet Place, whose most notable characteristic, after a while, was its noise; every area famous for being unpeopled fell before the consequences of its fame. The 6,000 tourists of 1966 had become 207,000 by 1985, and every other number had been scaled up accordingly. A shrewd local told me that he had purchased five acres of land for $25 in 1972; since then, the property had appreciated by 14,000 percent.

INDONESIA, OF COURSE, had taken none of this lying down, and in Bali, as in parts of Java, it was hard not to feel that, beneath even all the surface changes, the place had lost something of its innocence to the West. Almost every time I walked down an Ubud or Jogja street, I was arrested by a cheery voice and then by a dazzling smile. Where did I come from? What was my name? Did I need directions? Where had I bought my T-shirt? Did I know the story of the *Ramayana?* Could I not stop for a chat over tea?

Usually my interlocutor was a beautiful, slightly shady boy of college age with a ready smile and uncertain interests; a self-professed student or dancer, he nonetheless seemed to spend most of his days sitting around *losmens*, playing pool or taking

Aussie girls for scooter-rides. And though perhaps he half hoped for money or a favor, my new friend usually seemed happy just to sit around chatting about the wonders of the West.

The first topic to be considered was generally that of money: how much had I paid for my plane ticket, how much for the local bus, how much for a night in the *losmen?* The figures I delivered struck me as absurdly low ($8 for a twenty-hour bus ride, 60 cents for a hearty meal), but the Indonesian boys listened with the same fascination that I might have given to the tax returns of Howard Hughes or J. Paul Getty. Small wonder, perhaps. While I was in Java, the Jakarta *Post* advertised a dinner with Miss World in the capital that cost $4,000 a head; that was equivalent to twenty years' salary for the average Indonesian teacher.

Yet even as their unfamiliarity with money situated them inescapably within one of the poorest nations in Asia, my self-appointed guides to Indonesia also displayed a familiarity with things Western that could put many a Westerner to shame, in more ways than one. Their special subjects of expertise, like those of any bar-hound in New York, were sex, sports and show biz. One day in Jogja, a young bravo called Agus delivered a detailed and authoritative disquisition on the mating habits of Americans that started with his own beliefs—"Sexual intercourse before marriage, no good!"—and culminated with the startling conclusion: "In America, it's a case of 'no money, no honey.' Right?" That same day, in a garden restaurant nearby, I saw a local girl accost a sunburned Swiss student. What's your name, she probed gently. "Erik." She giggled. "Erik Estrada?" The Swiss man looked dazed. "*CHiPs,*" she explained admonishingly, but that was no help at all.

On my very first night in Java, as I tried to catch a good night's sleep on a bench in a railway station, I suddenly felt a hand on my body. I rolled off my suitcase pillow and looked at the sky. Dark. I checked my watch—4:10 a.m. Not quite myself, I took stock of the scene. I now, so it seemed, had not only a roommate, but also a bench mate. Eyes flashing, my slim-hipped new friend asked me where I came from. New York. His ardor noticeably dimmed. "AIDS!" he pronounced, and moved back a little. Firmly believing that this might not be the ideal time for a tête-à-tête, I nodded vigorously. But my potential companion was not so easily deterred. Did I like men? In certain contexts.

And women? Sometimes. Ah, he said, snatching up his own word as if it were a prompt, there are two kinds of woman, the soft and the hard. And so, in the darkened, empty hallways of a large railway terminal on a tropical island, at 4:30 in the morning, I was treated to a most persuasive treatise on the two kinds of woman, the soft and the hard, as epitomized—so my versatile lecturer told me—by Olivia Hussey and Grace Jones.

Of all America's ambassadors to the archipelago, however, the most popular seemed to be its athletes. When first I arrived in Kuta, I found the proprietress of my *losmen* and her husband staring intensely at a TV screen. I looked closer and found that the object of their attention was a college basketball game between Lamar and Villanova. In the same Balinese village, I heard, for the first time ever, a rap song celebrating the skills of Julius Erving. Two teenage Indonesian friends hotly debated the strengths and weaknesses of American soccer. ("Look at the mighty Cosmos," said one. "But recall," parried the other, "that all their stars were imported.") And the household god of the entire nation while I was there was an eighteen-year-old super flyweight whose admiration for "Marvelous" Marvin Hagler ran so deep that he had actually shaven his head and changed his name to Yoni Hagler.

Foreign names, in fact, seemed the most precious currency of exchange in Indonesia, magical coins to be traded with every emissary from abroad. Often, my initial conversation with young Indonesians consisted merely of a recitation of familiar names—Michael Jackson, Rambo, Larry Holmes, Madonna—delivered in much the same spirit in which two people, newly introduced, might fish for an acquaintance in common. Once, as I sat drinking tea and watching the sun come up over the rice paddies of Ubud, a local boy strolled up to me, smiled and sat down at my feet, as for a weekly tutorial.

"Michael Jackson," he began tentatively. "He African?"

"No. He's a Negro, an American black."

Nioman took this in. A few moments passed.

"Same with Lionel Richie?"

"Yup."

"Him Negro?"

"Uh-huh."

This, too, was digested in time.

"And Marvin Hagler Negro?"

"Yes."

"And Michael Spinks?"

"Yes."

By now we were gaining momentum. Nioman looked thrilled with his new discovery.

"And Muhammad Ali Negro?"

"Right."

"And Larry Holmes?"

"Yes."

"And Ronald Reagan?"

I paused for a moment, and Nioman looked alarmed. I tried to explain that though many a star of stage and song and sports arena was black, the President of the Union was white. Nioman looked incredulous at first, then crestfallen. I began to wish I had voted for Jesse Jackson.

DEVELOPMENT, IN SHORT, had come to Bali as crookedly as it had to many another such place, and most of the boys I met, having dropped out of school because their parents could not afford the fees of $3 a month, were unable to read or write in their own language, yet were fluent in English. By now, therefore, it had become a commonplace to portray the Western presence in Bali as a snake in a tropical Eden. Even in my small-town California home, a local library carried a tome entitled *Cultural Involution: Tourists, Balinese and the Process of Modernization in the Anthropological Perspective.* And when I consulted *Bima Wasata,* a pamphlet put out by the village of Ubud to explain its culture to foreigners, I found *Buta,* or the force of evil, defined as follows: "Evil power can be many things. It might be too much money from tourism, or the imbalance number between locals and visitors, or the local people who think about moneymaking work." All three kinds of evil, one could not help but notice, arose from tourism.

And the image of the virgin violated was all the more tempting in Bali precisely because the great distinction of Bali lay precisely in its purity, its innocence of suggestiveness; at its best, the island had the springtime grace of a virgin who does not need to understand the beauty or the weight she carries. Indeed, it was innocence, above all else, that the Balinese (like Prospero) deemed holy: children were venerated on the island for the very Wordsworthian reason that they were recent arrivals from heaven, the closest thing on earth to messengers from the gods. Thus it was strictly forbidden for anyone to touch a child on his head, and until the age of three, every infant was carried on the shoulders of his elders so that he would not have to come in contact with the impure earth. Many of Bali's most divine duties were entrusted only to virgins: a village that felt itself to be possessed would select two little girls, known as "heavenly nymphs," to don white dresses and perform the *sanghyang* dance, casting out evil spirits as they moved together in a trance, swaying to the rhythm of an unheard music. These days, however, the signs outside the travel agencies in Kuta shouted: "Virgin Dance! Only $5 (U.S.)!"

And though virgins might be the first victims to be sacrificed on the altar of tourism, others were sure to follow. Traditionally, the Balinese had always shunned the sea, believing it to be the hiding place of malefic spirits; today, however, the beach at Kuta was packed with local vendors and villagers in swimsuits who were more than willing to confront demons if it led to extra dollars. So too, one of the Gauguinesque beauties of Bali—celebrated by all its early visitors—had been the majestic unselfconsciousness of the local women as they went about their daily tasks bare-breasted. But in turfing the natives out of Eden, the West had supplied them with a fig leaf. After a series of Western documentaries in the thirties had tried to sell the tropical garden as Toplessness Central, Balinese women had been forced to follow the example of prostitutes and cover themselves up. Yet even now, local vendors did a brisk business in portraits of natural maidens undressed. And these days, ironically, it was the Australian girls in Kuta who sought to get back to nature by shedding their tops (to the amusement of the young Balinese and the consternation of the old), while the local girls wrapped themselves up against the invasion of staring eyes. Decadence, perhaps, could be defined as nothing more than the artificial embrace of what once had been natural.

YET STILL, NOW and then, Bali shone with a freshness newly minted. It had become a truism to call the island the "Morning of the World" but true the fact remained. For every morning, very early, while most of the foreign revelers were sleeping off the excesses of the night before, the island became herself once again. At daybreak, Bali took on the soft glow that bodies acquire in sleep, and the same sense of innocence inviolate.

Down by the long-sighing sea, Kuta Beach was empty, save for a lone fishermen or two casting their nets in the early light. Wind chimes sang outside the cafés. The lanes were drowsy with a gentle quiet. And one day when I walked at dawn to the beach, I saw a procession of villagers, dressed in their finest silks, carrying a flower-wreathed tower, amid a host of gilded parasols, down to the misty sea.

By 5:30, the sleepy lanes were already bright and latticed with light. Wrinkled old women walked through the dust with a queenly erectness, silks piled high atop their heads; soft-faced little girls, in spotless white shirts and burgundy skirts, skipped their way to school; teenage boys, shirtless brown bodies radiant with good health, finished the day's washing under the sun. In the mornings, Bali felt like a world reborn.

THUS I WENT back and forth, unable to decide whether paradise had been lost, or was losing, or could ever be regained. And my greatest problem with Bali was, finally, that it seemed too free of problems. In many respects, it struck me as too lazy, and too easy. A real paradise, I felt, could not just be entered; it had to be earned. A real paradise must exact a price, resist admission as much as it invited it. And a real paradise, like a god or a lover, must have an element of mystery about it; only the presence of the unknown and the unseen—the possibility of surprise— could awaken true faith or devotion.

At least, so I thought, the trekkers in Nepal had to hike and to suffer for their uplifting highs; even the tourist in Burma or Tibet had to tilt against the crazily spinning windmills of a socialist bureaucracy before he could collect his epiphanies. But the visitor to Bali was handed a gift-wrapped parcel of paradise the minute he arrived. After that, he had only to lie back and let the idyll present itself to him, demanding nothing in return. It was not just tropical fruits that were brought to tourists on a plate by slim, smiling dryads, it was the whole Bali package: massages, temple dances, the heart-stopping radiance of the local children. Every room came equipped with sunlight and birdsong. Every lane brought smiles. Extraordinary sunsets were shown every night on Kuta Beach, and free of charge.

I knew, of course, that for the locals, life here could be as troubling as anywhere else in the developing world. I had read all about the two most famous events in the island's recent history: the massacre of 3,500 locals in 1906, when the entire royal court of Denpasar had dressed up in all its ceremonial finery and walked, as if in a dream, into the gunfire of the invading Dutch, preferring mass suicide to surrender; and the maddened blood-letting that had swept across the island in 1965 during the convulsions that attended the end of Sukarno's rule by rough magic, when villagers, entranced, cut throats and smashed heads until as many as 100,000 people lay dead. Even in the most peaceful of times, medical care remained in the uncertain hands of witch doctors, and the press of vendors on Kuta Beach attested to the fact that, though the Balinese were not desperately poor, neither were they rich.

The story I heard from Wayan, an engaging, ever-smiling twenty-three-year-old boy who worked in my guesthouse, sounded typical. He had grown up, he told me one sunny morning, in a tiny village in the west. At seventeen he had got married, and soon after, he had been blessed with a son. But soon after that, his wife had forsaken him for another man. Wayan was left in a one-room house, with his mother, his father, his brother, his sister and his baby to support. There was no work in his village, so he had come to Kuta.

Did he think of remarrying?

No, he said, he was afraid of girls now. He lived only for his baby. But even that was not easy. He could make only $22 a month at the *losmen*, and he had to spend $5 a month just to take a *bemo* home to visit his baby. If he wanted to take home some cake for his child, that would cost more. As it was, his son, now three and a half, still wore the clothes he had been given when two. And Wayan himself owned only two T-shirts, two pairs of trousers and a pair of shorts.

Last year, to make things still harder, he had smashed his leg in a motorbike accident. The doctors, as usual, wanted to amputate; Wayan refused. But the treatment needed to save the leg had cost $250, and there was no way he could ever get that kind of money. He was frightened, he told me, always frightened that the people from the hospital would come and get him. What could he do?

A cynic might say that Wayan had rehearsed his hard-luck tale for the benefit of credulous tourists. Maybe so. But that made the fact of his telling it no less sad or importunate. And still, every morning, when he saw me, Wayan flashed me an ebullient smile. "Bali, paradise!" he exulted.

THERE WAS ALSO, as the trance-killings revealed, a more disquieting side to this island famous for its witches, its exorcisms, the nighttime howling of its unfed dogs (believed to be agents of the demons). Before I came to Bali, I had never met a girl with the passional rawness—the wild and windswept intensity—of a Brontëan heroine. But I found her, with a vengeance, in another Wayan, a twenty-year-old girl of Kuta (in Bali, the name is given to the eldest child in nearly every family, whether male or female). Often when she spoke, it seemed that she was clutching on to life with such urgency, such frantic desperation, that life itself would wish to escape from her furious grip.

One lazy evening, as we walked beside the sea under an enormous full moon, Wayan told me her story. At fourteen, she said, she had fallen in love, but when she refused to sleep with her boyfriend, he had gone off and found another girl. In response, said Wayan calmly, she had swallowed every pill she could find. She spent a month in the hospital, longing to die. At twenty, she continued steadily, she had found her first lover, a nice boy from Amsterdam; one month after he left, she had received a letter from his father informing her of the boy's death in an industrial accident.

These shadows hung about Wayan like dark attendant spirits. And when it came time for me to leave Bali, she asked, with unusual vehemence, if she could come to the airport to see me off. The reason, I discovered, was that she wished to deliver a chilling valediction. "Last night," she told me with haunted eyes, "I dreamed I died. I dress all in white and go away." I told her gently not to be worried by such dark thoughts. "I ready to be dead," she intoned. "I know. I have dream." But she had much to be happy about, I reminded her. "I am happy"; she nodded, looking down. "But I am also a lot sad. You come to Bali again, you not see me, because I dead. Last night I dreamed I dead."

For all that, however, the Balinese firmly believed that such spirits generally did not bother with foreigners, and, mostly, they seemed to be right. For most tourists, no shadows at all obscured the Balinese sky. Sure, the island might have a few hustlers and hellhounds, but for the most part it was as soft and welcoming as Miranda. In that sense, I thought, Bali had not matured into complexity, but remained in a state of sweet vulnerability. A real paradise, I told myself, should be the natural equivalent of an artistic masterpiece: it should have challenge and chiaroscuro, the fascination of what's difficult; it should yield new meanings on every inspection, awakening in its visitors something new and unexpected; it should bring a different meaning to everyone who saw it.

But Bali, for all the variety of its charms, was relentless in its charm, and it meant the same to everyone who came here. It offered paradise, and provided it. It was pretty as a postcard, and just about as deep. Only a special kind of person can remain for long in Paradise, making his peace with tranquillity. Most people, I suspected, took taking it easy pretty hard. Humankind, to invert Eliot, cannot stand too little reality.

IV

And maybe it was the ease with which Bali yielded to its tourist traffic or maybe it was something else—its dawning freshness, perhaps—but when first I came to know the island, I was sure somehow that the local culture had a self-sufficiency to it, a tough self-possession, that could withstand even the grasping hands and outstretched dollars of foreign intruders. And even as I was unnerved by the rowdy desecration of Kuta, I was constantly surprised to see how the Balinese seemed almost impervious to the corruption around them. Innocence, I thought, could be its own protection; seeing no evil was halfway toward feeling no evil. "There's nothing ill can dwell in such a temple," says Ferdinand. Later he tells Miranda, "'Tis fresh morning with me when you are by at night."

My hopefulness had been encouraged when I ran across a Javanese man on the banks of a stream in Ubud. Every Balinese family, he explained to me, was linked together by a *desa* in each village, and every *desa* was connected by a *banjar*. These units included every married man in the village and oversaw the welfare of the entire community: they financed local dancers and artists, distributed wealth to ensure that nobody in the area would be without food or clothes or shelter, and, most important, enclosed the locals within a magic circle of self-reliance. There was no police force on the island, the man went on; the people simply governed themselves with minatory memories of the gods. Nor, as I had seen, were there any bloated stomachs or tattered rags or broken huts in Bali—only fine silks, and houses laureled in flowers. Bali's happy system of agrarian socialism, embroidered by its spiritual gaiety, seemed truly to have brought it close to that golden age envisaged by Gonzalo, where there is "no name of magistrate; letters should not be known; riches, poverty, and use of service, none."

I reminded myself too that all paradises are the subjects of as many elegies as eulogies, and all accounts of travel, as Lévi-Strauss observes, "create the illusion of something which no longer exists, but should exist." For at least fifty years now, Bali had been the ultimate once-upon-a-time idyll, the traveler's favorite requiem. As early as 1930, Hickman Powell, author of *The Last Paradise* (the first book in English on Bali), was writing of the "modern Juggernaut that would kill Bali," and in 1937, Covarrubias had published his landmark study mostly, he wrote, as a monument to "a living culture that is doomed to disappear under the remorseless onslaught of modern commercialism." By 1941, Philip Hanson Hiss, while repeatedly announcing: "The Balinese are the happiest people in the world!" was already cursing the hotels that packaged Balinese dances as sex-appeal shows "not very different from Broadway or Hollywood." At the end of his paean, he had concluded, grimly: "The end seems inevitable." Over the last fifty years, some of those fearful nightmares had come true. But still the dream remained.

Indeed, according to many Bali watchers, the tourist trade had actually quickened and revived Balinese culture, given wood carvers a living instead of a full-time hobby, provided dancers with a larger audience as well as an incentive to excel. The famous *kecak* dance had been imported to the island by foreigners, as had the art of oil painting. The locals, moreover, had displayed an impressive gift for adapting their ways to the times: these days, the *leyak* witches who traditionally took the forms of pigs or monkeys or treacherous maidens were said to turn themselves into runaway motorbikes, while the couples who eloped, as Balinese tradition dictates, did so not on foot but in brand-new Hondas. The Balinese, indeed, were wonderfully matter-of-fact about their magic. If you live in L.A., a Balinese dancer once told me in California, you need a car to get you where you want; if you live in Bali, you need an art to get you to the sacred.

And across the street from Casablanca, where Tina Turner was shrieking out "What's Love Got to Do with It?," fifty Balinese men, in Kiwi Tour T-shirts, sat in a circle, practicing the chant of the *kecak* dance, the hissing, insistent curse that reminded me of nothing so much as the "Brekekoax-koax" chorus of Aristophanes' *Frogs*. Bali's frequent obliviousness to imported corruption seemed almost proof against it.

SO I HAD decided in 1984. But when I returned to Bali just eighteen months later, my faith was shaken, and my seesawing convictions about whether paradise could survive took what seemed to be their final turn, downward.

When I arrived in Kuta, the place was almost unrecognizable. Half its buildings were new, so it seemed, and the other half were under construction. In less than two years—no more than a blink in the eye of Siva—roadside stalls had been turned into flashy boutiques, tiny cafés into sleek Mexican watering holes. And as I walked down "Poppies' Gang," the dusty, narrow lane where I had stayed the year before in the Lasi Erawati, I could hardly orient myself for all the new additions. On one side of the field full of cows was a snazzy new singles bar, and on the other, a glassy café called Warung Transformer. Farther down the lane was a fresh two-story joint called Kempu's Café (offering pizzas, tofuburgers, beef tacos and three kinds of guacamole), and down by the sea a newcomer called Chip's that served hot dogs, hamburgers and piña coladas. More motorbikes than ever were racing down the unpaved road, throwing up water from puddles and forcing old women to back against bushes.

For fun-loving tourists, of course, the boom was a boon. And for the locals, the development may well have been even more of a blessing. As I walked down the *gang*, taking in all the changes, a woman waved frantically to me from the kitchen of Kempu's. I looked again and saw that it was the smiling proprietress of my former guesthouse, the Lasi Erawati. How did I like her latest business? she asked me with pride, gesturing with her head around the glittering café. She had also, she said, beaming, opened a whole new set of cottages farther down the lane. Everyone was flourishing. As she spoke, Madé and Madé, the two sweet-tempered young beauties who had served me tea every day the previous year, dazzled me with smiles from the Kempu kitchen. This was where they worked now, they said happily. And did I remember Wayan? I thought of the boy with the sad story, the faraway baby, only five articles of clothing, the $250 debt. He had struck it big, the girls chimed: he was now cooking burritos at brand-new T.J.'s.

Inside the Lasi Erawati, the number of surfing decals on the walls had increased, and the mosquito coils that had been handed out free the previous year had now to be bought from a booth next to the kitchen. A new line of arty postcards was also on sale, costing four times more than the old standards. And as I walked into my room, I heard desperate whispers from the other side of the wall. An unemployed surfer from Byron Bay was pressing his claim on the girl who ran the restaurant now, so it appeared, a slender, golden-limbed nymph who seemed the spirit of sunlight incarnate. Finally, they emerged and walked hand in hand down to the beach.

One feature of the guesthouse, however, seemed to be unchanged, and it was also one of the main reasons for my return: Reno, the fluffy dog who had sat serenely by my side every day the previous year as I wrote on my veranda. As soon as I saw him still lying quietly in the courtyard, I walked over and reached down to stroke him. Reno snarled, whipped round his head and snapped at my hand. Eighteen months was a decade in a dog's life.

Very much like Reno, the people of Kuta—especially the once demure girls—seemed to have suffered a sea change into something not so rich and strange. The shy teenagers who had looked after the boutiques now sported tight jeans and sunglasses; they had scarlet headbands above their mascaraed eyes, and they wore T-shirts that said "Proudly Australian" across their chests. They touched shirtless tourists on the arm, and giggled. Yet all the while, the real Balinese smiles seemed to be fading. Honey Villas. Eldorado. Rendezvous Inn. And what I was witnessing, I believed, was a kind of miracle in reverse: the most graceful people in the world, blessed with an unfailing dignity that beggared description, seemed, impossibly, to be turning hard, even ugly. Charisma. The Monte Carlo. The Pink Panther Club. With a shiver, I realized what it was that the names of the stores, like the girls at their counters, brought overwhelmingly to mind: the go-go bars of Bangkok and Manila.

"Misery acquaints a man with strange bedfellows," said Trinculo. And though I disliked the recitation of obligatory Bali laments, and though I could not help being pleased about Wayan's good fortune, I, like every other tourist, struck up my own lament.

ON MY FIRST night back in Kuta, I also came across the female Wayan whom I had met on the island eighteen months earlier. Now twenty-one, she had a smear of crimson on her lips, and her dancer's hands were painted with a shopgirl's nail polish. Around her waist was a gaudy white belt, and she had taken up jogging each morning to stay in shape. She too, I noted sadly, was beginning to look like a bar girl—and to sound like one. "My watch?" she said briskly. "Present from a friend in Darwin. My dress from friend in Sydney. My bag from my friend in Perth. You"—she flashed me a routinely lovely Bali Smile—"you send me straight-leg jeans from America."

A couple of nights later, when I accompanied her to a movie— to my horror and her delight, it turned out to be a Black Power kung fu flick in faded late-sixties Technicolor—she left at the end of the show holding hands with Terry, a happy-go-lucky electrician from Perth who had embarked, within four hours of arrival, upon fondling this fine piece of local talent.

Why did she not like Indonesian boys, I asked Wayan when I met her the following day. To Western eyes they seemed the very picture of gentleness and beauty.

Her smile faded. "I would rather"—she spat—"marry a dog."

WHEN I MADE my way up to Ubud, things seemed to have changed much less than in Kuta, though the place had certainly grown more crowded and had started to sprout *losmens* like mushrooms. And as I was meandering through the village, I came by chance upon exactly what I had hoped beyond hope to see: Madé Sri. She was walking along in a pretty rainbow skirt and a light blue top, her pile of sarongs still on her head. At ten, she had been radiant; at eleven, she had blossomed into one of the loveliest girls I had ever seen. As soon as she spotted me, she scampered over and blessed me with an angel's smile. We exchanged all our news, and I gave her a copy of *Time* for her English and a piece of chocolate cake from the Lotus Café. Madé, I said finally, guess what. I have a picture of you up in my office in New York. Why didn't you send me a copy? she demanded. I didn't have your address, I said. And, I added, looking around the one-road village, I pretty well assumed that you didn't have one.

"Wait just a minute," she chirped gaily, reaching into the bag in which she carried her temple scarves. She foraged swiftly through the bag, and then pulled out what she had been seeking: a stack of two-tone, heavily embossed business cards.

> Madé Sri Asih
> Handicrafts, sarongs, etc.

On the bottom was an address.
"This is yours, Madé?" I asked, foolish with incredulity.
"Sure," she sang out. "Why not?"

AND THEN, JUST as I was beginning to suspect that Bali had finally become compromised beyond relief or belief, and that the vandals were about to knock Prospero unconscious and claim his paradise as their own, the fates were kind to me: a shadow crossed my path, and I fell ill. I was struck down, indeed, by a mysterious ailment that laid me low with a sledgehammer force I had never known before.

For three days, I stayed in bed, too listless to eat or move or even think. And as I lay in my fairy-tale hut by the lotus pond, the tourist's Bali I had seen blacked out and the silhouette of some darker spirit of the island began to take shape. That night I heard no propositions or Top 40 tunes. But I saw a tailless cat walk across the garden, heard a cock crowing in the dead of night. A plump gecko scuttled up the wall of my room, past a demon mask fringed with human hair. Mosquitoes buzzed about my head. The midnight air was rent with the yowls of copulating cats. All night long, I heard the shrieking and yelping of wild dog-demons. The jungle felt close.

Cast out from the sunlit paradise that had seemed so compliant, I was borne back, so it seemed, into the night world of Bali, island of shadow plays and cockfights, sacred daggers and full moon rites. This was the Bali where artists wait to be visited in dreams before they cover their canvases with swirling druggy patterns; where villagers place dead cocks on their doorsteps to placate evil spirits; where a menstruating woman is shunned even by her husband as a thing possessed. In Bali, when witches come out from the dark, gold-toothed monkeys are seen on deserted roads at night, and headless giants. In Bali—twilight zone of the unrational—I had seen a holy cave full of bats, and a temple in the sea guarded by a snake.

In Bali, I had strange dreams each night. And gradually, through my fever, I began to catch the steady, keening undertone of this island of spirits (the aural equivalent, perhaps, to the undertow that carries several surfers to their deaths each year). I heard the jangled syncopation of the clangorous gamelan, weird, unearthly, psychic, resolving itself into no pattern that a Western ear could follow, but hammering away, with a dissonant and insistent tinkle, all through the narrow lanes of Kuta in the dark.

Strange, magical currents pulse through the whole of Indonesia, a hardheaded editor at *Time* had told me before I left. There was a beach in Java, an American girl had said, which washed away every body dressed in green: she had not believed it either, she said, until she visited the placc and felt her toe stubbing against something, and looked down to see a corpse, in green. There is a strange and poisonous plant in Indonesia (I read on the front page, no less, of the Jakarta *Post*) that blooms when the moon is full, and wards off black magicians, then vanishes again as soon as the moon grows small. "The unseen is all around us in Java," the enigmatic dwarf Billy Kwan had told the arriving Australian journalist in *The Year of Living Dangerously.*

And as I lay alone in the dark, I began to think about the secrecy of this whole mysterious land, a secrecy so deep that it seemed like sorcery. Indonesia is the fifth-largest country in the world, exceeded in population only by the three superpowers and India, home to more people than South Korea, the Philippines, Thailand, Hong Kong and Nepal combined. But how often was it heard from? And what did we know of it? There are more than 13,000 islands in the country, stretched across an area that could reach from Oregon to Bermuda. But what were they famous for producing? And how many Indonesians had I met in the West? Indonesia was far and away the largest Islamic nation in the world, with *twice* as many Muslims as Iran, Iraq, Syria and Saudi Arabia combined. Yet even in Muslim Java there seemed to be few mosques, the mythology was Hindu and its most famous monument (Borobudur) was Buddhist. What was driving this place and why did it shy away from the headlines? Where were the remnants of its longtime Dutch rule? Indonesia was the only country I knew of whose national airline gave no indication of its homeland and was named after a mythological god-bird. What was going on here? And what were these beautiful people weaving behind the screens of their eerie shadow plays?

And in a village courtyard, a huge moon hanging in the branches of the trees beyond, I watched as an old man patiently lit candles in the silence. A gang of bare-chested men burst out, in a trance, chak-a-chakking rhythmically, waving their arms about, sitting down in concentric circles and raising their hands to the heavens and shaking their heads wildly in the dust and all the time chuck-a-chucking furiously. As the chant mounted, the village mongrels let out a low growl, and backed away slowly. Limber, light-footed spirits in monkeys' masks jumped out from the darkness and leaped this way and that. Then two little girls, perhaps eight years old, slithered out of the darkness in a trance, dressed all in white, bodies swaying, eyes shut tight, twisting their tiny wrists together in a witchery of motion, fluttering their hands like snakes. And as the fairies rocked back and forth in a spellbound dance of exorcism, the gamelan continued its relentless ungodly wailing, the voices of its caged dark spirits clanging and jangling through the night.

I was delighted. Caliban was back, and the spirits were active, and both had survived even their shipwrecked visitors from abroad.

TIBET
The Underground
Overland Invasion

ONE MORNING in Tibet, I awoke before dawn and walked out from my tiny room onto a narrow, whitewashed terrace. The mountains before me were shadowed and huge. Feeling my way down a steep wooden ladder, I fumbled across a darkened courtyard and splashed my face with icy water from a pump. Then, while the world was still dreaming, I walked out into the inky streets, and traveled by bus, far, far out of town, past phantoms clomping through the blue-black alleyways, past the sleeping yak-hair tents of nomads, lit by tiny candles, past silhouettes of prayer flags flapping above squat, mud-brick houses, far, far across the high plateaus to a lonely hilltop monastery. There, in the chill of first light, some monks and nomads invited me to join them where they sat. Our breath condensed in the early air, as we shared rough bread and tea made of rancid yak butter and salt. Then, as the sun began to burn away the mist, a monk got up without a word and opened a door, letting me wander through the darkened chambers of the lamasery. Every one of them was heavy with the artichokey smell of butter lamps. Ancient scrolls were stacked inside glass cases thick with dust. Rows of flickering candles encircled placid Buddhas. Dog-eared snapshots of the Dalai Lama stood about their altars. In some rooms, in the darkness, small windows were thrown open to the bright, sharp air, framing the distant snowcaps against a brilliant blue. In others, the sun came down in shafts upon the chanting monks, flooding the room with light.

As the day grew warmer, I scrambled up a flight of stone stairs to the open rooftop, where the building's golden turrets stood out against the cloudless blue. And there I sat, through the sun-washed morning, writing and thinking and looking out on the barren plains below. No movement could be felt but the fluttering of prayer flags. No sound at all but the low-voiced murmurs of the monks, the sometime tolling of a prayer bell.

Later, after many noiseless hours in the sun, I scrambled down the hill again and caught a bus back to Lhasa. By then, the clean-edged light was starting to turn the "City of Sun" to gold, sharpening the orange of its flower boxes, the bright yellow of its temple walls, the clean white of its balconies, and gilding all the strange faces that moved through its central sunlit square— fierce-eyed Khampa bandits, skins almost black and strips of red cloth woven through their jet-black hair; leather-skinned Golok women in green bowler hats and yak-hide boots, prayer wheels spinning as they hobbled down dusty lanes; rough men from the mountains in broad-brimmed gaucho hats, the heads of bulls or carcasses of dogs slung over their sturdy shoulders; huge-eyed, hairless babies clinging to the backs of mothers whose 108 ritual braids, smeared in yak butter, streamed below their waists; traders and monks and mendicants, and purple-cheeked young girls with turquoise in their pigtails and brilliant smiles.

Then, as the shadows lengthened, I wandered back to my guesthouse terrace to watch the light leave the mountains. And then, once night had fallen, I descended the narrow ladder again to a cavernous kitchen bubbling with pots and tureens. In one dark corner, three pretty girls were chopping meat while their hardy sisters busily peeled potatoes; in the center of the room, an old man with shaggy white hair took the vegetables I gave him, emptied them into a large black frying pan, scattered spices all about and then, squinting through the flying grease, handed me back my bowl. Dinner in one hand and glass of milky tea in the other, I went back up to the terrace and watched the heavens fill with stars.

TIBET HAD ALWAYS been one of the world's secret places. For more than twenty centuries, its people had turned their backs on the world at large and resolved to live alone, hidden behind the highest peaks on earth, disengaged from the march of time. Four decades ago, Heinrich Harrer had wandered by chance across the seemingly impassable mountains and stumbled into the heart of secrecy; during his seven years of living in Tibet, he later reported, only five other foreigners were sighted there. Indeed, in all of history until 1979, less than two thousand Westerners had ever set eyes on the Forbidden Land—most of them members of the Younghusband expedition, and the rest mostly madmen or wild adventurers disguised as Chinese nomads. "Isolation," the Dalai Lama once wrote, "was in our blood."

In time, of course, such solitude had become not only self-sufficient but self-sustaining; gradually, Tibet had vanished further and still further behind the veils of myth. By now, indeed, the country seemed mostly to exist in the imagination, a lofty, otherworldly kingdom on the rooftop of the world, curtained by clouds, encircled by snow: Tibet was the home of the Abominable Snowman and the half-mythical Snow Leopard; Tibet was the mystical place known as Shambala or Shangri-La; Tibet was the magical zone that summoned Tintin in a vision and waylaid Sherlock Holmes during the three years of his "death." Even the historical details of the area's recent past seemed torn from some fabulous romance—the discovery of the Dalai Lama at the age of two, in a distant peasant's home, through omens and an oracle's dream; his rescue from an evil warlord, who demanded almost $400,000 before agreeing to release his divine subject; his ceremonial installation, amid regents and seers and rainmakers, on Lhasa's Lion Throne; his sudden assumption of political leadership at the age of fifteen, as China's occupation of his homeland threw him up against Mao Zedong and Zhou Enlai; and finally, most poignantly, the God-King's sad flight through snowbound passes, disguised and on a pony, into exile.

With that last turn, history had conspired with fancy and geography to render Tibet's seclusion absolute: ever since the

Chinese invasion of 1959, the Land of Snows had disappeared entirely. Visitors haunted by images of lamas blowing twelve-foot horns on snow-whitened mountaintops were forced to content themselves with visiting Ladakh, Nepal or even $200-a-day Bhutan. Tibet was glimpsed in dreams alone.

Just a few months before I arrived in China, however, Beijing suddenly decided to throw open the door to Tibet, for the first time since the invasion. And suddenly, the dreamed-of Forbidden Land, whose mystique had always resided in its invisibility, was placed on full view before the world.

By the time I got to Lhasa, it was still too early for many people to have registered the area's awakening; the bright, glassy lobby of the official, 1,000-room Chinese hotel reverberated with nothing but emptiness. But as I made my way across town, I found the narrow labyrinths of the Tibetan quarter jammed with nomads and pilgrims from every corner of the land. And as I wandered through their midst, I found myself standing, as in some Steppenwolf reverie, before a gaily colored board that read "Banak Shol Hotel, Happiness Road."

I walked inside. To my left was a tiny reception booth. By its side, scraps of loose paper were fluttering this way and that from an ad hoc bulletin board. Jean-Claude was selling his tent. Larry was offering the best black-market rates for unofficial currency. Inge wanted to get rid of her copy of *China: A Survival Kit*. Sign up here for a three-day jeep trip around the mountains! Or over here for journeys to Xigatse! Or here for bus rides to Nepal! And as I looked on in bewilderment, gaggles of shaggy foreigners bustled in and out of tiny passageways, while a band of Danes vanished up a wooden ladder. I scrambled after them, and up to the guesthouse terrace, there to be greeted by an even stranger sight: a dozen foreign pilgrims tanning themselves under the brilliant Tibetan sun, the men shirtless and bearded, cooler-than-thou in their cowboy hats and shades, their ladies in baggy pants and bangles, bright scarves wound about their necks.

Without a warning, like Alice through the rabbit hole, I had tumbled, so it seemed, into the upside-down world of the underground Overlanders, the tribe of countercultural imperialists that wanders the planet in search of cut-rate paradises. A few years ago, the hipster trail had stretched all the way from Amsterdam to Kathmandu, through Istanbul and Isfahan and

Kabul; nowadays, however, the professional drifters were beginning to converge on the hidden corners of the Himalayas and the
newly opened minority areas of China. And as I settled down
inside the Banak Shol, I realized that even this most esoteric of
hideaways was fast being turned into the latest way station of
the Denim Route. The only true democracy, D. H. Lawrence
once wrote, is Whitman's version, in which "soul meets soul on
the open road," and Lhasa was now being colonized by a free-
floating band of Whitmanic democrats.

Certainly, there was a Whitman's catalogue of characters in
evidence around the guesthouse corridors. There was a shabby
scientist who had received a grant from Washington to study
cloud formations, and another dubious fellow who had
unearthed some ancient maps of the secret monasteries of Lhasa
and was now planning a book on them. There was an expert on
Chinese music called R.I.P., who dressed from dawn to midnight
in a heavy forest-green poncho and a dark brown gaucho hat, and
told me, somewhat airily, that he came from nowhere, but com-
muted between Soho and Beijing—whenever, that is, he wasn't
living in South America and there was a soi-disant free-lance
photographer who had been traveling for two years without
deadline or destination. There was a Cambodian refugee in a
chic Parisian leather jacket and a soft sweater with sleeves rolled
up to his elbows, and by his side a blowsy American redhead who
confessed that eighteen months of budget traveling had cured
her for life of a love for vagabondage.

Just down the corridor was a quiet Chinese girl from Beijing
who had been allowed to become a painter because her father
was a high-ranking cadre, and a British sailor who had been
traveling for four full years with no companion except his shortwave radio (turned on each night at eleven to catch the news on
the BBC). There was a teenage historian from Cambridge, and a
social worker from Singapore. There was a pair of his-and-hers
fitness freaks from Boulder, Colorado—Mr. Good Health a gentle, bearded craftsman, Ms. Good Health a radiant cowgirl—
who were bicycling at a leisurely pace across the Himalayas.
And, inevitably, there was a whole school of German, Dutch and
Danish students who spoke gallingly fluent English and, more
gallingly still, enjoyed five-month summer vacations even, so it
seemed, into early middle age.

Next door to me lived a blonde from Hawaii who connected stereo speakers to her Walkman so that she could share the latest Talking Heads tapes with her neighbors while her tanned roommate swerved his skateboard frantically up and down the narrow guesthouse corridors. I took them at first to be an archetypal campus couple. But then one day, the girl referred to Tanzi as her kid brother. And later I gathered that she had only just graduated from high school. And later still, she happened to mention her parents, and I looked with new respect upon the figures beside us on the terrace—"Mom," I inferred, was the one in wild earrings and flamboyant pantaloons, "Dad" the fellow in ponytail and chest-length beard, puffing serenely on his peace pipe. Astonishing! Here were some genuine Children—and Grandchildren—of the Revolution! Here in fact were two whole generations of freaks, dropping out and hitting the road *en famille!*

The following day, on a bus out of town, I found myself next to a wonderfully high-spirited white-haired old lady from Pontiac, Michigan. Had she come here on a tour? I asked routinely. Certainly not, she declared with vigor: she was a card-carrying Communist, a supporter of Gus Hall and a solo traveler on her second inspection of the mainland. Her husband had died six years ago, she went on, watery blue eyes sparkling merrily behind her spectacles, and she had instantly decided that there was no point at all in sitting around and waiting to die while playing canasta with toothless widows in the country club. So, at the age of sixty-five, she had taken to the road in search of the socialist ideal. Since then, she reported cheerily, she had been to fifty-five countries, journeyed from Morocco to India by bus (via Iran, Afghanistan and the Khyber Pass), spent four months bouncing across the subcontinent on third-class trains and gone on four separate occasions to the Soviet Union. (Each of the latter trips had brought her somewhat closer to death, she noted, but the doctors in Estonia were simply wonderful, and the specialists in Siberia had saved her life more than once.) Now she was back in China to see how it measured up to Marx. "My heavens," she chuckled heartily as the bus lurched around a corner and a passenger in a wooden headdress landed with all his weight on her toes and another, runny-nosed peasant collapsed against her shoulder and a yak serenely ambled past. "Whatever would my friends say if they could see me now?"

SUCH WERE THE colorful souls that made up my world in Lhasa. But every morning, they, and all their world, were left far behind as I traveled alone to one of the distant mountain lamaseries, and basked in its spacious silences. All around me on the sunlit terraces was nothing but an elevating stillness, broken only by the distant thunk of a wood chopper, the occasional clang of a gong. Stillness too filled the narrow lanes of the monastery, where little girls sat frowning over serious tasks. Even the shaggy dogs stationed like guardians outside the lamasery gates seemed strangely charmed into quietude. I never once saw any of them beg, or bark, or squabble; they simply lay there, in the sunlight, twenty or thirty or more together, healthy and at peace. And so the days dreamed on: morning bells; murmured chants; blue sky on whitewashed terraces.

BY THE TIME I arrived in Lhasa, the Tibetan capital was still uncolonized enough to be rich in all the inconveniences that the Overlander needs to remind himself that "travel" is closely related to "travail." There were two small guesthouses in town, but each had only a few luxury $2 rooms complete with rough mattresses and thick straw pillows; otherwise, they offered nothing but communal dorms filled with tiny beds. Both places boasted taps in their yards, but that was all; to take a shower, one had to risk almost certain disease by braving the public bathhouse. The Banak Shol had a single toilet on every floor, but it consisted only of a hole in the cement, behind a door so rusty that even to try to lock it was to render one's hands bloody and gangrenous; besides, only one store in town carried toilet paper, and its supplies were irregular at best. Coffee and soft drinks were completely unknown in Tibet, and the only postcards to be found came in two sets of fifteen, at least twelve of which were close-ups of murals that might as well have been labels attached to cans of soup. To change money involved trekking through labyrinths of nameless alleyways to a desolate construction site, where a minuscule hut advertised the "Bank of China Lhasa" and presented nothing but a locked door (which opened, occasionally, after 3:30 p.m.); to visit the tourist office involved an eight-mile walk.

Yet even as Lhasa was forcing the Overlanders to turn themselves into locals—living dirt-cheap, washing in rural streams, eating at streetside stalls and camouflaging themselves in native garb—the Overlanders were quickly forcing Lhasa to turn itself into a rough version of the homes they had quit. Yakburgers had been introduced to local menus, and makeshift English-language schools were cropping up in guesthouse rooms. The tiny dive across from the Banak Shol had been newly fitted with a name— the Tasty Restaurant—and with a giant cassette player that filled the Himalayan night with the strains of Bob Marley. And blurring distinctions still further, a few local kids now sported cowboy jeans and chattered away in English as they bartered over pirated cassettes.

Yet most of these foreign developments, I had to admit, were really quite pleasant, if only because the secret fraternity that had gathered in Lhasa seemed an unusually directed and discriminating lot. These ragged gypsies had not come to Tibet by mistake, or en route to someplace else; they had come to Tibet. And their commonality of interests made for a special sense of community, even—or especially—in this almost perfectly alien setting. Before long, I had come to know just about all the fifty or so foreigners in town, and begun to feel at home in their home-grown world-within-a-world. One day, when I emerged onto the darkened terrace at dawn, I met Tomas, a soft-spoken engineer from Munich, and he invited me to join him for a quiet day at distant Ganden Monastery; early that evening, as I wandered through the central market, I found myself next to a skinhead Buddhist actor from London, and off we went together for a cup of tea. At dinner one night, Tomas introduced me to his friends from Zurich; at dinner the next night, I joined the skinhead in a debate with a Hollander on the merits of royalty. Sometimes I stopped in Yak Alley to chat with dysentery-stricken Diane, sometimes I listened to Hans as he described why "Communism stifles life, wherever it goes, and capitalism overstimulates it." The Nicaraguan problem was solved without difficulty at breakfast, and Reagan was summarily deposed. This was where to stay in Kathmandu, said one person, and this was where you could find old swords to buy, and this was when the bus leaves, and this was why Tibetan Buddhists wear yellow hats.

The climax of all these impromptu seminars, however, came at night, when the members of the Lhasa chapter of the Overland brotherhood gathered, like elders around a campfire, inside the dining room of the Banak Shol, and extended the oral tradition deep into the night. Assembled in the half-light over glasses of tea and bottles of beer, they bandied about strange names ("Gurkha Dave, you know, got busted for smuggling gold out of Nepal") and chattered away in a language all their own ("I carried a forty-five-pounder up to seventeen point two"; "I hauled a fifty-fiver up to fifteen point five"). Some of them hatched schemes for cross-country skiing in Tibet, others made plans to rendezvous for Christmas on the beach at Goa. One night, they gave critical ratings to the forgotten islands of Indonesia where visitors could sleep for 20 cents a night (fresh fish included three times a day); the next, they shared condolences about such intercontinental flea pits—the landmarks of the Denim Route—as the ill-named Chungqing Mansions of Hong Kong, the Bencoolen Street flophouses of Singapore and the hostels of Jalan Jaksa in much-despised Jakarta. And always, somehow, every one of them managed to affirm the golden commandments of the Overlander ("Thou shalt not plan. Thou shalt not hurry. Thou shalt not travel without backpacks, on anything other than back roads. And thou shalt not, ever, in any circumstance, call thyself a tourist").

More than anything, though, the travelers filled the mountain nights with stories, Homeric accounts of epic journeys, rife with monsters and marvels (and, in place of the Homeric formulae, catchphrases taken from the ubiquitous guidebooks of the Lonely Planet Company); accounts of life-and-death struggles with malaria pills or ground-breaking bouts of dysentery, of buses without floors and hotels without roofs. More conventional tourists may justify their travels by acquiring eye-catching knickknacks; the unpackaged tourists of the Overland Trail collect anecdotes instead, stories designed to induce pity and terror. Memento mori are their only curricula vitae. "When I was in Monrovia," a Frenchwoman began with practiced nonchalance, "the uncle of my driver was eaten, including his eyes and testicles." It was in Zambia, said a Briton of highly indeterminate means, that I first smelled a lion's breath. I knew the golfing champion of Zambia, piped up another; he died of Coca-

Cola addiction. And I in turn inflicted on the assembled company interminable accounts of sleeping in the jungles of Suriname and being molested in the temples of Upper Egypt.

It often seemed, in fact, that the principal aim of every Overland journey was nothing, really, but an exhaustive knowledge
of suffering (and not, alas, in the Buddhist sense); hard-core
Travelers felt "close to the natives" only when they were actually close to death. And so the litanies continued. "It took us
thirty hours to get here by truck from Golmud." "Oh, that's
nothing. It took me thirty-six hours, and the driver only stopped
once for food, and we all got food poisoning and for the rest of
the trip everyone was vomiting on the bumpy road." "No sweat,
man: it took me seventeen days by road from Chengdu—and
that was by post office truck."

The horror show to end them all, though, was said to be the
bus trip to Nepal; almost none of the foreigners in Lhasa could
conceal his excitement about an ordeal that was said to be the
last word in discomfort. Three months later, in a temple in
Kathmandu, I happened to bump into an Australian whom I had
last seen preparing for the ride. How had the trip been? "Oh,
n'bad. Took five dies. We niver stopped for food. Hid to find for
oursilves, y'know? One night we stopped at this plice to sty, but
thy didn't want us. But thit's where the droyver stopped, so we
slipt outsoid. Bloody freezing." And the scenery? "Yeah.
Couldn't see much, y'know?" (As for his five weeks trekking, his
account was even more heroically laconic. "Yeah, it was ixcellent! Freezing cold, couldn't move for four dies. Wint up to
Iverest Bise Cemp, met some Poles. Thy hedn't seen anyone in
forty-five dies, pretty plized to see us. The next die was the worst
storm of the winter. Thy lost a man. We thought we'd die." He
grinned. "Yeah, it was ixcellent overall.")

TIBET ALSO, HOWEVER, awakened a different, and more
unusual, kind of tale. A few months after I returned to New
York, I arranged one night to have dinner with a Canadian I had
last seen in the Banak Shol. "I ended up taking the bus to Nepal,"
he began, as we gathered in pinstripes in a midtown restaurant,
"and it was really, really rough—especially after the bus broke
down. We had to scrabble for potatoes in the fields, and at night
we had to sleep out in the open. To get a ride, we had to lie down

on the road in front of oncoming trucks. Yet somehow, you know, it was really worth it." Now a corporate lawyer in Manhattan, he began to speak more softly. "And one day, in Gyantse, I met a monk by the side of the road. He couldn't speak English. And I, of course, don't know any Tibetan. But just the way he looked, something in the way he stood there . . ." His eyes grew distant as the memory. "People gathered round him, and they began giving him gifts. They just couldn't help it. And me, I ended up doing the same. In fact, I spent the whole day just following him around. I couldn't do anything else." He stopped for a moment, shaking his head. "You know, it was really unreal. I've never seen anything like it."

Tibet, in fact, cast a curious spell over just about everyone who came here: even those who arrived as proud models of dispassion left as evangelists of the local cause. One reason for this, no doubt, was that after the bland monumentality and mechanical bustle of the rest of China, Tibet was, in every sense, a breath of fresh air; an antithesis to the communal vacancy of the mainland, and an antidote to it. The cities of China were drab and dusty and dour; Lhasa, by contrast, was a festival, a revelation, an explosion of brilliant flower boxes and golden symbols and gaily painted awnings. The dull-eyed Chinese were generally withdrawn, even sullen toward foreigners; the Tibetans, by contrast, were incorrigibly merry, with quick animation in their faces, ready at any moment to break into ruddy smiles that felt like benedictions. China, it was, ironically, that felt closed and remote; Tibet was jolly and rainbowed and welcoming.

Politically, of course, the contrast seemed even more abject: seven million Tibetans, reputed to be among the most pious and peace-loving people in the world, had found themselves assaulted by the forces of a billion Chinese ideologues who seemed to derive a perverse delight from violating the monuments of their faith. Lamaseries had been bombed to smithereens, sacred texts had been used as toilet paper. Children had been made to shoot their parents. Monks had been forced to copulate in public.

But beyond even the horrifying details of the genocide, there lay the deepest difference of all: China these days seemed to lack any semblance of a living culture or an abiding devotion to anything more than pragmatism; yet Tibet, in the face of terrible opposition, sustained a spirit more moving and uplifting than any I had ever seen.

All across Lhasa, this faith burned with a fervor that left me shaking. From daybreak until late at night, old men and old women gathered in crowds outside the central Jokhang Monastery, joining their hands above their heads and flinging themselves down to the dust again and again and again in a ritual three-part prostration. Along the desolate plateaus, pilgrims from the farthest corners of the country could be seen tramping for days or weeks or months on end in order to visit Lhasa, crawling through the gutters to perform their ritual circumambulations of the holy places. Around the monasteries, wizened old men labored patiently up rocky mountain slopes, leading grandchildren or great-grandchildren by the hand as they brought the monks all the money they could spare. And in the lamaseries themselves, now broken and open to the wind (only a couple of hundred monks remained in the Drepung, where once 10,000 had inhabited the largest monastery in the world), the holy men went unceasingly about their prayers. If ever they chanced to see a foreign visitor, they asked for one thing, and one thing only: a photograph of their leader, exiled from Tibet more than a quarter century before. "Dalai Lama" was all they said. "Dalai Lama."

Instead of being dimmed by the Chinese massacres, in fact, the calm intensity of Tibetan faith seemed only to have been strengthened by them. And Tibetan Buddhism was the first religion I had ever seen more impressive in its practice than its preaching. Back home, I had always harbored suspicions about the protestations of Tibetan or Tibetan-minded friends. Nor had I ever been able to follow the abstruse cerebrations of their doctrine. Yet the Tibetans I met—gentle yet tough, devout but fun-loving, masters of magic and machinery—thoroughly disarmed me. And the devotion I saw everywhere in their country moved me beyond words. Whenever I was alone in the Tibetan sunlight and silence, I felt that these were days of heaven and I would never know such purity again.

Almost everyone who had ever stumbled into this zone of mysterious magnetism seemed similarly stirred. When he arrived in Lhasa in 1811, disguised as a Chinese physician, the cranky British madman Thomas Manning disliked much of what he saw; nonetheless, he found himself confessing that in Tibet "everything excites the idea of something unreal." Upon first setting eyes on Shangri-La, the token cynic in *Lost Horizon* had let only one word escape, and that was "magic." Even the most jaded or strung-out of the foreigners at the Banak Shol surprised themselves, and me, by speaking of monks whose presence had left them silent.

TIBET, WE ALL agreed, was an inspiration to visit. And yet, if we had been honest about it, it would probably have been better had we never visited it at all. For the airy elevation of its spell tempted us all to overlook the one inescapable fact of our presence here: that the Chinese, by most accounts, had decided to open up the "autonomous region" not out of charity, nor out of genuine penitence, but for purely strategic reasons, both military and economic. They knew very well that Westerners could not resist paying any amount of money to penetrate the world's last secret, and they were hardly blind to the power of public relations. Thus, by opening up Tibet, Beijing was apparently hoping to give proof to the world of its enlightened tolerance; and by flocking to Tibet, we were in effect giving legitimacy to this show of good intentions. In our determination to be one step ahead of everyone else, we were like the vanguard of some invading army that, by racing ahead, is the first to trip the mines.

Many of the Overlanders at the Banak Shol made pointed gestures of sympathy for the local cause. They boycotted local transportation. They refused to patronize Chinese shops. They bought local maps in Tibetan, rather than Chinese, though neither script was intelligible to them. They even, by the end of 1987, began to urge the Tibetans on in anti-Chinese demonstrations. Yet still the fact remained: all of us were here only at Chinese sufferance, and our presence aided no one but the Chinese. Our money ended up in Chinese coffers; our visas were propaganda victories for Beijing.

In the process of making China richer, moreover, we were very likely making Tibet spiritually poorer; many observers believed that the Chinese, having failed to demolish Tibet by force, were now planning to destroy the place by exposing it to an onslaught of Western visitors. In 1984, China had tentatively allowed 1,500 foreigners into Tibet; by 1988, it was said, they would bring in more than 100,000 tourists. By now, therefore, even homesick Tibetans in exile were wary of returning to their motherland. Just before I arrived, the Dalai Lama himself had canceled his projected return to his people, in the fear that it would ultimately bring more harm than good.

Forty years ago, Robert Byron had written: "There can be few persons of sensibility whose heart is not with the Tibetans in their effort to remain the last outpost of any racial individualism on the face of the earth." His words were even truer now. But the Chinese invaders had begun to compromise that purity, and the newest invaders were threatening to finish it off for good. The "bitter lesson" of Tibet's sad history, the Dalai Lama once wrote, is that "the world has grown too small for any people to live in harmless isolation."

OCCASIONALLY, OF COURSE, it was possible to see that foreigners could bring a little solace to the exiled land. One day in Ganden Monastery, an old monk shuffled up to an Australian girl with the familiar plea, "Dalai Lama? Dalai Lama?" To my amazement, she reached into her bag, pulled out a color photo and gave it to him. Instantly, the monk's eyes filled with tears. He held the photo to his heart. He sat down and muttered to himself a prayer. Eyes tightly shut, he placed the picture on his heart, his head, his face. Then, drawing out a white scarf, he wrapped the photo inside it and set it down beside him with infinite care. For many moments, eyes still closed, he simply sat there, too grateful, or too rapt, to speak.

Yet as I looked on, the spell was abruptly broken. Please could she have, the girl demanded, two prayer scrolls in exchange. The monk, still moved, was happy to oblige. And at that moment, as so often in Tibet, what made me fear most deeply for the place was nothing but the unguarded openness of its people. After years of isolation, the Tibetans, for all their entrepreneurial skills, seemed achingly ready to welcome the world on any terms at all. As I sat on a local bus one day, wrinkled yak-herds in filthy cloaks bundled up and clapped their arms around my shoulders. At famous Sera Monastery, aging monks taught me how to say their chants, while novices asked, through smiles, if they could take my picture. And as I waited for the bus that would take me out of Lhasa, three jovial matrons bustled up to me and draped a traditional white scarf around my neck, then proffered a glass of Tibetan barley beer to send me on my way with happy memories of their land.

Such unqualified trust, however, was unlikely to be reciprocated. By now, even the most sympathetic pilgrims of the Overland Trail had grown so used to cutting corners that they could scarcely distinguish any longer between experience and expedience. They wanted to "live free" in every sense of the term. Besides, full-time travelers considered themselves accountable to no one but themselves.

One night, as we sat on the terrace of the Banak Shol in the starlight, an American photographer asked everyone to wish him luck as he descended for "the big battle." Almost an hour later, he emerged again, all smiles: he had succeeded, he declared triumphantly, in forcing the owners to accept his payment for his three-week stay, not in the Foreign Exchange Certificates that tourists were supposed to use, but in the "people's money" that was, in fact, worth 40 percent less. He had thus managed, he announced with pride, to save himself almost $20. The proprietors, a group of Tibetan girls who spoke little English but had hunted down blankets on request and given single travelers double rooms at no extra cost and offered their guests whatever bicycles they could spare, had threatened to call the police; but in the end, they knew, they were virtually powerless against a foreigner. "Man, I don't like all this chiseling kind of shit," declared the conqueror. "But, shit, if they'd hassled me, I'd just have shown them my American Express card."

At that, others in the audience were moved to recount their own victories in making money for nothing by selling desperate locals their Foreign Exchange Certificates. "I got a hundred sixty renminbi for a hundred FEC," said one. "Me too. One guy refused to give me more than a hundred fifty. We had to wait for half an hour. But in the end he gave in." "Jeez, man. I got only a hundred forty-eight." Through it all, an Indian boy remained pretty silent. Twice in the past week he had had things stolen from his bed; everyone knew that the thief had been a fellow traveler.

A little later, our conversation turned, inevitably, to the inevitable corruption of Tibet. Already, we lamented, two luxury hotels were under construction on the far side of town (one of them, a $30 million monstrosity, soon to be bought by Holiday Inn), and already there was talk of direct flights from Nepal and Hong Kong. A privately owned taxi firm had already set up business. Already, too, local children were beginning to ask for ballpoint pens, and greeting foreigners with shouts of "Hello!" There was already a copy of "Best Disco 84 Vol. 2" in the marketplace, next to the folk dentists and daggers and curled, yak-hide shoes, as well as a Junior League cap, and even a T-shirt stamped with the curious legend "Los Angeles 1985 Olympics."

Soon, the foreigners said, the place would be swarming with corrupting foreigners. Soon, we agreed, it would be full of people just like us. "Tibet is going to get real spoilt real fast," said a Canadian, between tokes of his Great Wall Grass. With that, he turned up his tape of "Born in the U.S.A." and prepared to let more fireworks off into the night.

One morning in Lhasa, I awoke to find snow blanketing the mountains, and a fine rain misting the town. As if in a dream, I made the long ascent up to the Potala Palace, whose thirteen white and brown and golden stories preside over the town with silent majesty. Inside, the secret rooms were heavy with the chanting of holy texts. The smell of butter lamps was everywhere, and flashes of a sky, now brilliant blue, outside. Banners fluttered in the wind, prayer bells sounded. Sunlight and silence and high air.

In some rooms, ruddy-cheeked girls and women in many-colored aprons bowed before monks who poured blessings of water in their hands; in others, ancient men placed coins and bank notes on the altar. And into the empty spaces, the slanted sunlight came softly, filtered through red or golden curtains. Uplifted by the chants, the smiles, the holy hush, I felt myself to be a clean and empty room, thrown open to the breeze.

And then came the golden afternoon. Then lightning over distant purple mountains. Then nightfall, and silence, and the stars.

YET THE GREATEST of all the sights in the Holy City, according to the wisdom of the Banak Shol, was the sacred rite known as the Celestial Burial. Each morning, at dawn, on a hillside five miles out of town, the bodies of the newly dead were placed on a huge, flat rock. There a sturdy local man, dressed in a white apron and armed with a large cleaver, would set about hacking them into small pieces. Assistants would grind the bones. When at last the corpses had been reduced to strips of bloody flesh, they were left on the Promethean stone for the vultures.

For Tibetan Buddhists, the ritual was a sacrament, a way of sending corpses back into the cycle of Nature, of removing all traces of the departed. For the visitors who had begun to congregate in larger and still larger numbers to watch the man they called "the Butcher," the rite was the last word in picturesque exoticism.

I was no different, and so one morning, I got up at four o'clock and walked for more than an hour through the night, crossing a field full of bones and wading through an icy stream that left my thighs stinging with the cold. By the time I arrived on the sacrificial rock, three Westerners were already seated, cross-legged, around a fire, murmuring Buddhist chants and fingering their rosaries. Twenty others stood around them on the darkened hillside, faces lit up by the flames. As the sky began to change color, three Tibetans picked up a body, wrapped it from head to toe in bandages, and gave it to the flames. Then, as the body burned, they handed some of us sticks of incense to hold, while the chanting continued. Afterward, with customary good humor, they brought us glasses of butter tea and chunks of bread the color of red meat.

Then they marched back to the rock, where the corpses of two more affluent citizens had been placed. One of the Tibetans tied an apron around his waist, picked up his ax and set about his work. As he did so, a gaggle of onlookers—most of them Chinese tourists from Hong Kong—started to inch closer to the sacred ground, chattering as they went. The man muttered something to himself, but continued about his task. Still, however, the visitors edged closer, giggling and whispering at the sight. The Tibetan stopped what he was doing, the gossip continued. And then, of a sudden, with a bloodcurdling shriek, the man whirled around and shouted again and, waving a piece of reddened flesh, he came after the visitors like a demon, slicing the air with his knife and screaming curses at their blasphemy. The tourists turned on their heels; still the Tibetan gave chase, reviling them for their irreverence. Terrified, the Chinese retreated to a safe position. The man stood before them, glowering.

After a long silence, the Tibetan turned around slowly and trudged back to his task. Chastened, we gathered on a hillside above the rock, a safe distance away. Before long, however, we were edging forward again, jostling to get a better glimpse of the dissection, urgently asking one another for binoculars and zoom lenses to get a close-up of the blood.

"Sometimes I think that we are the vultures," said a Yugoslav girl who had come to Tibet in search of an image glimpsed in a dream a decade before.

"Oh no," said a Danish girl. "It's always wild on Mondays. The butcher takes Sundays off, so Monday's always the best day to come here." She turned around with a smile. "On Mondays, it's great: there are always plenty of corpses."

NEPAL
The Quest
Becomes
a Trek

ITHIN MINUTES
of landing in Kathmandu, I found myself in Eden.

The Hotel Eden, that is, not to be confused with the Paradise Restaurant around the corner or the Hotel Shangri-La. The Eden was on the intersection of Freak Street and the Dharmapath, which was, I thought, the perfect location: at the intersection of hippiedom and Hinduism, where Haight-Ashbury meets the Himalayas. This, in fact, was exactly the kind of cross-cultural crossroads that I had hoped to find. For legend had it that Kathmandu was quite a trip—at once a time machine and a magic carpet—and I had come here to be transported. Not, however, to a dusty Himalayan kingdom, or even to a medieval community unchanged for many centuries. I wished to travel back no more than twenty years, and to be deposited in nowhere more exotic than a city of the spirit where people still regarded money as immaterial and youth as something more than a preparation for middle age. In Kathmandu I hoped to find the last stronghold of the sixties. And in the sixties I hoped to find a reflection of a younger and more innocent America, the land of idealism I was born too late to know.

At home, the sixties had long been the subject of embarrassed revisionism and packaged nostalgia. And where the counterculture had not been demolished, it had—worse still—been domesticated. Berkeley was now the province of born-again Christians and evangelical Reaganauts; the Haight had become a model of elegant gentrification. And all three of the cities in which I had recently made my home—Cambridge, Santa Barbara and Manhattan—had spent much of the last decade trading in their dreams for securities. The coffeehouses of Cambridge had been turned into croissanteries; Santa Barbara had shed its idiosyncrasies to become nothing more than a bright young thing for bright young things, the setting for a national soap opera; and whatever rebellion against fashion had once been found in Manhattan was now a fashionable rebellion and a rebellious fashion in a metropolis that had consolidated its status as the world capital of greed. As riches had been made, imaginations seemed to have been impoverished. Nonetheless, I had great expectations for Kathmandu—subject of Cat Stevens songs, longtime mecca of the hippies, sometime colony of the professional idealists of the Peace Corps. "When you are in Nepal," said the magazine ad for the Jhwalakhel Distillery, "the land of the spirited people, keep your spirit high with Ruslan vodka." The double pun on "high" and "spirit" struck me as exceedingly auspicious.

My hopes had been further excited just three weeks before my arrival in Nepal in, of all unlikely places, the Schwedagon Pagoda in Rangoon. Going there for the Buddhist Festival of Lights, I found myself in a state of holy enchantment. A great full moon rose behind the temple's soaring gold-leaf stupa; local families, all in their brightest silks, gathered for photographs by the side of golden Buddhas; tinseled shrines were lit up with halos of flickering candles. A local man waved at me from an antechamber, and I hurried over. Inside, a group of women was busily preparing dishes of vegetables and rice in one corner, while, at the center of the shrine, a Western couple sat smiling back their greetings. The girl was dressed in an earth mother's uniform of bandanna, thick sweater and jeans, her friend in dropout jumper and jeans. "This is a holy day for Buddha," explained our host, handing each of us some food. "And this, you see, is a custom of our religion." "We have a religion too," offered the foreign girl brightly. "It's called the Grateful Dead."

The pious Burmese gentleman did not seem delighted to hear of this worship of anti-Boddhisattvas, but I quickly warmed to the earnest, friendly pair. They seemed to be eminently gentle souls, and I could not help being impressed when they informed me that they had given up their jobs in Vancouver, their homes, even their proprietorship of a local Dead-head fanzine, in order to come to Asia for a year. Just to travel? No, they replied, they planned to work in an eye clinic sponsored by the Dead. Where exactly? Nepal. Perfect, I thought. Hessean journeyers to the East, propelled by a social conscience, a lifetime of Dead-mania, a kind of improvised innocence—this was exactly what I dreamed of finding in Kathmandu.

MY FIRST IMPRESSION of the city was delirious. I felt as if I had tumbled into the jangled and kaleidoscoped subconscious of an opium freak. Sweet incense wafted out of stores crushed raggedly together along dusty, crooked streets, and out from their walls hung horror-eyed masks, spinning prayer wheels, druggy thanka scrolls and revolving lanterns. Mirrors caught the light on shoulder bags, long dresses streamed from carved wooden balconies, scarves fluttered in the breeze, demons stared out of rice-paper calendars. On every side, irregular, nine-storied temples jutted up, and then were obscured by a flutter of pigeons. Squeaky-voiced elves chattered around the shrines where they peddled Bhutanese stamps, Niwari paintings, English chocolate. A ramshackle hut advertised the "Unique Typing Institute" and its only customer, standing patiently outside, was a cow. Everywhere, the dusty streets spun and whirled and revolved like a mandala. Freaks and flute sellers wandered in circles around a main square where long-haired men from East and West, hipsters and hawkers, hustlers and heretics, ricocheted counters off the sides of Carom boards. Snakelike icons wriggled from cardboard signs and elephant-headed gods sat in the middle of yellow-wreathed shrines and everywhere, staring down from walls and homes and streamers, were eyes, eyes, narrow, painted pairs of eyes.

Senses reeling, I caught glimpses, or glimpses of glimpses, of the freewheeling psychedelic fun house I had imagined from afar. A ponytailed Italian in a thick red waistcoat and silken Kashmiri cravat sat on a jewelry-store stool, studiously rolling a joint; when a girl asked him where she could get some hash, he looked up blearily, smiled and trudged off down the street on her behalf. He did not need to look far. Glassy-eyed vendors patrolled the length and breadth of Freak Street, walking in circles, talking in circles, muttering a steady litany: "Buy hashish. Buy hash. Buy hashish!" One dazed fellow sat in a dusty doorway intoning a steady monklike chant: "Hash. Hashish. Change dollars. Traveler's checks." Another entrepreneur, hands thrust into his pockets against the winter chill, fast-talked his way through his own unorthodox rosary: "Brown sugar, white sugar, coke, smack, or dope."

And Dylan was crooning "Isis" from the second floor of a dusty, red brick café and a few longhairs were shuffling down dark passageways into 50-cent-a-night flophouses. "Optic Nerve," said one shop; "Humor," said another. A crew-cut Western woman shuffled past in yellow-and-burgundy Buddhist raiment and sunglasses, while a man with a full-blown Maharishi beard stared over his pot of tea at anyone who would return his gaze. The shelves of the disheveled bookstalls were packed with *The Directory of Dreams*, *A Guide to the Tarot* and *Man's Eternal Quest*, and flapping against one of the clothes stores was a calendar put out by the "Eden Hashish House" ("the Oldest and Favorite Shop in Town serving you the Best Nepali Hashish and Ganja"). "Let us Take you Higher," offered the friendly ad. "Come visit us any time for all your hashish needs." Edens and hash houses had never, I imagined, been far apart in Kathmandu.

And peering out at me from every one of the open-fronted stores, the local shopkeepers were smiling back with warmth, but unsurrendered dignity. The Nepalis were said to be capable of great and penetrating intuitiveness. In Kathmandu, a friend from New York told me how she had been walking through Manhattan just two months earlier when a voice from behind her called out, "Are you an artist?" However did this stranger know that she was indeed an aspiring writer with a weakness for artists? Turning around, she had found herself staring at a man from the East. He came from Nepal, he said, and she should look him up there. With that, the mysterious character had vanished once more into the shadows.

My friend had indeed come to Nepal. And as soon as we met up, I assured her that the wisdom of the East would not be hard to find here. From the rooftop of the Eden, we could see the mountains bright in the clear distance, and, presiding over us from a nearby hill, shining in the clean winter light, the gleaming white stupa of Swayambhunath Temple. This, we decided, must be the site of our maiden pilgrimage. And so we headed off through a warren of dust-filled streets, past squawking, bright-eyed urchins, under lion-headed banners wishing everyone an auspicious New Year, and past the Jubilant Pre-Primary School. Soon, the noise of the city began to subside, and the air picked up an invigorating sharpness. We walked through an avenue of trees, past fields smothered with wildflowers. We passed a few local men going about their business, small but sturdy-looking fellows in the rough tunics and fezzes of the High Atlas Mountains. We walked over narrow bridges and across fields of yellow flowers and then, in the bright and cloudless winter afternoon, we began our ascent of the hill.

Just short of the top, we came to a Tibetan monastery, its sunlit white terrace empty under the brilliant blue. Calmness filled the place, and distant chanting from a prayer hall. We decided to rest on the terrace, and as we sat there, reading and writing in the sun, a monk came out and engaged us gently in conversation. He had been here many years, he said, but still he missed his home in Tibet. He much looked forward to hearing His Holiness the Dalai Lama at Bodh Gaya later this year. Would we care to follow him inside?

Slipping off our shoes, we tiptoed into the central chamber. The hall was dark, and along its two main benches two rows of monks kneeled in their thick red robes. Their faces were lit by candles as they bowed above their scriptures. The smell of butter lamps mixed sweetly with the scent of incense. The deep-voiced chants rolled around and around the hall, broken at moments by the tolling of a gong and the sudden low growl of the head abbot.

Quite a few of the monks, I noticed, were mischief-eyed little characters, scarcely nine years old, whose vigor in shouting out the chants owed more, it seemed, to schoolboy zest than to spiritual zeal. Often, in fact, they forgot themselves in furtive, impish smiles—only to be briskly brought back to the matter at hand by an elder's gentle, but decisive, slap. And as the muttered chants went on, I began to lose myself in wistful reverie. The strange smells, the hypnotic repetitions, the flutter of candles transported me. I felt myself carried away to distant lamaseries, whisked off to snowy mountain passes. I almost imagined myself back in Tibet. And then, without a warning, I felt my friend tugging urgently at my sleeve. "Look over there," she whispered. I did, and there, to my astonishment, one of the young monks was happily bouncing a startled-looking Pekingese puppy up and down on his lap. As soon as he saw us watching him, he giggled at his broad-faced neighbor. This jovial character responded by flashing us a huge and gleeful smile. His mouth was filled with Dracula fangs purchased at some local novelty store.

Through it all, the chanting continued like a spell.

II

The best deal in Kathmandu, I soon discovered, was Paradise. "Nepal, the Fantasting Country, has become a Promised Land," began the book of national facts and figures put out by the Ministry of Tourism and written by U. S. Thappa. Another of U.S.'s volumes was called, simply, *Paradise Nepal*. Little boys wore Paradise T-shirts, and Paradise Tours and Travels had to compete against both Shangri-La Tours and Shangri-La Treks.

Nepal was not, however, selling Paradise in the sense of Arcadia—a Balinese tropical playground filled with unfallen fruit and unfallen souls. Rather, it was offering Paradise in its highest, and most rigorous, form: Nirvana. The greatest bargains in town were spiritual accessories. Sweatshirts that said "Adidas," or even "Ddidas," cost a small fortune in Kathmandu, but thankas, prayer wheels and Buddhist calendars could always be found on sale. Day-trippers could take their pick between Nirvana Tours and Lama Excursions. Bargain hunters could try the Temple of Trade Pvt. Ltd.

Nepal, in fact, had cornered this side of paradise. For twenty years now, it had cashed in on being the closest place on earth to the remotest place on earth, a country just around the corner from Shangri-La. And if Tibet's charm lay in its remoteness, Nepal's lay in its availability; a veteran of the mystic market, it knew exactly how to sell itself as a wholesale, secondhand Tibet. Thus the magic title of the Forbidden Land found its way into every single brand name: local stores were stocked not just with handicrafts, but with Tibetan handicrafts, Tibetan paintings, Tibetan bells, Tibetan scarves, Tibetan pizzas.

Nepal had the additional advantage of being on the fringes of India, and where India was still the biggest spiritual department store in the East, Nepal offered an economy-sized convenience store with many of the same goods at even better prices. And the country's hybrid mix of Buddhism and Hinduism, with bits of animism thrown in, allowed it to offer not just lamas, and not just yogis, but lamas and yogis thrown together in every kind of combination. Billboards all across town offered enough Thanka Painting courses, Himalayan Buddhist Meditation classes, sessions at the Himalayan Yogi Institute and yoga/massage doubleheaders to keep every resident of Santa Cruz out of mischief for a decade.

"Shining Enlightened Mastery," proclaimed the poster to be found in nearly every bookstore. Underneath, the ad announced: "Sri Swami Prem Paramahansa will be sharing his wisdom. Intoxicated in the love of God and the Supreme Ancient Knowledge since childhood, Sri Swamiji will share the fruits of his most elevated life in 900 discourses on The History of Mankind and the Planet Earth." Enlightenment on the installment plan! Nine hundred lectures sounded like a long haul, but the Swami's subject was, after all, a big one (an earlier work in his canon had been entitled "Biography of a Tough Yogi"). And the Swami's "intoxication" would, I suspected, have no trouble in finding a responsive audience.

For the second-best deal in Kathmandu was still instant mind expansion, a stairway to heaven even easier to mount than religion: twenty-five pounds of hash could be purchased in parts of the country for all of 30 cents (four hundred pounds cost the same as a small tube of suntan oil). Religion and drugs had been the country's two great cash crops for so long now that nobody really seemed to care which one was sedative and which one stimulant. Religion was a drug to some and drugs were a religion to others. In Kathmandu some people lapsed into a narcotic haze and called it Buddhist serenity, while others had opiate dreams and called them visions. "Drugs" and "gurus," they told themselves, were almost anagrams; the high and the holy were virtual synonyms.

Indeed, the very fact that spiritual and secular trips could hardly be distinguished had itself become a major selling point. In New York, the Simone Travel Bureau advertised trips to the "magical land where deities mingle with common people and legends merge with Hindu and Buddhist spiritualism." "There is a place halfway between here and heaven," said the ads for Royal Nepal Airlines, where "Legends are Real." Even the airline's magazine sported the distinctly ambiguous title of "Yeti: Flight Tales." Within the pages of *The Nepal Traveler* ("which combines fantasy with very practical tips to trekking"), the same theme was struck again and again, as reverberatingly as a temple gong.

That same division was no less ubiquitous within the "Fabled Kingdom." The most cherished sight here was the Kumari, or Living Goddess, a prepubescent girl who was consigned to an upper-floor temple room where she served as a flesh-and-blood incarnation of a divinity; the most famous line about the place was Kipling's claim that "the wildest dreams of Kew are the facts of Kathmandu." Even the two national symbols, which had given their names to the capital's five-star hotel and restaurant, turned on this same ambiguity: Yak and Yeti, most earth-bound of creatures and most mythical. Nepal seemed to have one eye on the heavens and the other close to the ground.

This double perspective made, of course, for some double-edged blessings. Where sacred met profane, the result was often confusion. Earth's Heaven, the name of one local restaurant, was a case in point. Even the location of the Eden, which had so delighted me at first, was not so far from limbo: where the Dharmapath meets Freak Street was not only where East meets West, but also where self-sacrifice runs into self-indulgence. The next road along was the Ganga Path (or was it the Ganja Path?). Even so, I decided, all this was simply part and parcel of the sixties, a spirit that had claimed as many casualties as visionaries. Some doubtless came to Kathmandu to learn how to turn their experiences into epiphanies, but plenty of others planned to enjoy their vices more by learning how to call them virtues.

Yet what began to surprise me as I looked more closely at the town was not that religion or drugs were being abused, but rather that both of them seemed largely absent. Neither casualties nor visionaries were very much in evidence around Freak Street; neither wasted druggies nor starry-eyed dreamers flocked through the streets. Here and there, of course, I caught flashes of the spirit that had hit me so forcibly on arrival: dancing skeletons—icons of the Grateful Dead!—hung from the dark walls of some Tibetan temples and, in the abject darkness of the State Bank, I spied an arresting character in a ponytail with kohl around his green eyes, clad in an emerald Chinese jacket and a red coolie's hat. The Jasmine Restaurant did, as expectation dictated, have some old King Crimson anthems on its system, while a nearby health-food joint was selling Reality Soup. One salesman in Durbar Square kept up an impressively loud pitch of "A kilo of smack, a kilo of smack." Yet I could as easily have found all this in Washington Square.

Still, I assured my friend, we would at least find some strangeness in the "Tantric" restaurant in Durbar Square. Here at least was a Yin-Yang symbol hanging from the facade; here at least we would see dead-eyed hippies sprawled across cushions and munching hash brownies while they listened to Pink Floyd. As we entered the place, we shed our shoes, and as we sat down, we prepared to shed our inhibitions. The small round room was filled with smoke, and country-and-Eastern music wafted out of its sound system. On its floors were scattered pillows and divans; its walls swarmed with mandalas and thankas. This, I thought, must be an opium den, and my friend likened it to a womb. But there were no lamps and pipes beside every cushion, and no creative spasms rent the air. Yin was not in evidence; nor, to be frank, was Yang. Nothing, in fact, but a few well-heeled Italian tourists in their late thirties. We had traveled 8,000 miles only to end up, so it seemed, in a facsimile of the East Village.

Somewhat disappointed, I went back to the Eden to sleep. My friend, however, decided to stroll through the dreaming town. As she was wandering along Freak Street, a voice called out to her from behind. "Are you an artist?"

Amazed, she turned around. There stood the same man she had met in Manhattan just two months before! Noting that her smiling recognition of him was unreciprocated (an American girl was not often accosted in the streets by Nepali boys, but who knows how often a Nepali boy might accost American girls?), my friend pointed out that they had met only a few weeks before and half a world away. Her questioner recovered quickly. "Yes indeed," he replied, without missing a beat. "I feel that you and I have the same kind of power. I feel a strange kind of affinity with you. Tonight is a holy night. Come and see my apartment."

The circumstances were too remarkable not to agree. Fascinated, my friend assented, following the leather-jacketed young man through the darkened, empty streets. "I come from Tibet," he told her as they walked, "and my name is Lobsang. But you can call me Lobby."

They arrived at the flat, and Lobby turned on the light to reveal two large posters: one of the Dalai Lama, the other of Rocky. His family, he explained, were all Tibetan holy men, but the medallion he wore around his neck had been given him by Sly Stallone. He had, he said, sort of one foot in New York and the other in Nepal. Lobby got up for a minute to put on a Dire Straits tape, then edged a little closer on the sofa. He was an artist himself, he went on, and an actor and a writer. But he knew all about the mysteries of Tibet. He put a hand on his visitor's arm. Lobby certainly lived up to his name. His uncle, he said, was a professor at Columbia University, and Richard Gere was about to come and stay in this very flat. "I feel this great *chi* coming from you," he continued, warming to his theme. "I feel this great spiritual force. The only trouble is, your *chakras* are blocked." What could she do? asked my friend. Well, said Lobby, as it happened, he did know of a cure: an ancient form of Tibetan massage passed down to him by his forefathers from the secret Land of Snows. Would she like to give it a try?

III

In time, as I came to know Kathmandu better, I began to recognize that the swarming city I had seen at first was as much in the eye of the beholder as in the heart of the beheld. The whirling surfaces existed, no doubt, but they seemed to be no more than surfaces. Revelations both mind-boggling and earth-shattering did not in fact lie around every corner. But still, when it came to modest, modish pleasures, the place was not to be surpassed. I had the best enchilada of my life on Freak Street, and the chocolates in the stores seemed to have been sent special delivery from the heavens. As for the pies for which Nepal was famous, they exceeded even their reputation. Soon I established my own sacramental ritual: disappearing several times each day into the dark entrances of cafés—not just Mom's Health Food Restaurant and Aunt Jane's, but also Tibetan, Chinese and stateless restaurants—in order to devour extraordinary apple pies, almond layer pies, orange cakes, fruit cakes, lemon pies and more apple pies.

Nepal, of course, had long been famous for adapting to Western tastes and fashions with unparalleled swiftness and skill. In the forties, before the country was even linked to the outside world by road, Kathmandu was said to be *the* place in the Himalayas for cinemas and cars. The king at that time, Tribhubana (he of plucked eyebrows and scented breath), was a celebrated connoisseur of mail-order catalogues who sent porters across the mountains to bring back lounge suits and gadgets for the royal palace. In that respect, at least, little seemed to have changed. When I stepped into a local store in the ten-hut village of Tandi Bazaar in the malarial lowlands of Nepal, I found, on the counter, an issue of *The New York Review of Books*, nine months old, open to an article entitled "The Melancholy of Montaigne." And whenever Westerners staying in India felt homesick, a Nepali who lived in Benares informed me, they simply hurried off to Kathmandu.

"We Solve you all Travel Problems," promised Pawan Travels, "and make you Journey Easy and Funny."

Nepal's prodigious versatility was most apparent, however, in the smorgasbord of its menus, which could easily have put the United Nations cafeteria to shame. Every one of them, so it seemed, offered everything from borscht to quiche and sukiyaki to soyburgers. The Jamaly Restaurant served up "Mecxican food," Italian, American, Chop Suey, Moussaka, Curry and "Viena Schnitzel." Shiva's Sky, in the Continental section of its menu, provided "Mexican Takos," Vegetarian Chop Suey and Chow Mein. The Nor-Ling posted outside a twenty-six-line billboard listing its offerings, and beginning: "We offer delicious Tibetan, Italian, India, Nepal, Chinese dishes, minestrone soup,

Fr. onion soup . . . spagetti, lasagne, mousake a 'La' Greece . . ."
Everything of every nationality was available here—except
things Nepalese. When I asked a man in a candy store for
Nepalese chocolate, he looked distinctly put out. "We have
Indian chocolate, English, American, German. You can have
Thai chocolate. You can have Chinese marshmallow. But Nepalese, no. Here only international chocolate." And when I asked
another local what he served in his Kathmandu restaurant, he
answered crisply, "Indian, Chinese, Continental, German,
American, Mexican." And Nepalese? "No. Nepalese, very difficult."

LIKEWISE, EVERY KIND of conventional wisdom seemed available here—except, of course, the Nepalese. Nonetheless, I
refused to give up on what the brochures called "the land of
mystic delights." My guidebook assured me that a distinguished
astrologer could be found in Patan, by the name of Mangal Raj
Joshi. Little else was said about the sage, but that only added to
his mystery. And so, one bright afternoon, my friend and I hailed
an ailing "tempo" (the haphazard, three-wheeled vehicle that is
the country's contribution to the kamikaze art), and bumped
along rutted ditches and unpaved roads into the maze of alleyways known as Patan. Deposited at a corner in the middle of this
labyrinth, we looked around. No sage was in sight. No wisdom
was in view. Not even any animate life was apparent. Wandering
around a little, we came at last upon a German patiently trying
to rev up his motorcycle in the dust. How could we get to the
center of town? "Follow the paved road," he said cryptically.
"Always the paved road."

This we did, through serpentine passageways and lanes, past
grubby courtyards and old homes, until at last we arrived at a
central jumble of temples. Religious figures were on every side;
wise men, however, were not. Undefeated, we trooped into the
only restaurant in sight, the Café de Patan. After an apple pie or
two, we asked the waiter where we might find the famous Mr.
Joshi.

He stopped to think for a moment. "Astrologer," I prompted.
He considered the matter a little longer. "Go to the Golden
Temple," he said. "Ask at the Golden Temple."

The Kathmandu Valley contains more temples per square foot

than any other place on earth. Nearly all of them have gold on their stupas, gold in their spires, gold in some part or another. None of them has an English name.

Nonetheless, we were disinclined to ignore instructions that had been delivered in the best Hollywood Sage manner, and so we gamely wandered around temple after temple, all of them golden, all of them empty. Beginning at last to suspect that we were in pursuit of a golden fleece, we turned down a dark side street. There was a temple almost devoid of gold! This must be the place we sought. I went up to a gatekeeper. Did he know the astrologer?

Silently, he pointed to another guardian of the temple.

Mr. Joshi? I presumed.

"Ah," said the smiling young man. "Palmist!"

I nodded enthusiastically. "Hello, Mr. Joshi!"

The black-jacketed man said nothing. Instead, he turned around and led us through the temple, and out into a huge sunlit square filled with urchins, and down an alleyway, and through a narrow archway, and into a tiny lane and up to a small black door. It was locked.

"Joshi?" he asked a shopkeeper on the other side of the alley. The man motioned heavenward.

Without a word, our leader set off again, taking us past more golden temples, into more private courtyards, through long dark lanes and then at last into what looked like a barn. We stared around the place uncertainly, while our sibylline guide vanished up a wooden ladder. A minute or so later, he poked his head down through the attic opening, and motioned us up. Scrambling up the ladder, we adjusted our eyes to the half-darkness. There, standing before us in fez and dark glasses and shoeless socks, on the second floor of what seemed to be a stable, was Mr. Joshi, the Royal Astrologer of Nepal.

We bowed and respectfully exchanged greetings as the great man ushered us into his cell. I looked around the ill-lit, low-roofed little chamber with wonder. Its walls were covered with hieroglyphical calendars and dusty almanacs. Amidst these wizardly ephemerides hung portraits of King Birendra and his queen (clients both of the celebrated Joshi). Next to a blinding poster advertising Fujicolor film were some dusty glass cases filled with old volumes. All of them, I noticed excitedly, were about the "Soul." And then I peered a little closer through the half-light and realized they said "Soil."

"I have studied sixteen years in Benares Hindi University,"began Prof. Dr. Mr. Joshi, Ph.D. (as his business card identified him). "Also I have given lectures at Reading University in England, and at Northwestern University in Chicago." In what subject? I asked. "Astronomy," he answered, and the silence and the darkness deepened.

"I also was ten months in Texas."

"At the university there?"

"No." Silence. "I was an adviser at NASA."

The mystery around the hierophant expanded.

"And then," went on the sage, "I spent a month in Acapulco." The alarm on his visitors' faces must have been evident. "In Acapulco," Dr. Joshi continued with some asperity, "I was doing research. Into the Mexican system of astrology. I have looked at the Chinese system, the Mexican system, the Indonesian system, the Indian system and the Nepali system." And which had he found to be best? I asked, perhaps redundantly. "The Indian," he said severely, "and the Nepali."

We sat there in silence, unsure what came next.

"Would you have time," I tried, "to tell our futures?"

Silence. Dr. Joshi stared back at us. "There exist," he said, "three different systems," and he outlined their prices on a piece of paper.

"Do all three types produce the same results?"

The Royal Astrologer gave me a hard stare in the dark room. An uncomfortable pause ensued. In Nepal, I gathered, futures came in economy, business and luxury class; all three, however, transported one to the same destination. And if prudence ruled out the first-class fortune, protocol told us to spurn the cheapest.

"Maybe we'll try the middle type."

"Then it will cost two hundred fifty rupees for a chart," proclaimed the Royal Astrologer. I blanched. That was equivalent to $14, four round-trip bus tickets to Pokhara, forty pieces of apple pie or ten nights in a guesthouse, whichever came first. Dr. Joshi saw my hesitation. "Sometimes," he added disapprovingly, "I can give fifty-rupee student discount."

Happily we agreed on the second-class fortunes and asked him when they would be ready. In ten minutes, said Dr. Joshi in a voice full of portent, he would have to go to the Royal Palace. But if we would return in three hours, he would explain to us the rest of our lives. Fortunes, it seemed, were quickly ascertained in the shadow of the Himalayas.

Thus tantalized, the two of us wandered off into the alleyways of Patan, visited a Tibetan refugee camp, walked around Nepal's only zoo (where a mad white-haired Swiss woman with a Nepali by her side was cross-questioning monkeys and a bear was clutching the bars of his cage and sobbing helplessly), stopped in at a German café for some apple pie and made our way back, through the failing light, down dark lanes, across courtyards and up the wooden ladder to the sage's den.

Several customers were sitting apprehensively in the utter darkness of the soothsayer's waiting room. A chilling breeze came in through the open windows. Dr. Joshi, still shoeless, shuffled in and out, dealing with one life at a time. Then, at last, he motioned us up another creaking ladder into a tiny top-floor attic. "Here," he said confidentially, "we will not be disturbed."

Teeth chattering in the gathering cold, we hugged ourselves with our arms as we leaned forward to hear our futures. The Royal Astrologer peered at the mass of squiggles and signs before him in the darkness. "Generally," he began, "I have found that . . ." And then the door was flung open, and an old Nepali gentleman in a fez raced in and put on the brakes just a few steps away from the Royal Astrologer. Dr. Joshi turned to him, and the man poured out a series of inquiries. The two swapped sentences in staccato gunfire bursts, and then at last the supplicant fell silent and the astrologer turned back to us. Fumbling for his notes, he tried to collect his thoughts. Then he began once more to read the stars.

"Generally, I have found that the most important principle in your life is . . ." But this was all too much for the be-fezzed man, who was still hovering restlessly in the darkness, his future hanging precariously in the balance. Out burst another furious stream of questions. With a deep sigh, Dr. Joshi took off his glasses and rubbed his eyes. Then, in a calm voice, he laid bare the man's future. His monologue complete, he turned back, a little brusquely, to us.

"Where was I?" he wondered, putting back his glasses. "Where was I?" And then there came a fearful banging at the door, desperate and importunate. Muttering something hateful, the Royal Astrologer got up and trudged across the room to see what was the matter. Outside, in the corridor, stood a trio of wide-eyed petitioners—a woman and what I assumed to be her son and prospective daughter-in-law. The nuptials were on hold, I surmised, until some critical matters in the stars had been cleared up. The ever-patient Dr. Joshi listened to a few questions, fired off a few bulletins from the heavens and then, shutting the door, came back to us.

"Generally, I have found," he started up again, and peered more closely at my chart, "that every month, on the night of the full moon, you must fast."

I looked back at him in horror. "Okay," he added swiftly, "you must eat only vegetarian food every month on the night of the full moon."

With that he consulted my destiny again. "Also," he went on after a pause, "every month on the night of the full moon, you must meditate for one hour."

"One whole hour?"

"Okay, okay. Fifteen minutes."

By then, alas, our time was almost up. Our futures hanging in the balance, we went back out into the dark.

IV

In the end, perhaps, I came closest to the real Nepal when least I sought it. One evening, I went up to the roof of the Eden, from which, each morning, I watched the city come to life through the mist, as women shook their washing clean on rooftops and children skipped rope in the dust of tiny courtyards. Now the process was reversed. The dusk began to obscure the mountains, and lights came up all around the jagged scrawl of streets below. People thronged through the main squares as they went about their evening shopping. Scamps zigzagged with wild squeals across the narrow lanes. And I, far above, felt that I had indeed been taken back in some time machine to a Dickensian London in December, with gas fires lit against the dark afternoons, and rapscallions racing through a twilight bright with the promise of a coming Christmas. I felt a pang of some mysterious homesickness.

Drawn into the streets, now dark, I went downstairs and walked out, through the commotion of Freak Street and past the temples of Durbar Square and into the distant alleyways, now desolate and still. A few of the shrines were lit up, and occasional footfalls echoed through the crooked, cobbled streets. I felt myself again a child in Oxford. A sense of coziness emanated from the dark, of families at home amid chocolate and tea. Lights shone in second-floor windows, smells of cooking wafted out of courtyards. Yet all these rituals were shut off from me, and that, in its way, made me happier than anything. For the first time since I came to Kathmandu, I felt that the city had turned its back on foreigners and was going instead about its age-old ways.

As I wandered absently through the quiet lanes, empty save for a few beggars sleeping in the temples, I was roused abruptly from my daydreams by a vigorous greeting from a storefront. "Hello, my friend!" called a smiling little boy, waving animatedly in my direction. I strolled over to his shop, and we shook hands. Then he scampered up a narrow flight of stairs and I went after. On the second floor were two tiny rooms decorated in every spare square inch with thankas.

Inside this psychedelic den of visions, Pappy prepared some cushions for me on the floor and made a cup of tea. On the wall he pointed out some photos of his family celebrating Divali and then he went off to fetch a thick album of letters from all his satisfied customers around the world. He took me through the addresses and, with them, all the distant places of enchantment he hoped one day to visit. Then, in the manner peculiar to the bright-eyed, high-voiced little schoolboys who seem at times to run Kathmandu, Pappy launched into a solemn but confident disquisition on the Art of Nepal. Using the paintings on the walls, he described to me the difference between Niwari, Nepali and Tibetan thankas. He explained how Spanish tourists always went for the cheap kind of thankas, but Americans and Germans knew how to tell the sublime from the ordinary. And he told me that as soon as his English was good enough, he planned to make his fortune overseas.

Our tea finished, Pappy offered to take me on a night tour of his city. We walked outside, and through more narrow passageways. We heard an acoustic guitar floating out of a temple, we passed an open space that had been turned for the evening into a raucous outdoor disco. A couple of other engaging schoolboys who had entertained me earlier in the day called out their hellos. These versatile characters sold not only all three kinds of thankas but also Zen paintings, Hokusai prints and Aubrey Beardsley reproductions, while handing out a ten-page homemade pamphlet explaining Buddhist iconography. Pappy glared at his rivals with less good humor than usual, and hissed, "No good boys." Finally, we arrived at his family's house.

Putting a finger to his lips, Pappy guided me to a staircase. We crept up, making as little noise as possible, and then he led me through a corridor and opened a door.

There, inside an inner sanctum, sat fifty or so men on folding chairs, absolutely silent. We slipped inside, sat down and looked toward the front of the room. On a small color TV screen, a pudgy Indian actor was shaking through a parody of Michael Jackson's contortions in the "Thriller" video. We watched for a while, then tiptoed out again. There were fifty video clubs like that in the neighborhood, whispered Pappy. They charged 2, 3, 4 rupees. Some showed Hindi movies, some kung fu. Some offered 2-rupee admission for children. But competition was tough. And a VCR cost 50,000 rupees ($3,000), fully as much as a new house.

The real, behind-closed-doors Nepal, if this was it, did not seem so different from the Nepal that every foreigner could see. Which should have been no surprise. Only those who have money can afford not to think about money. ("Bankers talk about transcendental meditation, writers talk about money," as Erica Jong writes in another context. "Spirituality is expensive.") Nepal, however, was far from such a position of luxury. Illiteracy here was still higher than 80 percent and, in a country where there was often only one doctor for 100,000 people, it was not surprising, perhaps, that the average Nepali did not live much past forty. Monasteries and mandalas must be the least of the nation's concerns.

Tourism, of course, had brought many resources to the country, and Nepal had adapted to the trade with a remarkable resourcefulness of its own. In 1955, no road connected the country with the outside world, and there was only one restaurant in the entire capital. The first international flight arrived in Kathmandu only a year before men walked on the moon, and in the early sixties, only around seven tourists arrived each day. Since then, however, the number had rocketed up to 700 a day. Were there many touts in Kathmandu, I asked an American executive who often did business there. He chuckled. "Seventy-five percent of the country's GNP is in tourism," he said, "and the other twenty-five percent, I think, is in drugs."

The sudden boom had not, of course, been without its costs. Flocking to Nepal to find drugs, Westerners had left Nepal with a sad drug problem of its own: there were now 15,000 heroin addicts in Kathmandu alone, or one in every twenty of the town's young men. Racing to Nepal to find religion, Westerners had left Nepalis thinking of the spiritual in largely material terms: holy men nowadays demanded payment every time their picture was taken, while shrewd peasants had taken to selling pages of their sacred texts. Hurrying to Nepal for its mountain views, Westerners had left Nepalis with an expanded sense of horizon, and a diminished sense of wonder; since a tourist could offer a village bread man 2 cents for a roll, twice the local price, the bread man would reserve all his goods for foreigners. In time, the rice man and the vegetable man would likely follow suit. During the twenty years in which tourism had soared, the per capita income of Nepal had, incredibly, fallen. Today, a third of all the country's citizens earn no more than 15 cents a day.

"I am not very rich," a young boy told me as the early morning sunlight flooded the rooftop dining room of the Eden. "I do not want big job in the U.S. Small job okay." Wanting what the East had, the West, I thought, saddled the East with awareness of what it did not have. Trading dollars for dreams, the West brought notions of profit and loss to the levelheaded areas in the world. Rich enough to go native, the West came East to shed all its belongings, and the East scrambled in the dust to pick them up as they fell.

Yet still, I did not worry very much about Nepal. The Nepalis seemed to have a keen sense of how to endure the assaults of tourism, and even of how to gain from foreigners without seeming grasping. The country had contrived to receive foreign aid from America, Russia, China and just about everyone else. King

Birendra, graduate of Eton, alumnus of Harvard and reincarnation of Vishnu, had reportedly become fabulously rich thanks to a variety of concerns, most notably a pharmaceuticals firm that rejoiced in the inspired name of Royal Drugs. And if not exactly sagacious, the Nepalis certainly seemed savvy. An American friend who had joined a team traveling to the remote monasteries of Nepal in order to microfilm sacred texts before they could be sold told me that the Nepalese government had actually tried to charge the expedition for its charity. Even Edmund Hillary, the country's most famous foreign champion, had been forced to pay customs duties on the emergency medical supplies he brought in for the hospital he founded in Nepal.

Thus things remained in a fairly happy state of equilibrium. The Nepalese were not hard-sell hucksters, and the Westerners here were not hard-core hustlers. And though it knew how to live off the West, Nepal had none of the glossy seductiveness of Bangkok, the sometime worldliness of Bali or the wistful desperation of Manila. Kathmandu seemed a Shantih-town. The place still had an endearing wonkiness to it, a ragamuffin charm best exemplified by the schoolboy sages in brown pullovers and scholarly airs who operated most of its stores and cafés. The restaurants in Nepal offered every kind of national cuisine, and yet, by all accounts, every dish was pretty much the same. And every dish, so it was said, had pretty much the same effect. "The thing about the Nepalese," a New Zealander told me, "is that they're so friendly, and they're so keen to adapt to Western tastes, that they make dishes they don't have a clue how to cook. That's why everyone gets sick there."

Certainly the cuisine, though fantastically cosmopolitan, did not infallibly inspire confidence. At Suraha, a village with a population of less than 100, the guesthouses bravely attempted Western menus and promised "The gienic Food and Beverage." Yet Western heads turned, and so did stomachs, at the choice among "Noddle," "Plane Toast" and "Custurd." I never saw a single customer order "Vegetable Plow." El Parador in Kathmandu had a whole section of its menu entitled "Iodine-Soaked Salad" and including such items as "Fruit Salad in Wheaped Cream." Its "Bout of Plain Curd," I always suspected, might lead to a bout of something even worse. And just about every café offered Buffburgers, Buff Steak, Buff Tacos (everything, in fact, but Bufferin). I left Nepal assuming this to be a widespread misspelling of "beef." It was only later, in India, that I lear-nedthat I could not have been more wrong: "buff," in fact, stood for water buffalo, and beef was available in Nepal only in a couple of five-star hotels that flew it in from India.

All this, however, only added to the place's raggedy charm. El Parador was typical. I liked it most not for its improbable Span-ish name (in the Tibetan quarter of the Nepalese capital!), or for its four-course Mexican breakfasts, or even for its routinely scrumptious apple pies, but most of all for its management: a pair of eager and soft-eyed little boys, as irrepressible as they were irresistible. As soon as I sat down on one of the restaurant's divans, the nine-year-old maître d' came up to me and smiled expectantly. I ordered and he bundled off to the kitchen and shouted something out. Once, he returned a few seconds later bearing, not the expected pot of tea, but an eighteen-month-old sibling, whom he bounced up and down in his arms, tenderly nuzzled, and proudly displayed to his startled customers. Another time, the twelve-year-old proprietor emerged solemnly from the back, placed an Eagles tape in the restaurant's cassette recorder and, closing his eyes as he danced, broke into note-per-fect harmonies on "Lying Eyes."

Both parties seemed more than eager to accommodate each and every Western demand, however strange. One dusky after-noon, a Scottish fellow, apparently fresh (or something other) from a Freak Street transaction, lurched into the café. One of the boys greeted him with a smile. Did they have anything with bananas in it, asked the newcomer with a weird intensity.

"Banana pie," piped the manager. "Banana omelette. Banana pancake . . ."

At this, the customer suddenly swerved off in another direc-tion. "You got some girls here?" he demanded.

The small salesman was unprepared for this, but nonetheless undaunted. "We have Mexican breakfast. Cappuccino. Pies."

"Yeah, but have you got Some Girls?"

The host looked perplexed. They had tacos, he explained, and tea and also Tibetan pizza.

With that, the Scotsman angrily stalked out, and the boy

returned cheerfully to his task, never suspecting that the customer had wanted nothing more exotic than a Rolling Stones cassette.

EL PARADOR, THOUGH, was only typical of an air—unworldly, if not exactly spiritual—that seemed to suffuse the faraway land-locked kingdom. Flying to Kathmandu from India, one had to turn one's watch forward by exactly ten minutes (Kathmandu, quite crazily, was five hours and forty minutes ahead of Greenwich Mean Time), and the entire country seemed equivalently, and endearingly, out of sync. At Pokhara Airport, a suami tree served passengers in place of a waiting lounge. "His Majesty Felicitates King Bedouin I" was a front-page headline in Nepal's English-language newspaper, *The Rising Nepal,* one day in November. Its other headlines were "His Majesty Receives Tika," "Nepalese Cultural Night in London" and "Blood Donations" (about blood given on the occasion of Her Majesty's thirty-seventh auspicious birthday). Buried on page 5 of the six-page edition was the headline "Gorbachev-Reagan Meet: Most Important for Mankind's History."

The same newspaper also did a roaring trade in largely unintelligible ads, or notices that would have been better off unintelligible: "Avail golden chance. Learn or improve your English under the most unique. Method. Get register your self immediately." In a similar vein, the museum in the old Royal Palace proudly displayed the Royal Aquarium and several other personal effects of a profoundly unregal nature. On the wall were photos of the king as a bewildered-looking toddler ("The Royal Babyhood," announced the caption below) and of the king as a bewildered-looking child atop a bewildered-looking horse ("His Majesty Approaching the Full Bloom of Youth"). "Entertainment! It never stops at Casino Nepal!" cried the country's only center for gambling. Next to it was a sign denying entry to all Nepalis.

V

One sunny afternoon, I made my final attempt to conquer what was proving to be an even tougher peak than the southwestern face of Everest—the "Dreamland Nepal" of the travel agents. I happened to be walking along a sidewalk when a young roadside soothsayer, dressed in red-and-orange fez and heavy brown overcoat, looked up at me brightly. Then he extended his palm. I might, I thought, be looking at my future.

"How much?" I asked.

"As you wish."

"Okay, um . . ."

"Five hundred rupees."

"What did you say?"

"One hundred rupees."

"Ten."

"Okay."

I was convinced already of the diviner's shrewdness. With a lofty flutter of his hand, he sent off a minion to fetch a translator. Then he picked up my hand and, eyes closed, began sight-reading its lines. We remained in this unlikely position for many minutes, while a crowd gathered around us. Finally, a man appeared, in rags, with lank black hair falling to his shoulders and a king-size, straggly beard. This character's principal qualification for the translating job, I gathered, was that he spoke almost no English, and what English he did speak sounded very close to gibberish.

All systems go, the soothsayer went back into his trance and began rocking back and forth where he sat. Each of his staccato Delphic utterances the translator deftly rendered meaningless. "You need an anti-person," he said. And my domestic future? "You have two wives, three children." And my health? "Wear a copper bracelet." Gnomic outbursts kept on shooting out of the palmist's mouth, but the rest of my life was lost in transmission.

The episode was not the eye-opening illumination I had expected. But it was a happy enough fiasco. And the same was true of much in Nepal. The longer I remained, the more I settled into its cheery rhythms, the more I came to recognize the unlikelihood of finding any real magic here. The Eden Hash House calendar was only a decoration, I was told, a quaint curiosity from an age long gone. Pie Alley had been rechristened, by visitors more fastidious than the earliest Western settlers, Pig Alley. Boris, the White Russian who had been a dancer with the Ballet Russe, friend to Stravinsky and Cocteau, caterer to heads of state and, for thirty years Kathmandu's principal tourist attraction, had died just one month before I arrived. And these days, when a Nepali led tourists up into an unlit second-floor room, the transaction that ensued usually revolved around dollars, not drugs.

The door to the Kathmandu of dreams was finally slammed shut on me one evening when I went to the Up and Down, the capital's solitary disco (the only other night life in town, residents said darkly, was the Marine Bar at the U.S. embassy on Friday nights). At the bar, I met an Irish academic who had lived in Kathmandu on and off for years, studying its caste system. When he heard that I was staying on Freak Street, on the other side of town, he reacted as if I had said I was just off with some groovy cats to a love-in where the Electric Prunes were performing. Freak Street, he said, was history; the place where foreigners hung out these days was Thamel.

Chastened, I looked around Thamel. Certainly, the area was as full of life, even late at night, as Freak Street was dead, and in place of the handful of lesser-spotted derelicts to be found at the center of town, there seemed to be brigades of bright, clean-cut foreigners, in thick sweaters and sensible skirts, marching from the Zen Restaurant to the Third Eye boutique and back again. In contrast to the windblown, dusty refuse of the area around the Eden, these streets were clean almost; with their wood-walled coffeehouses and the Old Vienna Inn, they conveyed a spanking briskness reminiscent of Martha's Vineyard or Carmel.

Around the corner from the Up and Down, I came upon the Pilgrim Book Shop, a beautiful, brightly lit store that had coffee and tables and books on one side of a blond-wood partition and, on the other, coffee-table books. The place was a smarter version of the Harvard Book Store Café, or Kramerbooks in Washington, or any of the other chic confectioners serving food for body and mind in renovated malls from Ghirardelli Square to Covent Garden. It stayed open till midnight and played classical music on its system and provided the latest issues of *Interview, Connoisseur* and *The New Yorker* for patrons to leaf through over their Celestial Seasonings tea. "Are you American?" I asked the distinctly New Yawkish waitress. "Nah. I'm a little Japanese. A little Indian. A little Nepali." Very much Nepali, I would have said.

Not far from the Pilgrim was one of the area's most fashionable dining spots, packed with cheerful, well-dressed health freaks drinking beers to the sound of Billy Joel. Eavesdropping, I caught just enough to get a sense of great means and narrow ends. Software, I heard, and Tacoma. Volvo. Manhattan law practice. Jimmy Carter had been on the same trekking route two weeks earlier. Everest was booked until 1990. "The mountains were real awesome. Like, we were wowed."

Uppers and Downers, indeed. These guys hadn't left their heads in San Francisco, I thought unkindly. They weren't interested in communing with Nature, they just wanted to do lunch with it sometime. Having hoped to find myself in a Grateful Dead song, I had ended up instead in an Ann Beattie story.

And as surely as the eighties had eclipsed the sixties, so trekking seemed mostly to have usurped questing. These days, more people came to Nepal to improve their muscles than to expand their minds; the career path was held in much higher esteem than the spiritual path. "Food for Thought" was chalked up every day on a blackboard at the Lost Horizon Tibetan restaurant, I noted with excitement. But on the day I ate there, the message, from Herbert Spencer, said: "The preservation of Health is a duty. Few seem conscious that there is such a thing as physical morality."

So where were all the freaks? I finally asked the Irishman with some plaintiveness. The freaks? he howled. Where had I been for the last ten years? The freaks had been flushed out of Nepal long ago. First the government had made drugs illegal. Then they had begun making occasional raids on the Freak Street crash pads. Finally, they had called upon an instrument even more powerful than simple morality or muscle: economics. A one-month Nepalese visa now cost $16. A one-month extension cost another $23, and a third-month extension $35. Thus a three-month stay in Nepal now cost no less than an apartment in a fairly nice house here (or five hundred pounds of hashish, whichever came first). The only freaks still hanging out in Nepal, said the Irishman, were second-rate leftovers dressed in uniform costumes of individuation: jeans, earrings, baggy pants and "Jesus boots." But drugs were still available, I noted. "Sure," said the Irishman. "Anything drug-related is possible here. But it's a business now, not a trip."

The absence of drugs was itself no bad thing; what I mourned was the absence of the sensibility that drove some people to drugs and the searching that others undertook instead of drugs. The Peace Corps had left a few traces of its presence—in the apple pies and health-food stores—but even they seemed to have faded into the woodwork. Where, I wondered, were the idealists? Had they too disappeared? "Of course," said Tomas, a thoughtful former Magic Bus driver from Amsterdam who now worked here for CARE. "That was ten years ago. That age is past."

It seemed to be true. "Attention Travelers," said the sign posted on most of the Freak Street restaurant walls. "Ashramed out, Caféd Out, Caked Out, Biscuit'd out, Chai'd out, Gompa'd out, Chicall'd out, Tea'd out? Bored to Tears? Then why not volunteer to help out at the local clinic run by Mother Teresa's sister?" Only, it seemed, after every single other option had been tried and every pleasure exhausted might the time come for a little social conscience.

It served me right, I suppose: prosaic justice. I had come to Kathmandu hoping to find a refuge from the trends of Santa Barbara, Cambridge and Manhattan. But that, I realized, was like going to Newcastle if one were allergic to coal. For Nepal's great skill lay in mirroring Western ways and keeping up with the Western times. It was hardly surprising, then, that it had followed the example of any American dropout from the sixties: shedding its ragged threads, cleaning up its act, going through business school and settling down to a good steady income as a law-abiding, upwardly mobile member of the eighties. Its livelihood depended on it.

These days, indeed, the facts of Kew were the facts of Kathmandu. Communications had sent the world spinning around so fast that every wheel came around full circle. Travel far enough East and you'd quickly end up in the West; go across the globe and you'd find that you had never left home at all.

"Excuse me, sister," said a Nepali man to my friend when we visited Bodnath Temple. "You want to go to trekking?" It seemed a request as Nepali as apple pie.

CHINA
The Door
Swings
Both Ways

The beautiful young girl lies on a grassy knoll
daydreaming about her future price charming.
— *Opening line of a review of the movie*
The Bordertown *in the* Beijing Review, *July 29, 1985*

HE NEW
China—the China that has opened its door to the outside world
and is beckoning it inside with a smile—deals with its suitors in
Hong Kong. The New China is well aware that her longtime
seclusion has only inflamed the romantic illusions of the West,
adding the lure of the long-forbidden to the appeal of the mysterious. The New China also knows that many a dreamy admirer
will spare no expense at all to catch a long-denied glimpse of her
mist-wreathed pagodas and jade mountains; a courtesan's
expensiveness is, after all, part of her seduction.

So it is that the China Travel Service in Hong Kong, the New
China's official overseas agent, offers its visitor as many positions and permutations as a panderer, catering to every fantasy
with a variety of tours that range from the most basic, in-and-out
package ($1,000) to a host of more exotic options ($2,500 or
more). The China Travel Service will procure for a tourist hotels,
guides, flights and trains. For $17, it will get him a visa; for $25, a
visa overnight. "The Chinese are masters of supply and

demand," a British financier who did business in Beijing advised me. "They know exactly how to hit the right level."

The New China also prefers to keep its rendezvous with the West strictly organized and closely chaperoned, a series of blind dates on which the two parties may inspect one another from a safe distance, swap reassuring smiles and then go their separate ways, separately enriched. Nearly all the country's modern facilities are therefore confined to the well-roped trail of the Imitation Silk Route, along which groups of tourists are led as through some special museum exhibition. Traveling in China alone, especially without any Chinese language, was still in 1985 an act of folly. I, however, was willing to put up with any amount of inconvenience in order to be spared the red-carpet rituals of the guided tour—the picture-perfect vistas, the routine exchange of pleasantries with well-trained hosts and, above all, the infamous climax of every New China visit, the group of adorable schoolchildren welcoming Westerners with an impromptu chorus of "Jingle Bells." (Even a nine-hour day trip across the border included a "visit to a kindergarten where children will greet you warmly with laughter, hand-clapping, singing and dancing.") I therefore asked for nothing more from the China Travel Service than a $30 train ticket to Guangzhou, spurning even the extra $20 service that would ensure someone to greet me on arrival and see me safely onto the next train to Beijing.

Next morning, nursing a mild fever, I boarded an express train in Hong Kong. Three air-conditioned, soft-seated hours later, I got out in China. In front of me in the bright afternoon was a vast square, ringed by giant billboards and graying skyscrapers. Beside me, extending for block after block after gray, gray block, was the main body of the station. Along its walls were ragged clumps of people, sleeping, spitting, fighting, jostling, crouched on cases, encamped on the ground. All around was vastness and great vacancy.

Across the length of the whole great square, I could decipher not a single sign but one: "China Travel Service," inscribed on a drab gray building behind a barbed-wire fence. That, however, was all I needed. Hoisting my case over the barrier, I ducked under it myself, tramped across a courtyard and walked into the gray stone building. I found myself within a maze of shadowed hallways, musty stairwells, empty rooms. I passed through a frosted-glass door and was directed out again into another series of dark corridors. I stopped a passerby and was sent down another hallway. I found another official, and was pointed down a series of high school passageways, to a large room in which sat three small men. I asked them for a ticket to Beijing, and they pointed me out toward the station.

Back in the sun, I started walking across the square, past crowds and empty spaces, past bus stands and dollar-mongers, past more people and more empty space, along the side of the never-ending station, for ten minutes or more. Finally, halfway down the immense block, I came upon the departure hall. Inside, it was echoing and empty as the belly of a whale. Vast waiting rooms the size of auditoriums were utterly unpeopled. Grand staircases swept heavenward to more balconies. Long, long corridors led through unlit hallways that led into long, long corridors. The main hall, in which a few ragtag bands of nomads were camped, forked this way and that, into a garden courtyard, a nursery, a checkroom, a puzzle of bleak entrances.

Anxious to find anyone or anything that I could understand I began walking—around the hall, and through it, up the stairs and down a corridor, into an empty room, and out of it again. I walked along the length of corridors and around a balcony and through the garden, back around the hall, into waiting rooms and out of them, back up the sweeping staircase and down again. Everywhere it was the same: no English, no help, no good. I went back to a duty-free shop crammed with high-tech goods, and around again, and back to the waiting hall, and out. Nowhere any English, nowhere any help. I walked up, and down, and up once more. No English. No use. No good. Canton Station was a maze designed by Escher with considerable assistance from Borges—not dizzying like Tokyo Station, which buzzes with microchip lights and bustling armies, beehive catacombs and secret passageways, but impenetrable in the manner of an enormous tomb cluttered with overstuffed filing cabinets.

And so I walked around and around. Finally, after almost an hour, I suddenly caught sight of a Caucasian couple being led by a $20 escort onto a platform. Where could I get tickets? I called out as they disappeared into freedom. Booth Number 6, called back the guide; for foreigners only.

Back out in the sunlight, I set out again past more clumps of people, more dark entranceways, more empty spaces, until at last I arrived at a series of booths. The Arabic numeral 6 was written above one hatch, but the rest of the sign—an old piece of wood—was all in Chinese. In front of it was a long line that showed no sign of moving. People spat and looked up at the boards, pushed their neighbors, spat again. Minutes passed, and more minutes; the line grew larger and more restless. I looked all around, at large walls and departure boards: nothing I could fathom. I went up to a counter and was directed to another booth, and then to a third, especially for tourists. Where could I get a ticket to Beijing? "China Travel Service." "But they said to come here." "Only China Travel Service."

Picking up my case, I set off again, through the sun-baked square, over the wall and under the fence and up to the CTS door. By now, it was bolted. I looked for side entrances, but everything was closed. Tens, hundreds, thousands of people hurried through the square. Buses buzzed off down spacious boulevards.

Virtually dragging my case along by now, half exhausted from the fever, the heat, the confusion, I staggered back across the huge square, past the ragged groups, under the sun, past block after block after block, sweating as I walked, back to the ticket booths. Nothing had changed. Chinese characters swarming, no sign of English, certainly no movement. Spitting and waiting and blankness. Shouts, lines, chaos. I gave up. I would check into a hotel, no matter the expense, go to the CTS tomorrow morning, offer to pay $20—or anything they wanted—in exchange for their assistance.

Then, just as I was sitting down on my case to gather my strength for the walk back to the taxi stand, I caught a snatch of something familiar. "There is no other way. The sign says no more tickets. This ticket okay. Listen, I show you. You can ask anyone." "Ees no good. Thees second class. No good for touristes." I looked up. "But this the only way to go to Beijing. There is no other ticket." "Non. Ees no good. I do not want." With that, a scruffy young French girl turned her back defiantly to reassert her place in the motionless line, and a lanky, bespectacled young Chinese smiled helplessly in my direction.

The girl was crazy, he volunteered; the board at the front of the line explained that all tickets were gone, and he had a ticket he was willing to sell at face value. Face value? Sure—was I interested? In case I didn't trust him, he went on earnestly, I need pay him only when he actually put me on the train four hours from now. I shouldn't trust him, I decided, and he might very well put me on the train four years from now. But even that seemed preferable to a night at the station or a return next day to the mandarins of the China Travel Service. Gladly accepting his offer, I shook his hand, he invited me to dinner and we jumped into the nearest taxi.

Twenty minutes later, a doorman pushed open the heavy doors to the China Hotel. In its ads, the $100-million hotel promised to treat every guest "like a merchant prince" and inside it did indeed boast the studiously exotic elegance of a costly Manhattan restaurant. Lavish dragon hangings hung from its walls. Black marble pillars stretched up to its roof. The gift stores in the shopping arcade sparkled like chandeliers, and the shining, blond-wood tables at the cafeteria gleamed under bright modern lights.

This, explained my guide over $1.25 Cokes, was a symbol of the New China. As it happened, he went on, he was another. Not long ago, in fact, he had been stranded in a faraway village with a menial job—his reward for being an active democrat at his hometown university in Changsha. But then, only a year after his rustication, the ideological winds had begun to change. The Cultural Revolution had ended almost as suddenly as it had begun. Mao had died. Almost overnight, the country had begun to turn on its head. And suddenly, Joe said, he had found himself at its top. Suddenly, the very skills that had once condemned him—his free-enterprising spirit, his independent mind, his easy command of English—had recommended him to the system. Wasting no time at all, he had hurried off to Guangdong Province, the capital of the Gold Rush, and started to play the market.

Nowadays, he went on, he could get almost any job he wanted. An American oil company was currently employing him as interpreter and intermediary for 500 yuan ($150) a month— equivalent to the salary of twenty average workers. But he could triple his earnings whenever he wanted. He was only twenty-six, he said, but he already had his own shop, was already, in fact, a 10,000-yuan household, the country's equivalent to the millionaire. Would I like to visit his office?

Somewhat taken aback by such a grand display of wealth—this, after all, was the world's largest Communist nation—I readily agreed. Joe led me off to one of the hotel's elevators. Fifteen floors later, we got out in a paneled and carpeted corridor. At one end was an executive set of glass doors. Joe pushed a button, and a mellifluous chime greeted us with the tune, "Be it ever so humble, there's no place like home."

Home indeed! The office inside was plusher than any I had ever seen in Manhattan (not surprisingly, perhaps: many a two-room office in China, I later read, costs $70,000, twice as much as in New York). Leather chairs lazed around a comfortable lobby. Bright corridors gave off into kitchens and computer centers. Office windows offered penthouse views of the glittering city below. Everyone, explained Joe, was joining in on the mad search for oil in the South China Sea. Over there—he pointed into the illumined night—was the $100-million building built by BP. That ten-story monstrosity was Esso's headquarters. In the distance, the big skyscraper was the Garden Hotel.

He often chose to spend his evenings here, Joe explained while brewing up some coffee, because his own apartment was even smaller than this kitchen. Sometimes, he went on, he came here just to read *Time* and *Newsweek*, sometimes he listened to the BBC World Service; two or three times a week he did body-building exercises nearby. He had read much of Hemingway and Twain, and he had seen *On Golden Pond*, as well as *Daughter of the Miner* with Sissy Spacek. Also, of course, *Nightmare*. *Nightmare*? Yes, said Joe with a smile, it was a film about capitalism.

A few minutes later, good as his word, Joe took me back to the station and showed me to my berth on the Beijing train. Just as the train began to pull out, he wished me good health and asked me to call him on my way back. Then, very shyly, he pressed into my hands a bag of bananas and three Cokes, waving goodbye to me as I pulled away into the dark.

FOR THE NEXT forty hours, I lived inside a kind of merry peasant home on wheels, a fragment of the old China transported by the New. Opposite me in my "hard sleeper" second-class compartment sat a family of four, a middle-aged couple and two teenage sons. One of the boys had a withered hand and a T-shirt that said "Milano"; his brother had a shirt that said "Ferrari." All four were huddled over jars filled to the brim with what looked like eel juice, but was doubtless only strong tea, matted with an inch or two of leaves. On my side, one entire berth was given over to a huge box that said "Microcomputer"; another was occupied by a wiry man in his early fifties, with Schwarzenegger muscles over his string shirt, and a belt around his waist that said "U.S.A."; inside the third, most curious of all to my companions, no doubt, sat a scrawny, scruffy foreign devil in an ancient blue blazer from Harrods, a pair of old corduroys that grew grayer and smaller by the day, a blindingly bright scarlet T-shirt and a pair of $2 sneakers just purchased in Hong Kong. Over us all hung a friendly, down-home air.

Next morning, I awoke from a fitful, fevered sleep to see the mist beginning to lift above long green fields. Slowly, the carriage began to stir into life. Someone in the next compartment put on a radio that crackled into the treble strains of a lilting folk ditty. Someone else interrupted these melodious sounds with an instrumental version of "Yesterday" and "The Gambler." In the corridor, a ponytailed little girl sat on a fold-down seat by the window, playing cards with a smile-wrinkled man in a vest. The ever-busy matriarch across from me briskly handed out jars of broth to her troops, filling our carriage with the smell of noodles. The muscleman calmly broke open eggs on the bench.

Thus the day lazed on, and I fell asleep again, awoke, nibbled on bananas, read Mishima in feverish snatches, slept and awoke and slept once more. Outside, the landscape unscrolled itself like a watercolor by Wang Wei, field upon field dotted with the peaked triangles of bamboo hats, or the bent forms of peasants carrying buckets of water under T-shaped bars. Just before nightfall, I suddenly felt my body being shaken. I looked up foggily. A guard barked something out at me. I stared back blankly. He shouted something else. I gazed back helpless. A crowd began to gather at the door, whispers spread along the corridor. The guard looked around for help. Finally, the mob parted and a young man in spectacles stepped forward. The guard was offering me a first-class sleeper, he explained—it was much better for foreigners. That was very kind, I said, but please could he tell the guard that I was happy where I was? "He says that the first-class compartment is more comfortable for you. This is no good." "Thank you, but this is comfortable enough." At that, the guard looked unhappier than ever. More words were exchanged. Finally, convinced no doubt that it was better to leave the barbarian to his folly than to try to coerce him out of it, the guard padded off. He came from Mongolia, my amiable rescuer explained, and he had learned English at his university in Peking. Was there anything else I needed? Only sleep, I assured him, collapsing into Mishima dreams. When I awoke, I found that my new friend had slipped into the compartment to close the chilling window above me as I slept.

Next morning, a sense of festive anticipation crackled through the mobile commune as we drew into Beijing. From out of a nearby radio, Teresa Teng, or some sound-alike songstress, whinnied sweetly. The ponytailed little girl clapped her hands while her father smiled proudly, and the two of them sent paper planes shooting along the corridor. The Mongolian appeared again at my door, followed by an old lady who pressed upon me some tablets for my fever. There was much excitement, my new friend explained—during the night, my roommate from Hong Kong had been robbed!

A few minutes later, the train stopped and the crowds began pouring out onto the platform, hoisting boxes, handing cases through the windows, scrambling for room. Guiding me gently away from the mob, the Mongolian led me down long corridors and up stairs and across waiting halls and then out into the daylight and across another enormous square. Did I have a friend in Beijing? he asked. Not really, I gasped—just a secondhand invitation to stay with a correspondent for Agence France-Presse, whom I had never met. His fiancée in Hong Kong had told me to stay with him, but he knew nothing about it. The Mongolian looked surprised, but guided me nonetheless to one of the city's only public telephones and dialed the number I gave him. The phone crackled, he shot something out and then he was shot at in return. He put down the receiver with an air of anxious melancholy. It would not be easy, he said, to find my friend.

The only other name I knew in Beijing was the Peking Hotel. As soon as I mentioned it, my tireless guide nodded briskly, led me across an enormous street and delivered me onto a jam-packed bus. Two stops later, he led me off again onto another wide boulevard. By our side, at the end of an ambassadorial driveway, stood an old gray monument, sleepy and stately as an elderly gentleman at some interminable committee meeting.

I invited my savior to join me for some tea, but he reminded me gently that he was not allowed to enter such places. Thanking him warmly, I headed alone across the imposing courtyard. Inside, the building resembled nothing so much as a dusty castle deserted by its fleeing lords and left in the care of the servants. There were grand red carpets in the corridors, but they were torn. There were rows of gift-store display cases, but they were covered with dust. There were cavernous banquet halls on every side, but they were crowded with ghosts. Chamber after chamber was haunted by an air of lavish desolation.

For many minutes, I wandered and wandered through the endless lounges. Then I walked into another huge lounge, and found myself suddenly amidst a whole crowd of noisy foreigners, seated over small circular tables crammed with cups. Like their surroundings, the whole chattering assembly had a somewhat queer and old-fashioned look to it, as if it had just stepped out, a little the worse for wear, from the pages of Marguerite Duras. Bohemian girls from the Continent in baggy trousers sat back from their tables with the air of veteran café-goers, languorously letting smoke escape from their lips as they exchanged greetings with thick-bearded Quartier Latin types in pajama suits and Chinese slippers. Shifty-looking businessmen in shabby suits conferred in whispers. Mountebanks seemed imminent.

Collapsing into a chair, I treated myself to some tea dispensed by what seemed a British hospital canteen and picked up a copy of the *China Daily*. On television today, I read, I could watch "We Are the 8th Army Soldiers," "Accelerating the Ripening of Cotton," "Around the World: Beautiful Bulgaria," "Les Misérables" (a cartoon) and a show on knock-knees. On the radio, I could listen to "Australian Song: Spring Is the Season for Sheep Shearing" or "Vocal Solos: Offering a Bouquet to the Party." Strangely fortified by all this, I hoisted myself up and wandered out again to the main thoroughfare. Herds of bicyclists were streaming down the sides of a street as wide as the Pasadena Freeway; along the pavements, groups of green-clad workers chattered past rows of buildings lined up as formidably as poker-faced dignitaries at a May Day parade. Uniformed young soldiers walked together in animated schoolboy clusters, joking and pushing one another about; solitary peasants looked around in openmouthed astonishment. Wisp-bearded old men whose wrinkled faces seemed older than surprise shuffled past, looking at nothing but the ground.

A few blocks down, the main artery—so cluttered at its fringes, so empty at its center—gave way to the enormous open space of Tiananmen Square, the largest in the world. In one corner of the huge, but quiet, square was a pair of small stone bridges and a tiny gap, underneath a giant poster of Mao. Through it, throngs of visitors were streaming into a further courtyard. Falling into step with them, I entered the Forbidden City. The first thing I saw was a basketball court.

For several hours, still feverish, I found and lost and found myself in a leafy labyrinth of courtyards and pavilions. As I made my way unguided around serpentine turns and dragon-shaped detours, through sunlight and shade, I could relate it to nothing I knew except the Chinese emperor in the Marguerite Yourcenar story, "beautiful, but blank, like a looking-glass placed too high, reflecting nothing except the stars and the immutable heavens." Finally, more disoriented than ever, I staggered back to the Peking Hotel and tried another phone call. This time, surprisingly, my unknown and unknowing host answered the phone; more surprisingly still, when I invited myself to stay, he graciously acquiesced.

Twenty minutes later, a gliding taxi took me through broad avenues of tree-lined quiet, past an elaborate network of sentry posts and into the Forbidden City of the New China: Beijing's main foreigners' compound. Jinguomenwai reminded me of nothing so much as some bleak housing estate in a featureless British industrial town: block after block of numbered concrete towers, encircled by parking lots and vacant lots in which African kids played dustily and Muslim mothers wheeled prams. Behind them, stretching grayly into the gray distance, were more built-by-number blocks, a motorway, a hazy skyline. Within this well-guarded protectorate, my host explained, the expat community was obliged to live as if it were a commune like any other: foreigners did their shopping at the Friendship Store, their socializing at the International Club, their living inside this group of blocks, or one of two others.

That night, for dinner, we went around the corner to the Jianguo Hotel, a replica of the Holiday Inn in Palo Alto. Aliens, my host explained, did enjoy a little more freedom now than they had done in the past, but they were still kept largely under house arrest. A few lucky foreigners were put up in the splendor of the $150-a-night Great Wall Hotel (which offered on Friday nights "the romance of the Mediterranean . . . souvlaki, pastas, gnocchi"), and others could take $85 lunches at Maxim's. But the Jianguo was the place where most foreign residents usually ate. In the coffee shop, customers consulted menus on HoJo place mats while white-bloused, green-skirted waitresses circulated with refills of coffee and men in tall white hats cooked burgers; in the lobby, a girl clunked her way unhappily through "Beautiful Dreamer" and the theme from *Love Story*, while in the French restaurant, tuxedoed waiters with Parisian manners served us filet mignon, duck à l'orange and mandarin sorbet with peach slices. As we went on chatting, my host happened to mention that he came from California. In reality, he came from the next town up the coast from mine. And, as it transpired, he had been to college in my own hometown. As a matter of fact, we soon discovered, he had learned some of his political theory from my father. That was my first sign that Beijing was among the smallest of places, as well as the largest.

SCALE, INDEED, WAS the single great feature of Beijing: sheer monumentality. The city had little of the decorous dignity or stately grandeur of a Washington, D.C., or even a New Delhi; it just had bigness plain and simple. And the plainness and simplicity only heightened the bigness. Beijing's buildings seemed solid, unguarded, declarative, tributes in block capitals to the rightness of the Right Way. This was not, it seemed, a place that allowed itself the luxury of decorative flourishes or side-street nuances; it was a city of grand simplicities.

In Beijing, moreover, proportion was an expression of priority. The huge public buildings made concrete the assertion of a will that was public, an ego that was only collective; their effect was to state inarguably that the sum of individuals was less than the whole of the state. Beijing thus appeared to be both imperial and impersonal: a city drafted by committee. And this in turn made for a curious disjunction: while the public world here seemed constructed on the epic scale, the private was on the miniature. The place seemed built not for people but for abstractions. The streets were huge, but virtually carless. The official buildings were enormous, but the sidewalk stalls were cramped. The bureaucratic monoliths were gargantuan and yet, by all accounts, private homes were smaller here than anywhere else in the world. Everything, in fact, was topsy-turvily scaled, right down, and up, to a system in which more than a thousand million people were ruled by one twinkling four foot eleven octogenarian who liked to remain behind the scenes. Beijing seemed a Brobdingnag peopled by Lilliputians.

In recent years, of course, this vertical division had been further stressed and strained by a horizontal split. Erected like a Trojan horse within the very heart of the Old China was a New China, designed to encourage all the influences that the country had long worked hard to keep out: capitalism, individualism, fashion, freedom, the flash and grab of the West. The rationale was simple: China wanted progress, and progress meant the West. In return for giving foreigners a precious glimpse of the past, the country now hoped to gain a lucrative taste of the future; by attracting the outer world, it planned to bolster the inner.

Thus the world's largest country had started putting Mao's celebrated maxim—"Make the past serve the present, make the foreign serve China"—to radically new use. The Great Wall, established to keep out the world at large, was now being used to attract it. Foreign influences, long reviled as obscene, were now being welcomed. The little red book was now being rivaled by the big greenback. And as the country began hawking its tradition to the outsiders it had long distrusted, it also set about importing Western goods, methods and funds—everything, so it hoped, but Western values.

So far, the government had generally managed to keep its interactions with foreign admirers as ritualized and precisely choreographed as a Chinese opera. Foreign devils had been admitted—but only, so it seemed, in much the same spirit as the barbarians who had flocked to China for centuries to kowtow before the emperor. And thousands of foreigners, who had long had a soft spot for chinoiserie and old Cathay, were more than willing to comply with any and every demand in their eagerness to inspect a Middle Kingdom as romantic to them as Middle Earth. Thus, six years after the door had begun to creak open, ceremonial visitors were still flocking in to pay their respects. Just before I arrived in China, three wandering shepherds of Washington—Geraldine Ferraro, Robert Dole and Tip O'Neill —passed through to salute the birth of the New China. The day I arrived in Beijing, Richard Nixon, still regarded here as a hero who had helped to open the door, returned to pay a call on the ruling triad; not far behind him came Felipe González. Jerry Rawlings of Ghana followed soon thereafter, and Lee Kuan Yew of Singapore was celebrating his birthday at Confucius' birthplace. The Chancellor of Austria arrived in Chengdu just as I got there, and a steady train of panjandrums was lining up outside, waiting to file through the Great Wall, the Great Hall of the People and the latest version of the Great Leap Forward.

By now, of course, the New China had also agreed to receive official delegations, as well as just plain tourists (so long as they acted like diplomatic delegations). In 1985, in fact, tourism was 59 percent higher than in the boom year of 1984, and four million foreigners were crowding around the Great Wall (soon to be surrounded, no doubt, by a Great Mall). In 1982, the door had even been opened to individual travelers. By the time I was in China, however, facilities for visitors were still so limited that tourism remained largely a matter of tour group collectives being herded around local collectives (in the courtship of the West, as on any uncertain date, there was safety in numbers). China had opened up to the West—but it had done so, I felt, in the spirit of a girl who admits a suitor just long enough to accept his tributes before showing him the door.

Thus foreigners in China even more than other closed socialist countries such as Cuba or Burma still found themselves treated in the manner of deposed royalty, quarantined within their own sumptuous world-within-a-world. Foreign residents lived like diplomats, or prisoners, within their imperial—and imperialist —compounds; tourists, meanwhile, were transported around the country inside a kind of capitalist's *cordon sanitaire*. They were given special waiting rooms at airports, special reserved seats on buses, special carriages in trains. They traveled in their own taxis and sometimes their own planes, made merry in their own segregated discos. They paid specially marked-up entrance fees at monuments, and special 75 percent higher rates on trains. They even had their own kind of currency—the Foreign Exchange Certificate (FEC)—with which to pay for foreigners-only hotels and $50 foreigners-only taxis. And their only contact with the country came from Western-wise locals and jingle-singing children.

On paper, at least, China's "friendship offensive" was thus proceeding as planned; in practice, however, the delicate mating dance was charged with all the uncertainties that attend any young woman who lets herself be wined and dined while hoping that her admirer will be content with nothing in return but a farewell kiss. The Chinese were making friends as a way of making money; many Westerners hoped that by giving money, they could gain new friends. In the process, more than a billion peasants were suddenly being confronted by teams of butter-reeking round-eyes from the West, whose own intentions were confused by their dangerously wide eyes. Thus questions began to multiply. How far could the girl go without committing or compromising herself? What exactly was expected of her in return? What if her suitor, in his keenness to get closer, suddenly lost his head? And what if the girl, in spite of everything, somehow lost her heart?

IN THE DAYS that followed, I found myself constantly shuttled back and forth from one side of the curtain to the other. Now I was among peasants in the shabby streets, now with foreigners in their gilded cages. One minute the city would extend her left hand, and the next minute her right, and neither seemed to know what the other was doing.

MY FIRST FULL morning in the capital, I awoke before dawn and walked through the sleeping foreigners' compound to a nearby park. Inside, slow-moving ancients were ghosting their way through a daily tai chi ballet in the early light, while out from a small pavilion came the weird piping of ancient instruments played by a group of old-timers. Later, as the light came up, the rhythm for the city as a whole was set by the bicycles that wheeled along in leisurely brigades, pedaling, pedaling, pedaling with hasteless equanimity. Again the numbers were almost impossible to grasp: there were 5.6 million bicycles in Beijing and all of them seemed to be moving through the streets at once. But again, theirs seemed a casual motion, tranquil as the flight of swallows. Nothing smudged the grand serenity of the big city, neither cars nor airplanes nor horns; even in Tiananmen Square the vast quiet seemed scarcely dented by humanity.

Later that afternoon, I chanced down a small lane overhung with willows, a hushed place beside a river. Temples peeped up in the distance and above a wall. Along the noiseless riverbank, a solitary old man sat in thoughtful repose, some children clambered up a tree. The afternoon drifted past with the twittering hum of Indian summer. Later, in the drizzle, the Summer Palace was a moody vision of a long-ago canvas, half hidden and softened by the mist. In the golden twilight, back on the main street, men and women languidly batted shuttlecocks back and forth while old men looked on, arms folded, leaning on the seats of bicycles propped up against trees.

That evening, however, I was catapulted back into the other Beijing. I had managed to track down a local colleague, Jimi Florcruz, and he invited me to join him and a friendly bear of a Chinese student at Beijing's latest night spot, the city's greatest social revolution, said Jimi, in all his fourteen years of living here. So we drove over to the plush Lido Hotel and gulped down a few sandwiches at the Tenpin coffee shop (its menus shaped like their eponyms). Then we hit the new China's first set of bowling lanes. Nobody else was in evidence there, except for a few Filipinos who worked in the local hotels and a tiny Chinese girl who looked about twelve but was, I was told, a very important person—the country's foremost Taiwan-style singer. Jimi, who came here several times a week, dispatched the pins with elegant efficiency. The Chinese giant, a stranger to the sport, sent the balls hurtling through the air so that they landed with a tremendous crash somewhere in roughly the same province as the pins. The diminutive songstress was a marvel of precision. And I, to my surprise, bowled a 138, my highest—and if truth be told, my lowest—score in a decade.

THE NEXT DAY, Jimi pushed a Dire Straits cassette onto his tape system and drove me in his Honda through enormous streets to a large block of old apartments. Up a narrow flight of stairs he led me, and then up to a small door. A handsome old lady opened up, and, twinkling delightedly at the sight of her adoptive son, hurried off into the kitchen to cook up the vegetables he had brought. Meanwhile, her husband padded out to give us a formal welcome. He too was in his seventies, and he too was strikingly handsome, a patrician elegance in his unlined face, his thick white hair and his unstooped body.

The couple's small main room had the same look of well-cared-for poverty, the same poignant attic quality that I had often seen in Bombay and Havana, its few objects arranged with touching care. Motioning us to two chairs, the old man sat down on a narrow bed. Beside him, on a sideboard, reverentially covered by a dish towel, was a TV and a Betamax (brought back, I was told, by a nephew studying in Paris). Scattered around were a few old Bee Gees cassettes.

As our host began firing questions at Jimi about the latest news from Taiwan, America, the world, he handed me a stack of dusty old photo albums to leaf through. Inside, I was instantly transported back to the glamour of a vanished age—Shanghai, 1936—when the air was electric with talk of "democracy." In every other brown-and-white snapshot, proud young men, solemn in their horn-rimmed glasses, impeccably garbed in three-piece suits and sleek overcoats, posed gravely in front of statues whose erectness was outdone by their own; and in every other stamp-sized picture, their glamorous sisters and fiancées showed off the latest fashions from Wellesley or Milan. Every shot, moreover, caught the whole golden confederacy in a moment of splendid preparation—seated in rows before large houses, looking up from long tables at lavish banquets, striking Hollywood poses at some ski resort. This gentleman, explained the old man, was now an important professor in America, this man had followed General Chiang to Taiwan, this lady was a socialite in New York. Every one of them had fled—except, so it seemed, our gentle host.

And what about these X's, I asked, scrawled in crude ballpoint across some of the holiday snaps—were they the handiwork of some mischievous child? No, said Jimi calmly, this was the doing of the Red Guards. They had raided the house during the Cultural Revolution, confiscated all the pictures and pinned them up at the old man's institute as proof of his decadence. These were the only photos that the couple had managed to recover. The rest of their past had been destroyed.

A silence fell. Then the bright-eyed old man assured me that these days, life was much easier. He and his wife were free now to publish a Kuomintang newspaper, and to tell jokes about Uncle Mao. They were allowed to stage dances and plays (he directed my attention to their latest, color photos) to raise funds for democracy. They had even been told that they might be assigned another apartment. And the famous singer who lived next door was free to perform any opera she wanted—not just the four revolutionary scores permitted by Madame Mao. That brought her almost 100 yuan ($30) each month.

In its way, indeed, the family had made its peace with the New China. The couple's young grandson and his pretty fiancée (now sitting decorously, knee by knee, in the tiny room next door) were both members of the People's Liberation Army song-and-dance unit; their perky granddaughter, who was helping out in the kitchen, spoke English so well that the diplomatic services were trying to lure her away from a hotel (though the hotel refused to release her unless the manager's underemployed and underqualified daughter was also given a position in the diplomatic services). As for the old man himself, he had recently embarked on a new career as a translator. Though he spoke not a word of English, he had labored, with the help of the heavy dictionary Jimi had given him, sentence by painful sentence, through the whole of *Brian's Song*, the heartrending tale of a Chicago Bears running back who had died of cancer. That rendition had proved so wildly popular that now he had been commissioned to do the same with Ingrid Bergman's autobiography. He was also working on the lives of Bette Davis, Joan Crawford and Elizabeth Taylor. On his desk lay the proofs of Gielgud's memoirs.

Yet through all the tales of profit and progress, the Old China hung in the air like incense. Sitting together on the bed after lunch, the couple explained a little about how their world had changed. In the old days, they said, people had usually been more polite: often, two strangers at a bus stop were so busy saying "After you," "No, after you," that the bus would end up leaving without them both. And in the old days, they continued, not angrily but with a quiet wistfulness, people had had more respect for their elders, a greater sense of family. Nowadays, they did not know what to believe. With that, the old lady smiled and asked how long Jimi and I had been friends. We had met only yesterday, he explained, but we had worked together on stories for years. "Ah," she said, eyes twinkling. "An acquaintance of the spirit!" "No, no," broke in her cheerful granddaughter. "An acquaintance of the telex."

THAT EVENING, I went to a party in a palatial flat in Jinguo-menwai, where hot dogs and chicken were barbecued to the sound of the Temptations, and all the talk was of the video rental club set up by the couple at the Mexican embassy, and two girls just out of Radcliffe asked excitedly after common friends from Adams House.

MY LAST DAY in Beijing, I let myself just wander. Again, the overwhelming impression was of proportion askew: every other citizen seemed to be draped in shirt sleeves that swallowed up his hands, trousers baggy enough to fit three, jackets that hung around shoulders as if around an umbrella stand. In a sense, it seemed a version, in miniature, of the way that the individual never slipped snugly into the state here, but always seemed as removed from it as a spectator from the elaborate stagecraft of a Peking opera.

Indeed, the look that I came most to associate with Beijing was one of wide-eyed innocence, of peasants in ill-fitting suits gathered on the pavements, hands behind their backs as they peered around them, speechless and spellbound, at the stentorian monuments of the China both old and new. Sometimes I saw gray-beards simply gazing at a building in wonderment; sometimes I saw them gaping at the industrial-strength dimensions of an avenue. Often, I found them assembled in serene fascination on a sidewalk while a couple posed for a photo, or an Australian haggled with a vendor, or a Cadillac drove up to a foreigner's hotel. Along the wide thoroughfares, rheumy-eyed old men led toddlers in peaked army caps by the hand, each as unsteady as the other, and each, so it seemed, as stunned by the new world around them.

And if the Chinese often looked like tourists in their own

country (while foreign tourists had, in some respects, to carry themselves like locals), it was only fitting that the most visible prop in Beijing was also touristic: the two-lens Brownie box camera from the fifties, which every other person seemed to be wielding excitedly while family or friends posed in front of monuments. Three-year-old boys and girls gravely held hands before the Forbidden City poster of Mao as relatives clicked away furiously. A middle-aged woman struck a heroic pose in front of the Great Wall. Whole families arranged themselves next to a well-polished black sedan from the fifties placed by some shrewd entrepreneur in the middle of Tiananmen Square. And groups of men in fat, multicolored ties solemnly arranged themselves like soccer teams in front of watercolored cardboard backdrops of temples and misty valleys, hands on knees and faces severe. In every case, though, the process had an innocent ceremoniousness, a breath-held gravity, far greater, I thought, than what one might find among Kansans at the Lincoln Monument, or Greeks at the ruins of Olympia. In the eye of the camera—and perhaps only in the eye of the camera—the Chinese Everyman could place himself at last in the same frame as his state, his history, even his newfound sense of possibility.

THAT EVENING, AS the relentless pace of the bicycles let up and the light began to fade from the leafy lanes, I dropped in on the city's only social center for foreigners. A few tables had been set up on the sidewalk, under a decades-old sign that spelled out "International Club" in letters two-feet high. A row of Christmas lights strung out along the roof winked feebly in the dusk. Otherwise, the place was empty.

A couple of minutes after I sat down, however, two epicene young Chinese dawdled up and took their places beside me. One was dressed in skin-tight trousers, the other in a dark blue suit, button-down white shirt and collar-length long hair. The former plunked down a glass of beer before me, the latter placed a cigarette in my mouth. "American Club, Number One," said one. I nodded. "Break dance!" cried the other. Then he jumped up and began twisting himself around like a spastic. "Disco!" he shouted as he gyrated. "Disco! Break dance!! Disco!!!" cried his friend.

As I looked on, bewildered, one of the androgynes made kissing noises and the other performed an intricate set of hand gestures that seemed to connote plumbing. Then they began turning themselves into human spaghetti again. The next thing I knew, two plump girls, gaudily done up in lipstick, appeared at the table and plopped down on two more chairs. I stared at them incredulous. "Do It to Me One More Time" came scratching over the sound track from a turntable indoors. "Hubba Hubba" came on for the second time that night, and one of the Peter Pans began bouncing and jerking around in his chair, throwing his hands about and bobbing his head in a frenzy. His friend looked over at me for approval. "Disco!" cried the manic contortionist, jerking around like a madman. "Disco!" called his friend. "Break dance!" shouted the loony. "Break dance!" cried his partner. "Disco! Break dance! Disco!" they screamed together. Thus my first night with the new old China.

THE VERY NEXT morning, I went to the airport to catch a 10:15 flight to Chengdu. Upon arrival at the lonely barracks-style hangar, I was informed that the flight was full. I was also told that it was nonexistent. I was also sold a ticket and warned that the plane was running a little behind schedule. Still, said the woman at the tiny hatch that served as a ticket counter, there was a good chance it might leave at 4:30 p.m.

Thus I enjoyed my first taste of the inimitable CAAC, the airline service that had already become one of the great symbols of the New China. For in only a few years of operation, the carrier had already established itself as a kind of Icarus of the modern world, a legendary conqueror of the heavens shrouded in tales of planes that took off but never landed and others that touched down when it was time for lunch; of some hijackings that were "official" and others that were enigmatically not; of stewardesses who emitted frantic shrieks of terror in midflight and jets that had no covers on their overhead compartments, and so sent suitcases raining down on passengers' heads the minute they took off. "CAAC," Jimi had quipped darkly. "They serve you right!"

Through all this hapless mayhem, however, CAAC was said to be solicitous to a fault. One traveler told me how he had once been escorted, with smiling civility, to a seat that consisted of nothing but four bolts on the floor. When he protested, the

stewardess, ever anxious to oblige, hurried off to fetch a folding
chair and sweetly asked the passengers in the next row back to
keep the chair propped up for the duration of the flight. Certainly, the waiting room in which I found myself in Beijing
seemed to have been thoughtfully designed on the assumption
that it would often have to double as a living room. Canteens of
tea were set up to placate the impatient, while along the walls a
sign in English announced, more in sorrow than in anger:
"Thank you for your visit. Have a nice trip." On every side,
impassive locals were gleefully making the most of facilities that
were larger, and probably better, than any they could enjoy at
home. Nobody could hear the departure announcements, but
nobody really seemed to mind, since nobody really expected to
depart. "CAAC," so the joke had it: "China Airlines, Always
Canceled."

After only seven or eight hours of waiting, however, I suddenly looked up to see the people I had singled out as my flight
mates surging toward an exit. Without a moment's hesitation, I
joined the crush and pushed forward onto the tarmac. My first
sight of the carrier that was to take me to Chengdu—a rickety
707—did not increase my faith in CAAC. Nor did my survey of
the facilities within: airsickness bags, tattered seat covers and
just about nothing else.

The minute we took off, however, we were swept up in a
whirlwind of hospitality. Three or four stewardesses began moving up and down the aisles, dispensing paper fans to every
passenger as a gift. The minute they had finished, they turned
around and hurried back, dishing out souvenir plates on which
were brushstroked some delicate pastoral. The next thing I
knew, they were zipping past again, handing out trays on which
were neatly placed a box of orange wafers, a bag of "vegetable
fillings" and cartons of lychee juice. I had only just begun to
make inroads into these when the energetic ladies sprinted past
again, thrusting into already full hands a boxed assortment of
dried walnuts. Then, scarcely pausing for breath, they whizzed
past once more in a blur, seizing up the remains of the packaged
meal and tossing out a few more presents—a toothpaste-and-
toothbrush set to some people, a miniature key chain that doubled as a thermometer to others. Finally, lurching around
dangerously as the jouncing plane began its tremulous descent,

they careered up and down a final time, to pass out sweets and evaluation forms. By the time we had landed in Chengdu, I was thoroughly exhausted.

Yet hardly had I collected my case from the rickety shack that served as a baggage carousel when a young agent from a local travel service appeared before me in the darkness, hand extended; he had been sent, he explained, through the offices of my Beijing colleagues, to give me a ticket to Lhasa and take me to a local hotel. Shaking my hand with vigor, my guide ushered me into a waiting car. Then he jumped into the front seat. As the driver started up, Zheng swiveled around with a reassuring smile. "With its abundant rainfall, fertile soil and tranquil climate," he began, "Chengdu has been called a 'Paradise on Earth.' " I pondered this as we bumped along a potholed road past half-completed buildings, open stalls, a five-story Birth Control Center. The Dujiangyan Irrigation System, he commented, was marvelous. Silence again. He had read, Zheng went on, the works of Dickinson and Twain. "Her poems," he said darkly of the Belle of Amherst, "are very short. Very deep."

Upon our arrival at the Jinjiang Hotel, Zheng invited me, under his voice, to accompany him early the following morning on an unofficial tour of the Temple of the Marquis Wu. Next morning, sure enough, when I walked outside, there he was, waiting patiently in the early light. How had my stay been? Very nice. "Sausages are marvelous," he declared with feeling. "The whole place is very pleasant," I replied, caught up in the spirit of Ping-Pong diplomacy. "Thank you," he said. "With its abundant rainfall, fertile soil and tranquil climate, Chengdu is often called a 'Paradise on Earth.' "

A FEW DAYS later, in Lhasa, it came time for me to make my way back to Paradise on Earth. Reserving a seat on a returning plane was simplicity itself, I was assured by fellow travelers: all I had to do was proceed to the local bus station a few days before my departure, locate a foreigners-only booth and track down a CAAC official who could make a reservation. Managing this after only three visits, I even succeeded in securing a reservation. Just before I quit the office, though, I thought it best to ask when the bus for the airport would be leaving.

"Five-thirty."

"Five-thirty?"

The official nodded.

"Isn't that a little late, if the plane leaves at eight?" The bus trip to the airport, I recalled, took a good two hours.

He looked at me angrily. "Five-thirty in afternoon."

This took a moment or two to register.

"You mean the afternoon before?"

He nodded sullenly.

"You mean five-thirty in the afternoon for the plane the next morning?"

He nodded.

"That is to say, the bus leaves almost fifteen hours before the flight?"

This time he hardly bothered to nod.

"So we spend the night at the airport?"

At that point, he stalked away.

By 4:45 on the appointed day, the small bus station courtyard was already crowded with five dust-smeared buses, six times as many people as could fit on them and ten times as many as could fit on any CAAC plane. Tibetans in cowboy hats crouched on their haunches, wrinkled old women with turquoise braids stood fierce guard over Sharp radios. On the other side of the square, Chinese soldiers perched on boxes containing Sony TVs ("This Side Up" invariably reading upside down). The minute it was 5:00, all foreigners were guided with a frantic urgency to a special booth in order to get tickets for foreigners-only seats, and the whole dusty caravan began pulling out. Any tourist who arrived at the appointed hour of 5:30 must have found his stay in Lhasa extended by several days.

And so we bounced out of town, honking shepherds off the road, passing the curious gazes of weathered peasants working in the fields, bumping across the long, icy plateaus of Tibet, the mountains beside us sharpened by the gathering darkness, the cold lakes lit up by the dying sun. Foreigners in their reserved seats were squeezed between dribbling babies, runny-nosed urchins, champion expectorators and old nomads on the far side of death. Mauve-cheeked ladies sat in the aisles, impassively breast-feeding babies. Every few minutes, they were all brusquely pushed aside as the bus lurched to a halt and a herd of passengers scrambled out to relieve themselves.

Roughly two hours into this on-again, off-again progress, the bus bounced at last into an area that looked vaguely familiar. The airport! I looked around eagerly for signs of a makeshift inn. Seeing none, I grimly began steeling myself for a night of torment at the hands and feet of stampeding children (their only charm, I imagined, their ignorance of "Jingle Bells"). The other foreigners looked equally glum. "Keep your eyes open for the Holiday Inn!" cried one in a flight of antic bitterness.

And then, when least we expected it, the bus turned a corner, and there before us stood a gleaming rebuke to all our doubts: a spanking-new building with an airy lobby, bright modern lighting, a smart wooden desk guarded by uniformed employees. We were not alone in our appreciation. Hardly had the bus driver turned off the ignition than the Tibetan passengers and Chinese soldiers began throwing themselves headlong out of the vehicle like Kurosawa warriors storming a castle. Exercising skills refined at every rest stop, they stampeded off in the general direction of the desk, pushing each other to the floor, throwing elbows as they cleared their path, shouting, squabbling, shoving, spitting. Safely protected on the far side of the barricade, the hotel authorities serenely extended forms into the air. These the racing hordes grabbed and began filling out with desperate speed. The minute they were finished, the enthusiastic guests fought their way to the next line, where they handed in their forms and received others in return. These too they filled in speedily, before rushing off to another queue where they were assigned their rooms. In a fourth line, they paid up.

Thirty minutes later, I struggled out of the fracas and began walking down a carpeted corridor. Then, suddenly, I realized that I had no key. Throwing myself back into the press, I wormed my way again to the front of the line. "My key, please," I called out to a receptionist. She returned my gaze steadily; guests were not allowed keys. And if I wished to enter my room? "Doorkeeper," she said shortly, and went back to flinging out forms.

Wriggling out through shouts and shoves, I shuffled off, a little gloomily, in the direction of my room. The corridor was empty. I peered into some official rooms. They too were desolate. I went up to the second floor. The doorkeeper was nowhere to be seen. I tried the third floor. Silence. Then I returned to the first corridor. By now, it was considerably less empty—more and more guests were finding themselves in the same predicament as myself. The only solution, I decided, was to remain as fixed as a statue outside my door. The mountain would have to come to Mahomet.

Sure enough, a little later, a grumpy-looking lady with an enormous jangle of keys waddled down the corridor toward me. In a matter of minutes, she had located my key and, grimacing as she did so, had thrown open my door. There, to my astonishment, stood two tidy twin beds, a TV set, a bright modern reading lamp, a separate bathroom, a thermos of tea attended by two cups. Beside each bed was a pair of slippers.

I hurried inside and pressed the TV button. Nothing. Muttering angrily, the dungeon keeper shouldered me aside and pressed another button. As if by magic, the screen filled with static. I pressed each one of the channel buttons in turn: static, static and more static. A little disappointed, I turned to the lamp and pushed a button on its base. Again, a curse escaped the woman: impatiently, she pointed inside the lamp. No bulb. Next, I put my finger on the thermos for hot tea: not surprisingly, it had been chilled by the Himalayan breezes blowing through the open window. The cups beside it were filled to the brim with dirty water, or something a good deal worse.

My enthusiasm was beginning to subside a little when I heard a commotion in the corridor. I turned around to see a bearded young Frenchman, gesticulating animatedly to a beaming Japanese man with a goatee. Absorbed in their chatter, the two strolled inside, glancing only briefly at the number on the door. Then they stopped. Then they looked around the room, checked the number again, looked at each other, looked at me, looked at the truculent attendant. She stared back at me impassively. The Japanese man giggled. The Frenchman cried out something excitable. The three of us compared slips: sure enough, each of us had been assigned to the same single room.

We presented this evidence to the attendant. With a lackadaisical shrug, she summoned the Japanese man out into the corridor and, after another prolonged struggle with the keys, admitted him into the room next door. While she did so, his pretty young wife shot us a sorrowful smile as she was led down the corridor by another attendant on her way to a room that she would doubtless be sharing with some wild Tibetan mountain woman and a Panasonic.

As our jailer trudged off, with a satisfied grunt, to deal with other of her prisoners, the Frenchman and I gazed at each other in befuddlement. Then, with all the trepidation of a babysitter in a horror movie, I inched into the bathroom. There was a toilet there, but it could have been mistaken for a sewer. There was a naked wire strung across the room at neck level, perfect for decapitation. There were some dirty old towels hanging from the wire. There were taps in the sink, but no water inside them.

The sandals, however, worked perfectly.

"*C'est très bizarre, non!*" I said as I emerged. "*Mais non,*" cried the Frenchman, throwing up his hands wildly. "*Au Black Coffee Hôtel à Chengdu, c'est plus bizarre.*" This I did not doubt. Already I had heard a great deal about this infamous place, an unrenovated air-raid shelter that now served as a $1.50-a-night bordello where beds were laid out in the windowless corridors and guests could reach the bathroom only by crawling through a hatch. In the lobby of this now legendary underground haunt, a rock-and-roll band serenaded drunken couples, while well-fed sixteen-year-old girls spread themselves languorously out on couches. Keys, of course, were strictly forbidden. "*Un fois,*" began my roommate, "*je devrais attendre trente minutes parce que la gardienne lavait ses mains.*"

Sobered by that cautionary tale, we decided to minimize our comings and goings, as well as to synchronize them. Since it was now dinnertime, we quickly put this policy to the test, ventured out into the corridor in search of the dining room, sticking as close to one another as members of a chain gang. As we edged through the winding hallways, we found them crowded with other guests waiting to be admitted to their rooms. Finally, after many curses and collisions, we arrived at a huge assembly hall of a dining room. A sweet-faced girl was seated at a desk outside. She directed our attention to a piece of paper that said "Airpot Hotel." Below that curious inscription were eight rows of Chinese characters. We stared at the list for a while in despair, and then the girl smiled back her understanding and motioned us to follow her into the kitchen. Proudly, she pointed to a bowl of chicken and a bowl of vegetables. And what could we have to drink? "Yes," she said, smiling brightly. "Beer."

"Would it be possible to have some tea, please?"

"Yes, yes," she said, pointing to a bottle. "Beer."

"Thank you. But do you have tea, please? Tea." I did an unworthy imitation of the dainty movements of a deb at Brown's Hotel. The girl looked crestfallen. Deciding that it might be undiplomatic to remind her that Tibetans, according to Heinrich Harrer, drink two hundred cups of tea a day, I tried another tack.

"Does the Airpot Hotel have any soft drinks?" She looked confused. "Coke? Fanta? Lemon?"

Suddenly, her face brightened. "Beer," she pronounced agreeably. "Yes!"

"Do you have water?"

She was now the picture of happiness. "Yes, yes! Beer."

Drinkless, we proceeded to a table set aside for foreigners. There, the twenty-year-old student from Cambridge hell-bent on entering business school whom I knew from the Banak Shol was engaged in a dialectical session with the seventy-year-old Communist I had met in Lhasa. (He: "Did you have any problems during the McCarthy era?" She, eyes twinkling happily: "Oh no, dear. McCarthy was the one with problems.") As the meal proceeded, I began to think, for a variety of reasons, of Mao's famous injunction—"Self-criticism is like eating dog meat: if you haven't tried it, you don't know what you're missing." My cell mate, however, looked as if he knew all too much what he was missing. Recalling that he spoke no English, I suspected that it might be best for us to return to our room. We painstakingly mapped out an elaborate pincer movement for tracking down our elusive jailkeeper, and, a few minutes later, were rewarded with success.

Just as we were beginning to reacquaint ourselves with the pleasures of our suite, however, a young Chinese man in a corduroy jacket materialized at our door. He was round and bald and beaming. He looked at me happily. "Hindu?" I nodded, and he walked in, grabbed my head lustily and pressed his cheek against mine, kissing the space between ear and shoulder.

Then he turned to the Frenchman. "Karachi?" The Frenchman looked stunned. "English?" The Frenchman looked thunderstruck. "American? Japanese??" There was a long and terrible silence. "Hindu? German? Kar. . ." At this, the Frenchman wisely blurted out something about France. Our visitor turned around to me with a satisfied smile, then rewarded my cell mate with a kiss.

Niceties behind us, the stranger looked me in the eye. "I am porridge." Now it was my turn to look horrified. "Yes, yes," he said, thinking that I doubted him. "I am pirate." This was little better. "PIRATE!" he shouted out.

Through a leap of deductive reasoning, I came to two conclusions, neither of them heartening: (1) our guest was the beneficiary of the Airpot Hotel's unbending beer-only policy; and (2) he was the man who would be guiding our plane across some of the world's highest mountains just a few hours later.

Realizing, on both counts, that he was not a man to be crossed, I returned with new gusto to our small talk. Before long, the banter was proceeding swimmingly. The pilot told us his age, his wife's age, our ages. He reminded us of his age, and his wife's age. He taught us several Mandarin profanities, spitting out guttural sounds with angry nonchalance, then hissing as I tried to reproduce them. He volunteered, somewhat unexpectedly, that he had been to America, Russia, Karachi, Japan. He offered to buy my watch, then tickled me under the chin. He repeated his age, and his wife's age.

The spirit of jollity mounted. I gave him a guided tour of our amenities, flipping on the TV that did not work, pressing the button on the bulbless lamp. He chuckled delightedly. I whispered conspiratorially that the Frenchman was in fact a minority Muslim from Turkestan. He chortled with pleasure. I asked him his wife's age, and he whooped like a wild man.

Then, just as the bonhomie was reaching its peak, we heard a knock on the open door. There stood the girl from the dining hall. "Change money?" she offered, under her breath.

Smiling all around, she walked inside. Then she pulled out a napkin and, frowning with concentration, wrote down a number. The Frenchman stared at it in puzzlement, then scribbled down some numbers of his own. She scrutinized them for a moment, smiled with infinite sweetness and shook her head no. The pilot beamed at all parties with the air of a satisfied matchmaker.

Then, however, overexcited perhaps at the success of this cultural exchange, he began barking out numbers with the random frenzy of a bingo caller. "Twenty. Fourteen. Fifty. Thousand. Thirty. Sixteen. Seven." We stared at him in wonder. "Nineteen. Fifty. Four. Seven." What on earth was going on? "Fifty. Sixteen. Twenty. Thousand." Wild-eyed now, the Frenchman muttered something poisonous and scribbled down a few more figures. Again the girl shook her head no. Then, without a warning, the pilot broke off from his demented chant and tried to broker a four-part deal involving my watch, his watch, foreigners' currency and people's money. Foiled in an instant, he struck up again his terrible cry. "Thirty. Seven. Fifteen. Four." The Frenchman and the girl huddled together. "Nineteen. Forty. Three . . ." Then, just as the pilot's call was hitting a crescendo, the place was plunged into darkness. Lights-out at the Airpot Hotel!

As suddenly as they had appeared, the pilot and the girl vanished. Fumbling my way to my bed through the utter darkness, I heard a chorus of *merdes* as the Frenchman did the same. Since neither of us had any idea when, or whether, our plane would leave, I set my alarm clock for six. Next thing I knew, it shrilled me out of bed and I threw the light switch. Nada. Outside, the mountains were utterly dark. Dismally, I returned to bed. Just as I was beginning to relapse into sleep, however, there came a terrible banging at our door. I jumped to attention once more. Outside in the corridor, a hotel employee stared at me urgently. "Bus leave."

Driven like madmen, the Frenchman and I flung on our trousers, threw all our belongings into our bags, pushed some toothpaste toward our gums and, picking up our possessions, raced out into the corridor. Hurling ourselves at top speed along the hall, we careened into the lobby. There, we were brought to a sudden stop: the place was pitch black. Everything was motionless. A small army of Tibetans were seated on cases with the look of the damned, heads buried in hands or thrown back over their seats. For all we knew, they had spent much of the night in fruitless search for the doorkeeper or else had seen the rooms and elected to sleep in the familiarity of this plainlike space.

As we considered the melancholy scene, a hotel worker scurried up to us through the darkness. "Breakfast?" I thought bitterly of a choice between beer, beer and beer. "No, thank you." We sat down and waited. Maybe two hours later, the bus came into view, to be greeted by another mad stampede. We were driven to a terminal, then taken by another bus to a customs shed. There we waited for an hour or two before the plane arrived. After another short wait, we were told that it might be ready to leave.

THE INCIDENT AT Lhasa exemplified all the comic clumsiness of the New China's attempts to accommodate the West. But it also demonstrated its canniness. For at the airport, we encountered the package tourists who had been staying at a luxury hotel on the Chinese side of Lhasa; it did not seem a coincidence that they had been permitted to spend their last night in town (where they were paying 100 yuan a night) and had been driven to the airport only that morning, while we (who were paying 5 yuan a night on the Tibetan side of Lhasa) had been compelled to spend the night together with other improvident locals at the relatively exorbitant Airpot Hotel. Only the 30 yuan that came from every member of a captive and otherwise unremunerative audience could explain the erection of a shiny new hotel in the midst of a windswept plateau three hours from the nearest town.

The discrepancy also, however, revealed another hazardous strain in China's careful courtship of the West. For although the country had managed to keep package tourists successfully out of touch with the man in the Chinese street, it had not yet managed to bring the solo traveler to heel. And if feelings and finances were often dangerously confused at the larger level, the confusion was many times more explosive on the individual level, where finances had not been agreed upon, or emotions decided upon, in advance. The budget traveler, moreover, was resolutely determined to avoid the prescribed route, to scorn big hotels, to travel by train and to steal across any and every boundary between the cultures. Most dangerous of all, the backpacker sought at every point to make contact with locals—striking up deals and conversations without ever really troubling to distinguish between them. Floating around the country's bloodstream like a clump of bacteria, the individual traveler spread still further the contamination of individualism: not only did he refuse to be abstracted by being absorbed into a group, but he encouraged the same in those he met.

As it was, these impromptu meetings between locals and foreign individuals had already begun to subvert the rituals of official exchange and so to afford the individual a perfect revenge upon the system. To take just one example, the establishment of two separate but equal currencies—Foreign Exchange Certificates and "people's money"—worked wonderfully so long as foreigners and locals were strictly segregated. But as soon as the two parties mingled, their currencies were mixed together, and as soon as the currencies mingled, the foreigners' law of supply and demand came into devastating effect.

By 1985, therefore, the FEC was already worth 60 percent more than the renminbi with which it was supposed to enjoy parity, and a vigorous black market had arisen to fill the gap between theory and practice. Already too, rickshaw drivers had taken to loitering outside many tourist hotels, soliciting passing foreigners by rubbing thumbs and fingers together and muttering figures under their breath. Any tourist who wished to make a killing had only to reach an agreement by haggling on paper, in the manner of the Frenchman and the Chinese girl in the hotel, and the driver would usher him into his rickshaw and take him for a leisurely ride around the block. As he pedaled, the Chinese would casually slip some "people's money" into the tourist's hand, and as they went on, the tourist would press a roll of FECs into the driver's grasp. By the time the two had disembarked, a few minutes later, their positions were as good as reversed. The foreigner could now live as cheaply as a local, and the rickshaw driver as lavishly as a tourist. The only loser was the system.

UPON MY RETURN to Chengdu, famous "city of revolutions," I had more and more occasions to note how inevitable were these unscheduled meetings, and how incendiary. As soon as we arrived at the airport, the tour groups dutifully filed into their buses, while the four odd men out—I, the Frenchman, the Cambridge student and the Communist old lady—grabbed a taxi together and headed for the only tourist hotel in town, the Jinjiang. There we were informed that there were no suites available, no rooms, not even any dorm beds; we would have to find a flight out at the CAAC office. There we were told that the next seat available was on a plane leaving town three weeks from now; we would have to stay at the Changshi, the town's best nontourist hotel. There we were told that it was full (of delegations) and we would have to try the Black Coffee.

At this, the Frenchman, already all too familiar with the unorthodox facilities of that windowless prison, shouted out something passionate and went off to catch the next train out of town, regardless of its destination. The adventurous old lady picked up her three bags, cheerfully announced that her American Express card had been stolen two nights before and began trudging down a huge avenue toward the air-raid-shelter-turned-bordello. The Brit and I, however, decided to attempt another assault upon the Jinjiang.

Hailing a rickshaw driver, we recited our destination. He held up five fingers, we held up three. He held up four. We nodded, he rolled his bicycle up to us, and we took the five-minute ride to the hotel. Getting out, we handed him 40 fen (there are 100 fen in a yuan), and he pushed the money back to us. Again, the Brit gave him the fare, and began walking away. He hurried up and grabbed the Brit by the arm, thrusting the money back into his hand. His friends began gathering around. He shouted at us. We stood our ground. He shouted again. The Brit shouted back. The mood of the crowd started to turn ugly. The man poked at the Brit's arm, and the Brit pushed him back. There were shouts and threats. The Brit gave him the money again and he threw it on the ground. Alarmed by the mounting air of violence, I raced into the hotel and brought back a young gift-shop proprietress to serve as an interpreter. She explained that the man wanted 4 yuan. We told her that we had paid only 1 yuan for four people on the way over. The Brit handed over 40 fen again, and the man let out a shout. The girl, looking back and forth with rising alarm, told us that the driver was going to bring the police. Thirty or forty people had gathered around by now, some of them curious, some of them furious. The Brit threw 40 fen onto the ground and began walking away. The man spit at us. The girl, looking more and more miserable, said we would be taken to jail. The man hovered over us. The Brit cursed. The girl asked us just to pay 2 yuan and be done with it. We protested. The man circled around. At last, we handed over 2 yuan and, twenty-five minutes after the dispute had begun, the gang of rickshaw drivers shambled sullenly away.

As soon as the rickshaw drivers retreated, the Brit and I advanced into the Jinjiang to resume our siege. For more than an hour, we hurried up to each new attendant who appeared at the desk and repeated our appeal. For more than an hour, we were rebuffed. Finally, with a hearty curse, the Brit gave up and went off in search of a train timetable. I, as a last resort, decided to try that ever-helpful model of civic pride, Zheng.

Upon arrival at Zheng's office, however, I was greeted only by two young girls who could hardly contain their delight at finding someone on whom to practice their English, German and French. For an hour or so, we complimented one another on our proficiency in all three languages. Then Zheng reappeared. Chengdu was a Paradise on Earth, I reminded him, but I was being kept out of it. Predictably outraged, he summoned his troops, and the four of us returned to the Jinjiang. My cohorts marched up to the desk. I heard a few shotgun sentences. I saw a desk clerk try to save face. I was told that a room was available.

Thus, six hours after my arrival, I was able at last to settle down in a room. In the day that followed, I made a full inspection of the capital of Sichuan, the capital of the New China's agricultural revolution. In the proverbial "land of heavenly abundance," I quickly realized, I had emerged into an entirely different world from that of the capital. For in Beijing, the New China and the Old China seemed to be safely laid out side by side; in Chengdu, however, the two were as strangely mixed as if a color Polaroid had been superimposed upon a sepia-colored snapshot. The city's main arteries were crowded with vegetable carts and shops, and the shops were crowded with ancient vials and pounding ghetto blasters. At the head of the main street was the largest statue of Mao in the world and, around it, giant billboards commemorating the holy trinity of the New China— Sanyo, Seiko and Sony. *First Blood* was showing down the street, while in my hotel room I could listen, on the radio, to "Phoenix-Shaped Hairpin" at 3:30, move on to "Foreign Music: Thank you; Coffee-Bean Grinding; A Song" at 6:00, catch "Medley of Themes from Hawaiian Music" at 6:30 and hear "Instrumental: My Sweetheart: A Lovable Rose" at 7:30. Only half an hour later, the programming culminated in "Su Wu Tends Sheep." But when at last I did get my first, long-awaited taste of Chinese television, I found myself staring at a group of children dressed as cats and dogs, crazily swirling around a toy car. At the conclusion of this Dance of the Sugar Plum Comrade, on came another show in which real, animated cats and dogs merrily chased one another around, in honor, I could only assume, of Deng's most famous maxim ("It matters little whether a cat is black or white, so long as it catches mice"). A little later, a Hong Kong movie was shown, but it was soon thrown completely off kilter by a long and unusually frank topless scene—testament, I suspected, to some editor's erratic scissors.

Somewhat discombobulated, I went out into the bustling, light-filled streets. Chengdu and I, however, were never on the same wavelength. I saw a sign for a rest room and gratefully hurried in—to find an impassive matron crouching in a cubicle behind an open door. I bought a ticket to see some local acrobats in action—and went in to discover a huge screen blasting out a kung fu classic. I hired a rickshaw to take me to the Jinjiang and was dropped off, an hour later, in front of a small house at the end of a maze of back streets. And when I ventured into a local restaurant for my first-ever genuine Chinese meal, I pointed at a chicken, and was swiftly served a banquet for ten with a bill for twenty. Before very long, the meal had also succeeded in reuniting me with a traveling companion even more mercurial than the Frenchman—a fever. Thus I returned to Guangzhou in much the same state as when I had left it, at the start of my circular journey, fevered and fatigued.

THE GUANGZHOU THAT I saw now, however, seemed a very different place from the one I had left just a few weeks before, if only because my sense of China was radically altered. As I drove through the electric streets on my way back into town, I felt myself in a different country, a different century, from Beijing or Chengdu. On every side was a quickening pace, a flashing commotion, a boomtown dynamism and drive that could have put Bombay or Jakarta to shame. The boys who elsewhere rode bicycles were revving up scooters; the girls who elsewhere looked sadly miscast in ill-fitting costumes here struck worldly poses in their pretty dresses, nail polish and T-shirts that said "Superstar" or "Cute." I saw what looked like Sears, and it turned out to be the local Friendship Store. A notice in English advertised a "Motorcar Fitting Company." Signs, huge billboards, colored lights, pulsed through the brilliant streets. I could easily have believed that I was over the border in Hong Kong. Only one thing reminded me I was not: in the capital of capitalism, flashing neon is prohibited, while in the capital of southern China all the lights were winking furiously.

Passing through the electric doors of the White Swan Hotel, a glittering palace built on a lake, I entered a lobby graced with a tumbling waterfall and a beautifully landscaped three-tier garden of red bridges, ferns and tidy walkways. At the reception desk, rows of neatly lipsticked young ladies stood to attention, while a nearby pianist trilled her way through "Don't Cry for Me, Argentina." With a few brisk taps on a computer, a receptionist assigned me a room. At the elevator bank, a liveried attendant pressed the P button for me. Soothed by a melodious piano concerto, I was lifted twenty-seven floors closer to heaven. At the top, a floor attendant led me to a suite glittering with luxuries: a mini-bar; a set of boxed soaps and shampoos; a color TV that received two English-language stations from Hong Kong, in-house video and a channel devoted entirely to recording the facilities of the hotel; and a booklet describing the swimming pool, the tennis court, the babysitting service, the health club, the Hong Kong direct-dial phones and every other feature befitting a member of the Leading Hotels of the World. Then the lady pulled back the curtain and there—hey presto!—was a terrace and a blaze of lights.

Dazzled by this splendor of riches—two days earlier, after all, I had been staying in a bare cell on the windswept plains of Tibet—I hurried down to the lobby to inspect its facilities. Though it was 10:30 at night, the shopping arcade was still hectic with activity. Customers and workers buzzed in and out of the shiny Travel Office, the Telex Office, the one-hour Photo Developing Store. A Madison Avenue elegance graced the antique stores in the shopping arcade, and the bookshop was packed with everything from Gertrude Stein to Robert Stone. Tuxedoed men ushered guests into discos and nightclubs. And at the Buffeteria, well-fed customers were tucking into dishes called "Yes, Sir, Cheese My Baby," "Bacon your Pardon," "A Legitimate Beef" and "Ike and Tuna Turner." Not far away was a VIP entrance.

With Marxism like this, I thought, who needed capitalism?

BY THEN, I had also seen enough of the New China to appreciate that Joe, my first contact in the country, had been prompted by something more than simple philanthropy in giving me his train ticket to Beijing; though he had sold it at face value, he had been paid, and always would be paid by newcomers just stepping off the train from Hong Kong, in precious FEC. He had thus been assured of a tidy, riskless, 60 percent profit. At the same time, however, I had only to think back to the CARE package he had pressed upon me as I boarded my train to realize that Joe's canniness about his own well-being did not necessarily diminish his concern about mine. I therefore wasted no time in ringing up my former benefactor and arranging to spend the weekend with him on a tour of the New China.

As soon as Joe and his friend, a round-faced and bespectacled journalist called Wu, appeared at my hotel next morning, I explained how the CAAC meal and my ill-advised trip to the Genuine Chinese Restaurant in Chengdu had conspired to incite a series of revolutions and counterrevolutions within my stomach. Without a moment's hesitation, they whisked me off to the nearby apothecary market and there began enthusiastically pointing out deer antlers, turtle-shell juice, starfish and tiger bone ("In Guangzhou," said Joe, not very comfortingly, "people eat everything with four legs except a table. And anything that flies except a plane"). Some of these cures were mere superstition, he acknowledged: "the hair vegetable," for example—he pointed to what looked like a Brillo pad—was regarded as a panacea only because the Chinese word for it sounded like the ideogram for "making a fortune." But this, he went on—indicating some items in a jar and a drink—would make me healthy for life. Excellent. What did it contain? Oh, nothing much, said Joe: the edible part was bear's penis and the beverage was tiger's urine. It would cost me only 400 yuan for the former and 100 yuan for the latter. This, I thought bitterly, sounded very much like the English phrase for "making a fortune"; the miracle cure cost the equivalent of eighteen months' wages for the average worker.

Newly convinced of the relative merits of the New China, I dragged my bewildered guides back to the hotel and hurried off to consult its certified nurse—a matron who listened intently as

I described all my symptoms in exquisite and excruciating detail, nodded sagely at the end of my heart-wrenching monologue and then revealed that she spoke no English. When a translator delivered a rough summary of my condition, however, she again listened with a seraphic calm and then, without a word, pulled out three tablets, placed them in an envelope and handed them silently over to me. Five hours later, I was cured.

Back out on the jostled streets, Joe resumed his hymning of the booming energies of the New China. Some of these vendors made 2,000 yuan a month on the open market, he exulted, and one of them was said to be a millionaire. Once he had seen a man pull out 100,000 yuan in cash to pay for a truckful of produce. Guangzhou was so far ahead of the rest of the country that people came here all the way from Beijing just to buy, say, 1,000 pairs of jeans for 22 yuan a piece, each of which they could sell back home for 30 yuan. Many Chinese businessmen, in fact, had grown as active as the entrepreneurs of Hong Kong or New York—except, alas, that they were forbidden to ride planes. In the five days it took them to make the Beijing–Guangzhou round trip by train, the market often rose and fell precipitously. Still, in the new economic order, Guangzhou was unquestionably the capital of the nation. "I tell my friends," said Joe, "that in the thirties everyone went to Yenan, the center of the Revolution; now, everyone comes to Guangdong, the center of the New Revolution. In Shanghai, ten yuan is a lot of money; here, it's nothing. In Chengdu, I was once thrown into jail for staying in the Jinjiang tourist hotel; here, I can stay anywhere. In Beijing, people are interested only in politics, in power and prestige; here they want to make money."

That, he said, had always been the great problem with his country: lack of incentives. Why should members of a construction crew try to complete a 120-day project in 100 days? They knew they would get no extra money and no extra jobs; besides, their bosses would never give them bonuses in which they could not share themselves. Even now, there was no incentive to get educated: a taxi driver could earn in two days what a teacher made in a month. But nowadays, at least there were some inducements to work hard; there was more drive, more ambition, a greater will to succeed. People in the New China were ready to do anything, said Joe, to make money. In one province, two peasants had tried to sell off bottles of industrial alcohol, diluted to 60 percent, as booze. The result was twenty-two deaths. Recently, a more professional outfit on Hainan had been caught in a $1.5 billion scam, in which they had used Party funds to smuggle in 3 million television sets, 200,000 VCRs and 90,000 vehicles.

Politicians too were growing shrewder about courting the public. "Sure," continued the ever-fluent Joe. "Many people say, 'Democracy is hypocrisy.' Yet even baby kissing is better than what happened before, however selfish the motive. Sure, there are many sad effects to competition. But right now it is needed. Our people are lazy, inefficient. They don't want to achieve anything. The peasant is still poor, but now at least he has something to work for. And now he has pride in his heart."

Naturally, he went on, the New China could not solve all the problems of his country overnight. Some people resisted every kind of change. One local firm had invited a German expert to inspect their operations. At the end of his tour, the visitor had submitted a hundred-page report, accompanied by a promise to turn the company around if he were allowed to act as president for a few months. The company obliged, and the German promptly fired the vice president and the Party Secretary. Instantly, profits soared. In general, however, it was impossible to fire the Party Secretary. And if the Party Secretary could not be fired, neither could X, who was his ally. And if X could not be fired, it was difficult to fire Y, his rival. And so it went.

Indeed, said Joe, chuckling, the prison in which he had once spent two months was a perfect reflection of society as a whole. The entire place had been run on a basis of bribery, patronage and seniority. Only by befriending the senior convict had he managed to get a bed on the other side of the cell from the dreaded "shit pit."

At lunch, Joe casually tossed off the equivalent of an average worker's weekly wages on a sumptuous feast for the three of us, and then we returned to the clangorous commotion of downtown Guangzhou. The area was as crowded as Fifth Avenue on the Saturday before Christmas. In Beijing, Joe announced proudly, only 60 percent of the buildings in the central blocks were commercial; here, the figure was 90 percent. Shopkeepers paid 1,000 yuan a month just for a building overlooking the main street. And all about, he whispered, were the covert influences that flourished in the New China. Those men over there with the red armbands were the "Social Order Keepers." Many of the shoppers pushing through the crush were plainclothesmen, seeking out some of the 10,000 smugglers who worked the district, hawking watches, high-tech goods, porno tapes. Because of the 500 percent tax placed on luxury items, a VCR cost 18,000 yuan, and even a pair of sunglasses 50. Overseas Chinese, however, were permitted to bring eight luxury items into the country duty-free. "The government is too poor to buy new films," Joe reported with delight. "But the people can afford to buy all the latest videos."

At this, the quiet Wu spoke up. His great ambition, he shyly confessed, was to work as a journalist in Africa. Then he could send home luxury goods to his family.

Serenaded by the thumping disco beat of the theme from *Flashdance*, we threaded our way through crowded emporia exploding with consumer goods, high-tech radios, cameras, cassettes, more cameras, more radios, more girls in sun visors that said "Lover." The hottest items of all appeared to be those that added the lure of the long-forbidden to the appeal of the mysterious. Inside a cavernous record store, the most prominent tape on sale was "Peculiarities of English Usage." At the local bookstore, the front display was given over to the Paul Simon songbook and *The Ultimate Trivia Quiz Book*. On some of the shelves were children's versions in English of *Vanity Fair*, *Goodbye, Mr. Chips* and *The Helen Keller Story*. Upstairs, copies of *The Idiot*, *Oliver Twist*, and *Madame Bovary* were squashed between *The Dialectic of Nihilism*, *The Politics of Bureaucracy*, *Social Cohesion* and, best of all, *Beyond Dumping*. A customer could buy eighty copies of Dickens or Dostoevsky, however, for the same $50 it cost to purchase a single copy of *Human Society in Post-Revolutionary Cuba*.

Senses bombarded by this video arcade world, we repaired at last for some quiet in another of the city's grand hotels, the Garden Hotel (whose room keys came stamped with messages that read "I don't want to leave Guangzhou. Please leave me here"). As we walked past the hotel gift shop, Joe let out a cry, and pointed to a picture of Deng Xiaoping on the cover of a glossy magazine: we went in to take a closer look, and there, to my companions' delight and my amazement, was a *Time* cover story on China that I had written before leaving New York three months earlier. Impressed by this, my friends led me up to a lobby filled with huge armchairs, and as we munched on a selection of French pastries, they asked me to describe my impressions of a homeland that was still a little strange to them. In response, I rhapsodized at length about the sunlit lamaseries of Tibet, talked a little about the capital and then, by way of amusing parenthesis, mentioned some of the quirks of the fabled Black Coffee. At that instant, I happened to look across at Joe, my all-knowing guide to every deal in China. He was looking absolutely stunned. I stopped what I was saying. For many moments, he could not speak. Finally, he went on shakily: You mean that there were prostitutes there? I think so, I said; indeed, a colleague of mine had once been approached by a male prostitute on the streets of Shanghai. That left Joe quite devastated.

But prostitutes, he said after a very long while, existed only in the West. And even that he found hard to understand. In *Kramer vs. Kramer*, he had seen Dustin Hoffman meet a girl at a party and invite her home. Did that really happen? And if it was so easy to meet girls, why would any Westerner look for a prostitute? And was it true, Wu piped up, about the American man who had slept with 1,000 women in three years? Or the nymphomaniac who had slept with 500 men before realizing that her thirst would go forever unslaked and had therefore become a prostitute? And was there also much wife swapping in the United States? Wu had read about a Chinese couple visiting America who had been invited to a party only to find, to their horror, that they were expected to trade partners for the evening. Was that very common?

The Chinese, I had always heard, regarded sex less as something to do than as something to have done, and so be done with. And indeed, my friends delivered these questions with none of the smirking or swagger one might expect from young males elsewhere in the world, but rather with a great and somber earnestness. They seemed, in fact, to be delving into the subject in as fearful a way as I might ask about kidnappings in Beirut or the atrocities of the Khmer Rouge. Joe had clearly been much heartened by the American he had once met who had been traveling through China for thirty days with a Swedish girl. "He never kissed her, never once," reported Joe. "I said, 'That's incredible.' He said, 'We've both had enough of that kind of thing.' "

In China, Joe went on, it was difficult even to contemplate the subject. "We can say the words in English, but in Chinese we are embarrassed. We were worried when the lady in *Daughter of a Miner* was undressing. When I was at school, I got a sex education manual. I said it was for learning English. At first, when I read the book, I got excited. In college, we talked about intercourse position. But that's all. We are polite in China."

Even marriage, Wu volunteered, was not so easy in China. It was possible for a man to visit a marriage agency and find a partner for 2 yuan (quite a bargain, I thought, next to a bowl of tiger's urine), "but it is harder to find a flat than a fiancée." A typical couple could get an apartment, if they were lucky, of six square meters. Then too, he went on, there was an entire phantom generation of people now in their late twenties or thirties who had lost their best years to the Cultural Revolution. "They are very talented. If they just had a little education, they could do marvelous things. It's sad." Sadder still, perhaps, these "young old people" had never learned to be at ease with the opposite sex. And the longer they lived without contact, the less chance of contact they had. Many women in particular were turning bitter as they found themselves spinsters. But if they tried to find a husband, the man would dismiss them curtly: "Marriage is not only a product of love."

THAT EVENING, AFTER returning to Joe's office to see his stamp collection, I went back to my hotel room to take stock of all I had seen. In the course of the day, I had picked up a copy of the maiden issue of the *Shanghai Student's Post*, which proudly billed itself as the first English-language newspaper to appear in Shanghai since 1949. "The front page," the paper announced, "covers leading issues of the day—international, domestic, local and educational." Underneath that bold promise, the front page consisted, almost exclusively, of a large picture of Sissy Spacek, accompanied by a handwritten message from Sissy to her followers in China. On its inside pages, the paper described an "English Evening" in Shanghai in which four-year-olds donned skirts and then "filed to the center of the hall, saying in English,

'May I have the honor to dance with you?' " A column by one Hou Chen argued that vacations should be longer and then, cunningly citing the laconic example of ancient Sparta, that committee meetings should be shorter. On the following page, across from a history of Coca-Cola, were a list of dos and don'ts for eating with Westerners and short essays on the history of glasses, the Hovercraft, the waltz, UFOs and family-owned KYUS-TV in Montana, the smallest TV station in America.

Another magazine I had picked up, *Sight and Insight,* recorded a hailstorm of facts about the greening of China. The first fast food in Tiananmen Square. The first highway over the Heavenly Mountain. The first American movie shot entirely in China (starring June Lockhart). The first credit-card conference. That breathless litany took me back to all the headlines that had been pounding through the American papers in recent months, chronicling each and every surprising development within the land of Mao: the country's first beauty contest, its first sale of stocks, its first rock concert; a luxury resort built in the Valley of the Ming Tombs, fashion shows in Beijing, the arrival of a fleet of twelve Cadillacs for Party use, complete with bars, TVs and refrigerators. The government had even taken to trumpeting forth the country's first case of AIDS, as if it were proof that China had finally entered the twenty-first century. By now, moreover, six out of every seven Chinese families owned a television set. More Chinese had watched the Super Bowl than Americans. And China was already leading the world in American Express frauds.

Thus the get-rich-quick policies of the Cultureless Revolution were spinning ahead as furiously as the Cultural Revolution in reverse. Not only was the ancient behemoth turning, quite literally, on a dime; it was also turning overnight. So many cars had been put in the hands of so many new drivers that China was suffering 12,000 traffic fatalities a year, on roads that were still largely empty—in one typical day in Beijing, I had seen a bicycle crumpled under a truck, another truck lodged inside a tree trunk and two lots of crowds gathered around smashed cars. Likewise, the country was snapping up so many imports so fast that its trade deficit was rocketing up, in 1985, from $2 billion to almost $15 billion. As I thought of the shopping-spree frenzy of Canton, and of the feverish hospitality of the CAAC stewardesses, I began to understand why so many of the New China's guardians were worried that the girl was throwing open the door too far and embracing her admirer with an altogether unseemly warmth.

In some ways, indeed, the New China seemed like a head-strong young girl, so exhilarated by her new sense of power that she was determined to see how far she could take it, even though she did not know where she was going. Under Deng's new "socialism with a Chinese character," comrades were becoming mad for fads: men were parting with two weeks' wages to get their hair permed, women with two months' salary to have their eyelids doubled; people of both sexes were paying fifty times face value for tickets to fashion shows and thirty times as much for a porno tape as for a video of Chinese melodrama. Even the country's leaders were not immune to the blandishments of the West. Here were Premier Zhao Ziyang looking dapper in his tailored Western suits, Deng Xiaoping indulging his fondness for croissants and Deng's bridge partner, General Secretary Hu Yaobang, urging the people to relinquish chopsticks for knives and forks, on grounds of hygiene.

And through it all, the high-tech, open-market, westward-looking New China seemed to have a much clearer sense of the system it was abandoning than of the one it sought. As the government moved into the unknown, advancing by trial and error, stretching Marxism further and further without knowing quite where it was heading or when to stop, a quarter of the world's people were being turned around and around so dizzily that nobody was sure where anything stood. In the New China, money was still regarded as the source of all evil; but it was also now a source of much pride. One official slogan enjoined, "To Get Rich Is Glorious," while another exhorted, "Sacrifice for Socialism." One day Deng Xiaoping happily declared, "Capital-ism cannot harm us," and two months later he warned of the necessity of "combating the corrosive influence of capitalist ideas." The government reveled in its embarrassment of riches, even as it betrayed its embarrassment about riches. One day Maoism was enjoined, and the next day Me-ism, and the next day both, and the next day neither. Nobody knew anymore what was right, or what was wrong, or even what was left; the door, it seemed, was swinging wildly on its hinges.

I could only wonder what would happen when the honeymoon ended. Again and again in its history, after all, the long-xenophobic country had begun to open its door to the world, and then, in a frenzy of anxiety, had slammed it shut. In the mid-nineteenth century, the alien Manchu Dynasty had been rocked by a sudden rush of nationalism among the puritanical Taiping rebels, and 20 million people had died by the time China was returned to the Chinese. In 1897, the Emperor Guang Xu had encouraged Western commerce under the slogan "Chinese learning for the essence, Western learning for the application," only to provoke the Boxers into a fury of hatred indiscriminately aimed at all foreigners. Fifty years ago, Chiang Kai-shek's policies of free enterprise had prompted one American senator to predict that Shanghai would be "built up and up, ever up, until it is just like Kansas City," before they were reversed, with a terrible vengeance, by Maoism. Even with the blood of the Cultural Revolution still fresh, Deng's own reformist policy had already touched off a savage backlash, as conservatives began raising the cry of "spiritual pollution" and banning everything from Jean-Paul Sartre to Jonathan Livingston Seagull.

It seemed only a matter of time before an even more violent reversal erupted. Not long before I arrived, China had lost a soccer match to Hong Kong, and its supporters had gone berserk. What was most chilling about their bloodcurdling riot, though, was that the fans had chosen to direct their rage not at their team, or at their opponents, or even at the referees, but simply, and irrationally, at any foreigners they could find. They had smashed cameras, stomped on cars, crushed glasses. During my own trip, I had seen and heard about several fistfights between tourists and locals, a phenomenon unknown to me in all the rest of my travels. And by the time I got home, as the anti-reformist movement picked up momentum, pictures of my Californian host in Beijing were suddenly splashed across the world's front pages. Why? He had, I read, been evicted from China for growing too friendly with some local students.

ON MY FINAL day in China, Joe and Wu took me to see the area that had moved deepest into a deracinated future—the Special Economic Zone of Shenzhen. As soon as we crossed the fifty-four-mile-long border that separates the land of plenty from the rest of the country, we were definitely in another world. Shacks gave way to four-story homes, open fields to office towers. Esso signs sprouted up along the roads, and Cal Tex logos. Construction cranes jerked spasmodically over the skyline, hovering over buildings that lay under scaffolds like eggs half hatched. Not long ago, explained Joe, the sleepy fishing village had had a population of 20,000; now it was sixteen times that size.

In the beautifully landscaped area of Shekhou, we walked around rows of smart white condos, with red-tiled roofs, lined up, as if in La Jolla or Cassis, against a deep blue waterway. The trim little gardens exuded the surface-deep good health of a bright new singles complex somewhere in the Sunbelt. Every one of these units cost $20,000, explained Joe, and most of their residents were Japanese businessmen. "The Japanese tried to conquer us with arms, and they failed," he said. "Now they have managed to conquer us with trade."

Along the main shopping streets of Shenzhen, revelers and shoppers drifted among a Computerland store, an International Arcade and a forty-nine-story building, the tallest in China. We stopped for a snack in an ice-cream parlor decorated with a poster of Brooke Shields. Boxes of Fruit Loops crowded the local air-conditioned supermarket, Debussy was playing in a record store, the bookshop was filled with English textbooks given Confucian tags ("Words are words, but seeing is believing"). Not far away was a branch of Citibank, a country club, signs that exhorted "Time Is Money!" Even taxis, so notoriously difficult to find everywhere else in China, were here in abundance, and mini-buses too, one of which took us to the zone's latest amusement park, which came equipped with a roller coaster, a pagoda, a plush restaurant served by waitresses in cheongsams and a hotel with a lake beside it. Admission to the complex was 30 yuan, two weeks' wages for the typical peasant; in Shenzhen, however, one could pay in Hong Kong dollars. Indeed, if Guangzhou looked like a mirror image of Hong Kong, Shenzhen was effectively just a superior Hong Kong; most of the vacationers here had come over from the Crown Colony in order to make the most of splashy stores, high-tech offers, bright playgrounds even glitzier than those at home.

By the end of the day, all three of us were thoroughly exhausted. For thirty-six hours, we had been whirled and spun through the bright lights and frantic development of the New China as if through some furious washing machine. Now, on the way back to Guangzhou, we mostly kept quiet, alone with our thoughts. I looked out of the window to where the future was rolling in through the dark. Wu lost himself in a magazine, putting it down only once, to ask me, with quiet earnestness, "What do you think of sexual license?" Joe sat where he was, collecting his thoughts. Once he leaned forward to ask me if I knew Orianna Fallaci. Later, as we rolled ahead, he leaned forward again in the half-dark carriage and softly recited in its entirety "Shall I compare thee to a summer's day?"

It was almost midnight when we finished our farewell cup of tea at the White Swan, but the night around us was electric. As he took in the full splendor of the grand hotel—the waterfall, the sparkle, the bright lights on the water—Joe sat back and delivered himself of his final assessment. "When I was young," he began, "I wanted to change the government. I joined a hunger strike at college and I protested and I wanted to overturn everything. Now I see that it is better to develop, to work for oneself. I can see that evolution is better than revolution."

True enough, I said. But was he not alarmed by some of the influences pouring in through the open door? Did he not fear that the New China might spin out of control or else be spun back by reactionary forces? Might not the shy, age-old romance between China and the West turn suddenly into something more desperate and more violent?

He thought for a while, and then answered softly. Yes, he said, there was often much room for misunderstanding. These days, many old people looked to their roots, while many young people looked to the West. The two could no longer see eye to eye. They could not even speak the same language. Many young children, for example, used the English phrase "bye-bye." Their grandmothers, however, assumed that they were using the Mandarin phrase *bai bai*, meaning "bring your hands together and bow." Mistaking friendliness for insolence, the old women slapped the children, and the children decided never to be so friendly again. Still, said Joe, soon such problems would hardly matter: by the time he became a grandfather, the government's single-child policy would mean that many Chinese would not even know the word for "aunt." They would not understand what a "cousin" was. They might not even remember the meaning of "brother."

In any case, he concluded, everyone knew that everything in China was cyclical. "We tell Deng, 'Once you lose, you will be like Mao. Mao organized great reforms, and people called him a hero. Now the same people curse him.' I say to him, 'Deng, one day there will be a second Deng.' "

With that, Joe and Wu accompanied me to the hotel's electric doors and we said goodbye. Silently, the doors slid apart, and my friends walked out into the dazzled Western night. Silently, behind them, the doors once more slid shut.

THE PHILIPPINES
Born in the U.S.A.

I T WAS MY first night in Asia. I made my way from Bangkok's airport to the lobby of the Oriental Hotel, where I had agreed to meet my English school friend, Louis. A few minutes later, he swept in with a flourish, clad in a moth-eaten tropical suit fit only for some ancient tale of Maugham's and accompanied by Mike, a Canadian he had met earlier that day.

"Hey," said Mike, a veteran of the city, "I know a great place to eat."

I imagined some smoky opium den, dim under the light of a single swinging light bulb, thick with the back-door intrigue of wizened men at dirty wooden tables.

A few minutes later, a doorman admitted us to a super-luxury hotel, and Mike led us down a sweeping staircase, past a sparkling arcade of jewelry stores and through a pair of heavy wooden doors. Inside was an enormous room, done up to look like a plush red-carpet New England steak house. Every table in the place sported a tidy red cloth, a candle and a glittery setting of silverware. There must have been sixty or more of these nicely done-up tables in all. And every single one of them was empty. Across the length and breadth of the entire cavernous space, not a single person was to be seen, but one: a wiry, middle-aged Asian in a tuxedo, greasy hair combed unhappily across his forehead. Seated on a stool atop a modest stage, he had an electric guitar in his arms and a large black box at his side.

As we walked into the empty room, he suddenly came to life. "Hello, my friends." He perked up smoothly. "Good evening, and welcome." He tilted the mike in our direction. "My name is George, I come from the Philippines and I'm here to entertain you." With that, he turned around and flipped a few switches on his box. Moments later, as we took our seats, the soothing beat of a synthesizer and bass tangoed through the vast and empty chamber, and George oozed his way into "My Way."

Fighting back thoughts of Mikicide, Louis and I pored in gloomy silence over the menu. As we contemplated the selection —there was pizza, pizza or more pizza—our irrepressible serenader concluded a highly emotional rendition of "Feelings." A few minutes later, as our house specials were brought out from the microwave, he eased his way into "Strangers in the Night."

Seven more of these heartfelt dirges drifted through the echoing room as we munched into our cardboard. Finally, Louis pushed back his chair with an air of decisiveness and turned to the stage. "Hey!" he shouted out in the precious silence between songs. "El Paso." Our host looked back at us in perplexity. He frowned with concentration. For many moments, there was an uncertain silence. Then, face brightening, he called back hopefully, "Marty Robbins?"

"Yeaah!"

At that, the singer turned around to his mike, pushed a few buttons and twirled a few knobs. Out came the unmistakable, horseshoe-clopping rhythm of "Out in the West Texas town of El Paso . . ." written by Marty Robbins, made famous by the Grateful Dead. At that, Louis—former page to Queen Elizabeth II and flower of the British aristocracy—let out a wild yodel, tore off his jacket and raced onstage. Making him welcome with a smile, George pushed the mike in his direction, and, faces close together, the two of them launched into an exuberant rendition of "El Paso."

The minute they had brought the song to a rousing conclusion, Louis called out, "Casey Jones." George made a few adjustments on his machine, and then the grinning pair broke into an inimitable duet on that one too. Once that was done, they roared into Merle Haggard's "Branded Man," and then the Dead's "Mama Tried," and then Dylan's "It's All Over Now, Baby Blue," Louis sweating and red-faced by now, George as satin-smooth as ever. Every time Louis shouted out a title, George pushed a few buttons, and out came the pound and throb of the familiar chords. And so, for forty astonishing minutes, before a spellbound audience of two in the finest pizza parlor in Bangkok, George, the pride of Manila, and Old Etonian Louis chimed their way irresistibly through heartbreaking tunes of love and lonesomeness on the great open highways of the West.

THUS WAS I initiated into the joys of Filipino music. And thus I absorbed one of the Orient's great truths: that the Filipinos are its omnipresent, always smiling troubadours. Master of every American gesture, conversant with every Western song, polished and ebullient all at once, the Filipino plays minstrel to the entire continent.

Any tourist passing through the five-star palaces of the East is likely, indeed, to be serenaded at every step by Filipino crooners and songstresses. "Sultry Filipina Angel Joy Salinas" was playing at the Shangri-La in Bangkok when I was in town, while guests of the Hilton were invited to "lend an ear to three delightful and talented Filipina girls who comprise the Candy Bars." In Hong Kong, the Meridien, the Hong Kong Hotel and the Lee Gardens all boasted Filipino acts, as did the Hyatt and the Holiday Inn. "Special requests from guests are welcomed by most of the bands," explained the local tourist paper, "and it is very hard to catch them out with one they don't know." In the tiny East Malaysian port of Labuan, the only serious hotel in town "proudly presents . . . the Music Makers, direct from the Philippines." Even Beijing swung at night to Filipino rhythms: Los Magnificos were appearing at the Jianguo Hotel and some of their compatriots at the Great Wall Hotel.

Natural charmers, the Filipinos had long, I discovered, been masters of every aspect of Asia's "hospitality business." As early as 1950, Norman Lewis had found a Filipino band beguiling

Saigon with its version of "September in the Rain," and by now at least 3,000 Filipinos were playing the music circuit in Japan alone. In 1984, another 35,000 young ladies from the Philippines had entered Japan to work in other, less cheerful corners of the entertainment trade. And one day, when I opened up the Jakarta *Post*, I read that a local nightclub with the improbably cosmopolitan name of "Shamrock Copacabana" had been found guilty of smuggling in a foreign entertainer. The contraband performer was, of course, a female and, of course, a Filipina, and the article concluded with the curiously uninflected explanation—Muslim tact applied to Muslim tastes, perhaps—that foreign entertainers were always popular "because they could satisfy more customers by revealing their bodies during performances."

It was only natural, a school friend in Hong Kong informed me, that the Filipinos flourished as entertainers. They were blessed, after all, with a colorful sense of fiesta exuberance, a rare blend of Asian grace and Latin fire; they were also, he added, an uncommonly friendly and outgoing bunch—emotional, reckless, high-spirited. The Filipinos were the happiest people in all the world.

II

It was raining when I arrived in Manila, and dark. Smiling prettily, two girls at the airport desk led me to a bus and, as I entered, the driver greeted me with a twinkle. A few minutes later, he threaded his way through narrow streets and dropped me off at a small pension in the tourist belt of Ermita. I hurried inside through the downpour. The place was full, the family at the desk reported—but why not try another inn just around the corner?

Picking up my case, I wandered out into the dark street and began walking. The rain was coming down hard, but there was no way of staying dry under the awnings; the sidewalks were crowded with sleeping bodies. Women and babies were huddled on the stoops of storefronts, men were bundled up in doorways. Neon, half blurred by the rain, winked busily over shabby bars. "Hello, daddy!" short-skirted girls called out from open doors. "Hon, you want good time?" I reached an intersection and waited for the light to change. I give you girl, said a passerby softly, I give you hotel.

A couple of minutes later, I arrived at the recommended pension, dripping and disoriented, happy to accept whatever was available. A man led me up a creaking staircase. On the wall was a painting of the bleeding Jesus, and in the narrow corridor, a black-light portrait of a Bambi-eyed and huge-breasted topless Filipina. There were no locks on the door of my room, no sheets on the bed. Nothing, in fact, but a dirty mattress on which some previous occupant had scrawled: "I love you. Love R.S." A few inches away was a heart that said "Sheila." There was no water in the bathroom.

I did not care to pass much time in this melancholy dump and so, as soon as I had dropped off my things, I went out again into the streets. Finding my way to Mabini, one of the two main drags in Ermita, I began wandering through the rain. A man started walking rapidly by my side, offering to change dollars. A little girl clutched plaintively at my sleeve. At corners, lit up by the neon, tattered groups of people were gathered in clumps to sleep or to beg. I walked past VD clinics, rickety money changer's shacks, discount travel agents, run-down bars and nightclubs.

At last, I came to the Hobbit House, which I had heard of as the most interesting folk club in Manila. The dark room was almost empty. A middle-aged man played mournful jazz piano on a small stage, accompanied by a teenage boy on bass. Every other person in the place—the waiters, the bartenders, a sprinkling of customers—was a dwarf.

As soon as I sat down, one of the tiny waiters hobbled up to me, his small shoes heavy on the bare floor. Smiling his hello, he took my order. Then a waitress emerged from the darkness, shuffling along in three-inch steps and hoisting herself up onto a chair next to mine. She greeted me with a sweet smile, and we fell into conversation. Did she have any brothers and sisters? "Two," she answered with a sad smile. "But they big. I only one small."

Touched by her matter-of-factness, and a little discomfited, I remained hunched over my Coke. The door opened, and I swiveled around eagerly in hope of reinforcements. But it was just another huge-headed, grinning little man trying to sell T-shirts.

Then my waiter clomped over to my table and pulled himself up onto another chair. Four eyes closed in on me in the semi-darkness. Where did I live? asked the waiter. New York. Ah, he smiled, and burst into a few lines of "New York, New York." But actually, I said, I always thought of California as my home. "I left my heart in San Francisco," crooned the dwarf.

We talked some more in a desultory fashion, the waiter occasionally improvising a few songs over the moody piano music, and then I took my leave of the friendly pair. "Come back soon," the waitress called out after me. "And bring your companion."

The rain was still coming down in torrents, but I was not yet ready to return to my hotel room. So I walked the full length of the narrow street, exchanging helpless smiles with those huddled next to me in doorways, hurrying past pool halls and beer gardens and restaurants out of which I heard snatches of pop songs, acoustic guitars, jukeboxes. The handwritten cardboard signs that lined the streets were smudged by the rain, but I could still make out their messages. "Wanted: Young Attractive and Beautiful Sexy Dancer." "Wanted: Attractive Cashier." "Wanted: Sexy Karaoke Singers."

After ten minutes or so among these neon-lit shadows, I caught some pleasing music drifting out of a place called the Swagman. Inside, a six-piece band was playing on a modest stage, led by a pretty torch singer who could have been Streisand or Ronstadt in the dark. A kitty box for tips rested on top of one of the speakers. There were only ten seats at the tiny, semicircular bar, and I took my place on one of them. Next to me were two unaccompanied young ladies. Both of them gazed up with large, beseeching eyes.

I tried to concentrate exclusively on my drink, but I could not long ignore the penetrating stares on either side. Finally, I turned around to the girl on my left. She had glitter on her eyelids and her face was sweet and fresh, but her smile was not a cheerful one. We chatted a little, and she told me that she had two kids and a husband. But he could not find a job anywhere, so now she was working at the Swagman. I could think of nothing to say in reply. The singer onstage went into an aching version of "Please Release Me."

I turned to the lady on my other side, a small, matronly type in a sober green dress. She had two children also, she said, but then she had found out that their father was already married to another woman, and had eight other children at home. She worked in a factory, but the factory closed. So here she was in the Swagman, and once a month she saved up enough money to visit her mother on the far side of Manila, and her children. "My ambition," she said, "is to finish my studies in commerce. Then maybe I can own small business."

I did not know what to say to the unspoken appeals; I wanted to help but didn't know how, so I gulped down my Coke, wished both girls the best and hurried back out into the rain-washed street. There was time, I decided, for one more stop before I returned to my guesthouse.

I had exhausted most of Mabini by now, so I turned to the parallel strip, Del Pilar. There were fewer money changers on this street, fewer stores, and many more signs: "Wanted: Mama-san, experienced." "Hospitality girl wanted." "Wanted: A-Go-Go Girl or Receptionist with Pleasing Personality." The neon twinkled more frantically here, and the narrow lane was full of winking commotion. Loud music issued from the bars, and Western men stumbled out at intervals. Dressed-up girls and dressed-down girls called out invitations. Lights sparkled, neon lips flashed.

The glossiest joint on the street seemed to be the New Bangkok. Inside, Springsteen was deafening on a video screen, the stench of beer was powerful, cigarette smoke rose up from the barstools where foreign men dandled local beauties on their laps, bikinied dancers writhed on a tiny platform. In and out among the customers bustled a middle-aged Chinese lady in a cheongsam, anxious to make sure that everyone was enjoying himself.

A girl led me to a booth, and I put in an order for an orange juice. A minute or two later, I was joined by a different young lady, very prim in a smart gray dress with "Training" written in red across the front. Sitting down beside me and looking straight ahead, she drew a comb gravely through her short, sleek hair. Then, turning to me shyly, she asked if I would buy her a drink. Rosa was eighteen, I learned, and still in high school. Her classes lasted from 9:00 until 5:00, and she worked in the bar from 9:00 at night until 3:30. But she took off the nights before exams because she wanted to do well in her studies. She wanted to become a journalist.

Rosa had started working on Del Pilar only two weeks ago, she took pains to inform me, and she planned to work here only as a receptionist. She wouldn't wear a bikini, and she wouldn't be obliged to touch anyone. Dancers got an extra $3 a night, but she was content just to make 50 cents every time a customer bought her a drink.

Was the New Bangkok a good place to work? I asked. She didn't know, she replied earnestly; she worked at the Blue Hawaii across the street. Then why was she here? Because, she said, her elder sister also worked at the Blue Hawaii, as a dancer. And she could not bear to watch her sister put her arms around strangers or giggle as foreign men fondled her. So she came to the New Bangkok for shelter.

With that, serious Rosa turned to comb her hair again, and another girl, in a black bikini, stumbled toward us, tears streaking her mascara, turning her face into a sad and clownish mask. Lurching up to our booth, she let out a wail, then flung her arms around Rosa, burying her head on the younger girl's shoulder. Rosa turned to me, with a soft embarrassed smile, then turned back to the girl, put her arms around her and asked her what was wrong. Violently, the girl jerked back her head. "I hate millionaire," she blurted through her sobs, her eyes wild and vacant. "I hate money." She looked at me fiercely. "It's bullshit." Then she began to choke on her words. "I want Mamá." Her face twisted up again, she threw herself back onto Rosa.

Rosa looked over at me, confused, and then, telling the girl gently to stay put, she got up and walked away. The girl looked up at me, and through me, with hatred. Rosa came back, gave her a Kleenex and held onto her like a mother. A few moments later, the girl pulled back, dried her eyes and wiped her face clean. It was time for her to dance again.

As she walked off, an awkward silence fell. What was the girl's name? Rosa did not know; she had never met her before. And what was the problem? Drugs, she said; heroin. The thought made her silent. After a while, she spoke up again. "That girl," she said, "she reminds me of my sister. She does not take drugs. But when she gets drunk, she cries and cries. She does not like her life. And when she is drunk, she says what is in her mind, what is in her heart." Aren't you worried, Rosa, I asked, that the same thing will happen to you, working here? She nodded grimly. "I know. I think of my sister often. But I can keep control. I do not drink. I do not smoke. I will work only as receptionist. I want to reach my ambition." And you will really be able to avoid all this? "Yes," she said, nodding slowly and with shaky determination. "My ambition is to become a journalist."

Then the song changed, and the other girl staggered back again and threw herself onto Rosa as before, sobbing in racking spasms, blurting inarticulate curses through her tears. Solemn in her neat gray dress, Rosa kept hold of her, tender but uneasy. As she did so, the manageress came up, puffing on a long cigarette holder while she placed her hand on the hysterical dancer. "So," she said, giving me a sly smile. "You would like to take this girl home?"

SADNESS AND MUSIC were everywhere I looked in the Marcoses' Manila, smiles and rags. In all my travels, I had never seen poverty so open and so crushing. I had expected, from the travel brochures, to find grand hotels and glittery bars strung like jewels along wide boulevards by the sea. Instead I found a border-town seediness of beggars and whores. In the tourist district of Ermita, dead mice lay on the sidewalks like overturned trucks and men in old clothes urinated in the face of passing cars. The streets in the rain were littered with sleeping bodies, rotten with the stench of garbage and decay.

I moved on my first morning into a slightly better hotel, but often, even there, no milk was available at breakfast. Half of the local supermarket was taken up by a pharmacy; at the checkout stand, more brands of condoms were on sale than of cigarettes. The post office was a single booth, with cardboard boxes placed on the floor instead of slots; the line for stamps straggled along the sidewalk. Nearby, another, longer line had formed outside a sign promising jobs for able-bodied men in Saudi Arabia and Dubai. For women, I imagined, things were a little easier. Most bars or restaurants posted cardboard signs outside: "Wanted: Sexy Dancers, Receptionists." "Wanted: Hospitality Girl."

Within five minutes of my hotel, there must have been sixty or more of these places, beer gardens and bars and karaoke clubs where the customers sing along, all of them advertising live music, as well as some combination of "models," "actresses" or "campus girls," all "5' 4" with Pleasing Personalities." Typical of the Ermita style was Calle Cinquo, the restaurant where I stopped for dinner my second night in town. It was a fairly nondescript open-air beer garden, protected from the heavens by a thatched roof. There were not many customers in evidence when I entered, and only forty or so tables. But there were fifty-three waitresses in the place, all young, all dressed in bright skirts and prettily made up, most of them sitting around their tables, idly looking out into the street for custom. Meanwhile, lights flashed and guitars glinted on a large stage, where six pretty girls, all red-lipped with long earrings and shiny black hair, all dressed in matching yellow-and-black queen-bee outfits —three of them singers, two guitarists, and a sixth at the keyboards—zipped through record-perfect renditions of "Like a Virgin" and "High Society Girl," performing jazzy little steps in unison and flashing bright smiles at the scattered members of their audience. As soon as they had finished, another equally high-tech and professional girl group came on, and after them another, and then a fourth. "Girls Just Wanna Have Fun," the six-girl band chimed brightly, while outside, in the street, groups of men peered in over the fence, and women stopped to look at the signs soliciting more singers, more waitresses ("5' 4" minimum. Pleasing Personality. No experience needed").

All along the narrow streets of Ermita, hostesses in "U.S.A. for Africa" T-shirts or pretty dresses sat listlessly outside the entrance to their bars, staring imploringly at all who passed. The hospitality girls of the charm trade were happy, it seemed, to dance attention on any and every foreigner: there was a Chalet Suisse bar in Ermita, a Scandinavia, an Aussie Bar and the Australian. Richer visitors were even better accommodated. Within a few yards of Mabini were the Sahara Club, the Oasis, the Arabic Club, the Arabian Nights, the Sultan Café and the al-Chams. And all about were Japanese lanterns and bamboo screens and ryokans, the Michiko Karaoke Club and the Keiko Karaoke Club. "Unescorted Ladies Not Allowed" said the signs on most bars; others allowed them in, for a fee of $1.

Sometimes, the fallen dilapidation of the area could almost seem comic—I peered one night into the local bowling alley to see a frantic scatter of arms and legs at the far end of the lane every time a ball came down, and then a disembodied hand putting the pins back in place and rolling the ball back to sender.

More often, though, it was hard to raise a smile. The Waldorf-Astoria was a dingy little hole offering "24-Hour Dim Sum." Inside was Maxim's Café. "We are Exclusive Club" said another broken billboard, "but everyone is welcome."

With its rain-worn buildings and its palm trees windblown against a gray harbor, with its half-clad people lying in the streets and its air of careworn neglect, Ermita reminded me more of Bombay than anywhere else I knew. But the squalor here seemed more aching and more desolate. Unlike their Indian counterparts, Manila's beggars looked surprised by their newfound poverty and unaccustomed to it, lacking anything to support them as they fell. Never before had I felt such an overpowering sense of need—dirty, desperate, crying need; and never before had I felt myself so helpless. In Manila I learned for the first time all the grim sophistries of destitution and prostitution—the shame of giving a beggar only 50 cents, the shame of giving him nothing at all because there are too many others around, the shame of returning to the comfort of even a cheap hotel.

My own small hotel, like most of the businesses of Ermita, was guarded round the clock by two handsome young security guards in smart blue uniforms, guns set snugly against glistening gold buckles. As I settled down in the place, I often sat down in the lobby to chat with the cheery twosome. Manuel had three children, he told me, and he had christened every one of them with a name that began with an "M." He loved them, he said, but he envied me for being unattached. "Always problems," he explained. "Always thinking of my family. Always problems."

His colleague explained that he too had pressures at home. "I am fatherless," he said, "and my mother depends on me." Then he paused. "You have power," he said to me entreatingly. "Maybe you can help me get good job?"

I did not know what to say. "Sure," said Manuel, smiling brightly. "I come to U.S. I visit you there." I did not know whether it was crueler to encourage the illusion or just to kill it then. I smiled back sadly.

On my next night in Manila, as I took dinner alone in a tiny rock-video café, a girl dressed in a red headband and a long white T-shirt and almost nothing else began staring at me intently from another table. As soon as I looked back at her, she came over and sat down. She looked very young and very poor. I offered her some chicken, and she gnawed at the bone hungrily. "I have problem," she began. She had come into town only that morning, she said, bringing with her nothing but the clothes she was wearing and one other shirt and a pair of jeans that she kept in a Dick Whittington bag. She had no place to sleep, she explained with a tired, half-drugged smile. "My ambition," she said, "is to find a boyfriend." She smiled at me again. "To find a boyfriend—that is my ambition."

I HAD NOT known before I arrived in Manila that the tourist district was the red-light district. But then I had not known that one resident in every five of the "showcase of democracy" was reduced to squatting. I had not known that the $20 million government-run Manila Film Center, the grand creation of President and Madame Marcos, made its money by showing porno movies, uncut. And I had not known that across the street from the glittering pavilions of the Cultural Center of the Philippines, whose futuristic ramps and landscaped gardens were a gaudy monument to Marcos splendor, families were sleeping in bushes.

Before I came to Manila, I could not have guessed that more than a thousand families in what Imelda Marcos, Minister of Human Settlements, called "the City of Man" made their homes in the central garbage dump. And before I arrived in the New Society, I would never have suspected that a security guard, after eleven years on the job, received, for a twelve-hour shift, exactly $2.25. Actually, that was quite a good salary for Manila—$55 a month was as much as a long-standing government official could earn. Yet the horoscope in the government-run daily was telling its readers that for all those born on August 24 the likeliest occupations were "polo player, horse breeder, international playboy, jet pilot and travel mogul."

Until I came to Manila, I had not known that I was capable of social outrage. But then, one evening, one of my hotel security guards invited me home. We drove down Roxas Boulevard, the grand corniche that sweeps along Manila Bay and boasts the Hyatt, the Holiday Inn and many of the city's starriest discos; as we passed, I noticed people living on the center divider of the road, huddling against the rain and the wind in shacks no larger than a bathtub.

Ten minutes later, we got out in a street of run-down tenements in Pasay City and walked down an alley thick with refuse. At last we came to a concrete shack. My friend pounded at the door. A frightened-looking girl opened it, just a crack, and let us in. There were two dark rooms inside, but there was little in the way of furniture. There was no room for it.

Stepping over bodies, we made our way to the far room. On a sagging bed, a man dressed only in boxer shorts tossed and turned. Beside him, his girlfriend lay facing the other direction, her head lolling over the edge, her eyes bleary from the joint she was smoking. Between them lay a baby. Next to the bed was a mattress on which a woman was sitting and two or three children were uncomfortably stretched out.

In the other room, there was a bare sink, above it two bottles of brandy. On the floor, a couple of kids and a baby and three adults were sprawled across a mess of bedding. Above them, the concrete showed through the wallpaper. There was a picture of a black-and-yellow sunset on the wall, a photo of a girl torn from some calendar and a portrait of some human-faced dogs seated at a dinner table. To get to the bathroom, one had to crawl out through the window.

The kids, dirty-chinned and dressed in faded T-shirts, scrambled about the half-sleeping bodies. At the sink, the young girl who had let us in rolled joints. The man in boxer shorts got up, stretched, went over to the sink and knocked back some brandy. The kids bawled. It was nighttime, but nobody seemed to be sleeping much. Lulu, the girl on the bed, smiled up at me. She worked in a bar, so she spoke fluent English; it therefore fell to her to play hostess.

"What can we do?" she said, motioning toward the man drinking at the sink. "He is college graduate. Commerce. But no job." Her own position in the bar brought in a little money, of course, but she was twenty-nine now, and unless she joined most of her colleagues in going to Japan, she too would soon be out of a job. All the time she was speaking, her eleven-year-old son stared at me with bright eyes. Then he broke into a lovely smile. "Hip, hip, hooray," he cried.

THUS THE UNNERVING counterpoint continued: smiles amidst the squalor, and songs. In Japan, my previous stop, I had grown accustomed to living in a kind of mobile isolation tank; here, as I walked down the street, people looked me directly in the eye, and flashed me cheering smiles as they passed. The girls at grocery-store cash registers drew me shyly into conversation; the high-spirited boys who worked in my hotel showed me their college books. And all day long, from dawn to midnight, music buzzed through the streets of Ermita.

Usually, the songs that pounded out of the bars and jukeboxes were the latest Top 40 smashes—"Material Girl" and "Smooth Operator" and "Time After Time." There was also a steady supply of All-American favorites like "Country Roads" and "Hotel California," and nobody seemed to think it strange that Filipinos should be singing, "Take me home, country roads, to the land that I adore—West Virginia . . ." Sometimes the songs were played in the original recording, sometimes reproduced live, but with such high fidelity that it was impossible to tell if the sound came from jukebox or human voice. Either way, the sound was sunny and intoxicating. In Ermita, I felt as if I were living inside a Top 40 radio station.

I quickly noticed too that the talented Filipinos were able to turn their voices to any style or fashion. Yet they seemed most at home with sugarcoated Middle of the Road ditties: soft, straight-from-the-heart tunes, sweetened by pleasant melodies. There were forty-seven radio stations in town, FM and AM, but nearly all of them played the same AM tunes—easy listening as a background to easy living. I heard the Everly Brothers more often in Manila than ever before, and Simon and Garfunkel too; Peter Paul and Mary, and the Eagles. Country-and-western laments for lost love were everywhere too, and once, at a free concert in Rizal Park, I heard bankers perform duets from *Rigoletto* and miniskirted secretaries do arias from *La Traviata*. But in more than three weeks, I heard no hard rock, no New Wave, no eighties pop; no Talking Heads or Clash or even Twisted Sister—just ballads of heartbreak and high spirits, decorated with sweet falsettos and silvery harmonies.

The Number One hit while I was in the Philippines was, without a doubt, "We Are the World," the song recorded by the superstars of U.S.A. for Africa to raise money for the starving in Ethiopia. The anthem of hopeful charity had, in fact, become a virtual sound track to Philippine life. One morning, as I walked into Mister Donut for breakfast, the bespectacled college boy behind the counter began swaying rhythmically to the song as it came up on the radio. That same day I walked into a restaurant for lunch and heard Bruce Springsteen rasping his way passionately through the same plaintive refrain. The same appeal was drifting out of an open-air restaurant, sung by two young boys with acoustic guitars, as I walked down Mabini that evening. And at Calle Cinquo Restaurant that same night, cheers arose from the audience on two separate occasions as two different girl groups struck up the song's intimate opening bars.

On many a night, I could imagine nothing in the world more pleasant than just to wander through the streets of Ermita, catching the music that pulsed out of bars and beer gardens, hearkening to the siren call of caprice. One typical evening, I went to eat at Shakey's Pizza Parlor ("We Serve Fun") and was entertained by Euphoria, a tight, hard-driving seven-man group, six of whose members took turns on lead vocals. Every one of them had a beautiful voice and for every sad song—"I am just a poor boy/ Though my story's seldom told . . ."—they had a singer who could reproduce the exact pitch of the original recording. Then I dropped in at a beer garden where three women in Swingles-singers dresses and two middle-aged men in Travolta-ish black suits and white waistcoats danced their way through sleek, synchronized Manhattan Transfer–type numbers. Then I made my way to My Father's Mustache, a folk club where the waiters came dressed in three-gallon hats with sheriff's badges pinned to their chests and holsters around their waists. The walls of the place were decorated with sepia prints of American men in cowboy gear, and the theme song from *Bonanza* pounded out of the sound system. Onto the stage—designed in the shape of a Conestoga wagon—strode the Pony Express band, dressed up in Stetsons and bandannas. A fast-strumming banjo man, a fiddler and a girl with a tambourine careened into a roaring version of "Red River Valley," then raced into "Freight Train" (complete with choo-choo whistles). "Hi, y'all," drawled the lady singers after they had finished their overture, "we'd like to do a song by Hank Williams." Out came "Jambalaya." "Yee-hah," cried the guitarist. "Whooo-ey," called the bassist. And the fiddler played like the devil.

On my way back home that night, I found myself half skipping, so infectious was the happy music. And as I entered my hotel, I heard the receptionist breaking into a rendering of "We Are the World" so pretty that my heart felt like singing along with her.

III

"Where There Is Music," said a T-shirt in a Mabini gift shop, "There Can't Be Misery." "Music," said another in the same store, "Is the Medicine of a Troubled Mind."

Such wishful slogans were not difficult to believe so long as I was inside some folk-music club, watching a smiling singer under flashing orange lights. But as soon as I was back on the streets, amid the clutch of urchins and the cracked fences, it was harder to imagine that music could change the world. And as the days passed, the gray skies of Manila, its sense of peeling dereliction, began to wear me down. I did not know how to cope with the beggars, how to be of assistance to the large-eyed girls in the restaurants. I did not know what to make of the glossy ads for the Manila Casino (on Imelda Avenue), which offered free entrance to tourists and cried, "Game and Gain in U.S. Dollars. Watch that hot dice dance! Tumble at the table!" I needed some fresh air.

And so one day I took a bus out to Angeles City, the small town around Clark Air Force Base, one of the two American bases that help bind the ties between the United States and the only country it has ever directly ruled.

It was not hard to tell when we had arrived. For an hour or so, the bus drove through rice fields and small villages, past huts guarded by wide-eyed gamins. Then it drew up to an unkempt T-junction surrounded by vacant lots, gas stations and fading billboards. On one side of the road was Shakey's and Kentucky Fried Chicken; on the other a Dunkin' Donuts outlet ("Open 24 Hours. World's Finest Coffee") and a Drive-Thru Donut King. On the far side of the junction stood a rusted roadside shack called the Jailhouse Rock Disco and next to it the Café Valenzuela ("Pride of the Highway"). In the near gray distance gleamed the Golden Arches.

Inside, the walls of McDonald's were decorated in the style of an Arizona coffee shop; a faded picture of John Wayne; another of the Lone Ranger and of Chief Red Cloud; a drawing of a Typical Cowboy; a map representing "Guns of the West." Opposite me, frowning over his breakfast of burger and fries, was a big American kid, with blue eyes and a broad, open face. Above his snakeskin boots and jeans he wore a short-sleeved blue shirt made up of a collage of headlines from the New York *Times* and the Miami *Herald*. And seeping sweetly out of the music system I heard, yet again, the willful optimism of "We Are the World."

I waited to hear the end of the song and then went out along the town's main drag, the MacArthur Highway (sometimes spelled McArthur, sometimes spelled Hi-way). It was, I thought, the saddest-looking place in all the world—one long, gray strip of cardboard signs and cocktail lounges and beat-up bars with neon signs for beer in their windows, all lined by a rickety wooden porch. The stores had electric guitars in their windows, and "Harley-Davidson" warm-up jackets; sometimes they had baseball caps with "Playboy Club" on the front, or "Hillcrest Baptist Church"; sometimes they had army shields that said "Eternal Vigilance" and "Ready to Report" and "Pride in Uniform."

There were plenty of motels too, all with air conditioning, swimming pools and wall-to-wall carpeting, some advertising such additional frills as Betamaxes, Magic Mirrors, Drive-Thru service and free transportation to the base. There were also billboards advertising "bold movies" at the local cinemas. Mostly, though, there were bars—the Valley of the Dolls, the Spanish Fly, the Lovers Inn. The sign outside one of them said simply, "Wanted: Girls Immediately."

I could, I imagined, have been in any of the desolate small towns of the American West, where used-car lots and twinkling motels and dilapidated cafés run all the way out to the desert. But here there were not stores, but shacks; and here there were shanties, not houses, along the riverbank. There were "Pickup for Hire" signs in all the hardware stores, but there were also signs that said "Goat for Hire." And the children playing in the streets were not exactly All-American: the little boys bouncing tennis balls had black skins with Oriental features; the little girls at the candy stores were dark, but their hair was sandy.

As I continued looking around, a plane rumbled through the

heavens and a few minutes later it began to rain, pouring down hard on the stucco roof of the Question Mark Lounge, on Louisa's Patio ("Tourists and Returnees Hangout"), on the bar that promised Candy's Models and the Sunshine Café ("No Hustlers / Shoeshine Boys / Poofters / Dunces"). I hailed a jeepney (the souped-up secondhand U.S. jeep that provides mass transport in the Philippines) and took shelter on one of its benches, looking out into the grayness as we juddered past the Ponderosa Club, Mark and Donald's hamburger joint, the Harlem Disco A-Go-Go, Coney Island ("the All-American ice cream"). Most of my fellow passengers were little girls just out of school, eyes dark and faces bright in their tidy Holy Angels uniforms.

The jeepney bounced me off to the far side of town, and then turned around and took me back to the Friendship Highway. I got out, though the rain had yet to abate, and began walking again. "Born in the U.S.A." was thumping out of one of the bars, accompanied by a steady pattering on the rooftops. A gangly American teenager in a crew cut was leading a pretty little Filipina into one of the motels. Another tall man with a blond crew cut and a clean white shirt was marching purposefully through the downpour, a badge on his heart saying "Church of Latter-day Saints."

And as the rain kept coming down, I took shelter on the streetside patio. Beside me, under a falling roof, a jukebox stood forlornly against the wall. A teenage Filipina in pink curlers strolled out of a pool hall and pressed a selection. Then, as the first chords of "We Are the World" began to come through, she started to sing along with it softly, rocking her baby in her arms as the rain continued to fall.

THE PHILIPPINES IS not just the site of the largest U.S. military installations in the world. It is also perhaps the world's largest slice of the American Empire, in its purest impurest form. The first time I landed in Hong Kong, I felt a thrill of recognition to see the pert red letterboxes, the blue-and-white road signs, the boxes of Smarties that had been the props of my boyhood in England; upon arriving in Manila, I felt a similar pang as my eye caught Open 24-Hour gas stations, green exit signs on the freeways, Florida-style license plates and chains of grocery stores called "Mom and Pop." The deejay patter bubbling from the radios, the Merle Haggard songs drifting out of jukeboxes, the Coke signs and fast-food joints and grease-smeared garages—all carried me instantly back home, or, if not home, at least to some secondhand, beat-up image of the Sam Shepard Southwest, to Amarillo, perhaps, or East L.A.

Most of all, the Philippines took me back to the junk-neon flash of teen America, the rootless Western youth culture of drive-ins and jukeboxes, junior proms, cheap cutoffs, and custom dragsters. Many of the young dudes here, in their long hair and straw hats and bushy mustaches, had the cocky strut of aspiring rock stars, and many of the girls, saucing up their natural freshness, the apprehensive flair of would-be models. The jeepneys they rode, plastered with girlie pictures, Rolling Stones tongues, garish stickers and religious symbols, looked like nothing so much as graffitied pinball machines on wheels. And everyone here had a nickname (Wee-Wee, Baby, Boy and even Apple Pie), which made them seem even younger than they really were, little brown siblings to the big Americans across the sea. As it was, the average age in the entire country was only seventeen (in Japan, by contrast, it was over thirty). Small wonder, perhaps, that I felt myself living in a chrome-and-denim Top 40 world.

America's honorary fifty-second state had received much more, of course, from its former rulers than star-spangled love songs and hand-me-down jeans. The commercial area of Manila, Makati, looked not at all like Bakersfield or Tucson, but more like some textbook upper-middle-class California suburban tract. Jaguars lurked in the driveways of white split-level homes, maids sprinkled the lawns along leafy residential streets. The shopping strips were neatly laid out with a mall-to-mall carpeting of coffee shops and department stores. And though the area's jungle of high-rise office blocks seemed hardly to merit its title of "the Wall Street of Asia," it did resemble the kind of financial district you might find in the Sunbelt—the downtown area of Salt Lake City, say, or San Diego.

Baguio too, the hill station designed as a summer retreat for the American rulers—a kind of New World Simla—revealed the American Empire in a more pastoral mood. I could not easily discern the town's resemblance to Washington, D.C.—on which, many Filipinos proudly informed me, it had been modeled—save for the fact that both places had roads and trees, as well as a quorum of American servicemen, scientists and missionaries ("Most people in the U.S., I think," said a local cabbie, "are Christians and Mormons"). But Baguio was still a glistening vision of silver and green, graced with its own distinctive charm —white villas set among the thickly forested slopes of pine, quiet parks verdant in the mist. In the mild drizzle of a dark afternoon, the place had a cozy market-town feel of hot cakes and light rain; on a calm Sunday morning, the peal of church bells through the mist took me back to an English village. In Baguio, I settled down with an Elizabeth Bowen novel in the teapot snugness of a small café, and went on a gray afternoon to a crowded kiddies' matinee.

For all its silvered, foggy charm, though, Baguio did not seem to have the imperiousness of a British hill station, or its weighted dignity. And in much the same way, I did not sense in the Philippines anything comparable to the kind of stately legacy that the British, for example, had bequeathed to India. India seemed to have gained, as a colony, a sense of ritual solemnity, a feeling for the language of Shakespeare, a polished civil service, a belief in democracy and a sonorous faith in upstanding legal or educational institutions; it had, in some respects, been steadied by the chin-up British presence. By contrast, the most conspicuous institutions that America had bequeathed to the Philippines seemed to be the disco, the variety show and the beauty pageant. Perhaps the ideas and ideals of America had proved too weighty to be shipped across the seas, or perhaps they were just too fragile. Whatever, the nobility of the world's youngest power and the great principles on which it had been founded were scarcely in evidence here, except in a democratic system that seemed to parody the chicanery of the Nixon years. In the Philippines I found no sign of Lincoln or Thoreau or Sojourner Truth; just Dick Clark, Ronald McDonald and Madonna.

ON A HUMAN level, of course, the relation between America and her former colony was altogether more complex, and best seen, I thought, just by watching the slow mating dances that filled the smoky country-and-western joints of Ermita every night.

As I entered Club 21 one rainy evening, a small and perky Filipina in a red-and-white-checked shirt and tight jeans—a kind of dusky Joey Heatherton—was leading a country band through songs of lost love and heartbreak. The minute the group struck up the opening chords of another sad song, one of the American GI types seated at the bar, a craggy man in his sixties, six feet tall perhaps, slowly stood up and extended his hand to a pretty teenage girl in a white frock and white pumps. "Today," drawled the singer, "is the darkest day of my life," and the pedal steel wailed and the man put one hand around the girl's tiny waist and the other on her shoulder and led her, with great courtliness, through a slow, slow dance.

As the next ballad began, the vocalist went into a perfect Dolly Parton rasp, and a man in a bushy ginger mustache with sad eyes behind his thick glasses stood up, hitched up his trousers and walked over to a table in the corner where eight young Filipinas were staring idly into the distance. Crouching down, he whispered something to a beautiful young lady in a yellow-and-red ruffled skirt and she followed him back to the bar. "What's your name?" he said softly as they sat down, extending his hand. "I'm an American."

A couple of barstools away, another old-timer was gently stroking the long hair of his doll-like companion. "Hey," he chuckled, looking over her head to a colleague. "I'm going to marry her in a minute." And the band went through another plaintive ballad, then vanished through a back door that said "George's Massage Special."

A man got up from the bar and walked out, and as the door slammed behind him, his sweet-faced companion stuck out her tongue at his memory, then straightened her skirt and went off to sit in another man's lap. The door swung open again, and a lady came in with a basket full of roses. A red-faced Australian hailed her from where he sat and bought ten flowers. Then, very slowly, he walked around the place and, very tenderly, presented a rose to every girl in the room. The band came back again, and sailed into more sad songs from the West. "I warned you not to love me," wailed the singer, "I'm not going to be here very long."

If I had closed my eyes, I could have believed myself in Tucumcari, New Mexico, or listening to some jukebox in

Cheyenne. But my eyes were wide open and in front of me two couples were gliding around the dance floor, tiny arms wrapped around large backs as two pretty young girls, eyes closed, buried their silky heads in their partners' burly chests.

A couple of minutes later, the band went into a faster number. "Yee-hah," cried a man with the frame of a construction worker, standing up at the bar, shaking his fanny and pumping his elbows. He swirled a high school girl in high heels out onto the dance floor, and she flashed a smile back at him, shimmying like a dream. "Shake it," cried out the singer. "Yee-hah!" The dance floor started to get crowded. The Australian pulled his companion out onto the floor. Two girls in jeans began dancing together. A young girl in a flounced skirt swayed happily opposite an old girl with too much makeup. "Welcome to my world," sang the girls as they danced, smiling at their partners and clapping. "Welcome to my world." And as I went out, the singer was just breaking into a perfect replica of Loretta Lynn, while singing, with flawless anguish, "You know, it's only make-believe."

THE PROFESSIONALISM OF music in Manila had impressed me almost as soon as I arrived. But as I stayed longer in town, I was hit more forcibly by a different aspect of the local singing. It struck me first one night in Baguio, in one of the city's many "Minus One" sing-along pubs, where customers take turns coming onstage and delivering the latest hits, accompanied by a tape to provide backup instrumentation. "I would like to dedicate this song to a special someone," a girl was whispering huskily into the mike as I walked in. Then she adjusted the stand, put on her tape and proceeded to deliver a note-perfect version of Madonna's "Like a Virgin," absolutely identical to the original, down to the last pause and tic. Song complete, she whispered "Thank you" to the mike, sauntered offstage and went home with her special someone.

As the evening went on, the scene was repeated again and again and again and again. Almost everyone in the pub came up to deliver flawless imitations of some American hit. And almost everyone had every professional move down perfectly. They knew not only how to trill like Joan Baez and rasp like the Boss, but also how to play on the crowd with their eyes, how to twist the microphone wire in their hands, how to simulate every shade of heartbreak. They were wonderfully professional amateurs. But they were also professional impersonators.

When I walked into another pub down the street I got to witness an even greater display of virtuoso mimicry: the Chinese singer onstage was able to modulate his voice so as to muster a gruff warmth for a Kenny Rogers number, a high earnestness for Graham Nash, a kind of operatic bombast for Neil Diamond and a bland sincerity for Lionel Richie. His Paul Simon was perfect in its boyish sweetness. Yet what his own voice sounded like, and what his own personality might have been, were impossible to tell. And when it came to improvising, adding some of the frills or flourishes that his culture relished, making a song his own, he—like every other singer I had heard—simply did not bother.

"Sure," an American correspondent based in Manila told me when I mentioned this. "Music is definitely the single best thing here. But there's no way you're going to hear any local tunes, or variations on the recorded versions of the American hits. There's one singer in Davao they call the Stevie Wonder of the Philippines, because he sounds exactly—*exactly*—like Stevie Wonder. And there's another woman locally who's the Barbra Streisand of the Philippines. That's how they make it big here. You know one reason why the Filipinos love 'We Are the World' so much? Because it gives one member of the group the chance to do Michael Jackson, and another Cyndi Lauper and a third Bruce Springsteen. Some guy even gets to do Ray Charles."

Finally, in Baguio one night, I came upon a happy exception to the rule: a pudgy singer who slyly camped up Julio Iglesias's song "To All the Girls I Know" by delivering it in a perfect simulation of Iglesias's silky accent, while substituting "boys" for "girls." But then, a few days later, back in Manila, I heard another singer at the Hobbit House do exactly the same trick, with exactly the same words (and, a few months later, I was told, local minstrels were delivering the same song, in honor of the fallen Imelda, to the words: "To all the shoes I had before / I wore them once, and then no more"). Likewise, at a free public concert one afternoon I was surprised to hear a professionally trained singer transform the revved-up anarchy and energy of the Beatles' "Help" into a slow, soulful ballad of lovelorn agony. But then I heard the song delivered in exactly the same way, with exactly the same heart-rent inflections, in a small club in Baguio, and then again at another bar: all the singers, I realized, were not in fact creating a new version, but simply copying some cover version quite different from the Beatles' original. All the feelings were still borrowed.

This development of musical mannequins struck me as strange, especially in a country that understandably regarded its musical gifts as a major source of national pride. I could certainly see how the Filipinos' brilliance at reproducing their masters' voices, down to the very last burr, had made them the musical stars of Asia—the next-best thing, in fact, to having a real American. But as a form of self-expression, this eerie kind of ventriloquism made me sad.

It was the same kind of sadness I felt when I read that the national hero José Rizal had described his home as "a country without a soul" or when I opened *What's On in Manila* to find the first ad in the personals section begin: "I would like to meet an American. Looks are not important but he must be kind and cheerful." It was the same kind of sadness I felt when I went to Pistang Pilipino, the capital's main tourist center, and found that the highlight of its show of local culture was a splashy Hollywood-style spectacular in which chorus lines of handsome young men whipped through some brassy choreography and six-year-old girls in bikinis performed acrobatics while a fat man with greasy hair in an open shirt crooned "House of the Rising Sun." Mostly, it was the sadness I felt, when an intelligent Filipino friend in New York told me, with a happy smile, "Every Filipino dreams that he will grow up to be an American."

While I was in Manila, there was plenty of token opposition to the U.S. presence. Nationalists railed against the country's still justified image as the world's great center of mail-order brides and chambermaids. The Marcos-run paper, in a show of ill-considered braggadocio, printed Manuel Quezon's famous cry: "I prefer to see a government run like hell by Filipinos than a government run like heaven by Americans." And when foreign newsmen flooded into town for the election a few months later, an opposition paper greeted them as "two-bit, white-skinned, hirsute, AIDS-predisposed visitors." But the "two-bit," I thought, said it all. In the Philippines, anti-American guerrillas drew up their strategies in Michael Jackson notebooks. And a respected newspaper greeted the suggested removal of the American bases with the headline "Bye, Bye, American Pie."

IV

As the headline suggested, it was not just melodies that struck a responsive chord in Filipino hearts; it was, even more, the sentiments that pop songs expressed, the sensibility they revealed. One day, I managed at last to track down some examples of local music. To my surprise, nearly all the albums had titles like *Romantic Filipino, Romance* and *Hopeless Romantic.* And nearly all their liner notes were florid rhapsodies about hearts burning and eyes on fire, lovesick maidens and heartbroken men. All of Manila was saturated with this sense of overwrought passion and sweetness—emotions borrowed from love songs, convictions taken from a jukebox. The local coaches were called Love Buses, and there were Sweet Love Taxis too. Sweet Love Boat-Lines ran a Love-Boat to Zamboanga. The Sirens of Lost Eden were playing at Love City, and at Shakey's, Euphoria shared the stage with a group called Sweet Love.

Just one month before arriving in the Philippines, I had gone to California to cover a convention of high school cheerleaders, and there had found both walls and hearts decorated with Smiley faces and valentine symbols. After a while, I realized that the teen-queen gathering had, in fact, been an ideal preparation for the Philippines. For the entire country seemed to resonate to the high-spirited flightiness of a high school world, where tomorrow is another lifetime and hearts are made for breaking. The walls of Manila were plastered with red hearts, and the bumper stickers on jeepneys wailed: "It Hurts to Say Goodbye." Chatty sexism filled the media ("Sex in Space?" was the headline above an article on the possible return of martial law) and a kind of leopardskin looseness informed the TV listings (one typical show was called "Chicks to Chicks"). Local menus were tyrannized by cute tags (My Father's Mustache offered "Butch Cassidy and the Sandwitch Kid" and "Wild Beef Hickcock," while the Hard Rock Café had dishes called "GI Blues," "Star-Spangled Banner" and "Army-Navy," to go along with "Loving Spoonfuls" and "Johnny's B. Goode"). And the costume jewels of wisdom printed on T-shirts sounded like nothing so much as the catchy titles of pop songs—"Don't Let a Fool Kiss You or a Kiss Fool You."

All these, however, were contexts in which a kind of bubble-gum bumptiousness might be expected; what amazed me more as I looked more closely at the country was to see this poppy lingo applied to everything. Nothing was sacred. When first I saw the bumper sticker that said "I ♡ God," I took it to be a joke. But though it certainly reflected the happy-go-lucky exuberance of the nation, it was not, I gathered, meant to be funny. Nor was the jeepney sign that said "God is my co-driver." Nor was the huge billboard above the Aristocrat Restaurant ("the King of Fried Chicken") that announced: "Greetings to No. 1 Mother of the World on the 2000th Anniversary of Her Birth." The entire city was indeed planning to throw a super party on September 4, 1985, to wish the Virgin Mary a merry 2000th.

After a while, I was ready for anything. When I saw a sticker saying "Mother Dearest" on the fender of a jeepney, I assumed that it had a religious rather than a domestic significance. But who could tell whether Madonna Lingerie was named in honor of the Virgin or the Whore—especially in a country where both types were so ubiquitous? And as I rode the bus to Baguio, a lovely seven-year-old girl behind me sang along quietly with every determined word of "We Are the World," and a middle-aged lady next to me filled out one-word answers to a Bible Study quiz ("Can you describe the Holy Spirit?") while, in front of us all, a soft-core British spy movie flickered on a video screen.

Some of this was doubtless more glaring in the Philippines than elsewhere in Asia because the medium of mass culture here was American, its excesses neither dignified nor disguised by the exoticism of a foreign tongue. And some of it might have been a kind of Spanish trait—I had found an equally lush sentimentality in Cuba. But even in other English-language areas of the world, and even in other Spanish-American provinces like Honduras or Puerto Rico, I had never felt myself so relentlessly bombarded by what seemed to be broad satires, in somewhat shaky taste, of a nickel-and-dime culture—the products, one might have guessed, of a *Harvard Lampoon* parody of *Seventeen*. Every nugget of kitsch, moreover, was delivered quite without irony. "Come and see *Jenina*, a play on Child Prostitution," ran the breezy invitation in the anti-Marcos paper *Mr. and Ms.* The Family Club Theater in Dagupa City offered uncensored pornography. And one day, Manila's most respectable paper, the Marcos-run *Bulletin Today*, blandly reported: "Some films submitted for showing at the Manila Film Center were disapproved because they weren't bold enough. The producers had no alternative but to add more sexy footage." One of these movies, I read, "directed by a multi-awardee," showed its lead actress "making love to a lesbian, to the son of a semi-retired character actor and to a still very active character actor, probably the Kissing King in Show Biz." Another had a "lead actor sodomizing a bit player and ejaculating on the face of another bit player." Yet both, it seemed, were still too mild to satisfy the stern strictures of the Film Center (which charged four times the regular rate for its officially sponsored porn and denied admission to women in housedresses and men in sleeveless shirts). The Center's overseers, Mr. and Mrs. Marcos, were notoriously difficult to please.

Indeed, the jazzed-up jukebox sensibility that was so incongruous throughout much of the country was loudest of all where it was most incongruous: in government. Every political party so insistently used show biz that politics itself had come to seem nothing more than a party. And after a while in Manila, I could no longer distinguish between local show-biz characters, with names like Coy, Pepsi, Zsa Zsa and Bimbo, and local political figures, who were known as Joker, Teddy-Boy and Ting-Ting (the Chief Justice of the Philippine Supreme Court was called Dong Dong). Often, in any case, the two performed together on a single stage. The opposition to Marcos famously commemorated the assassination of its beloved leader by singing out the cheery pop tune "Tie a Yellow Ribbon Round the Old Oak Tree." The guerrillas of the Communist National People's Army had taken over a Manila studio to record an album of stirring guitar-and-flute folk ballads (to be played, no doubt, at 45 revolutions per minute). And the Marcoses' Foreign Minister was famous for his boogie-woogie piano.

The queen of them all, though, and the country's leading vocalist, was Imelda Marcos. Just before I arrived, she had organized a rendition of the national anthem sung "We Are the World" style, with pop stars imitating the country's favorite video right down to the hands they clapped on their ears as they took their turns at the mike. A little later, tapes emerged showing the First Family itself belting out the song for Ethiopia's starving in the midst of one of its abandoned bacchanals aboard a private yacht. And one day while I was in town, the *Bulletin Today* devoted much of its second page to printing, in its entirety, a song that Imelda, the former "Muse of Manila," had written, apparently to her husband, on her way to the funeral of Yuri Andropov in Moscow:

> I love you, I need you, I miss you, my love,
> I deeply love you.
> While I'm away from you an unbearable
> Loneliness overwhelms me.
> Because you are all I want.
> When I'm alone, I'm so hopeless and lost, oh my love.
> I need you beyond reason, my darling.
> I love you beyond life and my love will be yours forever.

Above and beyond such show-biz gimmicks, however, Philippine politicians conducted all their affairs, both public and private, with a noisy gossip-column brazenness, as if their only wish was to satisfy the cheering public. When B-movie actress Dovie Beams had released her kiss-and-tell story of life in bed with President Marcos, her beloved "Freddie" had retaliated, not by denying the rumors or protesting his innocence, or even by proffering excuses, but simply by splashing his own intimate photos of Lovie Dovie in the raw across the national newspapers. Here was Filipino openness and swagger, its fondness for the extravagant flourish, raised to the pitch of low art and high farce.

At the time I was in Manila, indeed, the Marcos Era was still rolling along with a boldness and broadness that could make a scriptwriter blush. The First Family itself featured a cast of characters stranger, or juicier at least, than any that fiction could conceive. There was the President, the Machiavellian macho villain who had put his monogram on every government institution and treated the national treasury as a personal checking account, and there was his First Lady, a former beauty queen with a scandalous past who proclaimed, "In the Philippines, we live in a Paradise. There are no poor people like there are in other countries," even as seven in every ten of her people, according to government statistics, were living under the poverty level. There was First Daughter Imee, whose boxer-playboy husband had been abducted by her parents because of his unfortunate first marriage to a former Miss International (now herself a leading opposition beauty—oops, politician), and there was the First Son, Ferdinand, Jr., now governor of Ilocos Norte, who was generally known as Bongbong.

The saddest aspect of the whole fiasco, however, was that these knockabout characters from *Dynasty* were stumbling their way through a tragedy by Sophocles. For swirling around the soap opera bouffe were all the darker ironies and justice-dispensing fates, the blood feuds and heaven-sent portents, of a larger-than-life morality play. By the time he was seventeen, Marcos had been charged with murder; while he was in jail, he had gained the highest bar exam scores in the country's history. After becoming the country's first reelected President, he had been challenged by an equally tough and resourceful wunder-kind, Ninoy Aquino—his fraternity brother, his close friend and, in a sense, his shadow self. After Aquino had been killed, Marcos had found himself hounded by the Electra-like figure of Aquino's widow, Corazón, a soft-spoken grandmother whom the people wished to cast as an avenging angel. True to the parable form, her name meant "Heart," her party was called Lakas ng Bayan (LABAN), or "People Power (FIGHT)," and her main supporter among the media was a Catholic magazine and broadcasting network entitled Veritas, or "Truth." Meanwhile, stargazing Imelda had been told by a soothsayer that as soon as an earthquake rocked a church and a crowd crossed Mendiola Bridge, the House of Marcos would fall (it did, it did and, finally, it did). And in the midst of all the murders and the mistresses, the profligate spending and the lavish conniving, stood a lonely one-man chorus with the Wycherley-perfect name of Cardinal Sin.

The melodrama was kept constantly on the boil, moreover, and the audience constantly absorbed in the political song-and-dance routine, by the restless rumormongers of the Manila cof-feehouses, who generated enough wild stories every few hours to ensure that the papers could run 40-point-bold headlines every day of the week. I was not in the Philippines long, but it was long enough to hear the thunderbolt that there was a move to impeach Marcos, and then the sudden bulletin that the President was going to call snap elections, and then the banner headline that there would be no elections after all, and then the wild claim that Imelda was going to be made Veep, and then the shock news that Marcos had decided to settle the election issue with a referendum in the National Assembly and then the screaming announcement that the National Assembly had decided to leave the decision in Marcos's hands. Every day, in fact, there came a new twist, a bizarre turn, a cliff-hanging invitation to the sequel. It was almost enough to make one forget that the plot was about a tyranny that had brought the country to its knees.

V

Whenever I got carried away by the thrill-a-minute frenzy of the political scene, however, the friends I made in Manila brought me back to the simple realities of a system that had reduced its men to rags and driven its women to brothels.

I first met Sarah, a waitress at Calle Cinquo, on my second night in town. A pious, stately girl from the countryside—both her sisters had joined a convent, and Sarah seemed to belong in their company—she had come to Manila, she told me, to study nursing. It was not easy to finance her studies, she went on, and many of her classmates took the easy way out. But she was determined, absolutely determined, to pay her way through college without compromising herself. "I have to work hard," she explained, "but I will do it. Step by step, Pico: that is how to live. If I am honest, I know God will help me."

Sarah's adamantine strength of will was sorely tested by her current job. Working in Calle Cinquo nine hours a day, seven days a week, she earned exactly $16 in the course of a month. Even that, however, was never guaranteed. Every now and then, the restaurant staged a variety show, and gave each of its waitresses three tickets to sell at $4.50 each—a small fortune for the average Filipino. If any of the tickets went unsold, the entire amount was deducted from the waitress's salary. Sarah lived in absolute terror of not finding takers for her tickets. Yet all the while, with her hacienda beauty and her dazzling smile, she also found herself constantly besieged by solicitations from foreigners who assumed, not without reason, that the waitresses themselves were on sale here. Every tourist, Sarah noted sadly, was interested in only one thing. "I do not blame them," she told me, with a soft smile. "But I still prefer my co-Filipinos."

Quite taken with Sarah's sweet-spirited warmth and innocence, I soon took to stopping off each night at Calle Cinquo for a Coke and a chat. Sarah always greeted me with a smile, and, though three years younger than I, she always lavished on me the benefit of her counsel. "You must always remember, Pico," she often told me, "that if you are good, God will reward you. You must always go step by step." At this she would flash me an earnest smile. "And one day I hope you will find a good wife, a lady who will always be faithful and true, a good lady who will always wait for you."

Before leaving Manila, I asked Sarah if I could send her something from the States. Just a picture of your parents, she replied.

THE OTHER OPTION open to most Filipinas was explained to me by Minnie, the best friend of the security guard's roommate, Lulu. The eldest of seven children in tough Pasay City, she had always been keenly aware of her obligation to help her parents support her siblings; her father, after a lifetime of working for the government, brought home only $55 a month. When she was seventeen, therefore, Minnie announced to her parents that she was going to start working in a bar. That way, she said, she could earn five times as much as her father, and put her younger brothers and sisters through school. Still, she warned her relatives sternly, "One bar girl in the family is enough!"

Ten years later, chirpy and long-haired Minnie, less than five feet tall and with the huge eyes of a teenage ingenue, was completely at home in every corner of the Manila demimonde. She smoked, she told me brightly, she drank, she did drugs. She played pool, she knew blackjack and she had two cupboards filled with clothes. She had been virtually addicted to gambling until, she said, at the age of twenty-five she had decided to take a "more responsible attitude." But still she could not resist playing bingo. And still she spent $2 every night having herself made up by one of the gay "billyboys" who set up shop at the back of the girlie bars. She was, she announced happily, a "one-day millionaire."

As a teenager, Minnie told me, she had once had an abortion. She had also once got married to a British executive from Papua New Guinea, who had given her, when he left Manila, a girlie bar of her own to operate. Unfortunately, she continued with characteristic nonchalance, the French International bar had sunk within a year ("No good girls"), leaving her with nothing but a series of abusive letters from the Englishman's Australian wife back home.

Throughout the bouncy melodrama, however, Minnie had always made good on her commitment to her family. She told me with pride, and told me again, that she had single-handedly paid for all the schooling of her youngest brother and sister. When her second sister had been saddled with a pregnancy out of wedlock, Minnie had paid for the delivery, the hospital stay and every aspect of the little boy's upbringing. No sooner had she come to know two Saudi Arabians in the bar than Minnie had managed to fix up a job in the Gulf for one of her cousins. And then, because the cousin had a police record, she had gone herself to the National Bureau of Investigations and taken care of all the paperwork for him. "I use my coconut" was Minnie's favorite dictum.

Thus Minnie's life careered crazily ahead, roller-coastering back and forth and back again between the bar scene and her family. One day I arranged to meet her for dinner, and she sauntered in an hour late. What had happened? Oh, nothing, she said carelessly, she had just been fixing up her sixteen-year-old cousin with a job. Where? At the Pussycat Lounge. And when was she due to begin? "Tonight," said Minnie, without much interest. "She lost her virginity last week. She is already dancing on Stage One."

On another occasion, I had arranged to go to a movie with her. Half an hour before it was due to begin, she breezed into my hotel and announced she couldn't go. Why? "Because my cousin, last night, after a fiesta, was stabbed." Was he hurt? "Yah!" she cried, eyes bright. "Dead."

Her ebullience seemed scarcely dimmed at all. I assumed, I said, that she had not really known her cousin. "Yah," she insisted, vehement. "He very close to me. He always bring me Mary Jane." But she did not seem very sad, I remarked. "Sad, yah! But what can I do? He was stabbed three times before, but always he survived. He was not a troublemaker. But at fiestas, especially on Sundays, there is always much violence."

Apart from her family, Minnie's most devoted commitment was to her religion. But here again hers was a festive, carefree, jeepney kind of worship. One Sunday she invited me to come along to a baptism. The father of the child, she whispered upon arrival, was a disk jockey on Del Pilar. Most of the others in the congregation were go-go dancers from his bar. The man's sister had to stand in for his wife, who had already left him. Yet all of them seemed pious in the extreme. I asked Minnie whether she ever had trouble squaring her lifestyle with her religion. "No," she piped, as bright and quick as ever. "God knows me. He understands why I do what I do."

Minnie had the Manila underworld entirely taped: wherever she went, she carried a Pro toothbrush and a lighter that said "Trust Me." But she was also experienced enough to know that she was growing too old to work much longer in the bar. Ever practical, she had now started taking courses in accountancy and shorthand. Her plan was to go to Stockholm to live with a friend who had married a Swedish man, there to practice bookkeeping. "Yah, I know it will be boring," she acknowledged. "But working in the bar, it is also boring."

When I asked Minnie if there was anything I could send her from America, she responded without hesitation, "Yah! Plane ticket. Manila–New York round trip." I assumed she was joking. "Why not?" she said, entirely serious. "You can say you hire me as maid. Tax deduction!"

MY THIRD LOCAL friend afforded me a glimpse into the other side of Manila life—the world of show-biz glitter and celebrity. I first ran into Mark one night at a typical Filipino affair: a ritzy PR gig in the glitzy Stargazer Disco, the city's hottest night spot, organized by Pepsi-Cola to celebrate the flop of the new-style Coke. As absurdly glamorous waitresses cruised the room in beige off-the-shoulder dresses, gold purses hanging from their necks, an emcee talked excitedly about the "Cola Wars" and a succession of the country's top pop stars stepped up to the mike and blasted out show-stopping numbers under swirling lasers and flashing lights.

While one of the routinely dazzling singers was strutting around the room, throwing her hands into the air and expertly going through the emotions, I commented on her professionalism to a brawny young guy in his early twenties beside me. His face broke into a broad smile.

"You think she's good?"

"Very good."

"All riiiight!" he exclaimed in a frat-boy voice, all smiles. "She's my wife." With that, he warmly shook my hand. "How you doing? You from the States? All riiiight!"

"Oh, you see her?" He pointed to a beauty who had taken over the mike. "That's Miss Beanie-Beanie. She's eighteen and she's not too bright, but she's real pretty, wouldn't you say? She won this kinda beauty-contest thing they have around here."

In between filling me in on the high jinks onstage, Mark explained a little about what he was doing here. Just a couple of years ago, he said, he had still been back home, at the University of Indiana. One day he happened to pick up a book on the music business. It sounded like a good deal, he thought, so he decided to give it a try. He didn't have much singing talent, he said, but he had managed to round up the backup band to John Cougar Mellencamp, and he had cut a demo. As soon as he heard the song, he knew there was no way he could make it at home. But he'd grown up a little in Asia while his dad was stationed over here, so he decided to come over and give it a whirl. First he tried Japan. No dice. Then he tried Singapore. No way. Then he came over to the Philippines, and someone here liked his sound and let him cut a record. One of his songs had made it to a Greatest Hits album and sold 27,000 copies, the local equivalent of a gold record. He must be rich, I said. "Nah," he said. "I got no percentage. No royalties. Anyway, it was a lousy record. . . . Oh, you see that guy onstage? He's the Lou Rawls of the Philippines. So anyway, one day I was at the studio and I found myself standing next to this incredibly beautiful nineteen-year-old singer. So I asked her out. I didn't know that over here you're supposed to court a girl. Hey, the only court I knew was a basketball court! Anyway, she agreed to be my girlfriend. So later

I asked her to get married, and—wouldn't you know it?—she said yes."

Thus, nine months earlier, Mark had moved to the Philippines, married to one of its leading singers and jobless. Well, he figured, he had nothing to do with his time; he might as well try show biz. The next thing he knew, he had been signed up to play host on a popular TV show: he had everything he needed to make it big over here, he discovered—an American accent and a faintly Oriental look (his father had married a Korean). So now, at twenty-three, just a few months out of college and equipped with nothing but a cheery sense of his own lack of qualifications, he found himself a national heartthrob. "You should come and see the show sometime," he told me happily. "It's a lot different from at home. It's real lousy.

"Oh, hey," he cried, as a greased-down kid with cocktail-lounge manners left the stage, "I'd like you to meet one of the other stars on the show. This is Marco. He's kind of the Julio Iglesias of the Philippines."

Three mornings later, I made my way to Mark's modest home in a quiet residential street in Makati. A maid admitted me to a modest ranch-style living room. Above the couch was a huge, black-lit portrait of a long-tressed nymph; next to the stairs was a painting of Jesus. A few minutes later, brushing his hair as he came and buttoning up his shirt, Mark raced downstairs, as happily flustered as if he were late for a final exam. We jumped into his Mitsubishi. His wife, he said proudly, had had to save up three years for this car.

As soon as we arrived at the studio, Mark led me past a mob of screaming girls and through a tiny back door marked "Strictly for Talents and Guests Only." Inside the backstage area, five teenage girls in fishnet stockings and black leotards were penciling their eyes in front of a mirror and practicing their moves. Nearby was a bathroom—a cubicle with a rusted shower tap and a dirty toilet that had neither a lid nor a flush. Farther in was a small auditorium—perfect, I thought, for an off-off-Broadway production of Beckett. But the place was alive. Rows upon rows of teenage girls were sitting behind a wire fence, squealing and waving posters. Meanwhile, onstage, a group was racing through "Dancing in the Dark," in preparation, I learned, for a Bruce Springsteen Sound-Alike Contest.

Mark stopped by a mirror for a couple of minutes while a woman dabbed some orange powder on him. Then he strolled over to his producer for a twenty-second briefing. "Hey," said a man who could have been found around any pool in Beverly Hills. "Just remember to say we're big. Everything's big and getting bigger." There were a few schoolboy giggles at this, and then the show began. Wasn't there a script? I asked as we took our places at the side of the stage. "Nah," said Mark, cheerful as ever. "We know the format by now. We just kinda improvise." With that, he went off to join his co-hosts in front of the cameras.

Between scenes, Mark hurried back to explain the setup to me. "The only veteran, apart from me," he said, under his breath, "is Frances. But she's getting kinda old for this. She's twenty-five, I think." The other female co-host was a stunning beauty called Rachel. "Yeah," said Mark, "she's seventeen. Her mother was a big star."

Rachel came over, and I asked her about high school. She left class at 10:30 every morning, she said, made it here for the 11:30 show and then got back in time for her 1:30 class. With that, Rachel wandered coolly back onstage. "She was gonna enter Miss Universe," Mark whispered, "but it's still a year too early."

Then I was reintroduced to Marco, the pint-size Julio Iglesias. "Marco got on the country charts last year," said Mark. "You know Freddie Aguilar had a hit in thirteen European countries? Too bad he never made it in the States. But hey, did you know that Shirley Bassey once came to sing here? And Menudo and Air Supply too. Matt Munro once recorded a song written by a Filipino." For everyone here, by the sound of it, the big time was just around the corner.

At that moment, a tremendous cry arose from the girls in the audience, and a pretty young boy in an unbuttoned white shirt sauntered onto the stage, crooning into a mike while a few lucky young ladies rushed across the stage and planted kisses on his cheek. "He's sixteen," explained Mark, "the son of Pilita Corrales, the Asian Queen of Music and a member of the Hall of Fame. She once sang with Sammy Davis, Jr., in Vegas." Off went the heartthrob and on came Hector Bautista ("Yeah, he's sixteen. Last year he won the Best Actor Award"). The next singing star was Pops Fernandez ("She's seventeen. She's the star of *Pent-*

house Live"). Then Cheska Inigo did a number ("Cute, isn't she? Only thirteen"). In between sketches, a few workers wheeled huge backdrops that looked like cinema billboards onto the stage, while other assistants handed the hosts handwritten messages on index cards to read offstage. Then Mark got up, told me he'd be right back and ran onto the stage, swinging his arms back and forth and lip-synching his way through Springsteen's "Dancing in the Dark." As he raced off, people patted him on the back and gave him their congratulations. "Yeah," he told me jauntily. "I'm no good at singing. But hey, that doesn't matter. I'm the host!"

After the show, Mark stopped off, smiling over helplessly at me, to sign the photos and limbs of the girls who had gathered around his car, and then we got in. "Hey," he said, "let me take you to lunch."

A few minutes later, we took our places in a shopping-mall McDonald's and Mark looked over at me with genuine affection. "You know," he said, "it's so great to have a conversation again. Most of my friends here, they're in the entertainment business. Or else they want some kinda favor from me. I really oughta apologize for my lack of proficiency in English. I kinda feel my intelligence is declining over here. My computer training, all that kind of stuff, it's getting real rusty." He stopped for a minute, reflective. "You know, I really kinda miss the States?"

"But over here," I said, looking at the girls who were giggling shyly as they stared at our table, "you're a superstar."

"Sure," he said, taking a bite out of his burger, "but you gotta remember this isn't the States. For the TV show, they give me thirty-five dollars a day. And my wife—she's one of the top entertainers in the country—she still has to appear at high school proms, department-store openings, promotional events, all that kind of stuff. Like the Pepsi gig. Right now, we're kinda excited: it looks like she might get a chance to attend a singing competition in East Germany. If she does well, she could become big in China, Russia even. But first she has to see if there's going to be an election."

"An election?"

"Sure. If there's an election, she'll do a few spots for the government."

"She likes the government?"

"Nah. But the opposition doesn't have enough money to pay her well. Anyway, she won't campaign for the government; she'll just do ads for them. No way you can afford to pass up job opportunities around here."

VI

A few days later, just before I left Manila, I finally had my chance to see all the pieces fit together—the people in the streets and the revelers far above, the constant smiles and the famous protests: the anti-Marcos opposition had scheduled a full day of demonstrations to mark the second anniversary of the killing of Ninoy Aquino.

The program began early in the morning, in the stately aisles of Santo Domingo Church in Quezon City, where Cardinal Sin delivered a fierce sermon decrying the systematic devastation of his country. Then Cory Aquino, whom the people were still trying to persuade to enter politics, walked shyly up to the stage. In a soft, quavering voice, she gave the people her heartfelt thanks. Her husband, she said, would have been proud, deeply proud of them. Then, fists raised silently in the air, the entire congregation joined together in a slow and stirring rendition of "The Impossible Dream." When it was over, a silence filled the church. Then, very slowly, the crowd went into a strong, subdued rendering of the banned national anthem, "Bayan Ko." As I listened to the brave, solemn voices of the two little girls next to me, and as I heard them singing of redemption with all their hearts, I felt strange tears coming to my eyes. Theirs sounded to me like the voice of a nation struggling to find a dignity adequate to its sorrow.

As soon as the song was over, however, everyone streamed out into the bright sunlight, and the requiem turned into a fiesta. The scene that greeted us outside the church looked like nothing so much as a rock festival. Vendors were hawking soft drinks and chewing gum. Other peddlers were doing a brisk business in T-shirts that said "I ♡ Ninoy," "Ninoy forever," "Ninoy lives in my ♡" and "Who Killed My Hero?" Yellow Ninoy balloons bumped together in the blue sky, and yellow Ninoy streamers fluttered in the breeze. Everyone was dressed in Ninoy yellow—

no matter that some of the yellow T-shirts had "David Bowie" on them, and one of them said "I Feel Terrific."

As the march began, and everyone surged forward, laughing and singing with their friends, waving their yellow signs in the sunlight, it felt more than ever like a happy picnic. The girls in their bright yellow shirts giggled among themselves, the boys proudly threw their fists into the air. Toddlers looked on from the sidewalk under sun hats that said "My Hero." Nuns, feminists, ragtag groups of students and other minority factions streamed smiling into the press of chanting yellow bodies. "I was a Breast-fed Baby," read one of the revolutionaries' T-shirts.

And so, waving placards against the "U.S.–Marcos Dictatorship" and chanting slogans, the whole bright mob flocked through the streets of Quezon City, past "24-Hour Go-Go Girls" signs, past billboards advertising the latest California high school comedy. When the rain began to fall, thousands of umbrellas came out, and not one of them was black.

In the early afternoon, the rain started to gather momentum, and as the yellow faction went off in one direction, I followed a more militant group, dressed all in red, in the other. For a few minutes, as we sang the "Internationale" and then started running, I felt a surge of adrenaline, the rising excitement of racing amidst a crowd of bright banners through the streets, hurled along by the mob, stumbling and tripping and speeding around corners as families sent confetti streaming down from their windows. And as we turned a corner and came into an open space where thousands of bodies had assembled from every direction, waving banners and laughing in the rain, I felt a dawning sense of wonder. But then the rally stopped for a few windy denunciations of the U.S.–Marcos Dictatorship, and a boy next to me went back to reading *Nicaragua for Beginners*, while a few college girls clustered around the latest issue of *Newsweek*.

A few minutes later, we were off again, charging through the downpour without a care in the world, excited children in the rain, running our hearts out for thirty minutes or more until we careened around an intersection and up to the Mendiola Bridge, right in front of Malacañang Palace. Ahead of us stood a huge barricade. On the far side of the barbed-wire fence, rows of stony-faced riot policemen stood stock-still, fingering their guns; behind them, men in masks silently brandished shields.

Just in case things didn't go on schedule, the policemen had brought reinforcements and brown bags filled with food. But it had already been decided that the demonstrators should shout and wave banners for no more than an hour and then disperse. So the foreign correspondents at the front lines started making plans for dinner and asking around for rides. And the masked revolutionaries cried out their rage for an hour. And then, as dusk began to fall, all of them quietly filed home for dinner. A little later, the riot policemen also packed their picnic bags and followed their enemies home. Marcos, I thought, had nothing to worry about; his enemies were blowing kisses in the wind.

AT THE RALLY, as so often in Manila, it was the happiness of the Filipinos that left me saddest.

Carefree and irrepressible to the end, they reminded me finally of one of those beautiful tennis players—Yannick Noah, say, or Vijay Armitraj—who delight their audiences with the sweet fluency of their shots, and light up the court with their grace and daring, and dazzle even themselves with their élan, yet, in the end, are always undone by their own lovely insouciance. It was sad that the Filipinos had been left with nothing to steady themselves except four hundred years of colonialism and the leftover knickknacks of a rock-'n'-roll culture. But sadder by far was the fact that they still had the openness and hopefulness —the happy innocence—to believe that rock 'n' roll was all they needed to change the world. "We Are the World" was especially popular, I suspected, because it was the ultimate anthem of pop idealism. It suggested that bright tunes could redeem politics; that high spirits and good intentions alone could bring food to the starving; that where there was music, there could not be misery.

And as I sat in the departure lounge of Manila International Airport, waiting to fly away, I heard for the last time, issuing from the sound system, the strains of the country's favorite anthem, affirming the limitless powers of faith. And I could not help thinking that even as the unguarded, sweet-tempered, friendly Filipinos kept on singing that they were the world, and they were the children, their own world was falling apart and they were too much the world, too much the children to resist.

VII

Thus I left the Philippines. But the Philippines did not so easily leave me. For months, I could not get the country out of my head: it haunted me like some pretty, plaintive melody.

In part, no doubt, this was explained by the world's sudden interest in the collapsing country. Just as I was beginning to write this chapter, President Marcos, in deference to U.S. pressure, held an election. As I continued writing, I heard snatches of news about the campaign: as usual, the voting was preceded by crazy rumors and as usual, the politicking was almost comic in its crudity (Imelda boasted that she had control of the bar-girl and "billyboy" vote because she used makeup better than Cory, while her husband's bullhorns boomed: "In these times of crisis, what this country needs is a man! A bull! A stud!"). As usual too, the balloting, though closely watched by a team of U.S. observers and more than seven hundred foreign journalists, was a free-for-all farce. Soldiers smilingly posed for pictures while tearing up ballots; voters happily admitted to accepting bribes; as many as three-million voter names were simply struck off the lists. But then, just as I was finishing this chapter, something happened: a friend raced in to announce that Marcos was gone. All my fears, it seemed, had been proven wrong. In the "smiling revolution," the very optimism, gentleness and tolerance that had long come to seem the country's greatest liabilities had proved to be its greatest blessing. With nothing more substantial than hope, faith and courage, the people had heroically brought off a non-violent revolution and recovered, as if by a miracle, their sense of possibility and pride.

Yet as the euphoria began to subside, I could not help wondering how much anything in the Philippines would really change. Cory Aquino was the purest and sincerest politician I had ever seen, yet even her fairy-tale ascent seemed only the flip side of the Marcoses' fabulous wickedness, a radiant and inspiring turn to be sure, but a turn that seemed still to belong to the world of a children's fantasy. I wondered too if Philippine politics would ever develop a real sense of gravitas or order, for even under Cory, it returned soon enough to show-business-as-usual, a made-for-TV drama filled with coffeehouse rumors, bungled coups and flashy gestures. Most of all, I wondered how soon the rainy streets of Ermita would change, and what would become of a people whose very buoyancy and hospitality lay at the heart of their vulnerability.

Once home, I made great efforts to keep in touch with the friends I had made in the Philippines. I never heard from Mark, though, and Minnie never replied to my letters—by now, I assumed, she must have gone off to Stockholm, or found herself another husband, or else just disappeared into some dark corner of the bar world. But Sarah, whom I had never met outside her restaurant, wrote to me as often as she had promised. Her letters were full of the sweet earnestness and solicitude I remembered. Most of her news, however, was sad.

> Pico,
> Merry Christmas and a Happy New Year. How's your parents. I know your so happy it's because your close to your papa and mama. For me it's so sad because I'm too far from my beloved parents. I'm lonely. Sorry, ha, if I'm telling you my problem. It is sad. I don't have job any more. That's why my Christmas and New Year's Eve is saddest.
> Pico, my friend, how can I finish my studies if my situation is like this? Who's the one to support my studies? Nobody, except me. You know me. I belong in a poor and uneducated family. It's better as you are. You are rich if you want to be, because of having permanent job.
> Well, Pico, do you remember the tickets? Well, here we are. We have more tickets to come. And that's when there begins a problem. Last Dec. 12, 1985, I go home to my boarding house. I'm crying because of no job. That date my 3 tickets were not sold. My salary in that month they will not give to me. Then I got mad. I hate them, all the employers in Calle Cinquo. I resigned. So here I am, no job, always crying, as if the world is to end. I pray to God that somebody offers to help my studies. As of now,

I'm looking for a job. Pico, I love my studies. I don't want to stop.

Please answer me wherever you are. May the Lord Jesus Christ Remember You Always.

Friendlove,
Sarah

On the day after Christmas, she was admitted to the hospital with a lung disease, Sarah wrote in her next letter, and two months later, she was still in bed. She had no job and no money for her medicine. But still she sent me a card and a prayer on my birthday. And at the end of her letters, Sarah always closed by sending my parents all her best. "How about more photos of your beloved papa and mama?" she usually signed off. "Please send me. Okey?"

BURMA
The Raj Is Dead!
Long Live the Raj!

ETTING FOOT at last in Burma, I looked around. A weathered little building, with monsoon stains smeared across its whiteness: "Rangoon Airport." A broken door: "VIP Lounge." A few girls under peacocky parasols, a few men in wraparound skirts, desultory in the steady drizzle. Across the length and breadth of the rain-swept tarmac, not a single other plane was to be seen. This, I suppose, was hardly surprising: Mingaladon, Burma's only inter-national airport, was not equipped to accommodate 747s, or even DC-10s. On a typical Friday, it received exactly one incoming flight.

Following me out of the creaking Fokker F-28 came fifty other shaken passengers, every one of them carrying an identical red-and-white bag bought at the airport duty-free shop in Bangkok. Within every bag—whether purchased by teetotaler, non-smoker or pleasure lover—was one carton of 555 brand cigarettes and one bottle of Johnnie Walker Red. Every visitor to Burma must bring such a bag, we had all been instructed by guidebooks, returned friends, the lore of the road; even the Burma Airways boarding card had pointedly reminded all embarking passengers: "PROCEED TO THE AIRPORT DEPARTURE LOUNGE AS SOON AS POS-SIBLE. TAX-FREE PURCHASES CAN BE MADE INSIDE." Identical red-and-white bags in hand, we trooped into the washed-out terminal.

Inside, several cheerful officials, trying hard to look grave, were lined up behind a long wooden counter like schoolteachers at a prizegiving. In the absence of formalities, passengers were invited to punch and pummel their way toward this central desk. A crush of bodies swept me forward, and I flung my health form toward an official. The scrum swayed and wobbled; I extended my Tourist Arrival Report in the direction of another official. Thrown off balance in the melee, and finding myself suddenly close to the front, I thrust my Customs Form at random into the air. A third official, unflustered and fastidious in his spectacles, plucked the paper from my grasp, asked a few questions, then handed it to a colleague. This fellow, in turn, copied down all the contents of my four-page form onto a separate form. The crowd shoved and shouted, and a soldier challenged an unfortunate who had brought no whiskey, only cigarettes, in his duty-free bag. A fifth man checked my carry-on case. What valuables did I have? None. How could that be? Curses rose up around me. Did I carry no watch? No glasses? No cuff links? By now, my third form, I was told, conflicted with a fourth, and a fifth would have to be completed. Did I have no wedding ring? Contact lenses perhaps? No spectacles? Elbows, passports collided. No American Express card? Not even a travel alarm clock? All, it seemed, were valuables; all had to be declared. An official began to add some of these items to my revised Customs Form and then, amidst a crash of voices, bodies, imprecations, to ask me, most cordially, to estimate the value of each piece. $5? $20? $7? Another official started rummaging through my bags, and then handed them to another for official inspection. Someone else gave me a copy of a Customs Declaration Form and a Currency Declaration Form and a Declaration Form, and told me that one had to be kept on my person and one had to be presented before every single transaction in Burma and one had to be shown upon departure. All of them, I noticed, already conflicted.

Then, as suddenly as they had converged, the officials released me, red-and-white bag in hand, through an old door bandaged with cellotape. Instantly, I was assaulted by a gang of waiting unofficials. 100 kyats for a carton of 555 cigarettes! 200 kyats for a bottle of Johnnie Walker Red! 270 kyats for cigarettes and whiskey! 250 kyats and a ride into town! 10 U.S. dollars for a taxi and a carton of 555s! 8 U.S. dollars and 100 kyats for . . .

I wasted not a moment; were it not for these black-market negotiations, I knew, I could easily find myself stranded at the airport indefinitely. Tourist Burma, ever eager to see the backs of foreigners, offered buses from Rangoon out to the airport; less pleased to welcome visitors, it ran no buses from the airport into town. Besides, it was illegal to bring kyats into the country and the only booth in the airport where local currency could be procured was closed.

A smiling man with pleading eyes and a greasy sarong led me outside. There, idling in the warm rain, were dozens upon dozens of cars, the youngest of them older than I. Battered Ford Fairlanes from the mid-fifties. Peeling Morris Minors from the Mountbatten years. Veteran Willys Jeeps left over from the war. Nearly all of them were gray, or green, or a khaki gray-green. Some had steering wheels on the right, some had steering wheels on the left and some, I'm sure, had no steering wheels at all. All looked like the final relics of some superannuated mobster.

Gently divesting me of my case, my guide flung it into the back of a 1953 Czech-made Skoda, ushered me happily into the back seat, and off we roared—or sputtered, rather, as the aging wreck gasped and creaked its way toward Rangoon. Every few minutes, it coughed up some phlegm and gave out completely. At that, the driver whirled around, flashed me a bright smile of helpless apology, jumped out, threw open the trunk, grabbed a container of water, flung open the hood, hopefully poured some water onto the engine, returned the container to the trunk, leapt into the car again and started her up. There were two dials on the dashboard, but neither of them worked.

Groaning and gagging, the Skoda bumped through wide avenues built for a queen. Above us, on an overblown billboard painted in faded comic-strip colors, a white-skinned woman with a fifties hairdo offered "English for Everyone." By the side of the road, broad driveways swept up to somber, white-pillared

mansions that now stood discolored and empty, their walls mil-
dewed, their gardens overgrown, moisture dripping from their
Kent or Sussex eaves. In the midst of all these tombs of Empire,
the Burmese went calmly about their daily rounds. On Thirl-
mere Avenue, monks in burgundy robes stood in line for buses.
Thick-spectacled old Indian gentlemen, with folded brollies and
ancient briefcases under their arms, waited to cross Windsor
Road. In the Landsdowne area, schoolchildren in spotless white
shirts and bright blue skirts sauntered, satchels swinging, home-
ward down muddy lanes.

Trying in vain to direct the dance of juddering jalopies that
careened like Dodg'ems through the collapsing city, policemen
presided over every roundabout, stern in their odd white shirts
with shiny blue buttons. A frayed notice board advertised "Public Latrines" and behind it the steeples of red-brick Victorian
churches poked into the sky. Shabby, dark little booths offered
"Cake and Snacks." Other solemn institutions, puffed up with
an air of earnest self-importance, stood unvisited along the
streets: the Military and Civil Tailors, the Foodstuffs and General Merchandise Trading Corporation, the Burmese League of
Moslem Women. Above us, on a Day-Glo cartoon of a billboard,
a dashing young couple—she a proto-Grace Kelly in white dress,
he a dinner-jacketed sophisticate—danced beside a goblet of
Super Star ice cream several times bigger than themselves.

At last, with an apologetic cough, the Skoda lurched up to the
Strand Hotel. Inside, behind a semicircular wooden counter, a
stern-looking woman pulled out a ledger thick with the dust of
ages. I filled in my name, my address and, most important of all,
the date on which I planned to leave Burma. A dirty-turbaned
man led me past grand and desolate assembly halls where groups
of schoolchildren might have gathered each morning for prayers.
A skeletal 1940s elevator creaked up its chute, the bellboy led me
down a naked, well-scrubbed corridor, a dungeon key turned in a
door and we entered my room: a hard bed with hospital covers, a
black *film noir* phone, a spartan tub in the bathroom, a Yale lock.
The turbaned man flicked a switch, and, lazily, a fan began to
whir.

"This is Burma," Kipling had written, "and it will be quite
unlike any land you know about."

BURMA IS THE dotty eccentric of Asia, the queer maiden aunt who lives alone and whom the maid has forgotten to visit. A quarter of a century ago, General Ne Win introduced his people to his own homemade political system—a slaphappy mixture of Buddhism and socialism. Almost overnight, he eliminated all private enterprise, expelled all foreigners and sealed up his nation's borders. Nothing should enter the country, he decreed, nobody should leave, and nothing should change. Burma is hardly a negligible little banana republic: it has as many citizens as Canada and Australia combined and its area is more than sixteen times greater than that of Switzerland. When Win took over, his country was the world's foremost exporter of rice, and even today it is rich with 80 percent of the globe's teak, vast quantities of rubies, even oil. Yet with one wave of his wand, its new leader managed to put the entire country to sleep. Ever since, the country had continued to slide further into poverty, deeper and ever deeper into the past. In 1974, it had emerged from its solitary confinement just long enough to announce its willingness to enter into joint-venture projects. But fully a decade passed before the first such deal was agreed upon, and it involved nothing more than the manufacture of obsolete German rifles for the Burmese Army. In Burma, Time itself had been sentenced to life imprisonment and History was held under house arrest.

Having seceded in this curious fashion from the world at large, Burma had retired, half monk and half misanthrope, to live amidst the changeless furnishings of the past. With the absoluteness that can come of isolation or idealism, it had also remained resolutely democratic in its mistrust of every aspect of the foreign, and the modern, world; an equal-opportunity recluse, it had no time for the West, no patience with the East. A founding member of the nonaligned movement, it was also the first to quit, charging that the body was no longer innocent of politics. The so-called Burmese Way to Socialism bore a fair resemblance to a one-way trip to solitary confinement.

For years, foreigners had been allowed to visit Burma for no longer than twenty-four hours. Recently, the maximum length of stay had increased to seven days. But Burma was hardly eager to attract tourists. Visitors were permitted to enter the country only by air. That meant flying into Rangoon. That in turn meant leaving from Kunming, Dhaka, Calcutta, Singapore or Bangkok. And the handful of carriers that plied these forgotten routes— the national airlines of Burma, Thailand, China, the Soviet Union and Bangladesh—did so only a couple of times each week. Arriving in Rangoon was difficult. Arriving at the right time from the right place was more difficult still. Managing to leave, exactly seven days later, for one's chosen destination, was nigh impossible.

I had enjoyed a taste of the Burmese Way to Socialism well before my arrival in Rangoon. At the Burmese consulate in New York, I had, in applying for a visa, submitted an Arrival Form, a Tourist Visa Application Form, another Tourist Application Form and three recent pictures of myself. A day had passed, and then a few more. I went back to the consulate to consult the man in charge. He was, he said with genuine courtesy, very sorry, very sorry indeed, for the delay. His country, he explained, did not have sophisticated technology. Were there no computers? "Oh no." Could we telephone? He shook his head sadly. What could I do? Well, he said, he could send a telex through New Delhi to Rangoon. But once it got to Rangoon, who could tell what would happen. I shrugged. He shrugged. Three more days passed, and then a week. I was due to leave in a matter of days. The man at the consulate handed me back my passport, minus a visa, and apologized. "Perhaps it will be easier in Bangkok."

As soon as I arrived in Bangkok, I hurried to the regally dilapidated Burmese consulate. Two men were sitting next to chaotically overcrowded desks behind a booth on a terrace marked "Visas." I would like to apply for a visa, I said. The office, they said, was closed. Could I get a form at least? The office, they said, was closed; I should come back the following day. I came back the following day. I would like to apply for a visa, I said. Where, one of the two men asked, was my plane ticket out of Burma? There seemed little point, I said, in getting a ticket out of Burma before I knew whether I could get into Burma. The two men shook their heads gravely. Soon, they said, the office would be closed.

A few minutes later, tucked away between snack shops and money dealers, I came upon a dusty, lightless little cell that looked like the back room of a warehouse. Inside, the Burma Airways head office was empty, save for a three-year-old boy wandering around vaguely among unpeopled desks. A few cheerless black-and-white posters of the homeland were stuck on the walls. A short typewritten schedule for such destinations as "Kathmadu" lay in an old Air-India folder. A postcard or two. Nothing else. Finally, a round-faced matron, huffing impatiently, shuffled up to the counter. I asked whether I could buy a ticket. She looked gloomy. It was difficult, she said. I asked why; she said nothing. At last, with lugubrious reluctance, she pulled out a Dickensian ledger and a fountain pen and entered my name on a list. Was that all? It had to be; after all, there were no typewriters in the place, and certainly no computer terminals. If I actually wanted to buy a ticket, she warned, I should go to Nepal Tours; their prices were much better than Burma Airways'. With that, she padded back into her room.

Proudly bearing my receipt, I returned to the two men at the consulate. The office, they said, was closed; I would have to come back the following day. I came back the following day. I would like to apply for a visa, I said. One of the men scrutinized my receipt unhappily. All right, he said. But he would have to warn me that his office could provide no staples.

HALF AN HOUR after arriving at the Strand, I turned off the fan in my room and walked across town to the central offices of Tourist Burma. There a middle-aged lady with black glasses, a severe bun and an air of hockey-mistress briskness began informing me of my rights. Tourists, she said, were allowed to visit only five places in Burma. It was possible to take the train, but—here she looked portentous—there were many delays. Given the seven-day limit, she did not recommend the train. Much better was to take a Burma Airways plane. An aircraft connected the country's four main sights each day.

She stopped and peered at me for a moment. Was I American? Not really. "Ah," she said with a relieved chuckle. "That is good. Americans do not like our ways here. Sometimes a plane will not leave because the pilot is sitting drinking tea. They do not understand that. They do not understand that here in Burma we live in the eighteenth century."

With that unsettling parenthesis, Miss Tourist Burma resumed her litany of rights. There was one good hotel in every town; it was not possible to stay anywhere else, unless one procured a special voucher from the Tourist Burma office. Often, she said, the office was closed. There was more or less one restaurant in every town (in the hotel), though Rangoon boasted two. And I should not on any account forget to list every transaction on my financial form. The gist of her message was clear: it was possible to choose any way at all of seeing the country, so long as it was the Tourist Burma way.

Thus reassured, I made my way back past cricket greens and stern libraries, regimental statues and white-columned institutes. Popping into a local bookstore, I found faded copies of Alistair MacLean, Angus Wilson and Trollope. Back at the Strand, black-tied men in curry-stained white coats were serving pots of tea on tarnished silver trays, accompanied by cardboardy pieces of cake last wielded, in my experience, by unsmiling school matrons at elevenses. One entire section of the menu was devoted to "Porridge." But the pièce de résistance of the hotel was clearly the five-course meal whose centerpiece was bacon and eggs. The bacon arrived in hefty black slabs as thick as expensive chocolate. I set to cutting into my meal, and a piece of meat ricocheted across the table. No wonder, I thought, Burma was such a cult favorite among my friends from British boarding school.

It all, I suppose, made a peculiar kind of sense. For in locking the modern world out, Burma had mostly succeeded in locking in the fading legacy of the long-ago outside world. By now, as a result, Rangoon had been turned into a sepia-colored daguerreotype of the Raj. And what had the Raj been in any case but a classically no-nonsense British institution, a public school writ large and transported to the colonies?

Rangoon had now, therefore, come to resemble a kind of cobwebbed, treasure-laden attic in the home of some imperial Miss Havisham, an anomalous old place cluttered with yellowed letters, ageless heirlooms and moth-eaten keepsakes left over from the days of Empire. The metaphor acquired an almost literal truth in the celebrated Lost-and-Found case at the Strand. The dusty museum case was a veritable treasure trove of ancient objets trouvés: ladies' fans and officers' cuff links; fin de siècle pince-nez and rusted fountain pens; grandfatherly razors that reminded me of Kipling's startling claim that, each night in the tropics, he was shaved by his servant while he slept; and all the other forgotten props of an age of vanished elegance when military men waltzed with memsahibs before repairing to the veranda for a drink.

By comparison, storied Raffles Hotel in Singapore seemed little more than a tourist's version of Empire, where sacraments were arranged as studiously as in some period-piece movie: plaques outside the rooms commemorated the stays of Coward and Maugham (and Arthur Hailey!); a home movie at teatime trumpeted forth the raffish history of the place; carefully framed pictures depicted elephants and mustachioed gentlemen; and a signposted trail guided visitors through a tale of the time a tiger was shot in the billiards room. In the Strand, however, the souvenirs were exactly where they belonged—everywhere in sight and nowhere in particular. Like Burma itself, the place brought to mind a down-at-heels wastrel who still preserved a misbegotten kind of propriety, dressing up for every occasion in a three-piece suit and hardly noticing that his clothes were ill-fitting and threadbare and a little sad.

And therein lay the country's charm. Having sequestered itself for decades from the splendors and sophistries of the modern world, Burma had continued to cultivate a suspicion of the new that was itself old-fashioned. Almost alone among the countries of the Third World, it seemed not to seek more Western sophistication, convenience and flash, but less. Burma was one of the only countries I had ever seen that was not goosestepping (to the sound of the Bee Gees) toward a brave new world of videos and burgers, but was content to mind its own business and go its own way. Having freed itself from servitude to the Empire, it had chosen to commit itself to a self-created ideal. Its dreams might seem wonky or zany or, worse than that, high- and simple-minded, but at least they were not shiny synthetic imports that changed with the seasons. "They do not need the glittering baubles described in the advertisement sections of American magazines," Norman Lewis had written more than thirty years ago. "The Burmese way of life has never been based on unnecessary consumption, and there is no reason why it ever should. It is as good as any, as it is."

The astonishing depth of Burma's innocence hit me fully only as I wandered around the capital. There were no high rises in Rangoon, no glass buildings or fast-food joints; there were no girls on sale, and no drugs. The massage parlors here offered massages (for innuendo, the shorthand of worldly corruption, was as absent as the corruption itself), and there was no danger, no meanness in the frayed and scruffy streets. Smuggled cans of Coke could, it was whispered, be procured for $3 at a few blue-chip black markets, but for the rest, one had to settle for rusty-capped bottles of "sparkling" Vimto that looked as though they had been fresh on the occasion of Churchill's final visit. It was rumored that one local newsstand carried *Time* and *Newsweek*, but copies could be purchased only by residents in possession of special vouchers—a possibility so remote that the official price of both magazines was 50 cents, a quarter their cost in every other country of the globe. As for the vendors who lined the roads of Rangoon, they offered nothing more topical than a three-year-old copy of *Good Housekeeping* and some dog-eared issues of *Reader's Digest*. I did notice the Snow White Pastries shop, the Flying Fish Store, and the Hope TV and Video Service. But the closest thing in Rangoon to a bright new boutique seemed to be a run-down shack with a wooden board outside, on which had been painted, decades ago, "Hollywood Beauty Parlor."

There were, I discovered, two English-language newspapers in Burma, *The Guardian* and *The Working People's Daily*. Each contained six pages, one of which was filled with lists of Model Workers Grade III, one of which concerned the minutes and seconds of sundry committees and one of which discussed, in elaborate detail, the world of golf. Both papers were entirely indistinguishable, and both were written in the featureless style of an *Izvestia* account of a town-hall meeting. For avid readers, however, that had to suffice: in Burma there were no libraries.

Television had come to the country in 1980, but both national stations came on the air only at 7:30 each night and closed down by 9:30. When I consulted the viewing schedule one day, the main attractions were "Augie Doggie and Doggie Daddy" and "Cat Happy Pappy."

A local cinema had decorated its walls with posters of such former triumphs as *A Man, a Woman and a Bank, The Story of the Mountain of Dreams*, and *The Girl in Gold Boots*. But when I went to the movies in Burma, the best picture on offer was an aging native classic. I paid my fee and entered. The place was almost empty. It reeked of spices and strong tea. A few children were slithering over parents and crawling under seats. Hardly had I sat down, however, when the few doughty souls around me sprang suddenly to their feet. A somber tune came scratchily up on the sound system and a few flags began flapping on screen. Then, just as suddenly—and well before the national anthem had concluded—everyone sat down again.

Frames flickered, numbers whirled and onto the screen came a Pathé-newsreelish documentary on Burmese dancing. For twenty minutes, a stately troupe glided, with precise delicacy, around a stage, and then the screen shook again, and shivered, and whirred, and on came the middle of the black-and-white main feature. Gangs of naked-chested hunks with caveman coiffures performed, somewhat ponderously, a handful of kung fu routines. A pair of perfumed Osrics tiptoed into view, swapping catty barbs about something or other. There was a marriage, and a parental heart attack. Two young lovers astride a motorcycle rode cheerfully through the empty streets of a travelogue-perfect Rangoon. A ten-month-old baby stared out at the audience in bemusement. The audience stared back, snickering. The martial artists, to dramatize their deaths, pounded heavily on their hearts and then, with a thump, keeled over. It was a violent genre, but the treatment seemed quite amiable.

Apart from such entertainment, there was just about nothing to do at night in Rangoon. A Burmese teenager asked me once if there were discos where I lived. Accustomed to such wistful inquiries and always ready to smuggle in a few images of the Good Life, I assured him that there were plenty of snazzy, loud, laser-beamed places. Then, almost rhetorically, I asked him whether he would like one day to see one. "What is the point?" he said quietly. "Why go to disco?"

Small wonder, then, that the only neon in town flashed above the heads of the giant Buddhas in the Sule Pagoda. For even as the streets emptied after nightfall, the central pagoda grew ever more frantic, jostling, high-spirited. Part bustling bazaar, part amusement park, part town square and part central shrine, it turned, each evening, into a beehive of frenzied activity. The neon lights blinked above the statues, prayer wheels with fortune-cookie compartments began spinning, groups of gossips clucked to themselves in corners, white-robed nuns knelt in silent prayer, palmists muttered, teenage kids tittered and paraded, what looked like an adult-education class recited slogans in what seemed to be a classroom, puppies for sale barked feebly and lines of citizens padded around antechapels wallpapered with photos of shaven-headed monks.

This, of course, was the metropolitan capital; as I traveled up-country, I realized that Rangoon marked the zenith of Burmese sophistication. Along the road to Mandalay, Burma's second city—its Leningrad or Chicago—the favored mode of transport was a horse-drawn tonga. There was a golf course in Taunggyi, but it was equipped with nothing but a tiny hut around which a few locals shuffled in their *longyis*. And Pagan, the country's main tourist sight—regarded by many as the most remarkable site in all Asia, with its thousands upon thousands of eleventh-century temples, golden and ocher and a blinding white, jutting up in lonely splendor across plains as flat and open as the scrubland of New Mexico—consisted of nothing but a puddly, one-lane village. One thatched hut had a sign outside that said "Post and Telegraph," but it was, in my experience, always open and never manned. The water that gushed out of the hotel taps was black.

In the entire country, I later discovered, there were only a third as many hotel rooms as in the Las Vegas Hilton. Most of them in any case were empty. I saw a few bearded, earringed young men accompanied by stringy-haired girls with sun-bleached shoulder bags. For them, it seemed, Burma was just another stop on a life they didn't want to get started; they were happy to go anywhere so long as it was not home. I saw some mad dogs and Englishmen who were paying tribute to the last outpost of the Empire and had come to inspect the national style of shabby gentility, and sometimes to incarnate it too. Beyond that, nothing.

THROUGHOUT ALL THIS, whether as cause or effect of its indifference to Western frippery, Burma seemed to bump along with a winning blend of merriment and strictness. If it was a malfunctioning guinea pig of fundamentalist socialism, that may have been because it was a model of strict Buddhism. And, one way or another, Buddhist precepts of compassion seemed always to subvert the rat-a-tat-tat of socialist slogans. One favorite sign, seen everywhere, advised: "Be Kind to Animals by not Eating Them." Another, on a hotel reception desk, implored foreigners to return the smiles they received. On a blackboard inside a tiny riverside inn was chalked up an even more plaintive appeal: "Please do not take photographs which create a bad impression for the village." And even more engaging than the boastful mottoes ("The King of Cars") daubed across the sides of bilious old wrecks were the injunctions of skewed firmness with which the authorities went about enforcing their regulations. "No Feet Wearing," said the sign at the entrance to every pagoda. "Smoking, Drinking and Flesh is Strictly Prohibited with in the Sikh Temple premises," read a sign outside a shrine, before adding, in a footnote that nicely covered an option ignored by the first injunction, "A Drunk Person is not Allowed Admission."

The signs, I thought, were apt reflections of their makers. For the Burmese seemed an uncommonly jolly and guileless people, not veiled or stealthy as other Southeast Asians could be, but sunny and open as their plains. Even the black marketeers had more mischief about them than malice. Generally, they approached me with respectful diffidence ("If I may, sir . . .") before treating me to a few housewifely maxims, a lecture or two on topics Burmese and an inquiry after my particulars ("If I am not being too inquisitive please, what is your age and where is your home?"). Only after the pleasantries had been observed would they get down to business. Could I sell some Johnnie Walker Red and a carton of 555 cigarettes? Would I like to exchange dollars? Could I buy them cigarettes from the Diplomatic Stores where only foreigners could shop? Should I not take a ride around Rangoon? Even then, however, a strict sense of decency was preserved: the irregulars cheerfully informed me exactly how much profit they stood to make before they fell into bargaining. Then, with undisguised pride, they chaperoned me toward their waiting chariots. "This," said the beaming owner of a 1952 Chevrolet, "cost only six thousand dollars."

Hardly was I installed in the back seat of one of these jalopies when a friendly rapscallion would hop behind the wheel, two of his cronies would bundle into the passenger seat, and off we would bounce through the sleepy streets, the Rangoon-squadders furnishing a running commentary of piquant perceptions, loony anecdotes and antic fables. Two topics were forbidden, they said: politics and drugs. But did I know that Ne Win was born in the same year as Reagan and Chernenko? And had I seen Rangoon's most efficient and prosperous industry—its black market? It was a wondrous thing, and indispensable. "Alas," said one shadow economist, "you can't just live on love and fresh air."

One day, during another such jaunt in an ailing thirty-year-old Morris, a typically amiable soul named Harry elected to deliver an irresistible defense of the system that had supported him, after a fashion, for eleven of his twenty-four years. "You," he said, "are rich and can buy many things. But we cannot. Therefore, if you buy for us, everyone is happy." Taken by this jabberwocky logic, I agreed to buy Harry some Burmese cigarettes. Instantly, his accomplice spun the wheel, and we whizzed—or rumbled, at least—across town to a hotel, where Harry instructed me to buy two cartons. Then we drove back to the Strand, and Harry, whispering prompts over my shoulder, asked me to get five more. The storekeeper objected; Harry stepped forward and fired back a riposte; the merchant protested; the two chattered excitedly; money was slipped from one palm to the next; Harry assured me that the manager had agreed not to enter the transaction on my currency form; I picked up the cigarettes, paid in dollars, and we left. Not everyone was happy, exactly, but the system seemed to work. Once outside, Harry addressed me as patiently as if I were a child. "In my country," he said, "it is, I am afraid, always necessary to bribe."

Many of Harry's confreres brought an equally wry and urbane sense of irony to the helter-skelter high jinks of their homeland, footnoting its antique anomalies in the Macaulay diction they had mastered at school under the British. A fast-dealing black marketeer who seemed to run an entire network of agents in Maymyo commanded the eternal fealty of his minions through nothing more than his honey-tongued English—"Mr. Ahmed," announced his followers with pride, "was educated at St. Albert's Mission School." A bookseller in Rangoon, as I tried to peddle a paperback copy of Mailer's latest novel, engaged me in a learned discussion on the prospects of the Great American Novel. And one bright afternoon, a withered old crone suddenly emerged from the shadows of one of the capital's lofty monuments to civic disrepair. "Money breeds money, brother," she began, tugging at my sleeve. "Brother, I ask for two minutes of your time, maybe three." She proceeded to make a spirited case for some ad hoc redistribution of income. Then, with Latinate decorum, she concluded by restating her principal theme: "You see—money, I believe, breeds money."

Most classic of all the Old World orators, however, was Lionel, the Anglo-Burmese guide who dropped epigrams and tropes in Chestertonian profusion as he offered to show me around Inle Lake. Thoroughly won over by his rhetoric, I stumbled outside before dawn the following day, and together we drove in the dark, through town after town of phantoms, to the water. There, as the light came up above the distant mountains, we climbed into a motorboat and began moving across the lake. Just as the sun appeared, a procession of boats came into view. In each one of them, twenty or thirty men were standing upright, propelling the vessel forward by rowing with their feet and, in the process, leading down the river a grand and golden bird-faced barge. After the floating monument had passed, trailed by boat after boat of chalk-faced votaries, hands prayerfully joined in the dawn, Lionel guided me around villages built on stilts in the water, showed me crops that grew on the lake itself, took me into huts where village girls wove Shan State clothing and temples crowded with Afghan-turbaned merchants. The highlight of the tour, however, and its grand finale, was a stop at the Taunggyi contraband market. "This," said Lionel, "is a necessary evil. Or, you might say, an evil necessity."

It was also a heterogeneous confusion. Tiny old ladies, puffing furiously on cheroots, sat guard over decaying cartons of Kodak film and calendars featuring photos of the White House; housewives, babies in bundles on their backs and faces whitened with *thanaka* bark, browsed through stalls, searching for tubes of French face cream; among framed pictures of old Burmese warriors there were jars of Nescafé, cans of Ovaltine, Mickey Mouse watches. Did I have a copy of *Noble House* by James Clavell? Lionel inquired. I didn't. He shook his head sorrowfully. "Here you could sell it for fifty dollars." How on earth, I asked, could anyone in Burma afford such luxuries? Fifty dollars was twice as much as a government clerk made in a month. "Oh, we have ways and means," said Lionel. "We have means and ways."

Indeed, the entire country seemed much too ironic or happy-go-lucky or simply good-natured to enforce all its ironclad regulations. At times, in fact, this affable land of xenophobia came to resemble nothing so much as a sitcom version of a socialist dictatorship. "In my country," reported one ebullient underground man, "the government has one eye open and one eye closed." The upshot of this Cyclopean state of affairs was predictable: the system frantically tripped over itself, got ever more tangled in its own red tape and finally upset so many pieces of furniture that every transaction became an under-the-table affair. In the chaos that resulted, there seemed to be more loopholes than laws, more dodges than directions. Thus the government insisted that visitors could stay no longer than seven days, yet freely allowed them to come for one seven-day stint after another. It demanded, and demanded again, that all transactions be noted down on a Declaration Form, yet when I presented an official with my form, which proved beyond doubt that I had availed myself fully of the black market, he punished me with no more than a helpless shrug. The government imported rice, and it exported rice. Tourist Burma gravely warned visitors not on any account to use Tourist Burma jeeps. And once, in the Taunggyi Hotel, I saw a Tourist Burma official, who had been kicked off a Tourist Burma flight, in despondent search of a shortwave radio: he was desperately trying, I gathered, to get in touch with the nearest Tourist Burma office twenty miles away. Naturally, there were no telephones.

Burma, moreover, seemed adept at confounding not only its own laws but also those of gravity and human nature, and, in fact, pretty much every theorem propounded by pundits and politicians alike. The Socialist Republic of the Union of Burma was neither strictly socialist nor unified nor much of a republic. But Burma it remained, and in its own inimitable fashion it continued to defy oblivion. It was among the ten poorest countries in the world, in per capita terms, yet it seemed to be cursed with little poverty and no starvation. It was decidedly backward, yet it boasted relatively fine schools and glorious, golden pagodas. One third of the country, the infamous Shan States, was a hornet's nest of political skulduggery where smugglers, Christian Karens, the Shan United Army, opium kings with armies 20,000 strong, remnants of Chiang Kai-shek's Nationalist forces and at least twelve ethnic groups (each with its own shadow government) fought against each other, the government and themselves. But that riotous scene was off on the margins of Burmese life, as remote and as ritualized as the thumping of bumptious hellions in some distant corner of the house.

Indeed, while battles had bloodied the fields of Indochina, civil and incivil wars had torn Pakistan, Sri Lanka, and India asunder, Singapore and Japan had given themselves radical face-lifts and China had swung like a murderous pendulum, Burma had kept serenely to itself, undisturbed by superpower rivalries or foreign interventions, at peace. And by abdicating from the rough-and-tumble of world affairs, it had, in effect, written itself out of the history books. One hot afternoon, as we drifted through Inle Lake, Lionel told me, almost offhand, that there had been some explosion the previous day in Rangoon, involving a few South Koreans. As soon as I could, I hurried to the British Council reading room to consult the local newspapers. Both *The Guardian* and *The Working People's Daily* delivered the same terse report: a bomb had exploded, three South Koreans had been killed. It was only two days later, when I left Burma, that I discovered that the story had pitched Win's land into the head-lines for the first time in twenty years. Small wonder. Sixteen visiting Korean dignitaries, including three cabinet members, had been killed by North Korean guerrillas; the South Korean President himself had only narrowly escaped assassination.

WHEN I RETURNED to Burma two years later, very little seemed to have altered. At the customs desk in the airport, mobs collided, calumnies were exchanged, forms were flung this way and that, hapless passengers were obliged to declare their pencils and their shoelaces. I stumbled out of the customs hall and a Tourist Burma official loomed before me to make an opening bid on my whiskey and cigarettes. By his side, a little girl started bargaining for my duty-free bag—not whiskey, not cigarettes, just the bag. After haggling in several currencies with an amused old man, I stepped into a 1952 English Tomahawk already occu-pied by two dazed British punks, and we lurched spasmodically toward the capital. *Herbie Goes Bananas* was playing at one cinema, and *The Terror of Mechagodzilla* at another. Inside the Strand, a blackboard apologized for the absence of all hot water this week. An ancient porter gave me a key ring, and it fell apart in my hands. I inserted the key into the lock, and the whole contraption got stuck.

Hardly had I stepped out of the Strand, a few minutes later, when a half-familiar voice hailed me from the darkness. "You were born in England," said a smiling young man walking up to greet me. "Your parents live in California. When you came here two years ago, you were wearing a brown cord jacket." Though doubtless few tourists had visited Rangoon over the past hundred weeks, I was nonetheless astonished. "Come, my friend," said Jain, and together we went to a nearby café.

The streets of Rangoon were somewhat brighter, a little quicker than I had remembered, lively with whispers and a bootlegged swagger. Inside the coffee shop, I saw a boy in a T-shirt that said " 'The Diana Ross Story' by Leonard Pickens Jr." and heard a tape playing "Riders on the Storm" by the Doors—or so I assumed until I listened more closely and realized that the acid-head anthem was actually being sung in Burmese (the Playboys, explained Jain, were sons of government officials; only they could afford to buy electric guitars and amps). Outside, Jain pointed out a few of the country's other developments: a new Datsun could be bought, he said, for only $40,000, and TVs were now available for just $4,000. A house could be purchased for $250,000. Some things, however, never change. When I asked Jain how people managed to afford such luxuries, he smiled. "Household goods," he replied, in a phrase last heard before the war, "and foodstuffs also."

Strolling in the warm evening through the fallen center of town, we sauntered past the Baptist Church and Gold Cup Café and Confectionery, wandered into a Hindu temple where we were hailed as dignitaries. Jain led me across the main park, and when we came upon three beaming young layabouts, he graciously provided introductions. I smelled liquor on the fellow's breath, and when we shook hands, they held mine slightly longer than seemed necessary as he stared at me imploringly. "Do not worry," Jain assured me. "They are not gays. They are just looking for gays to make love to." I registered my surprise. "Whatever is easier," he smiled. "They prefer girls. But they like what is easy." He himself, he said as we resumed our walk, had once been invited up to her room by a Spanish woman. But then she had told him she was married, and he, as a good Muslim, had been unable to conceal his shock.

And though the country seemed a touch more worldly than I had imagined, it was, for the most part, the same old, good old Burma. At breakfast the next morning, there was only one item on the menu: a five-course extravaganza that began with fruit juice ("Pineapple, please." "Only orange, sir") and concluded with fruit ("Banana, papaya or pineapple?" "Pineapple, please." "Sorry, sir, we are having papaya only"). There was only one telephone directory in the four-floor hotel, and it was three years out of date. I attempted a local call, but it was alternately cut dead or rerouted, so it seemed, through Gabon.

When I went to the Tourist Burma office, the stern lady of two years before greeted me as a long-lost friend, reminding me that it was most advisable to travel around her country by plane. Knowing as much from experience, I asked for a flight to Pagan. Sorry, she said, there were no flights. Burma Airways had only four planes and one of them had crashed last month. I asked for a train to Pagan. Sorry, she said, but the area was closed. An entire section of the country closed? "VIP," she explained cryptically; perhaps I would like to take the train to Mandalay? I quickly agreed and asked for a sleeper. Sorry, she said; all sleepers were taken. Because planes were scarce, trains were full. Perhaps a third-class seat would be satisfactory?

That evening, on a stiff wooden seat suited for nothing but the construing of Greek irregular verbs, I jounced through the long blue evening. Silent cracks of lightning illuminated the distant mountains. Across the broad plains a few oil lamps burned in tiny huts. The rest was darkness. Inside the carriage, vendors shuffled through the aisles, renting books to read during the journey or selling Bambi-like toys; outside, village girls slept by the tracks, bouncing up whenever a train approached and gathering by the windows to sell cups of water. By the time we got to Mandalay next morning, I learned that the local hotel was full. Perhaps I would be interested in a small room in a guesthouse?

That day, as I wandered through temples, I met a Burmese man who told me to give his best to his cousin in the Seventh-Day Adventist Hospital in Bakersfield, another who explained his plans for moving to Idaho. And as I descended from Mandalay Hill after watching the sun fall over the river, a middle-aged woman hopped nimbly into the back of my trishaw. "Make hay while the sun shines," she cried as she entered. As the cycle began moving, she winked broadly and advised, "Don't let the cat out of the bag." The next thing I knew we were riding together through broad avenues in the falling dusk and she was alternately cackling inscrutably and singing "Blue Suede Shoes" or other hits from the distant past. When at last we drew up to my hotel, the ineffable lady solemnly extended a skinny hand and, though it was the eve of a Buddhist festival in mid-October, declared, "Please give my very best regards to your parents and wish them, on my behalf, all best wishes for Christmas and the New Year."

That night I slept fitfully under a mosquito net which ensured that no bloodsucker would ever be more than two feet from my body. Shattered and scratchy by the break of day, I staggered out to join three other battered survivors on a bus to Inle Lake. The only hotel in Taunggyi was full; perhaps we would care to stay at the Inle Inn guesthouse? After an hour of bumping in a horse-drawn cart along quiet country lanes, we got out at a tiny rustic cottage and stumbled inside, famished and fatigued. Instantly, a young boy hurried out to greet us, and pointed meaningfully at a nearby blackboard: underneath a sign that read "Take a regard not to show braless and bare shorts in public places," it listed "Burmese Dinner" and "Roast Beef." "The Burmese dinner sounds very tempting." "I am very sorry, sir, but the Burmese food we serve in the evenings only." Oh. "May I recommend the roast beef?" All right. "Then it will be easiest for all your friends to have roast beef also."

As our host bustled into the kitchen, we collapsed gratefully into chairs. Two minutes later, however, another boy emerged, distraught. "Very sorry, sir, for roast beef we must go to market." No problem. "It means a wait of an hour." Fine. "Or longer." Okay. "You would like noodles, perhaps, sir, and maybe roast beef this evening?"

That evening, we had the Burmese dinner, seated on the floor around a lacquer table, by the light of a flickering candle, and feeling ourselves in a place of magic never to be known again. Afterward, we walked into the village and were led backstage at a traditional *pwe* where male actors were decorating themselves with rouge and lipstick, while families crouched on the ground outside. Next morning, before daybreak, we walked through the mist, where monks in bright red robes were filing silently from hut to hut with their begging bowls. And as we entered a boat on the lake and glided through the gathering light to see the golden temple on its annual trip downlake, we could hear, in the distance, the *pwe* going strong.

To get back to Rangoon, two hundred miles away, I traveled for six hours in a motorboat, one hour in a horse-drawn cart, another hour clinging to the sides of a 1946 Jeep crammed with fourteen excitable villagers, nine hours in a suspensionless army truck and fourteen more hours on yet another third-class overnight train. And when I got back to the capital, I found it giddy with the look of a happy children's toy, all its decaying buildings strung with lights in honor of the Thadingyut Festival, when angels light the path for Buddha to return to earth. That evening, as I walked among the carnival stalls, I suddenly heard a shout behind me, and turned to see the three boys whom I had met by the park waving me over for tea. Earnestly, they quizzed me about New York and the Live Aid concert, discussed the merits of Moshe Dayan's autobiography, assured me that Addis Ababa was the capital of Ethiopia and La Paz the main city of Bolivia. Then they told me about the life of Dr. Haing S. Ngor, hero of *The Killing Fields*, and showed me how to moonwalk (two months later, both rock 'n' roll and break dancing were officially outlawed in Burma). Finally, my new friends took me for a ride on a hand-operated Ferris wheel that revolved as slowly and as creakily as an ill-oiled gerbil's plaything. "Please do not think badly of us," said one of the boys, as, very gently, we rocked back and forth high above the city, gazing in the far distance at the full moon above the golden stupa of the Shwedagon Pagoda. "Please understand: we are pure."

AND BURMA'S SINS were so original, its freedom from self-consciousness so absolute, that it was indeed tempting to believe that it languished in some pre-fallen age of the world's infancy; by the limited standards of the world, Burma had never grown up. It was, I thought, a lost world in both senses of the word: a remnant from the past, but also a baffled child trying to make its way about an adult universe. And though it was customary to situate paradise in locations that were geographically far away

—Tahiti, perhaps, or the Seychelles—there was no reason why Shangri-La couldn't be hidden in the temporally remote. In time-warped Burma, all the grandmotherly saws seemed to apply: what you've never had, you've never missed; what you don't know can't hurt you; *les vrais paradis sont les paradis perdus.* The mustiest place I had ever seen, Burma was also, in many ways, the freshest, bright with an innocence close to self-possession, a diamond-shaped country in the rough. One of my school friends, a professional globe-trotter who took his holidays in every obscure land from Mozambique to Panama to Yemen, told me that Burma was his favorite place because it was, in a real sense, unspoiled; to his Christian eye, it represented a kind of Eden. And the last word in Norman Lewis's *Golden Earth*, itself the last word on Burma, was "Utopia."

The country was made doubly alluring, no doubt, by the sweet ache of nostalgia. Rue was in the air, and the mingled wistfulness of splendor recollected. All the props of the Golden Land were soft with an autumnal sense of yesterday, and every sentence seemed to begin with "once upon a time." "Once," a gentle Burmese soldier assured me, "Rangoon Airport was one of the great international centers of Asia. Now . . ." and his voice drifted off into regret. Once, as I awaited a plane at Inle, a prosperous-looking merchant sidled up and asked me where I came from. When I said England, a light came to his eyes as he began to describe the grand capital he had known as a boy. "Gosh," he said, "Rangoon was glorious. We had one of the best educational systems in Asia. We had dignity too. But now . . ." and his voice trailed off. And once, when I checked into the Strand, an aged porter asked me where I had been born. Britain, I answered. He replied with a crisp salute. "Rule Britannia," he intoned, without a trace of irony. "Britannia rules the waves."

The scent of elegy was most haunting amidst the pine-scented country lanes of Maymyo (named after some otherwise unre-membered Colonel May). The Motor Association Head Office was crumbling now, but still it took its place proudly on the main street beside the Golf Club Repairing Shop and Diamond Confectionery. Down Charing Cross Road and through Down-ing Street stepped horse-drawn victorias redolent of a gaslit London. And all around the hills were snug little half-timbered cottages with names like All in All and Fernside, tidy with flawless Cotswold gardens. The queen of them all, of course, was Candacraig (formerly the "chummery" of the Bombay-Burmah Trading Company), the boardinghouse where roast beef and vegetables were served at seven sharp every evening, and coffee was taken by the fireplace. From its balcony, in the misty early morning, I could hear the central town clock tolling with the same chime as Big Ben.

Filtered as it was through the gentling touch of memory, Burma had something of the poignancy of a book one might find in a secondhand bookstore, a hardback sold for 49 cents, which someone had inscribed as a present to a beloved and their future forever together. In Burma, I had found the India that my parents had known in their youth, albeit an India that had slept for ten thousand nights in the same old clothes. And in Burma I returned to the brisk spartanism of my own days at school in an England forever young.

After a while, however, I began to register a perplexing fact: Burma had been out of it for ages. A full decade before Ne Win had sent the rest of the world into exile, the prescient Norman Lewis had come to the country determined to see "the traditional Burma, with its archaic and charming way of life." If he waited any longer, he feared, it would be sullied irreparably by East or West, or else might simply vanish forever into "self-isolation" behind the Bamboo Curtain. Fifty years ago, when Orwell wrote his *Burmese Days*, the place was already a clubhouse of canned food and faded fashions where yesterday's promising young men read last month's copies of *Punch*. Even a century ago, the most famous lines ever written about Burma, by its honorary poet laureate, Kipling, were ruffled by the mild breeze of nostalgia:

> For the wind is in the palm trees, an'
> the temple bells they say:
> "Come you back, you British soldier;
> come you back to Mandalay!"

Burma had long lived in the past tense, I suspected, because Burma had long been preserving the memories of an Empire that had itself been built on memory. For decades, the country had accommodated the longing and homesickness of people in an alien land trying to re-create, however anomalously, every last feature of their old unforgotten homes. If the American Empire had to do with currency, immediacy, annihilation of the past, its British counterpart had been founded on continuity, tradition, a reverence, and remembrance, of things past. If the natives could not come to Britain, so the reasoning of the Raj had gone, Britain must come to the natives. Thus even at their prime, the institutions of the Empire had, in their way, been so studied and textbooked a re-creation of the homeland that they might have seemed almost a caricature. These days, Maymyo seemed a charming anachronism from an age long gone. Yet even when the place was new, it must have seemed a trifle backward-looking, a brave imitation of a world abandoned. Burma offered, in the end, a double romanticism: the nostalgic continuation of an age of nostalgia.

This evergreen outdatedness, combined with the country's remoteness from what is commonly called reality, had long consigned Burma to the farthest reaches of romance. So few reports of the country trickled into the world outside that Burma seemed to survive now only in the mind or memory: to most people, it was little more than the chime of exotic and evocative names. Mandalay. Kipling. The Irrawaddy. Even after my second visit to the country, I was tempted to think of it as a fabulous fiction: a Disney version of the Empire, called Yesterdayland perhaps, or some Hollywood set of an imperial ghost town. Burma had the beguiling sadness of an elegy; its charm lay in its ruined grandeur, its terminal inefficiency, its picturesque decay. Besides, it was always easy to romanticize what one left behind: childhood, or the past, or a country that seemed compounded of both.

That, perhaps, was the ultimate Western luxury.

"It's easy for you to talk about cultural innocence and integrity," said a foreign diplomat I met in Rangoon, a large man with a gentle manner who loved the country so much that he had returned for his second tour of duty. "But just go and look sometime at the Rangoon Hospital. Just look at it: the place is a charnel house." His voice, normally soft, took on an unexpected hardness. "I would rather die in the gutter than be admitted to that place."

And two days before I left Burma, as I waited for the plane that would take me back to Rangoon, and thence to the outside world, Lionel, my ever-ironic tour guide, ceased for a moment in his delivery of his country's madcap vagaries to call me aside for a minute. He was five days short of his sixtieth birthday, he said, and he was rich "only in children." Please, he said, please could I do him one small favor?

With that, he drew out from his pocket a crumpled envelope. Its address was folded and smudged almost to illegibility. Dimly, I could make out the name of a house in Essex. Please, said Lionel, please could I take this letter to his British uncle? As a Burmese resident, he was not allowed to send letters abroad. But perhaps I could take it for him and perhaps I could get it to his uncle. And perhaps, said Lionel, perhaps his faraway uncle could do something, anything, anything whatsoever—cut some deal or bribe some official or fill out some form—and somehow, sometime, free him from the slow and terrible death of his motherland.

SUDDENLY, LIKE
almost everyone else on almost every trip through Asia, I found
myself at Hong Kong's Kai Tak Airport. Quick with the honking
cries of energy and enterprise, pungent with discounts and deals,
Kai Tak is as much the Grand Central Station of the Orient as
O'Hare, according to Tom Wolfe, is the capital of America.
Hemmed in by skyscrapers, pressed down under sheer green
hills, its single runway squeezed into a spit of reclaimed land so
close to the sea that upon landing I saw a Lufthansa jet nose-
down in the water, Kai Tak is the spiritual center—and the
discount center—of typhooning Hong Kong.

Inside the sweaty and disheveled transit lounge, the expatriate
life was spinning around in all its wound-up frenzy. All about
was the bustle, the dash, the dynamism, of people passing
through, moving on, sloughing off old selves and picking up new
ones. Beefy bronzed men in tropical shirts tapped restless fingers
on briefcases as they waited to jet off to K.L., Bangkok, Manila;
imperial Brits in impeccably tailored suits marched with

a soft-spoken swagger through aisles where clipboard girls fussed busily about. Back and forth between bar and bookstore, bookstore and bar, eyes always open for an unoccupied seat or an unexpected offer, travelers from every corner of the continent circled and circled—smooth-faced Thais and straw-hatted Filipinos, groups of white-clad Japanese honeymoonies, ruddy Australians and curry-reeking Indians trailing all the possessions of this life and the last one and the one before that.

Departure signs clicked over, baggage carousels turned around, red-faced expats marched off to their commuter planes.

People on the rise, on the move, on the go.

MINUTES LATER, I was in a taxi winding along the narrow roads that snake through the hills of the "Mid-Levels." Below, in the distance, the city was a scintillant dream. Swerving up a steep incline, the car rolled into an underground garage complex and stopped by the side of three Mercedeses, a Rolls, a Porsche and a Ferrari. A noiseless elevator whisked me up to the eighteenth floor, and there, among the stars, stood Georges, a friend from Eton, tanned, barefoot and shirtless after a day at the office. Only a few months earlier, when last we had met, Georges had exhausted all his savings on a squat studio apartment amid the clutter and clamor of Greenwich Village. Now, thanks to an overseas transfer, he was living in a three-bedroom luxury apartment, with exquisite framed Thai prints along the wall, glass cases for his books, a twenty-first-century stereo system alive with green and scarlet flashes. Through his picture window we saw the switchboard lights of the city below, a thousand fireworks arrested in midflight, and, beyond, the illuminated curves of the world's most breathtaking harbor. Far in the distance gleamed the hills of Kowloon.

"You know," said Georges, leading me out onto his terrace in the soft autumn evening, "this place is really something." Below us, the curving road was lit up by the moon. The night was polished to a sheen and the breeze was warm. "It's not easy to leave," he sighed. "Seventeen and a half percent taxes. A free flat. A Filipina amah who comes in once a week to clean the place. Expat Services, Ltd., to take care of all my maintenance. Free holidays. All this." He swept his hand across the multicolored night. "That's why *gwei lo* never go home."

We stood outside and a breeze came up, as the nocturne soothed on. Below us, on the next block down, a roof was strung with colored lights. Bodies mingled and gyrated. The crystal tinkle of small talk drifted up to us, and, more faintly, the insistent bass of Tina Turner's "What's Love Got to Do with It?"

"You know," said Georges, talking slowly, "when you're ninety years old, and you're in your rocking chair, and you're talking to your grandchildren . . ." And, you know, he was right.

THE NEXT NIGHT, since it was Friday, we did what expats do on Friday nights. Georges invited two Chinese girls to join us for dinner at a soigné little café in Central, and we chatted about capital ventures and venture capitalists, futures and options, common friends from Harvard and London. Then, since it was Friday, we headed off to a party at the very top of the Peak. "Can I stop in at your flat for just a sec?" asked the girl from Morgan Guaranty. We did, and she put through a call to New York. "Oh. He's trading? Okay, I'll call again this afternoon, your time."

Into another cab we hopped, whizzing around and around the darkened hills, higher and still higher, around Mulholland twists and Côte d'Azur turns until the lights stretched everywhere before us and we were left upon their jeweled diadem. When last I had seen our host, he too was cohabiting with roaches and mass murderers in Manhattan. Now, high riser in a city of high rises, he lived at the top of the whole carousel. The designer shelves in his bachelor pad were elegantly bare save for a book by Adam Smith, a copy of *Competitive Strategies* and a pile of old copies of the *Far Eastern Economic Review*. The men at the party were expats, the girls, with one exception, Chinese.

A British banker approached a girl. "What do you think of the dollar?"

"As you know," said an American investment banker, "work takes up a hundred and ten percent of one's life here. There's no demarcation between business and real life. It's all business. That's all people do, all they talk about."

"Do you know Terry?" asked a local trader. "Sister's a Cathay girl?"

"We're definitely a golden company," said a Brit in computers. "Five hundred million in fifteen years. Sorry—could you excuse me for a moment? I've got to call New York."

And sometime after one o'clock, we wandered out into an evening gentler, more coaxing than any I could recall. The moon was so bright, and so bright the incandescence below, that the sky was the blue of faded denim. It felt like the last few minutes before daybreak, and I almost mistook the only diamond in the heavens for the morning star. Lulled by the sentimental muzziness of the faraway lights, buoyed by the sense of limitless possibility, I felt like wandering all night.

"It's a seductive city."

"It's a degenerate city."

FIRST AND FOREMOST, Hong Kong is an expat city, the world's great community of transients and refugees—less a community, perhaps, than a dervishing congregation of self-interests. In point of fact, forty out of every forty-one of the Colony's people are Chinese, not expats but exiles driven to the non-Forbidden City more by circumstance than choice. Yet still the expat seems to preside over the place, symbolically at least, as surely as the salaryman in Tokyo or the party hack in Moscow. The official face of the Crown Colony is white, its official voice the Queen's English. His Excellency the Governor administers the place, and its fortunes rest with the *taipan*. One of the major seats of power in the city—represented in my guidebook by a full-color photo—is still the loo at the Foreign Correspondents Club.

By 1985, moreover, negotiations had made formal what circumstances had long made inevitable—in 1997, Hong Kong would be handed over from Whitehall to Beijing. And with the signing of that agreement, reality had converged with metaphor, and the Colony seemed truly to be left in no hands but its own, directed by nothing save the force of individual will. An unregulated free-for-all, Hong Kong in 1985 seemed more than ever a kind of special economic zone for the international businessman, a giant version of one of those anonymous, convenient intercontinental spaces—the convention center, the five-star lobby, the departure lounge—where people can meet between flights to cut deals, have drinks, talk options. Offering all the amenities of a city with none of the encumbrances of a state, the entrepôt provided a perfect movable feast for go-getters, over-achievers and rootless ex-patriots—driven, self-making men with no allegiances except to the self. The Colony observed no ideology, after all, but laissez-faire, no law except that of the marketplace. It promised plenty of income and almost no tax. It honored no absolutes save profit and impermanence. And the only common denominator, the only *lingua franca* binding everyone together in Hong Kong—Chinese back-street tailor, British administrator and American investment banker—was money. "Business and shopping are the only things to do here," announced my Chinese colleague the day I arrived—making money and spending it.

And if the most concrete and convenient symbol of the city of concrete and convenience was Kai Tak—a hectic and duty-free and perennially overcrowded waiting room for the future—the most unvarnished was surely the Walled City, the six-acre section of Kowloon which had ended up, through one of the pieces of small print that are the Colony's history and destiny, policed by neither the Chinese nor the British. Now a kind of no-man's-land occupied by a neo-Elizabethan hugger-mugger of racketeers, drug dealers, gangsters and abortionists, the shark-toothed area seemed only a rawer version of the city all around—a freewheeling, free-spending center of free enterprise.

Where freedom meets money—that was the location of Hong Kong. And by 1985, the city had become the last wide-open settlement in the Wild East, the final El Dorado. This was where corporate cowboys came to lasso their futures, where fortune hunters flocked to pan for gold. "This is the second frontier," an advertising executive told me, excitement in his eyes. "Shoot from the hip," said his boss, stopping by for a brief strategic chat. "In Hong Kong," said a cabbie, "there's lots of freedom. You have money, you can do anything." And where anything goes, everyone goes, to be somebody.

THE MORNING AFTER the party on the Peak, I got up very early and walked into Georges' living room to find him doing what most expats do on Saturday mornings—calling his office in New York. On the other end of the line was another Old Etonian who was busy complaining that he could find no Old Etonians in New York, in part perhaps because nearly all of them were out East. "What we need here," this fellow bulled, "are more people like you—capable, confident, knows what he likes."

For British public school boys, of course, the Crown Colony had long been a first-class finishing school, or at least a tolerable halfway house fairly close to the tropics. Indeed, the expat life had first acquired its air of raffish glamour when I was at school, and nothing could seem more glamorous than raffishness. For though the best of our brightest might be expected to follow their paters into the Foreign Office or the City, the rest—the adventurers and apprentice ne'er-do-wells, the black sheep and white mischief-makers—were much better advised to respond to the ancestral call of "Go East, young man." In the East they could put to good use all the noble savagery they had mastered through flogging and fagging and firking at school; in the East, they could be rulers of empires. The East was opportunity, the East was escape. "The East," as Disraeli wrote in another context, "is a career."

At the only school reunion I ever attended, my daydreams of the expat life had come even more sharply into focus, in the shape of Charles, who had just flown in from Hong Kong, outfitted with a new air of knowingness, a matter-of-fact ease with the mysterious. As we gathered for drinks in the warm Berkshire evening, he entranced us all with schoolboy fantasies of the Orient. Working for Swire's, he began with practiced casualness, he received a free flat, free holidays, free flights on Cathay Pacific. How did he spend his weekends? Oh, usually, he flew off with a few expats to Bangkok for the night life and sometimes, that same night, they went on to Manila; on long weekends, they went to Bali. In the winter, expats went skiing in Japan; in the summer, they took over some forgotten fantasy island in the Philippines. And the food in Asia was terrific, and the weather was amazing. As for the girls, they were ravishing, and compliant, and dreamed of nothing but a British boyfriend! Even the miseries Charles described—dysentery in Kashmir, con men in Phuket, social diseases in Manila—sounded impossibly exotic.

In the years that followed, I often caught updates on the latter-day nabobs, supported by their Old Etonian ties and sustained by their imperial authority. Giles was a stockbroker in Hongers, Michael was a solicitor. Dominic from Tokyo and David from the Colony had just been on holiday together in Thailand. Mike had actually gone native and married a Chinese woman. Jamie was swanning around China playing free-lance writer. Jock was living it up in Bangkok, and Paul was starting his own company in Jakarta. Tim was in Seoul, which he loved —he kept one girl for official functions, one for more private occasions and a third for his visiting friends.

By 1985, moreover, as every other country in Asia had shaken off the fetters of colonialism, Hong Kong, the "Pearl of the Orient," seemed the last treasure left in the oyster that was the Old Boys' world. Etonians still crowded into the FCC, an American journalist complained, chattering away in their incomprehensible code of housemasters' initials and Latin tags; cocktail parties still buzzed with pukka talk of "bashes" and "punters." And one day, as I drove into town, I saw the Eton E. T. Language School hardly more than a scone's throw from the Anglican church, standing upright in the afternoon sun.

A couple of mornings later, I turned on the radio, and got another whiff of Empire in the commanding colonel tones of a well-educated Brit, calling up some chatty chappie on a talk show. Had the host happened to see the beauty contest on the television three days ago? he began with authoritative politeness. Well, not exactly. "I see," said the man, meaningfully. "Well! They gave the winner fully four seconds more than the others to do her toe touches!" The professionally euphoric host was not sure quite what to make of this. "So naturally," went on the caller, as if preparing his letter to *The Times*, "the girl won the aerobics section. Then they refused to release the score of the runners-up!" Half baked in the tropics, he warmed swiftly to his topic. "I was wondering whether you could perhaps use your good offices to look into this." Stunned, the host laughed nervously, and played for time. But the loony was unstoppable. "And do you know what the hostess was called?" The host did not know what the hostess was called. "Doh-doh!" said the voice triumphantly. The host rallied gamely. "Do-do." "Well, she said it Doh-doh, and, you know, that makes me think of . . ."

By 1985, however, the British presence in the city seemed all too easily represented by that voice of elegant irrelevance—a sort of polished character actor consigned to the margins of life and talking to himself unintelligibly in an enormous, echoing chamber. Hong Kong was still officially the Crown Colony, but the crown was slipping off and the Colony was slipping away.

The greatest hong in the city, Jardine-Matheson, had already moved its headquarters to Bermuda. The storied Repulse Bay Hotel, great bastion of old fogies and Old Hands, had been replaced by an eighteen-story megablock. The Peninsula, which still collected guests from the airport in a Rolls, was about to undergo a radical refurbishing. In 1985, for the first time in history, there were more Americans in Hong Kong than Brits.

Change, of course, was nothing new here; it had always been the only constant in the hyperactive Colony. Every seven minutes, the government erected a brand-new building, quite literally moving mountains and pushing back the sea and digging up new earth in its determination to keep up with the times. Nowadays, however, something else was changing, something deeper than the buildings. "In Hong Kong today," explained a Chinese banker from Harvard Business School, "to be rich is to be powerful. The two are the same." And as affluence had become the measure of authority, matter was superseding manner, and the great intangibles in which the British had long excelled—irony and wit, discretion and diplomacy, a sense of the mot juste and the *vin extraordinaire*—were fast being made redundant by the hard facts of money and technology. The ever-so-civil servant was being usurped by the stateless entrepreneur; the Empire was being eclipsed by the International Style.

The age of the Impersonal Computer was bringing with it, of course, an entirely new set of values. Quantities counted more than qualities now, function overruled form. Suburbs were beginning to swallow up cities. And as fast as the sun was setting on the Empire, it was being replaced by fluorescent lights. The Empire had always stressed character and distinctions; in the new technoglobal village, however, convenience and communications were everything, and the world was being made generic. Everywhere could be home if everywhere was homogeneous.

In 1985, therefore, Hong Kong, always one of the fastest places to adapt to the latest trend, was busy creating a new and serviceable identity for itself, sloughing off the superfluous niceties of Empire as it spun into a digital future. Already, the Colony boasted numbers as showy as the test scores of a teenage science whiz. There were more Rolls-Royces per capita here than in any other city in the world, more Mercedes-Benzes than in Berlin.

The new sixty-two-escalator Hong Kong and Shanghai Bank was reported to be the most expensive building in the world. And there were 1,500 men in Hong Kong worth more than $100 million, even though there were only 400 houses in the entire Colony.

The greatest numbers of all, of course, were always financial; in the Multinational Age, the top priority was always the bottom line. And here too, Hong Kong seemed eminently well endowed. For money infected the language of Hong Kong: the best place to eat, I was told, was "the poor man's nightclub" and the best thing to see was the "rich men's ghetto." Money colored the customs of Hong Kong: *kung hei fa choy* ("rejoice and grow rich") was the greeting exchanged by the Chinese, together with bank notes, during their New Year. Money informed the very sound of the city: the song of the moment while I was there, all too fittingly, was "Material Girl," which I heard again and again and again, pumped out by the sound system in McDonald's, blasting out at a party in Central, crooned by an entertainer in a Malaysian restaurant. Money, above all, was the opium of the masses: more than once in Hong Kong, I heard people acknowledge, "I like money." A little later, I read that up to 50 percent of all the Colony's psychiatric patients, most of them expats, suffered from "affluence depression." In Hong Kong, even the ironies were rich.

ON MY FIRST weekend in Hong Kong, I ended up doing what expats do on Saturdays, sitting stranded in the traffic jam that paralyzes the city as everyone in the center of speculators heads for the races. For the next day, though, I arranged to do what expats do on Sundays, cruising around the harbor on a junk.

As Sunday morning arose, however, a fine rain began to blanket the city, misting the quiet water below. And as I sat in Georges' luxury flat, gloomily watching the harbor erase itself below me, my hostess rang up: on rainy Sundays, she explained, expats tended to gather for brunches rather than launches; could I taxi around to her house in Happy Valley? Outside, in the drizzle, clumps of bright young American couples in Lacoste shirts and blue blazers, pantsuits and Reeboks, were lined up by the side of the road, waiting to hail taxis. They too, I assumed, were on their way to their own Sunday brunches.

As soon as I arrived at my friends' rambling home, I was led out onto the veranda, where expats were sitting around in wicker chairs, munching corn chips and drinking Carlsbergs as Elvis Costello songs floated between the ferns. Some "belongers" were working on the crossword in the Saturday *Herald Trib*, the closest you could get, I was told, to the Sunday New York *Times*. Someone assured me I could watch the NBA championship series on Tuesday evenings, someone else that I could hear the Top 10 of two years earlier on the radio. Someone else discussed the four-mile jogging track along Bonham Road and somebody reserved a block of tickets at the local cinema so that we could all go see the latest Woody Allen.

"Last night at a dinner party, a man told me how he'd just made a hundred thousand dollars U.S. A jockey rang him up before the race and told him he owed him a favor."

"When I came here, I really wanted to immerse myself in the Chinese community, speaking only Chinese, doing everything Chinese. And I was earning six thousand dollars U.S. and living on an island and all of my friends were Chinese. But then I started moving up in the world and earning more and more and now—well, now I live in an expat world."

"Ah, it's such a comfortable life out here. A car. Lots of rooms. A maid. It's so hard to move back to New York."

WHEN FIRST I visited Hong Kong, I could hardly imagine why anyone would want to go back to New York. For as the Colony threw over its imperial ties, it was coming more than ever to resemble a sweet-and-sour version of the capital of the modern world. Like New York, in its way, the orphan city was full of the street-smart bravado of a strutting young man in a hurry, a rags-to-riches Seventh Avenue shark who takes the world on, but only on his own terms. Like New York, "Chinatown East" valued volume and velocity; people moved quickly through the streets, and with purpose, pushing for space, shoving, struggling to get a step ahead. Like New Yorkers, Hong Kongers seemed to pride themselves on their rudeness, their impatience with the slow or sentimental ("Am I being courteous?" said the badge worn with black irony by the conductor on the Peak train who barked out orders and trampled on children as he kept the turnstiles spinning). Like New York, above all, Hong Kong seemed to prize energy before imagination and movement more than thought. The place had a one-track mind—and it was decidedly the fast track. Hard-driving and fast-talking, it ran on hard cash and quick wit, hard heads and quick kills. In Hong Kong, even Maxim's was a fast-food joint.

In that sort of environment, where statements were mostly associated with banks, values were rarely sentimental; everything, in fact, was a commodity. When first I visited, in 1983, the biggest deal in town and the center of the most furious bartering seemed to be the city itself; Hong Kong's very identity was being placed (as once Manhattan's had been) on the marketplace. And no sooner had China won the bidding than the world's most famous marketplace turned into a wholesale store feverish with the activity of a closing sale (Low prices! Moving soon! All stocks must go!). By the time I returned in 1985, the hottest place for young professionals was called 1997. A leading local racehorse had been christened 1997. And in the prime location of the Harbour Ferry departure lounge, the prize novelty of the store called 1997 (where every item sold for exactly HK $19.97) was a lumpy and ill-favored creature named the Rice Paddy Doll, a macabre variation on the Cabbage Patch Kid. This one, however, was not an orphan but an exile, equipped with a Hong Kong British passport and a sign that read: "I want to Emigrate" or "Immigration Department" or "I would love Australia." Already, so it seemed, the city had undertaken to turn its death to profit; already, it was flogging tickets to its own funeral.

Among the people of Hong Kong too, I met a pragmatism more no-nonsensical than any I had ever known before. In Hong Kong, cabbies were not the self-styled political pundits I had met elsewhere in the world, but self-appointed economists. And in their abacus vision of the world, even matters domestic were reduced in the end to matters economic. On my second day in the Colony, a driver took me around the main island, and when we stopped for lunch, I asked about his family. In the inimitable staccato English of the Chinese—spitting out syllables as if they were indigestible dumplings and speaking with the rapid urgency of a man holding on to a slippery bar of soap while fearing a fire alarm at any moment—he briskly filled me in on his principles of cost-efficient growth. He did not have child, because child cost money. Child also make wife stay at home, cut down income. He must take good care of wife, because wife bring good income. He need income. He work every day, twelve hour, but sometimes take Sunday off. He only have one job. Many people in Hong Kong have two.

I could not help recalling the Hong Konger I had met on the road who was making a year-long circumnavigation of the world. I had asked him which places had moved or impressed him most. Thailand was good, he answered; it was inexpensive. Greece was great; it didn't cost too much. Egyptians, they were all sharks. India, it was full of touts. With that, he cast his practiced eye around my room. This place was okay, he pronounced. But it should be worth a refund.

I did manage to find a snatch of romance in Hong Kong—at the Chinese opera. *The Cloud of Eternal Sorrow* was a ravishing pageant of water and air, through which was unrolled a watercolor vision of turquoise valleys and misty waterfalls. Swains chased sylphs through a brushstroked never-never land. Shaven-headed chamberlains and goat-bearded sages strode through a plot as brocaded and magical as that of *Turandot*. Every speech was fleet and fragile as light snowfall. A valiant warrior marched onto the stage, and English-language subtitles flickered on the blue velvet curtains framing the proscenium. "I am a hunter from Jade Mountain. My father's silver-maned horse is faster than the army's 3,000." Imprisoned, the lovely princess of his dreams could only weep beside her casement. "The palace is dark. The palace is lonely. The valleys are draped in a lilac shroud." The seasons drew on, and her pining grew more plaintive and more plangent. "The moon is so bright. These walls are so high. My heart is breaking." The curtain came down, and I went out into the night. Two old men, in white vests and black shorts, were playing go beside the harbor, while the water, purpled by neon, slapped against the docks. The moon was so bright. The walls were so high.

In life if not in art, however, Hong Kong, long the largest metropolis in the world without a museum, had its head screwed on very tightly. What good was tradition, it implied, when it came to moving ahead? When did sentiment ever contribute to profit? Who needed poetry when prose was so much clearer?

"Son was the most valuable long-term investment they possessed," writes Timothy Mo in his family portrait of Hong Kong exiles in Britain, *Sour Sweet*. "On maturity, the realization of this asset would be worth far more than the business would ever return."

IN 1985, HONG KONG was still, of course, much less advanced along the road to dehumanized pragmatism than Singapore, the *terminus ad quem* of the new order. The countries' airports alone, great centers of the Intercontinental Age, revealed the difference between a Babel present and an Esperanto future—Kai Tak was smelly, slovenly, vital with the cheery hucksterism of a sidewalk vendor in an alleyway crowded with laundry and kids; Singapore's Changi, however, with its automatic walkways and waterfalls lit by soft neon, its spotless jewelry stores and exquisite atria, its free telephones in fire-engine red and carpeted departure lounges, each with its own color TV, was the last word in flawless utopianism. Singapore, in fact, I always thought of as McCity, a perfect Platonic model of the Commonweal, as safe and efficient and convenient as McDonald's, and just about as featureless. With its multiplex cinemas, its look-alike office blocks and its theme-park restaurants, the city-state had set up an ideal of anonymous comfort in which everyone could live like an expatriate. And with its leafy, ranch-style homes, its languid, white-tiled malls, a blue sea in the distance and the plastic lyricism of a soft-rock jingle, Singapore resembled nothing so much as a California resort town run by Mormons. Hong Kong, by comprison, was chaotic, clamorous, dirty-fingered New York.

But still Hong Kong was New York only by comparison, and that was the great expat sorrow. For if the horror of New York is that it knows that it is the quickest city in the world, the sadness of Hong Kong is that it knows it too. Everywhere I went in Hong Kong, everyone I met was talking about New York—whenever they were not talking to New York on the phone. And the tone they adopted had the agitation of someone who lives to get ahead and fears that he is falling behind. "This place has the same energy, the same hustle as New York," a longtime settler told me at a party. "But it's unadulterated. There's no culture, no bohemians, no fringe. And in New York, people work so they can enjoy themselves. Here they work so—well, they don't really know why they're working. And in New York, people enjoy life even if they don't enjoy their work, or even if they're not working at all. Here work is life. There's absolutely no difference between the two."

In every café and penthouse, at every brunch and party, New York seemed to hover above Hong Kong as the sparkling apotheosis of all the values it enshrined: Speed, Money, Hard Dazzle. The hottest nightclub in town was Manhattan, the second best was New York, New York. A New York opera company came here once a year, said a Chinese girl from Harvard Business School, but they were never up to scratch; other cultural adornments of the *beau monde* never came at all. Luckily, she added, she would be taking a holiday next week in Manhattan. And some of this repeated frustration might only have reflected the glamour lent by distance, compounded by the wistfulness bred by exile. Part of it probably betrayed the congenital restlessness of the overachiever who finds himself at the top of his world and yet must find new worlds to conquer every day. Most of it, though, seemed to arise from the nervous self-doubt of the expat, who, ruling his small pond, can never forget that he succeeded only by seceding. Whenever I went to an expat party, I thought, with unkind irony, of the sign pinned up on every Hong Kong minibus—"For complainants, please call . . ." For everywhere, the lament continued. New York was prodigal, Hong Kong was only provincial; New York was cosmopolitan, Hong Kong was simply metropolitan; New York was everything, Hong Kong was nothing.

"This is a small town, amateurish," said a chubby Brit at a party, joyful because the next day would find him moving to Tokyo. "I want decency. I want professionalism. The East? It's awful here. I mean, I've been to Thailand and all the rest. But after one day of Asian villages, how much can you see? I know it's terrible, but I'm a businessman. I'm not interested in Asia. If I go away for two days, I can't read the *FT*."

SOMETHING OF THE great terror of the expat—to be trapped between the whirlpool of an incestuous foreigner community and the forbidding cliffs of an outer world that will always be alien—had come home to me in Brunei. Though the gold-plated sultanate was famous for its $350-million palace (complete with a telephone in each of its 2,200 rooms), its $15-billion surplus spread among a population about the size of Colorado Springs' and its per capita income, the highest in the world outside Kuwait, the only Neronian splendors I could find in its torpid capital were a multistory car park, a stadium, two overpriced hotels and a supermarket (which accepted American Express cards). Within two hours of arrival, I had exhausted its main sights—a tiny aquarium and a museum commemorating Winston Churchill on the grounds that Churchill had never been here—and was reduced to reading old copies of *Harper's* in the local library. In the streets, I saw tired-looking Mummies in sundresses leading whining children by the hand, and in the Grill Room (a pubby place with barrels of sherry on its walls and place mats representing the churches of Albion), red-faced Brits sullenly knifed their steaks while their Malay mistresses gaily chattered away. By my second day in town, I was beginning to see the same faces in the same places, and by my second night I was longing for the days to end. I stayed up till 1 a.m. to watch *I Was a Mail Order Bride* on TV and spent much of a morning reading the local phone book's essay "How to Use a Telephone" (Step #1: "Ascertain from the current issue of the Telephone Directory the number you wish to call"). That evening, at the Sheraton coffee shop, I saw the same Brit sipping what looked like the same $7 celery juice and paging his way through the same worn volume of Angus Wilson. I got on the next bus to the airport, and fled.

YET HONG KONG, I told myself, was in a different league; Hong Kong was a large international city that offered something for everyone. But even in Hong Kong, after three days in town, I began to find spheres overlapping, lines converging, my life noosed into a very small circle. All roads led to home. As I made the rounds of the expat circuit, I found myself playing the same party game of "Do you know so-and-so?" and then remarking, with an ease that left me uneasy, "What a small world!" So-and-so was at Jardine's and her friend was at Morgan Guaranty and she knew him from the *Asian Wall Street Journal*. At first I was excited to learn that a colleague from *Time* lived in the very next house to my school friend Georges. But soon it became apparent that everyone lived next door to everyone else. I had lunch one weekday—*chile rellenos* and Coke—at the place where expats have their weekday lunch—the American Club, forty-seven floors above the world. That night, on the other side of the harbor, in another world filled with young Chinese couples romancing under the stars, I saw my two expat friends from lunch, dressed in black-jacket Gatsby splendor, reeling out of the Regency Hotel in a swirl of laughter and drinks, a sequined Daisy Buchanan teetering along between them. I told Georges I'd like to introduce him to a journalistic couple I'd met in Manila. "Sure," said Georges, "I met him at a party two nights ago given by this girl who reads the news at ATV. Together with his friend Jack." "Really? I met him at brunch last Sunday."

Even the Chinese I met in Macao were silky men in beautifully tailored blue suits with courtly manners who might as well have been Old Etonians, or their neighbors. One told me that his daughters were studying in California. The other described how a friend had lost $2 million in a single afternoon at the casino.

By the time I had been in the Colony a while, I was no longer surprised that Georges, on his first day here, had chanced to meet a fellow from his house at Eton. Where? At a cocktail party, actually.

AFTER A WHILE, moreover, I gathered from party whispers that not all the Brits here were old school types, and not all the fugitives were Chinese. If most Chinese came to Hong Kong to flee the tyranny of classlessness, many Brits had come to escape the rigidity of class. Expatriation in any place is a shortcut to upward mobility, but in Hong Kong, where the British held symbolic sway yet the law of the commercial jungle obtained, the dice were even more loaded. Hong Kong had the jitters of an arriviste.

"I know this Welsh architect. He left a dull job in some grimy town and came over here. Suddenly he had maids, cars, an oceanfront villa in Repulse Bay. The firm paid for his children's schooling and for his private clubs. When his time was up, after thirty-six months, he was willing to do anything—anything at all—to extend his stay. Anything. He was almost begging."

One of the appeals of expatriation, I had always thought, was that it allowed one to treat real life as romantic; abroad, one could credit the lies one saw through at home. But one of the dangers of expatriation, I came to see, was that it tempted one to live the lies that would be seen through at home. Expatriation was often just evasion disguising itself as election. Expatriation permitted every john to become a sahib, and every girl to turn herself into le Carré's Lizzie Worthington, and both of them to flourish their new identities before people who could do nothing but defer.

"So this policeman comes here—just a regular British bobby —and all of a sudden here he is, with sixty men at his beck and call, two thousand subordinates in all. You can imagine the exploitation that follows."

Thus the trappings of expatriation became traps, and a freedom from attachments never did quite amount to detachment. Many Brits, I gathered, longed not so much to flee snobbery as to exercise it in a system in which they could at last be on the giving, rather than the receiving, end. Expatriation allowed them to get their revenge on Britain, even as they became more and more British the farther they got from home. Expatriation encouraged them to define themselves by their distance from the world around them, to make their very separation their identity and their exile their home. It did not seem a happy exchange.

"Most typical English people, middle-class, come here," explained a twenty-four-year-old Brit I had never met before. "Suddenly they've got an amah. And a fantastic flat. And a fifty-thousand-dollar-a-year housing allowance. And a salary five to ten times higher than they'd ever get in the U.K. And it's a fabulous life. And they also have the natives, who'll do anything for them and whom they can always treat as natives. I find it disgusting. I'm sorry, but I do."

But surely only a very few people fit into that category?

"I'd say about ninety-five percent."

ON MY LAST Wednesday evening in the Colony, I did what expats do on weekday evenings, heading off to the Culture Club, a private joint done up in pinstripe gray and black with a video screen in the bar playing old Bogart movies and sleek young beauties serving up "Nouvelle Japonesque" dishes (popular, I suspected, less because it was Japanese than because it reeked of Nouvelle York). By way of matters domestic, I and my three executive hosts discussed our home from home in the Colony, Cathay Pacific. I had chosen to fly with them, I said, not because they served free drinks in economy, or because they recruited their hostesses from all the Asian nations, but mostly because they seemed to be the only Eastern airline that stocked *Sports Illustrated*. Also, I added, I half hoped to meet the girlfriends of my expat school friends on the flights; most of them, by all accounts, were Cathay girls.

With that, the conversation perceptibly perked up. Of course, said my hosts; Cathay girls were the main reason for being here. Cathay girls were one's social life. Cathay girls were one's principal diversion. If one flew a lot—and one did, since one almost lived on planes—one couldn't fail to get to know a lot of Cathay girls pretty well. Swire's employees had the first pick, of course, since they worked for the same company, but every expat was in with a chance. The girls were bivouacked at the YWCA in Kowloon, but it was never hard to get around the visiting-hour restrictions. One of my hosts, by virtue of living in Bangkok, had a special expertise in the habits of Cathay girls from Thailand. They often went to a special Vietnamese restaurant in Kowloon, he said, but they could also be found at the Sawadee Thai restaurant, which was owned by a couple of Cathay girls from Thailand. The real Cathay aficionado, however, was said to be the absent Chris. He knew so many Cathay girls so well that on one celebrated occasion, he had stepped onto a plane and seen a girl he had once dated. Then he had looked up and there was another. And then a third. For the entire flight, like some figure from a Tony Curtis movie, he had had to keep his face hidden inside his copy of the airline magazine. Nowadays he flew only with Singapore Airlines.

Certainly, my hosts assured me, I could hardly leave Hong Kong without meeting a few Cathay girls. Come to dinner on Friday, one of them offered, and I'll round up a few Cathay girls to come with us to the Vietnamese restaurant.

"For girls," confided an American headhunter at another party, "you've got to go to the Chinese community."

"Funny thing, you know," said a British merchant-banker, shaking his head at lunch. "Most of my female friends here are Oriental. But all my male friends are British."

"You know, over here, you really become something of an experience freak," said an American sales executive. "You just get lost in your self-created universe. Did I tell you about the girls at the Regency Hotel in Bangkok?''

ON MY LAST night in Hong Kong, a Friday, I did what expats do on Friday evenings when there isn't a party to go to: I went out for a meal with some Cathay girls. But two of the girls, as it turned out, were flying that evening and the other was "kind of committed." Next time I came through, said my host consolingly, he'd come through with some Cathay girls for dinner. In the meantime, though, he could show me what expats do when Cathay girls are busy.

At the cocktail hour, we taxied across the harbor to the Regent Hotel and stopped off for a drink there. After dinner in Kowloon, we had a choice between the two places that expats haunt: Rick's Bar or Haley's Rock and Roll Club. The latter sounded more promising to me, so we walked through jumbled streets, letters wriggling vertically into the sky, people scurrying horizontally across the road, all of it a spiced pandemonium. We entered a small dark room. A wild-eyed Brit was jumping up and down on a piano stool and thumping out seventies art-rock songs on an electric keyboard. A long-haired Tamil was singing raucous backup and a couple of bespectacled Chinese who looked like Ph.D. candidates in physics were laying down some pragmatic bass lines. Expats in loosened ties and striped shirts were sprawled around the booths, extending lazy arms around the waists of passing Filipina barmaids. At some of the tables were a few Chinese girls, all ivory cool and Gucci hauteur, indulging their Chase Manhattan dates; against the wall were two British slatterns, eyes too black and skin too red and hair a little too yellow. When the singer told everyone to join in, everyone moaned, together and on cue, "Oh, Carol."

The maniac brought the song to a tidy conclusion and then stopped for a breathy intro to "Won't Get Fooled Again." "I'd like to dedicate this song," he began, "to Bank of America, and to its continued policy of lending money only to those who are unreliable." Wild whoops of laughter greeted the sally, and drunken cries of glee.

The night grew boozier and looser. More rockabilly financial numbers followed. A horn-rimmed Morgan Guaranty type in a blue-and-white-striped shirt and suspenders got up and laid an arm on one of the Filipina waitresses. He whispered something, and she pushed him away with a giggle. The next song, he tried the other barmaid, but she had been warned already. A few minutes later, he came lurching over to the British girls. One of them smiled as he whispered something in her ear, and, standing up, let him lead her through a dance. With that, she returned to her seat. What had he said? her friend asked urgently. "He gave me a thousand dollars [$120]." "What for?" "Just for agreeing to dance with him."

A little later, we left Haley's. My friend had to catch a 6 a.m. flight to Taipei the next morning. For business? No; not business, actually. He was off to see a girl. The same one he'd been to see in Taiwan last weekend? No, this one, as it happened, was different.

And next day, I too was back at Kai Tak, transit lounge in a city of transients, great thoroughfare of the continent. The expat life was spinning around in all its wound-up frenzy. People shouted out goodbyes, hurried to find spare seats, waited for tomorrow. Departure signs clicked over, baggage carousels turned around, red-faced expats marched off to their commuter planes.

People on the make, on the edge, on the run.

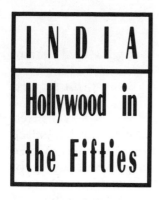

INDIA
Hollywood in the Fifties

 MEMBER OF *my family, I was told when I arrived in India, a handsome man in his late thirties with two children, had been given a year to live. He could not sleep at night, and neither could his family for his constant cries of pain.*

THE MOMENT WAS tense; a group of well-dressed dignitaries had assembled in the imperial palace. The country was in the midst of crisis; turbulence was all around. Then, suddenly, out into the center of the hall came an enormous birthday cake, and out of that popped our strapping hero, dressed as a Jesuit father and playing an antic tune on his fiddle. As soon as she saw him, our sultry heroine fell pouting to her knees. At that, the redeemer ripped off his disguise to reveal a white tuxedo, and the two began blurting out a duet while shaking their hips together in a copy of *Saturday Night Fever*. Instantly, there was joy all round. Scores of onlookers turned into blazered men and bangled and bejeweled houris, writhing and wriggling in unison.

The lead couple shimmied and slithered through a Fred Astaire and Ginger Rogers routine, arching their hips and flashing their eyes as they went. And everyone was happy, everything seemed good. There was plenty of singing and dancing.

Hero and heroine had met only shortly before. He had chanced to see her dragging an old woman through the dust of her palace grounds from the back of her snow-white Chevrolet. Hating such injustice, he had leaped into a horse cart and given chase. In the blink of an eye, he had overtaken the convertible and stood in its path and rescued the old lady. Little did he guess that this was the mother he had never known! And the girl was a princess, pale-skinned, pantsuited and voluptuous, while the man was nothing but a low-caste "tonga wallah." Yet when her eyes flashed with rage, he stared back unterrified. And so it was that their eyes locked and their hearts beat as one and they knew they could never live apart. The rest, in its way, was history.

Meanwhile, the entire country was ablaze with the flames of strife! For its people were under the thumb of a race of wicked despots from across the sea, white of skin yet black of heart. Already, the cruel tyrants had killed a thousand brave fighters at Amritsar; now, merciless fiends, they wished to drain the blood of every Indian in order to sustain their own soldiers. Outside their opulent club hung a sign—"Dogs and Indians Are Not Allowed." Inside, the shameless imperialists sat around a swimming pool, sipping wine as they ogled slinky girls in bikinis.

And then, without a warning and out of nowhere, who should come to the rescue but Our Hero? Sending his tonga crashing through the club's french windows, he rode into the pool to deliver an impromptu sermon in his heroic baritone; then, striding out, he seized a shaven-headed villain by the throat, forced him to drink Indian beer, kicked him into the water and began playing the drums on his head. And by the hero's side came Moti, the Wonder Dog, and behind them both the Wonder Horse, a silver stallion willing to risk anything in the cause of freedom. The Wonder Dog lifted his leg on the Empire. The Wonder Horse galloped this way and that. And the Wonder Man rubbed a foreigner's bloody nose into the detested sign until it blotted out one of the hateful words. Now the sign read: "Dogs and Indians Are Allowed." Jubilation! Ecstasy! Liberation! Joyfully, the crowd jumped up and followed its hero through a great deal of singing and dancing!

And so the humble tonga wallah led the downtrodden masses to freedom. He rescued poor babies, he lectured the oppressed, he brought speech to the dumb and made the lame to walk. He even, in the manner of a holy man, broke a coconut on his head. The dastardly British tried everything they could to stop him. They locked him up. They tied him up. They beat him up. They made him enter a gladiatorial arena and fight to the death the father he had never known. But nothing could stop him, neither Man nor Nature. Fearless in the fight for freedom, he burned effigies of Dyer and smashed a statue of Curzon. Like a good son, he embraced his father when he learned that he had been exchanged at birth for another. Like a good hero, he was ready at a pinch to wink and wiggle with his beloved. And like a good Hindu, he was as pious as he was playful: at his foster mother's grave, he sorrowfully performed all the appropriate devotional rites before scattering her ashes on the Ganges.

And so, like a god from the heavens, he brought justice and democracy and happiness back to the afflicted land. Right beat Might. Love conquered all. The people were redeemed. And always there was plenty of singing and dancing.

The masses called him "Mard" (He-Man).

Mard was the cultural event of the season when I was in India. "Mard," shouted the monstrous, many-colored hoardings that towered above the streets of Bombay. "Mard," proclaimed the huge trailers splashed across the newspapers. *Mard* was the subject of passionate debates and diatribes. A single name was on a million minds and lips across the country: Mard.

Mard was a match made in celluloid heaven. Its director was Manmohan Desai, godfather of the blockbuster, the Spielberg of the subcontinent. Its star, returning to the screen after too long an absence, was Amitabh Bachchan, the country's Clint Eastwood, Robert Redford and Sylvester Stallone all rolled into one. And Amitabh was not only India's leading man for a decade, and something of a risen god, and a personal friend of Rajiv Gandhi's, but also, now, a member of Parliament. The Wonder Dog, the Wonder Horse, a nationalist theme, a staggering $4 million budget—*Mard* had everything!

But it promised even more. It promised to bring king-size entertainment back to the giant screen. It promised, like *Rambo*, to reverse history, to redress the past and, once and for all, to render to the devil of colonialism what belonged to the devil. It promised to boost the prestige of the new generation of young politicians who belonged to the ruling Congress (I) party, exemplified by Amitabh. It even promised to come to the rescue of the embattled movie industry by punishing its hated rivals; fully $800,000 of the budget had reportedly gone to releasing the movie simultaneously across the country, a preemptive strike against the shameless pirates of the video market. And so, only days before Divali, the Hindu Festival of Lights, Amitabh came down like a god from the heavens into 250 theaters at once, a man of the streets, yet larger than life, here to bring law and order and romance—as well, of course, as a good deal of singing and dancing.

The response was titanic. Performances were sold out for days in advance at every cinema in town. Black marketeers did a roaring trade in heavily marked-up tickets. Those who were still unable to get in had had to content themselves with scratchily pirated videos. And the people rose as one to acclaim the spectacle. As the ads in the newspapers declared, "Record Crowds Hail the Man of the Masses!"

SUDDENLY, SAID THE *servant, just a few days earlier, the lady had lost consciousness. There was no explanation for it. "There was little blood," he recalled. "Nobody knew. It was a sweet death."*

INDIA, I HAD always thought, was humanity itself, an inflation of humanity, an intensification of humanity. The very scale of the place was fantastic: 16 major languages and 1,652 dialects and more than 2,000 castes and at least five main religions and 500 former kingdoms and thousands upon thousands of gods (many of them like humans, only more so). In India, the numbers alone were staggering—hundreds killed in each bus accident, thousands lost in a natural disaster, hundreds of thousands born each day. India, I often felt, was humanity itself, only more so.

Indian movies were India, only more so.

The Indian film industry makes twice as many movies each

year as its American counterpart. Almost 100 million movie tickets are sold in India every week. Nearly 5,000 touring theaters travel year-round from village to village—more mobile projection units, in short, than there are theaters in Britain. Recently, of course, the industry had been torpedoed from two sides—the sudden 1984 explosion of the Doordarshan government-owned television network, which quickly reached a viewership of more than 50 million people each night, as well as the mounting invasion of video (at last count, some 40,000 video libraries, together with 12,000 video-equipped coaches, had seized almost 60 percent of the movie market). Yet still the film industry continued unvanquished, grinding out 800 or more movies each year, in several different languages, from all parts of the country, most of them mega-shows that brought superstars and monster hits by the score to the giant screen. When it came to the production of dreams—or gods—India had the biggest, busiest, noisiest industry in the world.

It was hard to ignore. I flew into Bombay, late at night, and as my relatives drove me into town, I saw hordes of men in white shirts, hundreds of them, filing along the narrow road in the dark. Was this part of the Divali festival, I asked. "No, no," said my aunt. "Movies. The drive-in." She pointed out into the dark. And there, under the moon, sending images across the fields and over the tumbledown shacks, watched in wonder by hundreds of people beside the trees, was a silver screen.

As we drove into the heart of the city—still bustling less than an hour before midnight—we passed through a gallery of hand-painted, twenty-foot billboards screaming of the latest cinematic delights, and from all the cabs and shacks and shops I heard what I always think of as the sound track of Indian life, the shrill, squeaky lilt of a woman's voice delivering movie songs that spill out from radios and cassettes in an endless stream of good cheer. The tiny, hundred-yard street where I was staying, my cousins told me, was known as Hollywood Lane, in honor of all the movie stars who lived here. Another of my uncles, I was told, had just bought a flat next to Zeenat Aman, screen darling of the subcontinent. My grandmother was still putting up a pair of lodger-brothers who were still putting up thousands of rupees in the hopes of making more rupees out of movies. The legend was all around.

Early the next morning, I was awakened by a cry from the street. I went out to the balcony to see what was happening, and found a mustachioed impresario wheeling a movable merry-go-round from house to house, calling out as he went for customers. The four brightly colored cars in his sad-happy carousel had "Feat," "Empala," "Toita" and "Maruti" painted on their fronts, and on their sides, the names of movies. The same names shouted out at me from the streets, from the newspapers, from signs beside the temples. Hindi movies were everywhere in India.

But Hindi movies were everywhere in other parts of Asia too, especially where there was little else to be seen. I saw Indian films in village theaters in Nepal and Indonesia. I was cross-questioned about Amitabh by a middle-aged woman in Burma. I saw an Australian documentary on the Indian industry in Japan. "Nahi, nahi," sang the laughing girls in the shops of Bali whenever they saw me passing (in honor of the coquettish demurrals of Hindi-movie starlets), and when I sat down on a nearby beach, they collected around me in excited numbers. Did I know Amitabh? Was Dharmendra still married to Hema Malini? What was the story with Shashi Kapoor? I go to a Hindi movie every day of the week, even if I have to borrow the money, said a Balinese girl; I have 250 tapes of Hindi sound tracks, said a boy.

Even more surprisingly, Hindi movies were not just everywhere in Asia; they were everywhere in the world. A Turkish cabdriver once gave me a lecture on Raj Kapoor as we drove to Istanbul's airport at 4 a.m., while a Greek au pair in England once explained how she had first seen the Kapoors at home in her tiny island village. Raj Kapoor's *Aswara* was one of the most popular foreign movies ever seen in the Soviet Union, and in Eastern Europe the same filmmaker was said to be more famous than Nehru or Gandhi. I once saw a Hindi classic playing in Peru, and, five minutes from my office in midtown Manhattan, I once sat through a seven-hour double bill at the Bombay Cinema. "The Gulf, Mauritius, Fiji," recited a Bombay movie producer, listing some of the top markets for his films. In all, Hindi movies were exported to more than a hundred countries around the world.

By now, indeed, the Hindi cinema had penetrated every level of society, from critics to laymen, in First World and Third. Yet the movies' popularity remained strongest and truest in the heartland. All across the world, unlettered peasants who could barely follow the unsubtitled dialogue crowded each night into village huts to marvel at images of Amitabh. The Hindi cinema seemed to strike some universal chord in the common man, and in his longing for an uncommon redeemer.

MY SECOND DAY *in India, a man was asked about a close friend. She was praying, he said, and a candle fell on her. "After four days, she died."*

THE INDIAN FILM industry is the very model of a mass-production system. It manufactures films in masses, aimed at the masses, and distinguished largely by their mass. Every hero in the popular Hindi cinema is plump and every heroine chunky (as a sign of prosperity); so too every movie is overweight, at least two and a half hours long, with a minimum of six song-and-dance routines and a frenzied cornucopia of sex and violence, fights and seductions. The audiences for Hindi movies do not want just to see a love story, a crime melodrama, a musical, a domestic tale or a moral parable—they want to see them all, with every spice and every ingredient stirred together in a single epic concoction.

And what the audience wants, it gets. The Hindi movie industry is popular art in its highest, or its lowest, form; democracy in action. Filmmakers find out what the people want, and then produce it and produce it and produce it, ad infinitum and ad nauseam. Since four out of five Hindi pictures are never completed, risks are not encouraged. If an actor makes a hit with the crowds, he will be asked to star in almost every movie ever made; if a scene plays well—an actress emerging from the ocean in a clinging sari, for example—it will be ritually reproduced in picture after picture. Every movie becomes a mulligatawny stew in which all genres are thrown together to make what is known as a *masala* (mixed spice) movie. So too, the sound track of every film is a catholic cacophony of bouzouki tunes, Motown choruses, ancient ragas, rock chords, classical music from East and West and anything else that may stir up excitement. Novelty and surprise are no more prized in the Indian movie industry than in litanies or hymns. Formula is content.

Thus the big Hindi movies are mass-produced in assembly-line fashion. For twenty years, the same few stars have been moving their lips to the same kind of songs dubbed by the same few singers. All the stars, moreover, look just about the same: the men, Burt Reynolds look-alikes to a man, their beloveds, the spitting image of Cher after a decade of heavy meals. And all the movies feature much the same plots, the same sequences, even the same sets (some Bombay residents pull down $6,000 a month by hiring out their bungalows to a succession of different movie crews).

Thanks to this unvarying sameness, the principals themselves must often be as omnipresent as the deities they impersonate. Thus the facts grow ever more fantastic. Shashi Kapoor has at times been signed to act in 140 films simultaneously, and many actors routinely whiz each day from one set to another, and then to a third (sometimes delivering the lines from one movie in another, without, it seems, adverse effect); the leading song-writers have to churn out the scores of two entire musicals each week; one moviemaker is so busy that he has to direct his films over the phone; and the main playback singer, Lata Mangeshkar, has completed 30,000 recordings—a world record—and even now, in her late fifties, produces the same high, girlish tones as when first she conquered the scene more than thirty years ago.

Hindi movies even have the same audiences time after time. A large percentage of their revenues, a critic told me, comes from "repeat viewers." "Many people are going to see *Saagar* ten times," he explained. "You mean," I asked, incredulous, "that they'd rather see *Saagar* ten times than see *Saagar* nine times and *Mard* once?" He smiled indulgently at my innocence. "Of course not: they will see *Saagar* ten times, and they will see *Mard* ten times."

There were, of course, many practical reasons for this deadly consistency. Foremost among them was the heterogeneity of the audience. There is probably no country in the world more diverse than India, divided as it is by races, religions, regions, castes and a jangled kaleidoscope of special needs. Romu Sippy, a Bombay producer, gave me an eminently sensible explanation for why the tried way was the true way. "Mythological films are not popular," he said, "because they offend the Muslim people. Regional films are okay, but they cannot appeal to people who do not speak the language. If you make a *dacoit* [bandit] movie, you miss out on the South, where they don't have *dacoits*. Western-ized movies may be popular among the educated young people of the cities, but what about the rickshaw wallah, the small vendor, the villager? If you get an Adult Certificate [equivalent to an X], you miss out on the young audience. If you make a good, clean film, it may be well received by the critics, but commercially it will do nothing. Even a little sex is likely to offend the orthodox Hindu in Uttar Pradesh who goes to see a film first to find out if it's suitable for his daughters. The only thing that all people can relate to and understand is *action*."

Heaven help any filmmaker who chooses to depart from this scheme. "There's no corporate financing here," explained Sippy, "no insurance. Every commercial film is independently pro-duced." His unspoken implication was spelled out for me by Iqbal Masud, perhaps the leading movie critic in Bombay. As a tax commissioner for thirty-seven years who had long moon-lighted as a critic, Masud had seen the business from both sides of the tracks. There was only one way, he explained, for pro-ducers to raise the $1.75 million needed to bankroll a typical blockbuster: black money. As soon as they were backed by mobsters, producers could guarantee a good return on their investment—by paying a respectable businessman $50,000, say, to lend his name to the film, or by slipping a few critics $4,000 each for their appreciative notices. Having had their projects underwritten by gangsters, however, the producers were hardly inclined to risk failure in the service of High Art.

And so the logic of filmmaking proceeded, as simple as ABC or QED. The producers knew what the masses liked. They also knew what they could do. It did not take a master syllogist to work out the bottom line.

Sippy, in fact, evinced little embarrassment at the compro-mises the form demanded. "Look," he said straightforwardly. "The intelligence of the average moviegoer in India is that of an eleven-year-old. That you must always remember. Look at *Mard* and you'll see what I mean. The Wonder Dog puts up his paw and whistles. It's just berserk. Another movie was made in which a dog has flashbacks, and the whole movie—the whole damned movie—was shown from the dog's point of view. There was even a background song sung by the dog, saying, 'Oh, my master, you left me and I miss you.' In the end, of course, the dog avenges his master.

"Yes, I know that in the West you have Lassie, Benji, the Lady and the Tramp. But this is just crazy." Maybe so, I thought. But in the West we also have *E.T.* And *Jaws*. And R2D2. America has sent Bugs Bunny as its emissary to every continent, and installed Mickey Mouse as a patron saint in many a Third World land. The Paramount head office once cabled Cecil B. De Mille that "what the public demands today is modern stuff, with plenty of clothes, rich sets and action." And the United States does not have a 65 percent illiteracy rate, or half its population living under the poverty level.

As we went on talking in his Bombay office (a plush carpeted place on the second floor of a fantastically run-down old house, its polished shelves full of books on Hitchcock and Sam Goldwyn), Sippy laid out for me, with a craftsman's clarity, the nuts and bolts of an Indian movie. In every case, he said, there must be a hero, a hero's friend (often a clown), a heroine, a vamp and a villain (I thought of *The Two Gentlemen of Verona*). If the hero was rich, the heroine was poor, and vice versa (I thought of *Romeo and Juliet*). If there was a poor hero, he had an aging mother; if a rich heroine, there was a strict father (*Much Ado About Nothing*). And the poor must always conquer the rich (*Coriolanus*).

"Look at Manmohan Desai," he continued. "All his films have the same pattern. Always there are two brothers who get lost in childhood—one good, one bad." (I thought of *King Lear, The Comedy of Errors*.) "Then they meet in adulthood, and fight one another, and then they gang up and kill the villain." What about the women? "Yes," he said, a little impatient at my simplicity. "The good brother loves the heroine. The bad brother loves the vamp. And if he's very bad, at the end he will save the hero's life and die." And all this was unvarying? Well, he added, sometimes there were three brothers. "And every successful Hindi film has a vendetta," he went on. "Action and a vendetta." Oh, and one more thing, added Sippy—all Indian movies are nothing more than *The Taming of the Shrew*.

And then, of course, there was the formula fairy tale about the wicked queen with the poisoned apple, and the rogue who steals into the sleeping beauty's bedroom, and the princes who are raised as shepherds and must prove themselves in battle, and the god who suddenly appears onstage, and the nearly murdered girl dressed as a boy who wakes up next to the decapitated clown, and then the grand finale where everything is resolved, and everyone is reunited, and twenty-eight plot strands are brought together, and love wins out, and hero marries heroine, and children are returned to parents, while the country is rescued from its conquerors. But that was *Cymbeline*, and they hadn't turned that into a Hindi movie yet.

Just about then, though, Sippy, having itemized all the right moves of the Hindi formula movie, took me by surprise. "In America," he said, "it's not so different, is it? I have seen so many versions of *First Blood*. Look at the Chuck Norris picture *Missing in Action*. There are lots of replicas."

I thought back to the offerings of the summer just past. Most of the movies advertised in the papers had been teen-pix sex-comedies—the bastard progeny of *Porky's*—and horror movies spun off from *Halloween, Halloween II* and *Halloween III*, themselves the linear descendants of *Psycho*. There were the usual Clint Eastwood and Burt Reynolds pictures in which the stars played their usual larger-than-life selves. There were some third-generation musicals and shoot-by-number Bond flicks. But the biggest hits of the summer, as usual, were the Stallone action sequels (full of formula patriotism and common-man heroism) and the latest pastiches from the Spielberg factory. Nearly every big picture was simply a combination of big names (Redford and Streep, Streep and De Niro, De Niro and Duvall, Duvall and Pacino, Pacino and Sutherland, Hepburn and Nolte, Nolte and Murphy, Murphy and Aykroyd . . .), or a remake, or an out-and-out, in-and-out exploitation movie.

As I was thinking this, there came a knock on the door, and a servant brought Sippy the latest issue of *Variety*. He turned quickly to the box-office listings, and we pored over them together. At the top was *Commando*, and beneath it a battalion of look-alike action movies, the sons of Rambo, the grandsons of Bronson, the Western cousins of Bruce Lee.

"AH, THESE PEOPLE," *said my aunt as we drove past the beggars and slums of Bombay on the day after my arrival. "It makes you shed tears. Real tears."*

THE INDIAN MOVIE industry is the biggest, the most popular, the closest to the heartland of any in the world. But the American is still regarded as the best. Hollywood, not Bombay, is the capital of glamour, the nerve center of show biz, the source of every trend. And so, quite sensibly, Bombay takes its cues from Hollywood; what goes down well in America goes up quickly on the screens of India. And what is today in India is tomorrow around the world.

Sometimes, I learned, the Indians take no more than a label from America (Satyajit Ray shoots some of his movies in a complex called Tollywood, and a typical Hindi movie stars "Sunny" and "Jackie"). Sometimes they simply appropriate a kind of trend (while I was in Bombay, the cover story of the *Illustrated Weekly*, the grandfather of Indian magazines, its *Saturday Evening Post* or *Life*, discussed India's new generation of "movie brats," who "bring to their craft a remarkable understanding of celluloid and a professionalism rarely seen in the industry"). Sometimes, the Indians take over a great notion (creating the "curry Western," for example, simply by dressing up Amitabh in a cowboy hat). Sometimes, they even lift specific tricks—a chase from *Raiders of the Lost Ark* here, a plot development from James Bond there, now a camera technique from *One from the Heart*, now a dance sequence from *Saturday Night Fever*. Often, though, it is easiest to pilfer the entire movie.

The heist was managed easily enough, an editor of a movie mag explained. By hook or by crook, through contacts in the West or relatives in the Gulf, each of the Bombay movie moguls got hold of a video of the latest Western hit. Often, they were in possession of such tapes within two months of the movie's U.S. release and before it had even been shown in Britain. No sooner had the last credit rolled across their screens than they furiously set about cranking out frame-by-frame remakes. Thus, for example, five separate replicas of *Death Wish* had assaulted the screens of India almost simultaneously.

Other American tricks could be deployed in post-production. Telling me of a "lovely" article in *The Hollywood Reporter* about the use of teasers and trailers, Sippy said that he planned to follow the precedent of *Rambo*, which had been previewed to the public through teasers in 1,000 different cinemas. Promotion could likewise benefit from the wisdom of the West. One of the most popular ads in Bombay during my stay showed a hairy-chested he-man waving a gun while flames erupted behind him; on another billboard, an incredible hulk with scars on his chest and murder in his eyes straddled the world under the legend "He Is the Answer to Every Challenge." These two like-minded movies were certainly well advertised, I thought, as I saw the same image staring down at me from hoarding after ad after hoarding. Only when I turned to an entertainment newspaper and there found three separate full-page ads showing bestial he-men bestriding the world, bloodied, bare-chested and brandishing a deadly weapon, did I realize that all the ubiquitous ads were not selling just two movies, but several: one image served all. If Rambo did not exist, the Indian moviemakers would have had to invent him.

The process of turning an American movie into an Indian one was not very difficult, Sippy explained, but it did require a few changes. "The Americans like a straightforward story line," he explained, "something uncomplicated. An Indian audience likes everything complicated, a twist and turn every three reels." In addition, he continued, the Indian hero had to be domesticated, supplied with a father, a mother and a clutch of family complications. "Take *Rambo*, for example. Rambo must be given a sister who was raped. He must be made more human, more emotional. His plight must be individualized—not just an obscure vendetta against the system." Also, of course, there had to be some extra flourishes. "The average U.S. movie is only ninety minutes long; the average Hindi picture lasts a hundred and forty minutes. So we must add singing, dancing, more details." And since even kissing, not to mention nudity, had long been banned in India, explicitness and expletives had to be toned down, while suggestiveness had to be turned up. "Let's say a Western movie shows a typical society woman. In the West, she will sleep with ten different guys, and everyone takes it. But in India, we will make her just a high-society lady. We want puritan characters." Even so, the buxom puritan would doubtless be obliged to play much of the movie in miniskirts, wet saris and nighties. The Indian adaptation would, in effect, be faithful to its model, but bigger, broader, louder. In the Indian cinema, nothing succeeds like excess.

Thus the skill in producing Hindi movies lay less, it seemed, in making excellent pictures than in deciding which ones could be profitably copied. The obscure Hemingway-sister movie *Lipstick*, for example, had been popular, because it featured the two favorite themes of Indian movies, rape and revenge; Bronson movies were always good, since they turned on vigilantism; more surprisingly, Erich Segal's *Man, Woman and Child* (thanks, perhaps, to its domestic focus) had inspired two adaptations. Sippy himself was famous for his version of *Seven Brides for Seven Brothers*. Another perfect candidate for translation, he said, would be *The Natural*. "Just change baseball into cricket," he explained, "and it's a perfect Hindi movie. The dying father. The heroine and the vamp. The bolt of lightning from the heavens. The hero who somehow triumphs." And the implausibility of the original was, if anything, more a help to the adapter than a handicap. "How can you believe that the guy's in a stadium with a hundred thousand people and he can see one bloody woman standing up? But it's stirring."

I mentioned *Flashdance*, which had just arrived in Bombay, as another seemingly ideal source for a remake. It had, after all, a poverty-stricken, dark-haired girl with a gift for suggestiveness and a soulful, slightly fat-faced hero. The heroine had a lonely fairy godmother and a friend, the friend had parents who rallied round her during times of stress. The movie also had a likable comic figure, a pair of cartoonish villains and a potential Wonder Dog; lots of neon glitz and a rush of titillating song-and-dance sequences that had nothing to do with anything. It even had an inspirational it-pays-to-dream story line and a moral. "No," said Sippy, "it's too subtle for the Indian audience. It's too understated. At the end, for example, Alex leaves her audition and simply embraces her boyfriend; in India, the scene would have to be spelled out."

I received a more personal angle on the differences between the Eastern and Western approaches to filmmaking one day when I happened to run into Persis Khambatta, the only Indian actress to have recently made it to Hollywood. An unofficial repertory company of Indians is always on hand to stock the quiet art-house movies of James Ivory and Ismail Merchant, or to fill any PBS series about the subcontinent; Shashi Kapoor and Saeed Jaffrey, and more recently Victor Banerjee and Art Malik and Roshan Seth, are coming to seem almost as ubiquitous in "quality productions" as John Gielgud or Alan Bates. But these characters play to small audiences in small movies that show in small theaters. Khambatta, by contrast, had followed the golden brick road all the way to *People* magazine.

When I met her, however (feeding info to a gossip rag; even bad publicity was better than no publicity at all), Khambatta did not seem to be on the ascendant. She was, in fact, returning to the Hindi cinema. When I asked her about this—it sounded a little like going from riches to rags—she made a virtue of necessity, perhaps, by donning the sackcloth demeanor of an ascetic anxious to draw closer to her roots. The offer to return to India could not, she said, have come at a more propitious moment; at the time she received the call, she explained, she was cooking Indian food and all her thoughts were of the homeland. The summons seemed like a good omen. "I have to touch the ground of India every year," she continued. "I want to marry an Indian guy and come back here for good. I have to." On and on she raced, unstoppable. "Yes, the others in the industry think I'm crazy. But I need India. I want to be here. This Hindi picture I've just finished shooting is a great *masala* movie. I get to cry. I get to laugh. I get to dance. I play a schoolgirl in braids and a seducer. In the West, acting is all a matter of control. Here it's all emotion. Indians have a lot of guilt, lots of emotion. In the U.S., the more control, the more excellent; here I get to sob and sob and sob." And when, in the course of shooting, she had had to grieve over her film mother's coffin, said Persis, she simply looked across the set to where her real mother was standing, and the tears came freely.

There were, perhaps, a few other reasons for this sudden rush of patriotism (even as I talked to Persis, another Prodigal Child was returning to India—Bhagwan Rajneesh, who was being deported from the United States amid charges of fraud and clouds of rumors about free-love orgies and drug running and now proclaimed that the motherland he had quit only three years earlier was the greatest country in the world). Before our conversation was over, Persis had reeled off for me, unsolicited, all the movies she had made in Hollywood. Only two of the titles were familiar—*Nighthawks* and *Star Trek*—and in the latter, the most famous of her roles, the Wilhelmina model and former

Miss India had been forced to play the entire movie with a shaven head, an indignity to which I could hardly imagine Jessica Lange or Kathleen Turner submitting. Though she had certainly cornered the market on Indian females, Persis herself admitted that she was seldom offered more than one role a year. And that was always the part of an "exotic."

IF THE INDIAN industry was Hollywood made thirty times larger, however, it was also Hollywood turned back thirty years. For one thing, its production musicals still operated on a superstar system, still reveled in Busby Berkeley–style show stoppers and still favored grand religious themes with epic casts. For another, it had spawned a whole shadow industry of fanzines and gossip rags, *Cine Blitz* and *Filmfare* and *Movie* and 600 others that diligently bit the hand that fed them. Now, moreover, it was being challenged for the first time ever by television. "It's just like Hollywood in the fifties," said a Bombay producer, boasting that TV would simply inspire moviemakers to fight back with bigger and therefore better films. "It's really like Hollywood in the fifties," said a leading movie critic, pointing out that the early movies of the Indian cinema, full of Cowardian repartee and Shavian wit, had given way to musical spectaculars. "The scene is just like Hollywood in the fifties," said the editor of *Stardust*, the biggest movie mag. "There are affairs! Love children! Abortions! Even bigamy!"

The moviegoing public seemed equally old-fashioned—even when it came to foreign films. At the Regal cinema in central Bombay ("the Home of Great Motion Pictures"), the big hits of the past year had been *Gone with the Wind* and *Ben-Hur*. Around the corner, one of the few other English-language cinemas in town was showing *The Sound of Music*. And one day I turned to the *Times of India* to consult the movie page and there found a new release advertised as "one of the all-time great love stories." Farther down, I discovered that the movie in question was the doggy Disney cartoon *Lady and the Tramp*.

HOLLYWOOD AGAIN CAME to mind the day I visited Film City, a studio complex on the outskirts of Bombay. The skies were a brilliant blue above the scrub hills, and the dry ridges seemed a perfect vantage point for a posse to scan the horizon for stray Indians. Inside the run-down complex ("We Solicit Silence," said the sign at the entrance), nine or ten movies were in production (some of them doubtless featuring exactly the same actors, in much the same roles). Taking a seat on a sunlit patch of grass, I spent the next couple of hours watching the filming of a complex, if formulaic, pas de deux that would grace a movie called *Pyaasi Raat* (*Thirsty Night*).

A few men held up reflecting mirrors and a couple of assistants stood behind small cameras. Three bigwigs sat on director's chairs. Twenty or so others stood around getting a free taste of saucy entertainment. The principals, I gathered, were a pretty young girl in red thigh-length boots and heavy makeup, wearing a short dark blue frock that left her midriff bare, and a rotund swain dressed from head to toe in spotless white, with a T-shirt that declared, with brute simplicity, "Break Dance."

The scene called for the girl to approach the man, shaking her hips and wriggling her breasts. She was to slink up behind him, curl her body around his, stroke his face and put her uptilted head first on his left shoulder, then on his right. He was to break away, sending her into a frenzy of frustration. The scene picked up again with him standing contemplative against a tree (the same tree, I thought, heart beating, that had served as a love nest in a thousand Hindi movies through the ages). She had to approach him again, wind her body around his and then, pinning him against the trunk, lift her head for a kiss. When he recoiled, she was to push him down to the ground, hover over him where he lay and then, as she leaned down to kiss him, lose her balance so that the energetic couple would tumble over and over in the grass. This complicated movement was set to some capering melody, and throughout the contortions, the actress had to lip-synch (with the emphasis on lips) a tune sung by Lata Mangesh-kar, or someone exactly like her.

The two went into action. "Come on, Kammy darling," urged the behind-camera choreographer—a slinky, very dark lady in sunglasses and a negligent robe—as the onlooking crowd tensed with excitement, "Vikky love, get closer." The two writhed together uncomfortably as the music bounced merrily along. Cut!

Out slithered the choreographer to give Kammy a few lessons in wriggling and flouncing. "Shake your hips like this, lovey," she began, and toss your hair like this and narrow your eyes this way, and open your lips that way. When you rub against him, touch him like this; when you fall on top of him, tumble like this.

She danced back behind the camera, and Kammy practiced her moves. The onlookers stared on happily. "More sexy, love," came the choreographer's cry. "More sexy. Like this!"

IT WAS NEVER difficult, of course, to mock the Hindi cinema, to find fault with everything from the coarseness of its moves to the poverty of its imagination. Fairy-tale plots, broad innuendos, unquestioned piety, heroes and villains, a weakness for spectacle and a shrewd determination to give the groundlings what they wanted—all, of course, were the essence of Chaucerian or Shakespearean art. But Hindi movies remained—critics forbid!—irredeemably vulgar. They were as fat and fleshy and cartoonish as the characters they celebrated. They played—no, pandered—to the lowest common denominator in mankind. Why on earth did they always have to be so loud, so bright, so broad?

One answer, perhaps, was that they were reflections of the world around them. Movies were everywhere in India. But then everything was superabundant in India: signs, shrines, spices, smells, men, gods, beggars, cows, sobs, titters, marvels, horrors and more marvels. India itself seemed all perpetual motion and emotion, an overfull, overbright, overdone triptych by Hieronymus Bosch. Here was life, not on the grand, but on the epic scale, the Human Comedy, the Human Tragedy, played out on streets filled with too many people, too many feelings, too many schemes. India itself was simply too much.

The country's recent history alone was something of a tumultuous spectacle, piled higher with incident and thicker with Tragedy, Comedy, Melodrama—proliferative plotting and nonstop action—than any movie on earth. In the few months before I arrived in India, its longtime, risen-and-fallen-and-rerisen Prime Minister had sent her army to storm a sacred golden shrine, and then had been killed by her own bodyguards. Her son, who had never before held office, became Prime Minister. Riots had swept through the capital; men were burned alive, whole settlements were put to the torch, trains rolled through the countryside piled high with bloody bodies. Five weeks later, a cloud of poison gas had escaped from a chemical plant, killing thousands as they slept, in the worst industrial accident in history. Three weeks after that, the world's largest democracy had held a national election. A typhoon in neighboring Bangladesh had killed as many as 20,000 people and swept whole islands into the sea. An Air-India plane had suddenly, inexplicably, fallen from the heavens, and 329 people had been killed, in one of the worst airline disasters ever recorded. A peace agreement between the Hindus and Sikhs had been reached at last, following which the moderate leader of the Sikhs was promptly assassinated by his followers. Meanwhile, civil war continued in Sri Lanka, there was more unrest in Assam and each day brought news of another politician gunned down by turban terrorists.

Yet this constant explosion of eventfulness was, if anything, even more unrelenting on the small scale. For the sights of India are, to a large extent, the streets themselves, and the streets are chaotic open-air stages presenting life in the raw and humanity in the round. Through the avenues of Bombay stream sadhus and shamans, bullock carts and cows, rickshaws, rusty Ambassadors, turbaned men and veiled women, three-legged dogs, two-toed beggars, buses and bicycles and rites and sights and more people, more soldiers, more cows. Bleeding into this pandemonium is the confusion of the temples—not, as a rule, havens of meditation and quiet, but the Indian compendium all over again, a bombardment of sights and sounds and smells, monkeys, flames, chants, offerings, holy men, pilgrims, wonder-workers, musicians, more rites, more sights, more people. The streets of India are swollen with an embarrassment of riches, a richness of embarrassments. And it is on the streets that millions live, make love, defecate, and die.

This sense of febrile hyperactivity clings as tenaciously to Indians as the smell of curry. It assaulted me, indeed, before I had even set foot in the country. No sooner had I stepped into a Bombay-bound Cathay Pacific flight than whole mobs of Indian families began crashing into the cabin behind me, loaded down with VCRs, trailing in their wake five extra pieces of hand luggage, or maybe six, straggling a crush of miscellaneous loved ones and possessions. And no sooner had any of them sat down than they began shouting across the aisles at their children or calling out to relatives or standing up again to order the mostly Chinese cabin attendants to bring drinks and then more drinks. The kids started slithering over seats, their mothers raced to the bathroom, the men took up permanent residence in the aisles and began crying out gossip to friends and presumed enemies several cabins away. The attendants tried to restore order and send people back to their seats, and the scheming and the screaming only mounted. The passengers ordered more drinks and second meals and vegetarian meals and second vegetarian meals, and the attendants told them that none were available. The demands grew louder, the attendants told them to be quiet. The passengers bawled, the attendants snapped. Shouting matches broke out, and all the while, tens of families kept trundling inexorably through the aisles, transporting curries, heirlooms, squalling kids, more pieces of luggage, and then some more. Before long, the arguments turned into all-out, ten-decibel warfare. The attendants shouted their orders, the crowds milled all around. And through it all, a solemn Sikh looked around the cabin sadly, and began philosophizing, as only an Indian can, about mass hysteria. Where did it come from? How was it caused? What did it mean?

Not surprisingly, this sense of fertility run amok had also seeped from the country's textures into its texts. "Indians," John Russell wrote shrewdly, "are prodigious, irrepressible, never-tiring talkers." They are also, he might have added, fabulous raconteurs and rhapsodists, storytellers and sermonizers, purveyors of small talk and big; the garrulous gurus are only the most celebrated examples of the country's indefatigable speechmakers, their books less often written than transcribed from the hundreds of thousands of words they spin out of their mental loom each year. The whole country, it often seems, suffers from a kind of elephantiasis of the imagination; it teems and seethes, Babel-like, with texts on the subject of mortality and divinity. There is no place for the lapidary in India, and irony is quickly lost; amid all the agitation and animation, the only appropriate forms are rhodomontade, litany, hyperbole and exclamation. India's national epic, the *Mahabharata*, fifteen times longer than the Bible, is the longest poem ever written.

Nor is it ever possible to detach oneself from the whole clangorous Indian gallimaufry. Its smell seeped into the third-floor apartment where I stayed, its street cries penetrated the walls. When my car stopped at an intersection, a man carrying a limp child appeared by my side, an amputee began pounding on the windows. When I walked out of a serene Victorian library in central Bombay, a swarm of beggars was instantly around me, unaccommodated and bare. All doors were flung open in India, all boundaries collapsed: everything was thrown together in the streets. And next to this 3,000-ring circus, with a cast of thousands of hundreds of thousands, appearing in your neighborhood twenty-four hours each day, the overcrowded and impossibly melodramatic movies begin to make a little sense. They even begin to look rather small.

FOR FOREIGNERS, WHO do not have to live with the consequences, India's whirligig of earthly horrors and delights may often be the greatest show on earth. "India has everything," said a Yugoslavian girl I met in Tibet. "India is life on the stage," said a Canadian sitting nearby. "India is so different," said a Swiss designer. "I see many good things, also many bad things. The people are so generous, and so selfish." Every trip through India was to some extent a magical mystery tour into chaos and color and commotion. India might not be the easiest or loveliest place in the world, most travelers agreed, but it was surely the most shocking, the most amusing, the most overwhelming; the happiest, and the saddest; the most human—certainly the only country, as Geoffrey Moorhouse writes, "where superlatives were as much in order as adjectives anywhere else." India had everything, and its opposite; and if the West often struck me as a masculine culture, dedicated to assertion, virility and power, while Southeast Asia seemed feminine in its texture, all softness, delicacy and grace, India was both, and neither, as grotesque and fascinating as a hermaphrodite.

Small wonder, then, that India freaked out its visitors, and psyched them out, more than any other place I knew. One night, as I slept in a tiny inn in Kyoto, the screen door was violently pulled back and in stumbled a young Chinese photographer from Hong Kong. Taking one look at me, he registered my origins and began raving. He had just arrived, he said, from the land of my forefathers. "Varanasi," he said, spitting out the name. "They call it a holy city. But it is a filthy city, a stinking city, a city full of shit!" He had had enough, he said, more than enough of "silk men" and a holy river that was only a large-scale bathroom. He had had enough of cosmic dirt. He had had it up to here with the world's most persistent touts. He had had enough of being hounded and harassed. He had been taken, he said, for $350. He had been in India for six weeks, he went on, and six weeks was enough—no, more than enough. He could stand it no longer. And he wanted to go back, and he could talk of little else.

I could to some extent sympathize with his muddle. For few countries engage the sympathies more powerfully than India. Yet so many opposites are so haphazardly blended together in India that it is hard to be unequivocal about anything. Contradiction provides the only consistency—in the people's preservation of a British legacy they are glad to have sloughed off, in their fierce devotion to the clans whose pressures they resist, in the tangled intensities that bedevil every foreigner and find most eloquent expression in the agonized surveys of V. S. Naipaul. To many foreigners, every Indian seems a god or a demon; that, in a sense, is how India possesses them. "And are you liking India?" asks an Indian in Don DeLillo's *The Names*. "Yes," replies the narrator, "although I would have to say it goes beyond liking, in almost every direction."

ALL NIGHT LONG, *I heard, our relative howled and howled with pain. What he was going through, said my uncle, one would not wish on one's bitterest enemies. The cries never ceased.*

AS I ATTENDED more Indian movies, I came in time to discover another of their special pleasures (to be found in the West only at Coppola or Stallone or Boorman movies, or in such freak stunts as *The Long Riders*): the thrill of totting up the recurrences of a single surname in the credits. One poster advertised: "F. U. Ramsay presents Tulsi Ramsay and Shyam Ramsay's *Saamri*, with photography by Gangu Ramsay." Another show was made by Ramesh Sippy, assisted by Vijay Sippy and Al Sippy and produced by G. R. Sippy (none of them, of course, related to Romu Sippy, the producer I met who financed movies directed by his brother). In Rajasthan a pair of voluble rickshaw drivers started reciting the names of the First Family of Indian cinema (their Redgraves or Carradines) as if they were the thousand names of God: "Shashi Kapoor, Shammi Kapoor, Anil Kapoor, Raj Kapoor" (mercifully, they left out Tiger Kapoor, as well as Prithviraj Kapoor, the patriarch of the clan, whose image was shown, reverentially, before every one of Shashi and Raj Kapoor's movies). And so the list went on indefinitely—Satyajit Ray begat the director Sandip Ray, Dharmendra begat Sunny Deol, and Lata Mangeshkar's only rival, and possible successor, as the voice of India, was her sister, Asha Bhosle. After Dimple Kapadia struck it rich as a seventeen-year-old actress, up popped a look-alike sister called Simple Kapadia. Before long, one of my young cousins dryly remarked, there would doubtless be a Pimple Kapadia.

On screen too, the movies invariably paid their respects to the all-powerful and omnipresent Family, which had a way of turning every business into a family business. Mard, for example, had been supplied with a real father and mother, an adopted father and mother, a disguised father and an intricate set of duties to his motherland. "To me," intoned the hero in his famously resonant voice, "Mother is everything." His girlfriend knew she could expect to play only second fiddle in the orchestra of his emotions. And the same would be true of the Indian Rambos, I recalled, thinking back to Sippy's description. Even newspaper horoscopes—the movies' first cousin when it came to mass-producing dreams—tended to focus their advice, not on love affairs, but on family affairs.

The Family, indeed, seemed the strongest of all the forces organizing India's swarming congregation of subsets. It was the power that arranged marriages. It was the binding force that protected people from the centripetal pull of the masses. It was the last word in Indira Gandhi's *India.* And not only were the clans all-powerful; they were also huge. The typical Indian family tree resembles a banyan whose tendrils stretch in every direction and whose roots are cast halfway across the country. The family is the source of identity, and the extended family is the source of an extended identity stretched far and wide (in India, identity seems not to be diminished by being subjugated to a unit, as in Japan, but only strengthened). A typical sentence in India would begin: "Jaygopal's brother's sister-in-law's cousin," and the figure in question would be treated as a brother, worthy of the same affection, open to the same demands. Before long, therefore, the family itself began to seem as many-headed and undifferentiated as the flood it had sought to dam. Family planning had never enjoyed much success here.

With Indian roots myself, I was, perhaps, more aware of the power of family here than in other Asian countries where it was no less suffocating or strong. Nonetheless, it seemed to me that in India the force took on a decidedly Indian flavor. I was amused to find that the Indians had smuggled into English such terms as "co-brother" (to designate one's sister-in-law's brother) and "cousin brother" (to denote the sex of a first cousin, and, better yet, to draw the cousin as close as a brother). In some of the local languages, the terms were even more precisely defined, with separate words for a father's elder and younger brothers and special terms for uncles on one's mother's and one's father's side, as well as words to distinguish between mother's sisters and uncle's wives, blood uncles and uncles by marriage. Though India had a hunger for absolutes, it swarmed with relatives; before long, everyone came to seem related to everyone else.

The enveloping tightness that resulted might be responsible for much of the country's warmth, the hospitality of its embrace; but it also seemed to lie behind many of the country's antagonisms. If the large family made for an extended sense of alliance, it also made for an extended sense of enmity; thus a grievance against one Muslim would vent itself in an attack on all Muslims, a suspicion of all Sikhs assert itself in a mistreatment of one. If there was safety in numbers, there was also terror in numbers. So too, a typical office worker was often trussed up so tightly within an entangling net of obligations to this relative and that one, this one's friend and that one's in-laws, that he had no option but to ignore the general public, leaving the general public with no option but to make demands upon relatives of its own. In the end, the extrapolated sense of identity could smother an individual as much as it protected him.

Much of this, no doubt, was explained—and largely excused perhaps—by Hinduism, with its notion of collective identity. If all are simply parts of a single great Oneness, every individual is related to every other in the Family of Man. One touch of Siva makes the whole world kin.

This all-pervading sense of affiliation was brought home to me in a wonderfully Indian way. Early one morning, I boarded an intercity bus, and found myself next to a gentle civil servant. He could not speak much English, but he summoned every syllable he could recall in order to welcome me to his region and to wish me well. He was not a rich man, he said, or an educated man. But he was a pious man, a Brahmin, rich in his belief. I need never fear, he assured me, for my Atman would survive the death of my body. It was all in the *Bhagavad-Gita*. He had followed the *Gita*'s injunction, he went on, by giving his son the name of God (so that in calling out to his son he felt that he was calling on God). And as he continued, struggling to share increasingly complex metaphysical truths in a language that he clearly found difficult, I commended him on his gallant conquest of English. "Oh yes," he said happily, "your child learns English in school." This was not what I had expected. "What I am saying," he explained, "is that your son learns English in school." I looked daggers at him. Was he making some licentious insinuation about my private life? Or, worse still, trying to marry me off to his daughter? "You see," he went on, taking pity on my clueless-ness, "I say 'your child' and not 'my child' because we are all one. If he is my child, he is also your child. And if I say 'your child,' I am not suffering from pride."

In India, then, even complete strangers were related. But the connections did not end there. One sunny morning, a gardener in Bangalore invited me into his tiny hut. He had only one small room, and its simple decorations caught at my heart: American calendars that showed chocolate-box flowers, swans in flight, blond kids holding hands on a bench. The only other adornment in his modest hut was a large photograph of a beetle-browed lady, and of a couple at a wedding maybe forty years before. His wife had died five years ago, said the man in halting English, and ever since, he felt that he had lost his senses. He never wished to leave his home again; her memory was all he had to live for. And in the corner I noticed a humble shrine, richly decorated with pictures of the elephant-god Ganesh and other religious keep-sakes. There too was a picture of the departed woman, to which each day her husband faithfully applied fresh makeup.

Where the soul was immortal, no relative ever died; the family just kept growing and growing.

But even there the clan did not draw the line. For not only did the dead dwell among the living, but so too, as the gardener's hut reminded me, did the gods. And the issue was further complicated by all the fakers and fakirs and holy men and charlatans who walked the streets, saying that they were nothing less than gods in men's clothing, and adding, sometimes, that the same was true of all of us if only we would awaken to the fact. As the temples merged with the streets, the gods began mingling with mortals. In India, life danced with legend as gracefully as Krishna with the Gopis.

In the face of this ever-swelling swarm of gods and people and relations, a typical Indian could easily feel dwarfed—either buried within the exfoliating structure of the family or simply lost inside the shuffle. But unlike the Japanese, who seemed to have acquiesced in the sacrifice of personal identity, quite a few Indians appeared to hunger for it. Educated Indians are famous for their worship of degrees and diplomas, and for their preoccupation with keeping up with the times, and with the Patels. Many middle-class people I met seemed frankly unembarrassed about presenting themselves as walking entries for Who's Who, and some, I heard, even went so far as to print up calling cards that read "BAABF" (Bachelor of Arts—Appeared but Failed). In India, line jumping had been turned into a fine art, and one-upmanship a popular pastime. This was again, no doubt, symptomatic of a culture that is not by its nature reticent or retiring. But I suspected too that intrusiveness breeds pushiness and that where the pressure of huge numbers and frightful odds is intensified, so too is the longing for distinction.

STILL, I HEARD, *day after day, my relative could not pass a night without screaming out his pain.*

WITH PERSONAL DISTINCTION so elusive amidst the press of the all-consuming crowd, many a common Indian of the masses could only look upward—to the heavens, or to the giant screen. It therefore seemed no coincidence that many movies took their inspiration from traditional myths, throwing fantasy and reality together as liberally as any Shakespearean romance. And it seemed only fitting that every film began with a consultation of an astrologer and a holy *muhurat* ceremony that included the singing of religious songs and the ritual breaking of a coconut.

For in many ways, the movies fulfilled a role scarcely different from that of religion: to an audience not grown too cynical for belief, they brought heroes who were avenging angels, heroines who were full-breasted goddesses.

Thus the divisions between make-believe and reality, between reality and myth, became increasingly foggy. Appearing before the people again and again as a redeemer, with a face five feet high and a ten-gallon gift for heroics, an actor might well disappear within his divine role, hastened on his way by the latter-day mythmakers of the gossip rags. Off screen, moreover, superstars really did live in the manner of all-powerful gods; for his role in *Mard*, Amitabh had earned $500,000, as much as an average Indian would make if he worked for 2,500 years.

When an actor died, therefore, it seemed as if a god had died. While I was in Bombay, the actor Sanjeev Kumar, then in his late forties, suddenly passed away. Within twenty-four hours, the national television network had cobbled together a twenty-five-minute tribute to the Everyman who had come to seem like something more. Rajiv Gandhi issued a public message of sympathy. Thousands gathered outside Kumar's home to pay their final respects, some of them sobbing uncontrollably; and, within three days of the death, a government motion was raised to name a street after him. As had happened on a far grander scale when Sanjay Gandhi died in a plane crash (his demise changing his status from widely suspected rogue to full-fledged martyr), it had taken death to confirm Kumar's status among the immortals.

The greatest figure in the pantheon, however, was Amitabh. His divinity had been recognized even at birth, hagiographers noted, when he was given the name of the mythical King of the Land of the Pure. In 1982, when he suffered a near-fatal accident while performing a stunt, the whole country was stricken: one man walked three hundred miles backwards to persuade the gods to spare his hero, while thousands of people gathered outside his hospital to pray for his recovery and the Prime Minister herself canceled a foreign trip to rush to his bedside. When at last the fallen star arose from his deathbed, many took it to be a kind of resurrection. "God Is Great—Amitabh Lives!" said the signs on the streets; they could as easily have said "Amitabh Is Great —God Lives!"

To his new part, as to all the others, the resurrected star rose like a hero. Every morning, he held mass prayers at home before thousands of prostrate devotees, and the word went around that he could heal the afflicted. When the Hindi cinema released its first 3-D movie, it was Amitabh who came on screen beforehand to still the worries of startled moviegoers and give the project his blessing. Even a respected newspaper asserted, in a peculiarly Indian allusion, somewhat askew but nobly Shakespearean, that "Amitabh continues to stride the scene like a modern Colossus." Why, even his name, in Sanskrit, meant "Infinite Life"! Much of this reflected nothing more, perhaps, than the power of images on an unsophisticated audience ready to take their gods where they found them (the towering hero was often shot from below in order to increase his stature). But it also seemed to reveal a deeper, more widespread hunger for heroes. I could think of no American star who could command the same kind of worship from old and young, rich and poor, housewife and illiterate villager.

Except, perhaps, for President Reagan. With that fact in mind, it was hardly surprising that Amitabh had exploited his status as a god—and extended it—by standing for office. At least one other star, Sunil Dutt, had joined him in the ranks of the Congress (I) party. Their main antagonist, the head of the largest opposition party, was N. T. Rama Rao, who had come to prominence by playing the Indian Superman, Lord Rama, and many other deities in 292 mythological movies. Rao's predecessor as the country's leading oppositionist was M. G. Ramachandran; he had risen to the top politically through acting in 100 films in none of which he died.

In America, however, such former actors as President Reagan or Clint Eastwood effected a smooth transition to politics simply by transferring the tricks and tactics of self-promotion—a confident manner, a soothing voice, an ease before the cameras, a sympathy with the crowds—from one arena to the other, while at the same time taking pains to downplay the less than dignified roles for which they had originally won their fame. In India, by contrast, the process, like everything else, was much simpler and much larger. Amitabh had to do nothing but extend his godlike demeanor from the screen to life, and then from life to politics; he occupied the same role in fact and in fiction. In India, after all, both movies and politics were effectively responding to the same basic need: for a figure broad enough and huge enough—mythic enough, really—to transcend all divisions of region and religion, to tower above all earthly problems like a god.

Early one morning, as I drove through Delhi, I caught my breath to see a giant figure looming over the city in a central open lawn; it was, I learned, an eighty-foot-high statue of Indira Gandhi, erected to commemorate her death. The only comparable figure was Amitabh, standing ten feet high on the posters for *Mard*. As actors turned into gods, and gods into politicians, it was only logical that politicians were turning into gods, and then into actors. Indian politics, as Edmund Taylor noted forty years ago, "are the dream life of the masses."

Small wonder, then, that the hottest topic of intellectual discussion while I was in India was Rajiv Gandhi's manipulation of video dreams. His role as a celluloid hero had begun, by all accounts, at his mother's funeral. For four straight days on national television, the young man had enacted the scene beloved of Hindi movies (and featured in *Mard*): that of the bereaved son—handsome, soft-spoken, a little ill-starred— standing at his mother's bier, dutifully performing the appropriate rites amidst the threat of more violence and the odor of revenge. Twelve times the new leader had circled her funeral pyre and each of those times, so the pundits said, he had picked up another 10 million votes. Then, out of her ashes, he had arisen like a phoenix to lead the country to peace. Ever since, he had kept himself constantly in the eye of the camera, so constantly, in fact, that local wags—and they are never in short supply in India—had rechristened prime time "Prime Minister time." Shrewdly, however, Gandhi tended to present himself, not as a leader delivering stuffy speeches, but simply as another regular guy, playing with his children, talking to workers, mingling with the people as easily as Henry V on the eve of Agincourt. An ordinary man, in short, in an extraordinary position—like Amitabh, say, or a god.

Thus the biggest and most popular family drama in India continued to be played out by the First Family itself. For thirty-five of its thirty-eight independent years, India had been ruled by a single clan, which passed down the prime ministry from generation to generation as if it were a scepter. And through all the years, the House of Nehru had kept the public enthralled with a domestic soap opera quite as eventful as anything in the movies—first shy Indira's emergence to take over from her heartthrob father, and then the rise of her shady younger son, and then his sudden death and his wife's battles with her mother-in-law, and then Indira's violent death and the sudden emergence of her quiet elder son, who found himself opposed by . . . his sister-in-law. Foreigners might balk at this mom-and-pop version of democracy, but many Indians seemed thrilled by it, and reassured that the entire country was run, like so many of its businesses, as just another family business, attended by all the usual familial tensions. In its creation of a democratic monarchy, the ruling household made the entire country seem like one big happy, and unhappy, family. Indira Gandhi, in fact, was known to many of her 600 million constituents as Amma (Mother), a mother to the motherland (in India, as Salman Rushdie has shown, even metaphors go forth and multiply, while myths and parallels proliferate fantastically). And already, many of the new Prime Minister's supporters were beginning to call him by the affectionate pet name of Raju.

HER HYPOCHONDRIACAL FRIEND, *said my aunt, had recently told her that for the first time in her life she was feeling well. Three months later she died.*

OF ALL THE unlikely opposites that the Hindi cinema promiscuously brought together, however, the most surprising was its blend of sensuality and sententiousness. Certainly, there could be little doubt that the most arresting feature of the industry was its unremitting sauciness; thanks to the longtime prohibition of kissing, filmmakers had devised endlessly inventive ways of showing nothing at all, and everything: lovers who never quite made physical contact spent two hours on screen lustily dancing around couches, toppling into rivers and, of course, slithering around trees. Thus the movies, which bodied forth all the lip-smacking, hip-swinging salaciousness that was generally kept under wraps in India, had become a virtual catalogue of the varieties of irreligious experience. In one film I saw, hero and heroine animatedly sucked popsicles inches from one another's face. When next we saw them, they were bouncing up and down on a well-oiled carousel. As soon as the lovely nymph lay down, the movie cut to a shot of a panting man jacking up his car; and whenever the maiden walked around the room (her dress, of course, was filmy), she let her hand fondle an erotic sculpture or two. By Indian standards, however, all this was mild. "Should I give you tenderly / Something like coconut water?" asks one throbbing hero. To that his heaving lady answers, "When he satisfies his hunger with a fruit / Honey flows where he has entered the fruit."

All this, I thought, was fair enough in popular art, and universal enough too: not for nothing did ads for comedies, horror movies and teen pix in the United States invariably come appointed with girls in bikinis (and not for nothing did the people who scorned those "exploitative" shows hurry to the art cinemas to see the latest from Bertolucci, Pasolini or Oshima).

But the engaging idiosyncrasy of Hindi movies was that every one of them seasoned its gaudy provision of sleaze with earnest homilies. "Tamil films are all sex and violence," said a Tamil uncle of mine. "But still they manage to get everything in: crime doesn't pay; love conquers all; all's well that ends well." Hindi movies were no different. For 140 minutes, the screen was a racy riot of the polymorphous perverse in which every dress was clingingly wet and every symbol phallic. Then, in its final scene, the movie would suddenly provide its final thrust: a moral. The aforementioned popsicle sucker, his amours complete, cried, "We've got a duty to our motherland!" and the same exercise in ingenious naughtiness was full of such clinchers as "A diamond is a diamond—even in mud."

It came to seem, therefore, as if every single movie had been co-produced by the local equivalents of Jerry Falwell and Bob Guccione. When I consulted the ads in the papers, I found one that offered "an Explosive War of Principles," another promising "Woman's Thrilling Assault Against Man's Lust." One picture solemnly pledged to show how "Truth saves from the trouble and untruth ruins," while another vowed to address the question "Are Women Considered to Be Cheap?"—with the question mark drawn in the shape of two breasts. "Sensible, sexciting teenagers" was the quintessentially Indian offering of that quintessentially Indian film *The Blue Lagoon*, Malayalam-style. The same disarming division was carefully observed off screen. There had been a near riot, I heard, when ardent movie-goers learned that a favorite actress had not, as her director claimed, been a prostitute in real life. Yet Sridevi, one of the hottest actresses of 1984, thanks to her teases and wiggles and full exposures, claimed in all seriousness to be a virgin.

In some contexts, this moralized debauchery might sound hypocritical, reminiscent of the Saturday-night libertines and Sunday-morning churchgoers of a Tammy Wynette song. But hypocrisy implies a real discrepancy between public and private selves, and in India, where all opposites are flung together into the same helter-skelter confusion and dichotomies are, if not united, at least entertained simultaneously, the term seemed hardly to apply. Besides, the movies were only providing a bigger, bolder, more colorful and immediate version of the very mix of gin and tonic that pervaded the society as a whole. In one railway bookstore, I saw *The Life of Mahatma Gandhi* next to Jackie Collins's *Hollywood Wives;* the most popular English novels, I found, were still those of Ayn Rand, mistress of self-important philosophizing, and those of Harold Robbins, master of wish-fulfillment smut. Along the streets of the cities, those billboards that did not lay bare the fleshly torsos of the movie gods and goddesses were likely to offer maxims: "Lane Driving Is Sane Driving," "Small Family Is Happy Family," "Don't Play with Fire / The Consequences Are Dire" and—my favorite—"Let Us Solicit the Serenity of Silence (Blow Horn If You Must)."

So before one vilified the blend of worldly and otherworldly attractions to be found in Hindi movies, one had to recall that this was the home of the voluptuously carnal goddesses of Khajuraho and the phallic *lingam* of Siva, the birthplace of the *Kama Sutra* and of all those other Tantric arts in which sexual union was seen as a means of spiritual discipline. In a country full of symbols, the sensual had often, no doubt, been the most immediate and apprehensible model of the spiritual. Masud, as ever, was succinct. "Every movie producer is trying to seduce the public," he said. "Some by sex, some by religion." The best tactic of all, by the sound of it, was to make religion sexy.

———

"THERE IS NO hand, there is no foot," said an old lady, itemizing her ailments. "There is no leg. So what is there? What to do now? What to do?"

THE THIRD AND final great titillation in Hindi movies, as strong in its way as either sex or religion, was simple, filthy richness. Whenever the camera was not focusing on its stars' physical assets, it was usually lingering, with no less licentiousness, on their liquid assets; at one point or another, the actors always moved in a fairy-tale world of fancy cars and white-columned mansions and laser discos.

In part, this was just a visible manifestation of the basic assumption of all movies. "The people want illusions," explained Sippy. "They want palatial lifestyles. There's no way that the average man's going to see a cabaret in his life, so he wants to see it in the movies. And how else is a villager ever going to see a disco?" If Hindi movies were tattooed as promiscuously with brand names as a Judith Krantz novel, it was for much the same reason. The lure of entering behind the closed doors of the wealthy is everywhere the same: one wishes both to marvel at the gowns in their closets and to smirk at the skeletons clattering by their side. In India, moreover, this double purpose seemed quite consistent with the country's mix of sensualism and moralism, its voyeurism made righteous: the movies deified the rich, and then went on to show that they were no different from you and me. Democratic monarchy, you might call it.

Yet in India, this lavish display of consumables had a particular poignancy, because luxury goods were almost invariably foreign goods. The portly heroes drove Mercedes-Benzes. They flashed Nikons at the camera. They decanted bottles of Johnnie Walker and showed off copies of *Time* on their coffee tables. And the poignancy was further redoubled by the fact that the government imported no goods whatsoever, and assessed an enormous import duty on all foreign goods that were privately imported; thus, foreign substances had the lure not only of unattainable luxuries but also of forbidden fruit.

The lust for foreign goods—"crazy for phoren," as the local phrase had it—was therefore intense. "You can say that above wine, women and song," a Bombay critic had told me, "the great dream of the Indian intellectual is to go abroad. He hungers for it. Even I feel more at home in New York or Paris than in Bombay or Delhi." For those at an even greater distance from the West, the desire was, if anything, even greater. I saw this most touchingly in Arvind, a twenty-four-year-old hotel worker whom I encountered at a camel fair in the deserts of Rajasthan.

The day on which we met had begun in a typically Indian fashion. I had got up at 4:30 a.m. (in a $1-a-night dorm that took in new sleepers at irregular intervals throughout the night) and hurried to the Jaipur bus station to get a bus to Pushkar. No tickets were available, said the man at the kiosk, until five minutes before the bus left. I waited for an hour and a half, then asked for a ticket. How, asked the man in the kiosk, could he sell me a ticket only five minutes before the bus was leaving? After much ritual gnashing of teeth and tearing of hair, I was finally allowed on the bus. There, I was cheerfully informed that it did not go to Pushkar at all, but stopped only at Ajmer, eight miles away. When we arrived at Ajmer, therefore, I should get off and look for another bus to Pushkar. When we arrived in Ajmer, I got off and was told no bus to Pushkar existed; I would have to take an auto-rickshaw. I walked out of the bus station and enlisted the aid of two of the less persistent of the local rickshaw drivers. How much to Pushkar? $10. I'd give them $5. Fine, they said, but they couldn't take me anyway. I would have to take a taxi. And where could I find a taxi? At the train station. And where was that? On the other side of town. Could they take me there? Of course, they said, quoting an exorbitant price. I haggled them down to something absurd, and off we went.

As we passed at a leisurely pace through Ajmer, my drivers decided to try to supplement their business. They made a bid for my jeans. They promised to sell me a girl. They offered to give me a girl in exchange for my jeans. Finally—and not a moment too soon—we arrived at the train station. No taxis were in sight. The taximan was not here, my chauffeurs happily pointed out. But for some more money, they would help me find him. How much more? They mentioned an absurd price, I agreed on something ridiculous, and off we went. At long last we arrived at the taximan. How much to Pushkar? $10. I would pay $5. The man shook his head. I would have to take a bus. No problem, said the boys with the rickshaw: for some more money, they would take me back to the bus station. They suggested a ridiculous price, I beat them down to something enormous, and off we went. En route, they offered to buy my watch and tried to sell me a girl.

At last we returned to our original starting point, the bus station. Of course there was a bus to Pushkar, I was told. Over there. I stood in line for twenty-five minutes and then was told that it was the wrong line. I stood in another line for thirty minutes, and then observed that it was not moving. I decided to take a taxi. Walking out of the bus station, determined to learn from experience, I hailed a horse cart and asked him to take me to the taximan. Okay, he said. One dollar. Fifty cents, I said. Okay, he said, and drove off without me. At that point, I heard some excited cries behind me and saw the two boys with whom I had already done business. How much to the taximan? They quoted an enormous price, and I beat them down to something outrageous. Off we went.

My clothes, and the ladies of Rajasthan, still unsold, I was taken at last to the same taxi driver as before. $7, he said. $5, I said, provided that we go right away and I don't have to share. Fine, he said, ushering me into the back seat. His custom assured, he then closed the door and strolled off to enjoy some tea. At last he returned and off we went.

Perhaps five minutes later, the driver stopped again and got out. We were, I noticed, again at the bus station—the home from home that I was now visiting for the third time in the morning. After a considerable delay, my driver returned, trailing a family of unhappy-looking passengers. This quintet was thrown on top of me, and off we went.

Sometime before we arrived at Pushkar, the taxi driver stopped. Cars were allowed no farther, he said: not to worry, though, the tourist tent was only a short walk away. I got out and began walking. Twenty minutes later, I stopped one of the many cars careening down the forbidden road. How far to the tourist tent? A mile and a half. Could he take me there? No: the distance was too short. Still, he said, I could take a shortcut by way of that distant temple over there. I walked and walked to the temple, passing through narrow streets made virtually impassable by 20,000 pilgrims. How far to the tourist tent? I asked a passerby. Two miles. Which way? Away from the temple. I walked a little farther, and stopped another man for directions. The tourist tent was very close, he said, pointing to a street obscured by crowds. I labored along, guided by some more people, and walked down an endless driveway. At last, the tourist tent! Oh no, I was told when I walked in, this was the tourist bungalow. The tourist tent was on the other side of town. How far? Four, maybe five kilometers.

I spent the next hour moving in ever-widening circles, under a noonday desert sun, all my worldly possessions in my hands, directed this way and that by villagers who spoke no English, villagers who knew the word for "right" but not for "left," villagers who happily steered me to the tourist bungalow, villagers who shook their heads in abject pity. Pushkar was more crowded than any place I had ever seen. I stopped another taxi. I would pay well, very well indeed, I said, to be taken to the tourist tent. He was not allowed to go, said the driver, but he would be happy to look for another car. He found it. I would pay well, very well, exceptionally well, I told this second fellow, to be taken to the tourist tent. It was too close, he said. And besides, look at the crowds! It was at that point that a young man appeared, saw my plight and, courteously identifying himself as a part-time employee of the tourist tent, offered to show me the way.

That evening, by way of repayment, Arvind invited himself into my tent for a chat. It was one of those strange exchanges, peculiar to the Third World, during which I sensed that it was not just my company that appealed to my newfound friend. For it seemed to me that each of us was a symbol to the other, both to be cherished and to be put to use (a double irony here, since I, completely Indian, served Arvind as an image of the West). And all evening long, an unspoken request seemed to hover in the air. The happiest aspect of traveling in the developing world is that it allows cross-cultural exchanges in which each party can give something to the other. Yet the fact that both parties have something to gain from the giving is surely the saddest thing about traveling in the developing world. On both sides, it pays to be kind.

Arvind told me that he was twenty-five years old and worked in a hotel not far away. As I could imagine, he went on with pride, his job was wonderful, for it afforded him the greatest luxury in all the world: the chance to talk to foreigners. Once, he said, a Swedish man had fallen ill in his hotel and Arvind had taken him to a doctor and put him up at his home and nursed him back to health. When the man returned to Stockholm, he had sent him $1,000; when Arvind's first son had been born, he had sent another $250.

As I could imagine, Arvind continued, he was the envy of even the wealthy. The sons of rich men offered him as much money as they could spare, or anything else he wanted, if only he would do them one small favor: let them shake the hand of a European girl, or even sit by her side for a moment. Arvind looked kindly on such ambitions; he had actually slept with a French girl, and with another tourist from Spain.

Yet still he had never been abroad. And abroad, even the next country in Asia, had acquired for him an ineffable luster. His great dream, he said, was to be hired by a VCR importer, one of those black-money makers who paid men to go to Singapore and Bangkok to bring back video machines they could sell for vast profit. If only he could meet the right man, said Arvind, he might be able to spend at least a night in Bangkok.

Twice he had come close to making it abroad. His grandfather, a professor of linguistics, had promised to take him to a conference in Europe. But then the old man died. A friend of Arvind's had even got as far as the University of California. But no sooner had he arrived than his father died. Two hours later, his mother died. That was the end of his California studies.

Arvind's plight was hardly unique, of course; I had met scores of Arvinds in Indonesia and Nepal and China and, most heart-rending of all, in every closed country from Burma to Cuba to Nicaragua. The inconsistencies of this longing in a country full of nationalism had been explored by Satyajit Ray in *The Home and the World* in which the hero of the Swadeshi movement, aiming to eliminate all foreign goods, smokes only foreign cigarettes and travels only first-class. That too, however, was hardly unique: the anti-Western dictators of African countries (followers of that great non-Westerner Karl Marx) proverbially drove Mercedeses, while President Sukarno, to name just one, had turned his back on the West in a fit of nationalism and decided to make Jakarta a great modern metropolis—by stocking it with Western hotels and conveniences. In a movie like *Mard*, the cry of patriotism was a great rabble-rouser; but the great audience-pleaser was still the parade of foreign goods. Evil was foreign, and so too was the good life. That was a contradiction common to just about every developing country.

What did seem unique in the Indian regard of things Western, though, was its divided loyalties toward different kinds of West. For much of the world, India remained the greatest symbol of the British Empire. Yet modern India, especially under Rajiv, was hell-bent on following the way of the future, generally considered to be the American way. More even than Hong Kong, therefore, India, great amalgam of a hundred races and religions, was torn not just between tradition and modernity, but, more specifically, between the British and the American Empires. To paraphrase one of the country's most-quoted heroes, Matthew Arnold, India was caught between two worlds, one dying, the other struggling to be born.

This strange sense of divided loyalty informed every aspect of middle-class city life. My college-age cousins spent much of their time trying to get hold of records by Bob Dylan, Don McLean and Simon and Garfunkel; yet when it came to reading, they clearly felt most comfortable with P. G. Wodehouse and C. P. Snow. The central monuments of downtown Bombay were still unofficially known by their upstanding imperial names (Crawford Market, Flora Fountain, Victoria Terminus), though increasingly they were being besieged by Waikiki fast-food joints and Pac-Man restaurants. The streets of Bombay were, in fact, a chaos of mixed origins and competing influences—over here Caesars Palace and the Hollywood shop and a sign for mango juice in a "freaked-out box," over there Lady Diana Tailors, the Jolly Stores (serving "lovely pop-ice"), Textoriums galore and, most dignified of all, the Nota Bene "Cleaners of Distinction." Some of the pop-cultural artifacts, of course, were British—the Beatles and Wimpy Bars were popular too. But even they were British borrowings, after a fashion, from American models. America might represent riches, glitz and success, but Britain still had the monopoly on sophistication and class. People spoke of getting a few bucks to buy some fags.

I spent only a week in India in 1984, but more than once in that time, I was asked whether it was true that Gary Coleman was dead (*Different Strokes* and *Here's Lucy* were the only foreign shows on Indian television at the time). That same week, however, a lady in Ahmedabad shyly approached me for information on a different kind of West. "Do they say still in England 'old chap' and 'old man'?" she asked. The question was not for her, she quickly added, but for a fifteen-year-old boy of her acquaintance who was determined to get his British manners exactly right.

In time, of course, this mix was beginning to change, and India seemed, in its slow and elephantine fashion, to be sloughing off some of its musty Edwardian past and taking on more of the bright new futurism of America. Thirty years ago, a British accent might be the main selling point in a negotiated marriage; now the best draw of all was an American green card. In my parents' day, every bright student went to Oxbridge; now, as my cousin prepared for his GRE exam, he told me how one classmate had gone to Kansas, and one to Columbia, one to UCLA and one to Indiana. Rajiv himself, the country's great Everyman, had been educated at Doon School, India's grandest version of the English public school, and had followed his mother and his grandfather to Oxbridge; now, however, he stood as an apostle of the new, computerized, yuppie way of knowledge—the American way. One fairly typical Indian patriarch I heard about memorized a classical English poem every day (he had all the wartime speeches of Churchill down by heart), and made his family read *The Times* of London over breakfast, retire after dinner to read biographies of Asquith and reassemble at nine o'clock each night to listen to the news on BBC World Service (a treat he had missed, he boasted, only four times in his sixty-one years). When his son finally got to Cambridge, however, he had been so shocked at the absence of cummerbunds, Apostles and Conan Doyle streetlamps that he had suffered a nervous breakdown.

The sad story served, among other things, to highlight what was perhaps the strangest of all the features of India's relations with abroad: that many of India's dreams of the outside world, whether British or American or even Soviet, were curiously dated. Neither Don McLean nor P. G. Wodehouse, after all, was notably popular on the streets of London or New York. But in this land of dusty stairwells, Humphrey Bogart–style black telephones and Ambassador cars unchanged for twenty years, they fit right in. And even as "jolly good"s still echoed around the gentlemen's clubs, the movie mags trafficked in a fast talk full of "groovy gals and guys." The respectable daily newspapers still followed the sober and august example of *The Times* of London, hardly recognizing that their model had itself become zappily popularized, and to that extent Americanized; the glossy new magazines took their models from America, but here too they seemed somewhat behind the times, *India Today* appropriating the red border and structure of *Time* but investing it with some old-fashioned fast-and-Luce rhetoric, while newborn *Debonair* billed itself as the Indian *Playboy* but still adhered to a fifties sensibility of black-and-white modesty. "No, I'm sorry, Miss Brasenose," said the caption under the cartoon in *The Statesman*, one of India's most respected papers, "but 'coitus interruptus' was not the first Roman governor of Ireland." The slightly jejune nature of the joke, its Latin atmosphere, its provision of its heroine with the name of an Oxford college—all this gave even a semi-daring crack the somewhat musty and cobwebbed air of a Victorian schoolroom.

That skewed and displaced quality seemed peculiar to India. For where Thailand, the Philippines, Nepal and Bali all excelled, in their different ways, at re-creating every rage from the West, India simply naturalized them. The most obvious example of this was the half-erudite, half-errant English still spoken in many educated quarters of India. But more recent examples were everywhere. India had not imported McDonald's, as most countries had done, but had created instead its own fast-food emporia, Pizza King and Big Bite, which offered hamburgers without the beef. India did not have Coca-Cola (it had been outlawed in 1978 after the company refused to disclose its formula), but instead offered Campa-Cola, which took its name, its logo and its concept from Coke, though sadly not its taste. Just so, the commercial movies borrowed their props, their symbols, even their plots from abroad, yet finally produced something that was strangely old-fashioned and thoroughly Indian.

Even many of the foreigners who came to India came, after a while, to seem Indian. This process had begun when some of the eccentric Brits of the Raj, as described by Paul Scott and Gerald Hanley, had decided to go native. It had continued with those flocks of Western believers who had come over to India, donned orange robes and taken to the ascetic life. Even today, many of the bohemian vagabonds who drifted around the country in huge numbers seemed, in their beaded and sandaled and ragged forms, to have taken on something of the poverty and shapelessness of the country around them. In Thailand, or Indonesia, or Japan, I suspected, such transformations were almost unknown.

Thus, just about every influence here was ultimately assimilated into the heterogeneous Indian rush. In Bombay, the U.S.S.R. Books and Periodicals store was just down the street from the Cambridge Lending Library, and around the corner from the Yankee Doodle American Dream Pizza Parlor; on TV, two of the most popular shows were a version of *Dynasty* and an adaptation of *Pride and Prejudice*, both turned into their Hindi equivalents. China, I thought, preferred to keep visitors out; many Southeast Asian countries invited foreigners in, with an ambiguous wink and a smile; Japan smilingly greeted visitors at the door and appeared to admit them without ever really doing so. India, by contrast, took in all the hordes and simply swept them up in the undifferentiated tide.

AN ORDINARY MIDDLE-CLASS *child had been kidnapped, I was told. One year after his disappearance, his parents chanced to see him in a marketplace, dressed in rags and working as a cripple for some latter-day Fagin. By then, however, it was much too dangerous for them to try to get him back.*

JUST BEFORE I left the country, I made one last attempt to clarify my understanding of India's relation to the West, as reflected in the movies, by returning for a final chat with Masud. A typical Indian gentleman of distinction, he invited me to join him one leisurely Sunday morning for breakfast at the Cricket Club of India, a club in the great British tradition. We ordered some toast and a pot of tea and talked beside a sunlit pitch on which white-flanneled cricketers went through their motions with lazy grace. All the hubbub of Bombay was screened out in the quiet morning; we could almost, I thought, have been in Oxford, in a tranquillity broken only by the diffident thump of bat meeting ball, an occasional polite scatter of applause. A few girls in polka-dot dresses and high heels rambled around the pitch in the warm sea breeze. On the horizon were the steeples and towers of the red-brick Gothic buildings left by the British. And through the mild sunny morning we chatted about *Gremlins*, disco, the effects of PR.

Cinematically speaking, said Masud, the Western influence on India fell into three rough categories. There was the Hollywood Raj of Attenborough and Forster. There was the familiar disco culture of America ("Downright soulless and vulgar," he said, since it had been transplanted with no understanding of its context or meaning. "At least *Flashdance* has a certain lightness, a humor, a poetry. But go to Studio 29 here, an imitation of your Studio 54. It's pathetic"). Most salutary of all, in Masud's opinion, was the third category: the effect of the German and French thinkers on dissent, from whom many young Indians had learned their rebelliousness.

The first two traditions, both popular and in their way romantic (the British a relatively straightforward romance of elegance and class, the American a matter of instant gratification and cheap thrills), had obviously colored the commercial cinema. But the effect of the third was most apparent in the so-called parallel cinema. These were the art movies of the educated elite, pioneered by Ray and continued by a whole generation of young directors trained at the Film and Television Institute of Pune, South Asia's only film school. Although Ray had tried to fashion a rigorous cinema at once sophisticated and close to the heart, creating in his *Apu Trilogy* a true voice for rural India, many of his successors were determined intellectuals who concentrated exclusively on their nation's social problems. They had no time for escapism, no patience for clownish song-and-dance routines; they wanted to bring droughts to the screen, and caste tensions, poverty and subjugation. Often they wanted simply to shake their fist at the society around them. "You read the newspapers and you feel totally helpless," Govind Nihalani had told the *Illustrated Weekly*, "so you try to select something by which you can express your anger."

The art movies were the equal of anything put out in the West—in part, perhaps, because they had taken so much from the West. Ray, after all, had spent time when young around Jean Renoir, while Kumar Shahani had assisted Bresson. The angry young men acknowledged, even boasted, that they took their cues from Eisenstein, Godard and Fassbinder (though not, curiously, from the one director whose careening intensities and cheerful grotesqueries seemed tailor-made for the Indian scene —Fellini). They quoted Kafka and referred to Jancsó and Genet.

Even the name they gave to their movement—the New Wave cinema—was taken from the Continent.

Masud, I imagined, must be a champion of these thoughtful alternatives to the commercial formulae, if only for the relief they afforded after a day of gaudy pantomimes. I was wrong. He had once been an admirer of the New Wave, he explained to me. But all too often, its products proved to be pessimistic, self-indulgent, derivative. "These films are very intense," he continued. "But they do not take up the human thing. The new cinema has fallen into its own kind of orthodoxy. They all make films like Godard or Bresson, but they do not convey the reality, the humanity, the warmth of India. They do not bring out the feel of what is happening in India. All these directors are artists. But they are removed from the people. At least in the commercial cinema, there is a connection between the director and the audience; in the New Wave, there is no connection, no sense of the day-to-day experience of the average filmgoer. These films are forms of abstraction. In the West, it is possible to abstract oneself from one's environment, to concoct a film-within-a-film. But in India, you cannot do that."

Yes, said Masud, people like himself might appreciate the nuances and flourishes of the New Wave. But they were part of a tiny minority. "The commercial filmmaker exploits the people," he said. "But he also entertains them. He knows what they want, and he gives it to them. But with the parallel-cinema makers, it is all imagination: their films are good only for critics and a few people in the cities." In their way, he added, the serious directors were no more guided by integrity and originality than the commercial directors they mocked. "These directors are living off their earnings from the West. They train themselves in Western technology and then make films to please Western audiences."

He closed with a powerful example. "Three days ago," he said, "there was a New Wave film on TV about the poverty in Bihar. My two servants, who are from Bihar, walked out after thirty minutes. Why should they want to see that? They have already seen it—in real life. They came to Bombay to leave all that behind!"

I was at first somewhat skeptical of this line of reasoning. But a couple of months later I had a chance to see some of the most acclaimed of the New Wave movies when the Festival of India came to California. Leading the pack was a movie about campus unrest called *Holi*. It was, without a doubt, the least entertaining movie I'd seen in years.

The film established its mood in the first five minutes, and there its development ended. It began with a group of nihilistic students sitting around in a dilapidated hostel, drunk and with nothing to live for. Full of angry energy, they shouted and ran around. The graffiti on the hostel walls said "When? Why? Where?" The students shouted and raced around some more. Along the corridors was painted a huge question mark. The kids screeched and shouted. On one wall was the word *kal*, meaning both "tomorrow" and "yesterday"; a student spat on it. The kids shouted and screamed. Then they sang a song. "For one thing we pray / To witness doomsday." Later they sang another song. "No affection, no love / No virtue, no sin / No hope, no direction / No intention, no purpose / No direction, no goal." Then they pelted a visiting speaker with rotten fruit and ran around screaming and shouting. Then they tortured a fellow pupil. Then there was a suicide. Nobody could accuse *Holi* of subtlety.

Yet few could remain unaware of *Holi*'s strident aspirations to subtlety. It was full of showy overhead shots and very long takes. It had the nice device of containing forty-five single takes and a central take that had forty-five parts. It was designed to be symmetrical—it began with the kids drinking beer and concluded with them smoking dope. It was performed by a group of nonprofessionals who improvised as they went along (not for nothing had its well-educated director dedicated his first movie to Brecht). And the whole picture was, I thought, a farrago of borrowed gestures and secondhand beliefs. It had all the blank anger of a punk movie with none of the bravado. It had all the brutality of a kung fu movie with none of the extraordinary stunts. It had much of the behaviorism of *Lord of the Flies* but none of the point. I did not mind that the movie was boring, repetitive and crude. But I did feel cheated by its unspoken assumption that it was addressing a serious problem with serious candor, bravely fighting despair with despair. More than anything, I recoiled from its air of self-importance; it seemed in more ways than one a sub-Continental kind of movie.

True to Masud's claim, however, *Holi* seemed to find its ideal audience in America. It had been shown at the Museum of

Modern Art in New York and had been praised, with some bemusement, by a critic in *The New York Times* who mistook the whole setting for a coed high school and, failing to understand it, chivalrously tried to find something to praise in it. Many viewers in California felt they could relate to its shock-therapy anarchy, its vision of a society in ruins. They found it clever, intense, realistic. They may even have enjoyed the cafeteria song-and-dance routine that was at once a sneering parody of Hindi movies and a rip-off from *Fame*, by way of *Rock 'n' Roll High School*. But I wished I were watching the mad singing and dancing of *Mard* instead. And had I been a regular Indian, besieged by chaos, struggling to survive, surrounded by corruption and poverty and noise, and in no position whatsoever to enjoy the allusions to Buñuel and the virtuosity of the swiveling camera, I would have bitterly, desperately wished that I were seeing *Mard. Mard* at least had a happy ending.

TEN DAYS AFTER *my arrival in Bombay, my schedule called for me to go to Kathmandu for ten days. When I arrived back, a young cousin of mine picked me up at the airport. The relative who had been in such agonized pain, he said, had died. And two days later, the man's healthy old father, shaken by the tragedy, had followed him to the grave.*

THAILAND
Love in a
Duty-free Zone

ELCOME, MY friend! Welcome to Bangkok!" cried the small man in sunglasses hurrying toward me, hand outstretched and smile well-rehearsed. Outside the dumpy single block of Don Muang Airport, the tropical dusk was thick with sultriness. On every side, lank-haired, open-shirted cabbies were whispering solicitations. Smooth-skinned soldiers were fingering $100 bills. Girls in loose shirts slouched past, insouciance in their smiling eyes.

"Have a good time in Thailand!" offered the signs inside the terminal. "Have a good time in Thailand!" said the boards on the back of the baggage carts. "Bank of Love" read the sign on the back of a minibus.

"You wait for official government bus into city?" my new friend demanded.

I nodded.

"Very good!" He slapped an arm around me, half comrade and half conspirator. "I am official government guide." By way of proof, he pointed to the official government badge he wore on his heart. "Johnny," he explained, then whipped out an official government form.

"Okay," he began, frowning over his form. "Your name? Your country? Where you stay? Business"—he gave a quick leer—"or pleasure?" Every answer Johnny repeated to himself, syllable by syllable, then painstakingly copied down on his form. For that, I was most grateful. Clearly, Johnny was completing some neglected formality, or taking down some information required by the tourist police, or, at the very least, giving me the receipt I would need when I boarded the bus. Clearly, he was trying to save me, or rescue me from, trouble.

Sure enough, as soon as his interrogation was concluded, Johnny ripped out his chit, handed me a receipt and grinned expectantly. "Ten dollars!" I smiled back. I had, I explained, paid for my bus ticket already.

Johnny looked decidedly unnerved. I had not, he suggested, paid for the official government service already. Then, with the weariness of a much-tried bureaucrat, he opened the thick black folder he was carrying and began flipping through its pages. Finally, he stopped at a black-and-white passport photo of a sloe-eyed nymphet. "Miss Joy," he explained. "Tonight. Three hours. Miss Joy take you everywhere in Bangkok. Car included." I looked a little dubious. "Official government service," he continued. "Very good service. No problem, my friend."

This was indeed a thoughtful offer, I said, but perhaps a guidebook might serve my needs as well.

"Miss Joy Number One girl," Johnny shot back, with more than a hint of tartness. Of that, I hastily assured him, I had no doubt, but still I felt obliged to decline. "I think, perhaps, tonight, I might, actually, want to rest."

"No problem, my friend," the incorrigible smiled back. "Miss Joy come to you hotel. Eight o'clock? Eight-thirty? Nine o'clock?"

"That's very kind. But, well, I think, perhaps, you see, I might, very possibly, have to do some work tonight."

Johnny looked stricken. "Only ten dollars," he protested. "Number One price. You go into town—no good price." Then he returned to the smirk that was his specialty. "Drinking, dancing . . . anything you can do."

Impressive though this bill of rights was, I begged off.

Johnny's official government bonhomie was fast disappearing. "Okay," he said, wincing. "Look. I give this you free." He scribbled down a phone number. "Official government place. You go to hotel. You talk to office. Say Miss Joy."

"Well, er, actually, no, thanks. Maybe if I change my mind, I can call your office later."

At that, Johnny slammed shut his ledger and trudged back, muttering, into the gloom from which he had emerged . . .

. . . And out of which appeared, just a few seconds later, another beaming local, papers dangling out of an overstuffed folder as he hustled over toward me. Pointing to his badge—he too, it seemed, was an official government guide—he invited me to deliver a rough summary of my agenda. Anxious not to whet his hopes, I told him vaguely that I had many meetings, conferences, appointments, commitments.

"My friend, why you no have fun in Bangkok? Many nice ladies in Bangkok."

Of that, I said, I was sure. But I would be happy to take it on trust, I was starting to say . . . when, with a magician's flourish, he pulled out his dun-colored folder and began riffling through page after page of official government soft-focus, four-color glossies. Languorous limbs on heavy carpets. Silky legs on velvety sofas. Pouting lovelies splayed across satin sheets.

"Here." He settled on a young lady who seemed to have conquered shyness. "She very beautiful girl."

That was beyond dispute.

"Beautiful girl graduated from college," he went on.

"In physical education?"

"We have three massage," he continued relentlessly. "A, B, C."

I decided not to ask whether these corresponded to the Bachelor's, Master's and Doctor's degrees, respectively. This was all most interesting, I assured him, but I'd nonetheless have to turn him down.

"You no like Bangkok? Very good place."

So it seemed. Already I was convinced that the city welcomed visitors with open arms. And already I could see that its service industries were exceedingly well developed and its authorities admirably eager to please. But by the time a third official government tout approached me with the novel invitation: "My friend. You no like birdwatching?" I was inclined to suspect that ornithology was not among his interests. And when at last I entered the airport bus, the driver who took me for an official government ride lost no time at all in urging upon me the merits of a special hotel and, by happy chance, a nice young lady he happened to know.

II

I had long been wary of big bad Bangkok. It was a city, they said, whose main industry was recreation and whose main business was pleasure. Wickedness, by all accounts, was an art form here. For not only were all the seven vices, and quite a few others, embellished, expanded and refined in Bangkok, but they were also coupled with all the seven graces. In free-and-easy Bangkok, so legend had it, half the women were pros and half the men were cons. Everywhere in Asia, the Thai capital was spoken of in whispers, with the fascinated horror that attends a shadow Saigon. It was, by common consent, the best place around for procuring anything and everything illicit—smuggled goods, fake Rolexes, pirated cassettes, hard drugs, forged passports and IDs. And the Thais were famous for their gentleness and grace.

"Ah, such a charming people," mused Alan, a kindly sixty-nine-year-old British photographer-eccentric I met in Bali, "and yet the streets of Bangkok are really so terribly wicked." Once, he said, he had been approached on the sidewalk by a man offering Number One king prawns; when he accepted, the man had led him down a shady side street and into a dark café, served him the promised prawns and then presented him with a bill for $100. ("I must say, though, the prawns were awfully good.") Another time, he reported, a monk had taken him out for a drink and then had asked him pointedly whether he was sleeping alone, adding, "I am very nice man!" "Imagine that!" cried Alan with an innocence only strengthened by his knowledge of the world. "And he a monk! But still, you know, the Thais are really such a charming people."

Of all the unlikely resources husbanded in Bangkok, however, the most famous were potential wives. Two days after meeting Alan, I ran into another Brit in Bali, who was, by profession, "how shall I put it—a smuggler." No stranger to the blackest of markets, this character assured me that along the roads of northern Thailand $35 would buy a boy for life, and $50 a girl. I had also read that at village auctions virgins were the pièce de résistance. And it was common knowledge that the principal crops grown in certain parts of the country were young girls sent by their families to the bars of Bangkok to make fortunes they could plow back into the community as soon as they resumed their rustic lives. Indeed, said one Thai gentleman, talent scouts roamed the northern villages, offering families $150 for every prospective B-girl. "Here," he reported happily, "everything is for sale. Even human life."

The government itself seemed hardly bashful about advertising the skin trade. The Yellow Pages alone listed 100 massage parlors, and 350 bars, in every corner of the capital. Brochures circulated around the world, enticing packs of male visitors from Japan and Germany and the Gulf on special sex-tour vacations with the assurance that in Bangkok "you can pick up girls as easily as a pack of cigarettes" (those who found even that too onerous could select their companions from photo booklets before leaving home). In the city itself, accredited tourist agencies organized expeditions around Bangkok's most breathtaking natural wonders—its pretty shopgirls. By now, in fact, an estimated 60 percent of all the country's visitors came only for the dirt-cheap sex, and more than a million girls were waiting to oblige them. And since their international reputation—not to mention their gross national product—depended on the mass production of pleasure, the authorities made sure that the fantasy business was the best-run industry in town: well organized, fastidiously tended and lavishly displayed. All the playboys of the Western world made for Bangkok, and Bangkok was increasingly made for them.

Of late, of course, a terrible shadow had fallen over the business: crowded with bar-girls, heroin addicts and men who were gay just for money, Bangkok had the perfect conditions for an epidemic of AIDS. By the spring of 1986, six people had already died of the syndrome, and four of them were foreigners. Yet where countries like Japan had responded to the threat with a panic-stricken decisiveness and talk of testing all who entered the country, many Thais seemed content just to shrug off the danger. The public health minister himself had requested agencies to exercise discretion about publicizing AIDS statistics so as not to damage the tourist trade.

And indeed, the minute I entered my Bangkok hotel, I found myself surrounded by consumers of the Bangkok Dream. Simon, from Durham University in Britain, had first visited Thailand a couple of months ago and had now returned, he said, with a sly smile, for no reason at all really, and for how long, he didn't know. An Indian who was entwined in the snack bar with a couple of local ladies told me, rather shyly, that he had collected photos and tapes of almost a thousand Bangkok girls as souvenirs of his annual visits. A black man from the South Bronx explained that he was here on an extended R and R break from the pro basketball league in Australia. "People come here for different things," explained a male nurse from San Francisco. "Some people come for the temples. Some people come for the deals. Some people come for the sex." He pronounced this last with such disgust that I was moved to ask what he had come for. "Girls," he said, hardly pausing. "Fourteen-, fifteen-year-old girls. I've already been to Sri Lanka and Korea, but this is the best place to find them: the girls are real fresh here, straight from the hills." Noting my look of bemusement, he went on to explain himself. "Look," he began earnestly, "I'm forty-two years old. I'm losing some hair. I could lose a little weight here and there. I'm not getting any younger. But I don't want no thirty-five-year-old woman. I want to marry a girl who's twenty-two, twenty-three at the most. In America, none of them girls are gonna look at me. But here—here it's different."

No less typical of the city's supplicants was twenty-one-year-old Dave, who had arrived three months ago on vacation from the University of British Columbia. By now his tertiary education was a thing of the distant past, his ownership of a local bar a prospect for the perpetual future. Bright with ingenuous good nature, Dave had somehow managed to bring sincerity even to Sin City. Not long after we sat down to dinner, he leaned over in my direction. "Just look at these beauties," he whispered, gesturing toward the waitresses. "And you know something? They aren't even working girls." His own girlfriend, he confessed, was "out at work" tonight.

As soon as we had finished eating, Dave volunteered to serve as my Virgil through the inner circles of Bangkok's inferno. The best introduction to the city, he declared, was a pilgrimage to the heart of the Patpong Road, a mess of more than fifty look-alike bars set along two narrow lanes, designed with nothing in mind but the bodily pleasure of foreigners. We could try the Honey Bar, or the Pink Panther, or the Adam and Eve—they were all the same. But we might as well go to the Superstar.

And so we did. At the door, a scantily clad young sylph flashed me a soft smile, led me by the hand to a barstool, pressed her body lightly against mine, urged me to order a drink. As soon as I did so, she threaded long and languid arms around me, brushed lustrous, sweet-smelling hair against my face, inclined my straw into my mouth, tickled her lips with her tongue and whispered sweet nothings that could not have been sweeter or more full of nothing. Then, gradually, gently, all sidelong glances, kittenish giggles and seraphic smiles, she glided through a cross-questioning as ritualized and precise as those delivered by immigration officers deliberating whether to allow one entry. "Where you from? Where you live in Bangkok? How long you stay?" Give the right answers, I quickly discovered, and the response was immediate.

"Where you live?" asked a bewitching, orange-bikinied houri.

"Metro Hotel."

"Oh," she said, "sexy eyes."

All my reservations confirmed, I had, I felt, been transported back to some B-movie image of Saigon, 1968. Behind me, a jukebox with a throbbing bass pounded out "Do It to Me" and "Slow Hand" and "Da Ya Think I'm Sexy." A psychedelic light show on the wall fuzzily gave off a deliquescent blur of naked bodies mixing and mingling. On a platform behind the bar, a handful of beauties went through the motions of excitement in body language that needed no translation. Their reflections kept them company in mirrors behind them, above them and in front of them. And distractedly gawking up at the dancers from their barstools were rows upon rows of burly men in white bush shirts and crumpled trousers, Australians and Germans and Americans. As they looked on, every one of them bounced a giggly girl up and down on his lap, pawing soft limbs, stroking spare parts, slurring endearments. For purposes of identification, every handmaiden had a number on her breast.

Though Bangkok was famous for its narcotic properties, I did not sleep well that evening. All night long, from outside my room came the sounds of giggles and slamming doors, heavy feet padding after light ones down the corridor. And sometime before sunrise, I was abruptly awoken by a call from a hotel employee. "I miss you," she purred. This was strange, I thought, since I had not yet had the pleasure of her acquaintance. "I see you last night," she moaned. "I love you very much. You no remember me—the one with black hair and brown skin?"

She was indeed no different from all the others. Everywhere, at every time, it was the same: intimacy on the grand scale. Wherever I looked in this huge and hazy city, scattered harum-scarum along its main roads, were hundreds upon hundreds of short-time hotels, girlie bars, sex shows, massage parlors, "no hands" restaurants, pickup coffee shops, brothels, escort agencies, discos and—following as surely as the day the night—VD clinics. At one end of town gleamed the showy crystal palaces of the Patpong Road, at the other their tarted-up country cousins on a street known as Soi Cowboy. Between them, around them and on every side there seemed to be bars with videos, bars with shows, bars with dance floors, Swiss and American and German bars and special Japanese-language bars where businessmen from Tokyo could pay a flat $110 for a full night of entertainment, no holds barred, no strings attached. And in and out and all around were massage parlors, small massage parlors, back-alley massage parlors, massage parlors that were three-story pleasure domes as luxurious as Las Vegas casinos, each one equipped with one-way mirrors through which its customers could watch, unwatched, up to 400 masseuses seated in a huge glass tank, knitting, filing their nails or turning their deadened gaze to a TV screen. For the sake of convenience, these girls too had numbers on their breasts.

As a young, unattached foreign male, I found myself caught in a swarm of propositions. When I entered a taxi, the driver offered me "a private girl" (to which I was tempted to reply that I was a private man). When I stopped at a street corner, in the midst of a monsoony downpour, a shabby young man thrust upon me a soggy Polaroid of the girl he owned. When I peered into a barbershop, I was asked—nudge, nudge—whether I would like a private room. And everywhere I went, I heard from the shadows a busy, steady buzz of "Sex show. Sex show. Sex show" as ceaseless as the song of cicadas in Japan.

Nowhere, it seemed, was I safe. I checked into a tourist hotel and found that it was a "knock-knock" place, which provided girls, along with Cokes and pay phones, in the lobby. Many of these houses of good repute, I later discovered, took the liberty of sending spare girls, uninvited, up to the rooms at night. Even first-class hotels posted notices observing, with all regretful courtesy, that guests in single rooms would have to pay double since it was assumed that they would not, could not, be sleeping alone. And in the up-country city of Chiangmai, when I sat down to breakfast in my respectable hotel, video screens in every corner of the room began blasting out images of groping, groaning bodies squelching together in unfocused ecstasy. I had to take the moans of venery together with my toast and tea.

The search for a late-night bite was no less of a rude surprise. I had heard far and wide of the snack bar in the Grace Hotel, but its claim to fame had always remained obscure. No wonder. Walking around the corner from the Grace Clinic, I parted with $2 just to enter the hotel's darkened basement. Inside was a coffee shop of sorts, but it was unlikely to be mistaken for Denny's. For although the entire room had the All-American look of a high school cafeteria with the lights turned out and three jukeboxes blasting simultaneously, goodies were the last thing on sale here. On every side of the room sat girls of every shape and size, in miniskirts, leather pants, bulging sweaters and tight jeans. Some wore sun glasses in the near pitch-dark, some flashed smiles with gold teeth. One wore a T-shirt that said, quite simply, "Man." And the girls did nothing except sit around. They smoked and smoked. They chatted without interest. They paced and listlessly prowled. They banged buttons and pounded knobs at an electronic game called Video Hustler. And all around them circled schools of men, mostly Arab, some in djellabas, some in threadbare jackets, some in shirts cracked open to the waist. Many were aged, or rheumy-eyed, or ill-smelling. One was a hunchbacked dwarf wearing huge, black-rimmed spectacles. All eyes were open for a smile. Nobody was drinking coffee.

What else did Bangkok have to offer? I turned to the official government tourist magazine, *This Week in Bangkok*. Four pages were devoted to such agencies as the Darling Escort Services (which provided "educated ladies who come in many different languages to help you get around or get down"), a smattering of cocktail lounges ("Welcome to our real paradise," offered Madonna) and a bevy of massage parlors ("Experience unique courtesy only Thai girls can offer"). The next page featured a list of VD clinics, and the next a group of barbershops and beauty salons ("Guarantee full satisfaction," "Expert lady barbers for men"). The following page listed eight more escort agencies ("For lonely visitors to find the most beautiful, sensuous or sexy partner," cooed Eve. "So easy. Just call us"). Most of the rest of the tourist magazine was given over to a five-page listing of bars and clubs, and to such specialty clubs—Bangkok was nothing if not an equal opportunity employer—as Gentlemen (providing "gentle boys for gentlemen"). One entire page contained nothing but photographs of "special friends."

The magazine did, however, reserve a little space for mention of the Rotary Club's annual fund-raising extravaganza, which it acclaimed as a must for the entire family and extolled in the tones generally reserved for folkloric spectacles. This traditional event came with the blessing of the city's mayor and of a spokesman from the Prime Minister's office. Ah, I thought, a celebration of some of the country's distinctive customs.

Indeed it was. The charity affair was held in the Patpong Road. It featured an elaborate outdoor beauty contest involving a gaggle of lovelies from the area's bars, undressed to kill. The bars themselves were thrown open to the daylight so that any pedestrian could peep inside, where a harem's worth of damsels were wiggling and writhing on cue. The booths that lined the streets offered drinks with girls, dances with girls, or girls with girls. I could, I thought, be only in Bangkok.

The city, in fact, made me decidedly squeamish. Just to be exposed to such a society was, I thought, to contract a kind of social disease; just to be here was to be guilty. Not for nothing, I told myself, did "Thailand" mean "Land of the Free." Taken in by Bangkok's willingness to take one in, I felt myself outraged; Bangkok was dangerously easy, was my dangerously easy conclusion.

III

Thailand offered a good deal more, of course, than just the sex trade. My first week in the country, I took a night train to the north, watched darkness fall over the rice paddies, felt a hot tropical breeze against my face, saw great sheets of lightning break across the land. Next day, at dawn, I followed a vaulting, cross-eyed hill tribesman up steep hills and through a butterflied jungle, and that night, in an animist village, I watched, by the light of a single candle, as the local headman, reclining on pillows, filled himself with opium, then played a weird kind of bagpipes, while jigging his way through a discombobulated dance in the guttering light of the shadows. Never had I felt myself so close to mystery.

Yet even then, I could not help recalling the Dutchman I had met in Corsica the year before. When he had trekked into the Thai jungle, he told me with pleasure, the hill tribesmen, though conversant with no dialect but their own, had greeted his group by spelling out "Welcome" with the tops of Coke bottles. And in nearby Chiangmai, a quiet center of tribal handicrafts, there was little doubt that the West was coming through loud and clear. Teenage girls sat on the hoods of muscle cars on the town's main drag, while Nike-shod jocks revved up their Yamahas. Singers in hot-pants were lip-synching Top 40 tunes on screens in the Video 83 store, and across the street from Burger House, a neon sign advertised a bowling alley. A local Christian girl invited me to dinner, then sat at the table reading Maupassant. And early one evening, as dusk began to fall, a lazy-eyed rickshaw driver gave me a guided tour of his hometown. "Ah," he said as we bounced past a fallen hut where a wanton was combing her thick black hair, "no good place. Suzie Wong."

In the capital, of course, the Western influence was even more pronounced. Like every tourist, I was fascinated by the city's famous weekend market, a spicy department store of the subconscious that offered such niceties as rabbits for sale, and iridescent fish, crunchy grasshopper snacks and an evil-smelling wizard's brew of delicacies whipped up, so it seemed, from a recipe in the Wyrd Sisters' Cookbook. But the locals who were crowding the narrow aisles had no time for such common-or-garden fare. They had come to savor the real exotica: bright orange toy guitars; a bowling shirt that read "Rick's Carpet Center, Granada Hills"; and posters, fluttering along the sides of ramshackle stalls, of Jennifer Beals and Phoebe Cates—the newly canonized goddesses of the Orient—sitting in Mustangs, showing off UCLA letter jackets or simply carrying themselves as embodiments of the Promised Land. The largest crowd of all congregated around a craftsman who was meticulously brass-rubbing Maidenform ads onto T-shirts.

Bangkok, in fact, had a glamour and a sparkle that far out-shone those of Bombay, Casablanca, even Athens; smartly done up in art nouveau restaurants and chandeliered super-luxury hotels, it glittered with a fast and flashy style that would not have been out of place in Paris or San Francisco. Yet more than anywhere else, Bangkok reminded me of L.A. Not just because its 900,000 cars were forever deadlocked, or because its balmy skies were perpetually smoggy and sullen with exhaust fumes. Not even because it was, both literally and metaphorically, spaced out and strung out, sprawling and recumbent and horizontal (where New York and Hong Kong, its true opposites, were thrustingly, busily, ambitiously vertical). Mostly, the "City of Angels" reminded me of Los Angeles because it was so laid-back (in topography and mood) as to seem a kind of dreamy suburban Elysium, abundantly supplied with flashy homes and smart-fronted boutiques, streamlined Jaguars and Mexican cafés, fancy patisseries and even a wood-and-fern vegetarian restaurant (complete with classical guitarist and James Bond on the video). Down every puddle-glutted lane in Bangkok lay pizzas, pizzazz and all the glitzy razzmatazz of the American Dream, California style: video rental stores, Pizza Hut and Robinson's, pretty young things looking for sugar daddies and trendy watering holes with Redskins decals on the window and tapes of "This Week in the NFL" inside. In an inspired Freudian slip, one dingy hole-in-the-wall even promised "VDO."

It had been during the Vietnam War, I reminded myself, that Bangkok had first become celebrated in the West as a factory of dreams, a cathedral of sex and drugs and rock 'n' roll. So why should I be surprised that much of what remained resembled the bastard child of America and Indochina, a sad and shaming reminder of a difficult liaison? "My whorehouse," says Paul

Theroux's Saint Jack, "was a scale model of the imperial dream." The skin trade did indeed seem to underwrite the metaphor. For although the Patpong Road and the Grace Hotel were not exactly offering Love American Style, they were tricked up, even more than every other hopeful business, in all the hard and made-up finery of America. The bar girls were clad in Lee jeans and K-Mart tops; the songs on the jukebox were American, and so were the shows on the video. This was not, like the Philippines, a former American colony. Yet on any given day, the flashdancers of Bangkok could saunter from the Travolta Boutique to the Patty Duke Barbershop, then move from the Manhattan Hi-Tech Store to the Club Manhattan to the Manhattan Hotel (or the Florida, the Atlanta, the Reno, the Niagara, the Impala or the Miami). And on any given night, I could travel from the Don Juan Cocktail Lounge to the Honey Hotel, and thence, by way of the Lolita Nightclub and Disco Duck, to the Je T'Aime Guest House. One typical bar in Chiangmai advertised that this was "where expats do it," before sniggering, "Come once and you'll come many times." Another joint down the street featured a crooner who sang "The Streets of London," but changed the words so that a lament for the plight of the poor, the lonely and the homeless became a lurid, blow-by-blow account of a Thai girl bringing a foreigner to orgasm.

And everywhere I went in Thailand, were even more graphic examples of the country's relations with the West: here a ruddy-faced foreigner lumbering along the street hand-in-hand with a feather-skinned lovely; there a plump pale arm around slender brown shoulders in the back of a red-lit, three-wheel taxi; here a middle-aged executive cutting some deal on the sidewalk with a doe-eyed Lolita; there two sloppy-shirted, unshaven tourists nuzzling a pair of dancing girls in a restaurant, while the nymphs tittered fetchingly and put flowers in their suitors' thinning hair. Whenever I visited temples or museums or silk shops or historical sites in Thailand, I saw almost no sightseers, no scholars, no hippies from Oregon or honeymooning couples from Manhattan—nothing, in fact, save these oddest of bedfellows. And this curious parade of Occidental Adams and Oriental Eves (to cite the clever title of a story written by a local Brit named John Cadet) seemed a moralist's gift, a symbol-monger's delight. For what more perfect emblem could be found of the brash and brawny West buying the favors of the gentle, fine-boned East? The shy, sleepy-eyed Siam that had once enticed rhapsodies from Coward and Alec Waugh had now, so it seemed, been reduced into nothing but the land of Thai sticks and the setting for *Emmanuelle.*

IV

My first reaction to Bangkok was shock; my second was to know that shock was not right, but I didn't know what was. "Those who go beneath the surface do so at their own peril," wrote Wilde, and the more I looked at the bar scene, the more my vision blurred.

The system of kept women was no import, an English-educated Thai lady indignantly assured me; it was an honored tradition for men here to relieve their wives of certain pressures by spending a few nights now and then with concubines. Many husbands, in fact, participated in a kind of "scholarship" system whereby they paid a young lady's way through college in exchange for her occasional services.

Nor was the system new. Peter Fleming had come upon a Grace-style coffee shop while traveling through Manchuria in 1934, I read. And a few years later, well before the war in Vietnam, his brother Ian had noted that while tourists in Bangkok were courting trouble by escorting Thai girls in the streets, the problem was that they didn't understand the right procedure: if they went to the nearest police station, an officer on duty would gladly provide them with suitable names and addresses. Nor did the system pander exclusively to the West: a recent American guidebook, choosing its verbs carefully, pointed out that by 1983 "Asian [single male] visitors to Thailand outstripped American." Besides, the girls of Bangkok always insisted, nothing could be more exciting than a boyfriend from abroad ("Thai men no good" was their constant refrain). Queen Sirikit herself once told a friend of mine that the word for foreigner, *farang*, was synonymous with all that was wondrously exotic.

Before very long, in fact, I began to discover that the ubiquitous couple of Bangkok—the pudgy foreigner with the exquisite girleen—was not quite the buyer and seller, the subject and object, I had imagined. In many cases, I was told, the girls did not simply make their bodies available to all while they looked at their watches and counted their money; they chose to offer their admirers their time, their thought, even their lives. The couple would sometimes stay together for two weeks, or three, or thirty. They would travel together and live together and think of themselves as lovers. She would show him her country, cook him local delicacies, mend his clothes, even introduce him to her parents and her friends. He would protect her from some parts of the world, teach her about others. For the girl, her Western suitor might prove the mature and sophisticated companion she had always lacked; for the man, his Eastern consort could be the attentive, demure and sumptuously compliant goddess of his dreams. He would obviously provide material comforts and she physical; but sometimes—in subtler ways—their positions were reversed. And as the months passed, sensations sometimes developed into emotions, passions settled down into feelings. Often, in the end, they would go through a traditional marriage in her village.

Thus my tidy paradigm of West exploiting East began to crumble. Bangkok wasn't dealing only in the clear-cut trade of bodies; it was trafficking also in the altogether murkier exchange of hearts. The East, as Singapore Airlines knows full well, has always been a marketplace for romance. But Thailand was dispensing it on a personal scale, and in heavy doses. It offered love in a duty-free zone: a context in which boy meets girl without having to worry about commitments, obligations, even identities. Love, that is, or something like it.

V

As I returned to the bars, I steadied myself against their mounting equivocations by noting that at least some of the girls were as hard and fast as their propositions. These creatures of easy virtue were indeed no more than what they seemed: all artifice. Their pleasure was strictly professional, their "darlings" dangled in all the wrong places. They could be touched in any place except inside; they would extend themselves to any man who entered. When money was mentioned, their soft gaze turned hard; when a fat cat came in, their eyes irresistibly wandered; and when the closing hour finally arrived, they took off their glass slippers and turned off their tricked-up charm. In all of a second, these temptresses could shrug off or reassume their serviceable grace; in a single night, they would sleep with three or four customers. Did she enjoy what she did? "Ah," croaked one husky-voiced young girl who had been dancing with extraordinary abandon. "It's a job."

Kai too was bracing, almost reassuring in her toughness, her freedom from questions and qualms. Managing her life with brisk efficiency, she delivered a breakdown of all the relevant figures—bottom lines, profit curves, spreadsheets and the rest —with the scrupulous poise of a recent graduate from the Harvard Business School. Her body, she explained, was a worthwhile investment. She made $10 an hour teaching Thai classical dance. By comparison, she took home only $4 an evening from working in the bar, seven hours a day, seven days a week, twenty-eight days a month. But if she managed to snag a partner for the night, she could get $20 at least, more than an average Thai worker makes in a fortnight. And what job offered better perks? She could stay in the finest hotels, learn about—and sometimes travel about—the world, be wined, dined and feted, procure free tickets to every disco in town. Bright lights, fast cars, affluent white knights from abroad who were prepared to whisk her hither and thither—she could have them all. In return, she had to do very little. Just dance, flirt, kiss a little and sleep much of the day. "It's a business," she concluded matter-of-factly. "You understand me, I show you good heart."

All this was simple enough: these girls were unillusioned about the trade they were plying, and it was nothing more than a trade, usually of body for money. Yet all too often, the young ladies of the night were not so conveniently transparent: many, in fact, seemed not to be counterfeiting, so much as enjoying— for profit—a kind of frolicsome high spirits that actually came naturally. Their lust for lucre was real, but so too was their charm.

Take Nitya, for example, a lovely round-faced minx with hair that fell to her waist and a smile that could stop hearts from beating. That she could support herself just by drinking in the glamour of the big city was such a delight to her that she could not help but chatter uncontrollably. Her English boyfriend, who lived in Saudi Arabia, had been visiting her, she told me, for four years now. He sometimes sent her money and he always brought her presents. "Once," she said, eyes alight with pleasure, "I say I want video machine." And? "My boyfriend give me it. Otherwise I angry." Wasn't that a little conniving? "Why?" She pouted. "Some man give girl house. Five hundred thousand baht [$20,000]. Video only fifteen thousand baht [$600]. No problem."

A happy incarnation of the imp perverse, Nitya was jubilant at the effects of her appeal, and her appeal was only kindled by her jubilation. Sure, she admitted, she often got her sister to write her letters to her boyfriend. But she knew that he loved her, or needed her, much too much to abandon her. Once he had flown all the way to Bangkok only to find her in a hospital delivering an Arab-featured baby. "He cry, he very angry," she recalled, in the excitable staccato of bar-girl English. "But he cannot go." Once he had visited and found that her passport was filled with recent stamps from Denmark, Sweden and Germany. "He sad. He ask me why I hurt him," she cheerily reported. "What can I say? I was wrong." He walked out on her. But pretty soon he came back, as she knew he would. In any case, she assured me, she was always kind to her boyfriend when he visited, and she still wrote letters to his seventy-year-old mother in Glamorgan. "No problem," bubbled Nitya exultantly. "No problem."

Indeed, for every girl who opened herself up like a cash register, there seemed to be forty others who had about them more curious purity than seemed good or right. These were not the dull-eyed whores or jaded trollops of street corners, but coltish, puckish young kids, blessed often with a friendly, fresh-blown sweetness, sensual but not too far from innocence. And though they might be hardheaded, hardhearted they usually were not. Some, to be sure, were human calculators, some were blazing-eyed tigresses, all were polished charmers. But many, at heart, seemed nothing more than mischievous schoolgirls. When their favorite song came on, they could not help jumping up, singing along and dancing with their friends. And most of the rest of the time, they were to be found in a slumber-party mood, holding hands together, swapping stories about boyfriends, playing children's dice games or chattering on about Mamá and Papá. Many were country girls more pious in their Buddhism than the city's sophisticates, and many brought an uncomplicated zest even to the rigors of the job: one girl showed me the book that she had studied every day for a year in order to learn English, another told me that she had spent three months paying $10 an hour for Japanese lessons after learning that yen flowed more freely than dollars or Deutschemark.

So even as they went about their very adult trade, the girls who worked in the bars seemed little in more ways than the physical: hard and easily hurt, they were just experienced enough to know how to turn their innocence to advantage. Their sauciness was shy, their bashfulness was brazen. One minute, they would stroke a foreigner's hand to gauge what kind of job he had; the next in order to show him real affection. One minute, they were repeating endearments imperfectly picked up from some American movie; the next, forgetting themselves, they would admit to daydreaming about the right man or a fairy-tale future. They loved the *Star Wars* movies, many of them confessed, but their all-time favorites were *Rocky* and *Flashdance*. Because they showed that dreams come true.

INEVITABLY, THIS ELFIN wish for happy endings rubbed constantly against the details of the lives they led. Nearly every girl had a tale to tell, and nearly always it was the same one. She grew up in a village in a family of twelve. A local man came along when she was in her early teens and promised to make her rich ("Thai men no good"). He said she would make her fortune, but she ended up making his. He said she would be "a maid," then forced her to become a slave. She bore him a child, she returned alone to her village, she worked without joy or profit in the fields. Now she could support her offspring only by coming to Bangkok. Who looked after the child? "Mamá." Did her still devoted parents know what she was doing in Bangkok? "No. I tell them I work in boutique. They know I work in bar, they kill me." Sometimes there were hazards in her job: a boss would force her to sleep with him, or lock up the bar and screen blue movies. But she could always find another opening, another show. In the countryside, she could earn only $15 a month; here she took home thirty times as much, leaving her more than enough to send $100 each month to her little brother or her widowed mother.

One day, she hoped, she could make enough money to return

to her village and raise her child (though, schoolgirl to the end, she squandered her cash as soon as she got it on discos and flashy clothes). And one day, she hoped, she would fly off to live with her husband. After the wedding, he had been forced to return to Australia, or California, or Holland. But he promised, he really promised, to send her a visa. The plane ticket, he wrote, was in the mail.

Sometimes, there were variations on the standard theme: Somchai had been bustled out of Phnom Penh by her uncle as soon as the town was stormed by the Khmer Rouge and had landed up in Bangkok, penniless, uneducated and unqualified; Vaitnee had been studying at a local university when Papá died, forcing her to drop out to support Mamá. And some of the tales might have been fact, and some of them fiction—in the half-light of the bar, who could tell?—but it was hard not to shiver, just a little, when Somchai said that she was frightened of sleeping alone because ghosts from Cambodia came back to her in the night; or when Vaitnee admitted that her favorite night of the month was the night she returned to Mamá, and was lullabied to sleep as if she were once more a little girl.

Together with their anthology of sad stories, all the girls cherished, as souvenirs, their albums of photographs. These were invariably small and tatty things, their plastic covers adorned with pictures of a smiling kitten, or a cartoon bee. Inside was a heartbreaking gallery of treasured moments: Pen, for example, in a hundred places with a thousand men, her face always smiling, her eyes sometimes red in the flashlight glare. Usually, she was dressed in a bikini, or simply a pajama shirt, and her companion was fully clothed; sometimes she was nestled in the lap of a shirtless Westerner, sometimes her hand was draped around him. In most cases, they were sitting in a bedroom or a bar. "This man from Switzerland," she explained. "This me in Phuket. This outside bar. This very good man. He give me kangaroo bag. This," she said proudly, pointing to a portly, disheveled character in his late forties, "my boyfriend."

Their other most precious mementos were the letters or postcards they received (translated for $2 a shot, and sometimes answered too, in the great tradition of Samuel Richardson, by a man who hung around the entrance to the Grace Hotel). These too recited the formulae of uncertain affection as ritually as thank-you notes. "I still think of the time we spent together," they always said. "I hope I will see you again soon," they usually continued. "I love you," they invariably concluded. A Pakistani sent a greeting card showing two blond lovers in a California sunset. Bart from Holland wrote, "I love your mind, your body. You are all that I want in a woman." A firm in New Jersey replied, in Xeroxed typescript, "We are sorry to inform you that Mr. David Jackson, to whom you wrote, is no longer employed by this company. We sincerely apologize for any inconvenience this may cause you."

ONE AFTERNOON JANJIRA invited me to see her room. Down a dingy alleyway we went, and up some narrow stairs. She turned a key and let me into a tiny, ill-lit cell, bare except for a mattress and some bedding on the floor (the mattress for her, she explained, the sheets for her roommate—a loquacious, lipsticked transvestite from Laos). A stale loaf of bread sat on a small table; underneath was a bowl of old water. Mickey Mouse grinned down from the bathroom. On a shelf above the mattress, Janjira kept her most valuable possessions: a savings account book and a crumpled manila envelope stuffed with letters. She didn't sleep here very often, she said by way of apology.

Two pieces of decoration dominated the place. Above the mattress was a two-by-one-foot framed glossy photo of Janjira completely naked, with the hands of a clock attached to the glass. Her face was her fortune, I knew, and her picture, she implied, was her résumé. The only other furnishings were two three-foot-tall stuffed animals, with cartoony faces and silly smiles, suspended from the ceiling. Why keep these? I asked. She turned a little bashful. Sometimes, she said, she took them down and slept with them in her arms, one on either side of her. "I dream I have one little girl," she said. "And also one little boy."

Yet the system had little room for such indulgences. What it promised was something more then sex, but a good deal less than security. The girls were to offer love for a price; the men to return it for a while. Both parties were to swear eternal love for a week, or maybe a month. Constancy, like everything else, could be imagined into existence. But let affection or desperation or yearning intrude, even for a moment, and you were lost. Bangkok was home to what was truly the oldest profession in the world: of love, where there was only uncertainty.

I first met Ead in the corner of a bar, dressed in a housewife's buttoned-down frock and white sneakers that looked like a pixie's playthings, gravely keeping to herself. I was surprised to find a shrinking violet in this place of wildly blooming orchids. And doubly surprised when Ead, as we began to talk, swallowed a couple of pills. For what? "The doctor say I think too much." Of what? Sometimes of her seven-year-old daughter, sometimes of her present calling.

As Ead went on speaking, it became clear that her sorrow lay in an intelligence that could not easily accept the paradoxes of her life: unless she gave herself, she knew, she could not enjoy herself; but unless she kept something of herself to herself, she could not survive. Worse than that, she was still old-fashioned enough to chafe against the moral complexities of her position: unable to respect herself, she found it hard to trust herself. So, like many of her colleagues, she kept on reminding me of all her acts of charity, as if to remind herself. Once she gave her boss $1,000, she said. Again and again she reiterated that she had slept with only seven men in thirteen months. Two men had proposed to her. Another had said he would fly her to Hong Kong. A fourth had promised to open a bar just for her. "But," she said, eyes shining, "I no have good luck."

To me, it sounded as if she had all the luck in the world. But as she continued, I began to see that she—like any girl who could not happily give herself over to pleasure or profit—was entangled as fatally in the cat-and-mouse game as the men she attracted. These girls were looking for love in all the wrong places, receiving every proposal except the one they might be tempted to accept. For the men they encountered in bars were generally sweet-talkers, lonely transients, "butterflies" who flitted every night from one flower to the next. So Ead had to remember not to forget herself, had to force herself not to believe the compliments she heard. If her self-respect depended on accepting praise, her sense of self-protection bet he said that to all the girls.

For the sensitive bar girl, then, there was only one thing worse than attaching herself to a man she despised, and that was finding a man she really did care for. Ead's Swiss boyfriend had told her she meant everything to him and they had spent three weeks together. She never heard from him again. For six weeks she had gone everywhere with her Australian boyfriend, who had said they should get married. But now he was back in Sydney, and she did not know when or whether he would return, whether he would ever send for her, whether he was back with a girlfriend or a wife. She had thought about spending $500 to fly to Australia, just so she could be sure. In the meantime, in a mood of self-mutilation, Ead had cut off her long hair. "I think," she said simply, "I have broken heart."

VI

Such quicksand compacts were by no means peculiar to Thailand, of course. I had already met Phuong from Vietnam in Graham Greene's *The Quiet American*. And as I chugged upriver to the ancient capital of Ayutthaya, one bright autumn morning, I opened Greene's *The Honorary Consul* to find the Bangkok bar girl incarnated once again, down to the last jot and tittle, by Clara from Argentina. Here was the same sad taste in clothes, the same unhardened girlishness, the same easiness with deceit, the same ability to set off a hundred emotional guessing games—in short, the same centaurlike creature, half hooker and half ingenue, who saw nothing wrong with marrying a nice man while carrying on with a client.

And there she was again, the elusive meretrix, in Japanese Mariko, the obsessive focus of John David Morley's *Pictures from the Water Trade*, and there once more bodied forth unforgettably by half-Malayan Teena Chang, the girl at the heart of Paul Scott's *The Chinese Love-Pavilion* who drives her lover mad, even after her death, with her teasing duplicities. In Manila too, courtesans become consorts in almost exactly the same fashion.

Yet between those two scenes was a world of difference. For in seedy and improvident Manila, the bars were the fast-buck stuff of a puritan's nightmare; while in high-tech and prosperous Bangkok, they were quicksilver riddles, less alarming for their sleaze than for their cunning refinement, embellished by the country's exquisite sense of design, softened by the ease of

Buddhism, invigorated by the culture of *sanuk* (a good time). In Manila, girls tried to sell themselves out of sheer desperation; in Bangkok, the crystal palaces of sex were only extra adornments in a bejeweled city that already glittered with ambiguities.

In Bangkok, moreover, the ambivalence of the girls only intensified the ambiguity of the bars. For no gaze was direct, and no smile clear-cut in the city of mirrors. And the mirrors were everywhere: one-way mirrors walling the massage parlors, mirrors lining the ceilings of the "curtain hotels," mirrors shimmering in the bars, pocket mirrors in which each girl converted herself into a reflection of her admirer's wishes. Look into a bar girl's eyes, and you'd see nothing but the image of your own needs; ask her what she wanted, and she'd flash back a transparent "up to you." Everything here was in the eye of the beholder; everything was just a trick of the light.

Even language in this scene began in time to resemble a dance of a thousand veils. The girls referred to themselves always as "ladies" and talked of their beaus as "boyfriends," though many, in sad fact, were hardly boys and seldom friends. If they wanted money, the ladies asked their boyfriends, not to "pay," but just to "help" them. And if ever a man gave his coy mistress a compliment—if ever he told her that her eyes smiled or her smile had secrets in it—she would brush him off, with a mixture of sadness and skepticism, and dub him a "sweet mouth." Yet in her very next breath, she would gaily assure him that she had a "good heart," and so did he.

In the netherworld of Bangkok, then, nothing was sure, nothing secure. Names changed, relations shifted, people and places evaporated. All certainties were dissolved in the soft city of hard questions; it was easy to say what it wasn't, difficult to know what it was. Bangkok was a riddler who declared, in all candor, "I am a liar."

One girl in the bars told me she was twenty-five, though she was really twenty-nine and was born, in truth, thirty-one years ago. She could not speak English, she told me in faultless English. "How old are you?" I asked a girl who was new to the scene. "She," interjected another, "she only twenty-one." "No," said the first. "Twenty-three." "But two days ago," I protested, "you said nineteen." And two days ago she had also told me that she did not like this job, that she was unhappy amid the city's bluff and bluster, that she missed her family in Chiangmai. Now she was clapping and dancing as enthusiastically as all the others.

I asked three dancers the time, and none of their answers matched. I heard one girl say she had worked in the business for fifteen days. No, two years. In actual fact, a year. I looked for a girl called Noy and was told by her best friend, Ead, that Noy was a false name based on a nickname, and her surname had changed anyway now that she was married. I went back to the bar where I had met her, to find the place gone, and all the people changed. And some of the girls here looked like boys, and the most impossibly feminine of all—long of leg and husky of voice—were not girls at all. Janjira's hair in her photos was sometimes red, sometimes long, sometimes curly, sometimes black, sometimes short, sometimes brown, sometimes straight. "Who is that boy in all the pictures?" "My brother."

VII

Bangkok's intricate blend of dynamism and languor had long intrigued me. But as I spent more time in the country, Thailand began to betray other combinations I found more difficult to square. For savagery and grace were so cunningly interwoven here that beauty often seemed brutal and brutality itself quite beautiful. At official performances of Thai classical dance, sketches that featured lissome girls making supple turns were juxtaposed with others that showed off bruising, but no less sinuous, displays of sword fighting. Meanwhile, bouts of Thai boxing resembled nothing so much as ritualized ballets, in which two agile boys bowed their heads before the spirit of the ring, then pounded each other to the accompaniment of weird pipes, ominous drums and a steady chanting.

Late one evening, as I wandered through the streets of Chiangmai, I came upon groups of men flinging themselves through a game of volleyball played entirely with head and feet. Their suppleness was a marvel. They somersaulted and pirouetted, making corkscrew pivots in the air; they lunged and twisted high above the ground; they dazzled with their slinky acrobatics. Yet all the while, feet kicked faces, heads banged nastily together. And all around the dusty floodlit square hung a cockfight air of menace.

The Thais, wrote le Carré, are the world's swiftest and most efficient killers. Yet executioners would shoot their victims through gauze so as not to offend the Buddha, and monks would strain their water through their teeth so as not, by chance, to harm a single insect.

But at least, I thought, there was one clear-cut division here, in the Manichean setup of Bangkok. The city's two most common and appealing sights, after all, were its holy men, in spotless saffron robes, and its scarlet ladies. By day, the monks evoked a vision of purity, of hallowed groves filled with golden novitiates; by night, the whole grimy city felt polished, renewed and transformed as sequined girls sang the body electric. At least, so I thought, this day-and-night division would ensure that good was good, and evil evil, and never the twain would meet.

But no. For after a while, I began to notice that, as the whores were engagingly girlish, the monks seemed endearingly boyish. I saw them poring over Walkmans in electronics stores with shopping bags slung over their shoulders, puffing ruminatively on cigarettes, playing tag with their friends in temple courtyards. Once, on venturing inside a monastery on a drowsy afternoon, I chanced upon a group of monks, with beautiful faces, huddled, in the cool shadows, before a TV set that was blasting out cartoons. Then I registered a deeper confusion: some monks, I gathered, were criminals on the lam, while others scattered blessings each night upon the go-go bars; many bar girls, for their part, paid regular visits to Buddhist temples, joined palms together whenever they passed a shrine and knelt in prayer before undertaking their bump and daily grind. Finally, quite flummoxed, I was coming to see the girls as something close to martyrs ("72 prostitutes rescued," proclaimed *The Nation*), and the holy men as something close to con men (the Bangkok *Post* told how five monks had killed one of their fellows with axes and knives, because he dared to criticize them for shooting another monk during a party).

Thus the real sorcery of this dizzying place was that, before one knew it, it could work on one not just a physical but a moral seduction. For here was decadence so decorous that it disarmed the criticism it invited; amorality expressed with the delicacy of a ballerina's nod. And amid such a guiltless marketing of love, righteous indignation could only bounce off the mirrors and the shadows. Slowly, I saw, the city would unbutton your beliefs; gently, it would unbuckle your scruples; coolly, it would let your defenses slither to the floor. Buddhism did not forbid pleasure, the Thais kept saying—just the infliction of pain. So why find shame in enjoyment, and why take enjoyment in shame? What is so harmful or unnatural in love? Must sweetness be seen as a kind of laxness? And not see sex as an act of communion? *"Mai pen rai"* ran their constant refrain. No matter. No sweat. Never mind. "Everyone make love," cooed sweet-smiling Nitya. "What is so wrong? No problem, dahling, no problem."

VIII

And for all my unease in Bangkok, I could not deny that it was quite the most invigorating, and accommodating, city I had ever seen—more lazily seductive than even Rio or Havana. For elegance here was seasoned with funkiness, and efficiency was set off by mystery. Sugar was blended with spice. On Sunday mornings, I often went early to the Temple of the Dawn, and spent several noiseless hours there, surrounded by Buddhas and gazing at the gilded temples that lay across the river like slumberous lions; the minute I grew hungry, however, I could jump into a ten-cent local bus and savor a delectable lunch of watermelon juice and spicy chicken while watching Eurhythmics videos in a spotless air-conditioned café. In the evenings, I would sip Twining's tea from porcelain cups in an exquisite teak-tabled restaurant, soothed by the sound of George Winston, then saunter outside to find the wind blowing around the sleeping canals and three-wheel *tuk-tuks* puttering through the tropical night.

Bangkok was the heart of the Orient, of course. But it was also every Westerner's synthetic, five-star version of what the Orient should be: all the exoticism of the East served up amidst all the conveniences of the West ("It seems to combine," a fascinated S. J. Perelman once wrote, "the Hannibal, Missouri, of Mark Twain's boyhood with Beverly Hills, the Low Countries and Chinatown"). And all the country's variegated Western influences seemed, finally, nothing more than decorative strands that could be woven at will into the beautiful and ornamental tapestry of the country's own inalienable texture ("We provide attractive Thai, Australian, Japanese, Chinese, Swedish, Dutch,

Danish, Belgian, Austrian and French girls," offered one escort agency. "Also handsome and nice boys [gay] entirely at your service"). The Thais, moreover, seemed to know exactly what their assets were—melting smiles, whispering faces, a beseeching frailty, a luxurious grace—and exactly how to turn those virtues into commodities that the West would covet. The carnal marketplace known as the Grace Hotel was, to that extent, aptly named. "Experience unique courtesy only Thai girls can offer."

In the end, then, the lovely doubleness with which the bar scene enthralled its foreign votaries seemed scarcely different from the way in which the stealthy East had often disarmed its visitors from abroad. For had not the Buddha himself said that all that we see is illusion? And had not the war in Vietnam turned on much the same conflict between straight-ahead assault and tricky depth? Perhaps its truest representation, Tim O'Brien's *Going After Cacciato*, had, after all, suggested that the struggle on the battlefield, as in the mind, opposed the usual hard slog of war with the phantom forms of imagination. And in the war too, the result had been the same. Bombs could not annihilate shadows; guns could not demolish mirror images. Strength could not deal with what it could not understand. Throughout the fighting, the Americans had held their own by day. But the Vietnamese had ruled the night. So too, it seemed, in Bangkok.

Ultimately, then, it began to seem no coincidence that Thailand, the most open and most complaisant of all Asian nations, was also the only one that had never been conquered or colonized. The one woman who *never* gives herself away, D. H. Lawrence once wrote, is the free woman who always gives herself up. Just so with Thailand, a place, quite literally, more ravishing than ravished. For though it was known as the "Land of Smiles," the smiles here really gave nothing away; Thai eyes often seemed to laugh, and Thai smiles shone with the light of all that was left unsaid. Many years ago, some Americans had tried to unravel the mystery by calling the Thais "the nicest people money can buy." But even that seemed too simple a summary of the country's opacities. And even now, the Thais, with a gentle smile, continued to confound their visitors from abroad. A Westerner was not exactly in the dark here; just always in the shadows.

The effects of this silken sorcery were clearest, perhaps, in the alien residents who studded the country. For the expats I ran into in Thailand were very different, by and large, from the industrious yuppies who crowd Hong Kong, the vagabond artists who drift through Bali or the beaded seekers who traipse around India. A surprising number of them were underground or marginal men—professional renegades, mercenaries, free-lance writers, drug dealers, proprietors of girlie bars, men (and only men) whose wanderlust was spent. And all of them, in their way, seemed to have slipped into the city's resistless lifestyle as into the tempting embrace of a goddess. By now, therefore, they seemed almost stranded here, immobilized by their addiction to cheap drugs, to memories of the war or to the same "soft beds of the East" that had once seduced Mark Antony away from his official duties. "This," said Emmanuelle, "is a place where doing nothing is an art."

Yet the hardened expats were at least victims of their own worst selves; visitors to Bangkok with even a touch of naïveté were more likely to fall prey to their better impulses. For the bars provided a perfect setting in which susceptible visitors could lose themselves in thinking they had found themselves, shadow-loving their mirror girls, playing hide-and-seek with their consciences. They tempted their subjects to exchange ideals for fantasies. They teased them into circles of self-doubt. And they invited them to ignore the prudent spinster's voice of reason, in favor of the coquettish flirtations of pride—I am the one who can save her, I only think of her as a daughter, she really does care for me. Girls with dreams trigger daydreams in men, and make them feel like boys again.

One man, Ead told me, had stayed with her for five weeks, and had never laid a hand on her; when he left, he had given her a video-machine. Others I knew invariably kept up two girls at once, in the hope that they would fall in love with neither. But even that seemed something of an illusion. And on my third day in Thailand, the Bangkok *Post*, ever sagacious about the salacious, ran on its front page a pointed warning from Auden: "Men will pay large sums to whores for telling them they are not bores."

Yet still each day, the would-be conquerors kept flying into town in droves, old men and young, Arabs and Australians and Americans, on pleasure or a kind of business. Some of them had come many times before, some still had a first-time innocence. And as the airport bus left Johnny behind and drove past the Garden of Eden, Ltd., they could still be seen in the half-light, poring over crumpled pieces of paper (this is Soi Nana, the sex show is here), asking whether the girls were pretty and clean and safe, and concluding, with somewhat shaky assurance, "I think I'll relax this evening with a good Thai massage."

And all night long, in darkened hotel rooms across the length and breadth of the city, from the Sukumvhit Road to Suriwongse, uncertain foreigner and shy-smiling girl kept whispering a ritual litany amidst the mirrors and the shadows.

Do you really like me?

Do I really like you?

Why did you choose me?

How much? How much? How often?

When again? How much? Why not?

You have good heart? You will write to me soon?

Can you? Will I? Should we?

No problem, dah-ling. No problem.

JAPAN
Perfect Strangers

HEN FIRST
I set foot in Japan, baseball fever was sweeping the country.
Every radio in every cab, so it seemed, crackled with play-by-
play commentaries. Blackboards had been set up outside electronics stores to provide passersby with inning-by-inning
scoreboards. Huge Sonys in tidy blond-wood cases filled every
departure lounge in Narita Airport with faultless images of the
game of the moment. And the games and the moments never
ended: from dawn to midnight, the screen was filled with one
mega-montage of half-familiar images—high fives and hyperactive electronic scoreboards and the swaying of fans to caterwaul-
ing organ music, and men circling the bases, half-mythic figures,
in many cases, from my boyhood, like Reggie Smith. "Baseball
School for Children" was on one network at noon, pro baseball
was on another at 7:04 p.m. and the All-Japan National High
School Championship was being featured on the government
station for nine hours each day.

At 9 a.m. on the opening day of the high school championship,

I settled down before a TV set in a Kyoto coffee shop. Already, Koshien Stadium outside Osaka was filled to capacity with 55,000 fans, screaming their appreciation of opening ceremonies worthy of the Olympic Games. Trumpets sounded from the ramparts. Squadrons of girls trooped onto the field in perfect formation, waving flags. Then the teams themselves marched in, goose-stepping together, hands swinging rigidly by their sides, faces turned bravely in the same direction. The Education Minister came on to throw out the first ball. And for the next two weeks, thousands of people across the nation took time off work or closed down shop in order to follow the High School Championship. This was not, it seemed, a land that believed in half measures.

Baseball, indeed, was everywhere I looked in Japan. In the narrow streets of Tokyo, I saw children working and working to perfect their moves, and along the wide boulevards, businessmen were lined up in batting cages to refine their skills against pitching machines. Soft-drink machines incorporated games of baseball roulette, magazines offered readers in Hiroshima the chance to "meet your Carp." Half the little boys across the length of the country seemed to be sporting Giants caps, and every day brought seven different newspapers dealing with nothing—nothing—but sports. Earlier in the summer, a colleague told me, he had been on a photographic assignment in a Buddhist monastery outside Kyoto. Gradually, and patiently, he had won the trust of the head monk. Finally, once the sacred rituals were complete, the holy man had been moved to give his visitor, as a token of his appreciation, a poem. Oh, and one more thing, the monk had added: Were Yogi Berra and Mickey Mantle still playing in the major leagues?

"Baseball is the All-American sport," marveled Tina, a horse-trainer from Seattle who was bicycling through Japan. "But they're more fanatic about it here than they are at home." So indeed it seemed. In America, baseball was only the national pastime; in Japan, it was a national obsession.

JAPAN'S WHOLE-SCALE, WHOLESALE importation of things American was by now, of course, a universal cliché: students taking courses in Beginning Incongruity or Irony 101 could revel in a treasure house of easy absurdities and crazy juxtapositions, the silliness of signs for "Jerry Beans" or "Gland Beef," the almost willful absurdity of calling a video arcade "We'll Talk." In the hip young streets around Shinjuku Station in Tokyo, a department store (called American Blvd.) advertised "Jeans" in one area, "Accessories" in another and, in a third, "American Spirit"; the coffee shops nearby were mostly decorated in the borrowed nostalgia of American Graffiti, aglitter with shiny prom-night music and retro-mythic images of American Dreamin'. Tokyo's strip joints, where blondes were at a premium, were called U.S.A. or Campus City, and the magazines I saw at newsstands seemed ready to adopt any title at all, so long as it was English. Their contents were entirely Japanese, but their names were *McSister, Miss Hero, Fine, Belove, More, Say, Here, With* and, more alarmingly still, *Lemon;* in the well-endowed Adult section, I saw *Big Man* and *Bachelor, Mr. Dandy* and *Cool Guy* (this last including a bold promise on its cover: "Guaranteed Fully Ellection").

Only three days after my arrival in Tokyo, I made the statutory pilgrimage to Mount Fuji. The holy peak, as legend dictates, was veiled behind a screen of clouds that sometimes thickened, sometimes parted, sometimes drifted across the top to register the mountain's changing moods. Up at the Fifth Station, old men with backpacks and walking sticks, waving flags of the Rising Sun, made their final preparations for a long, emotion-filled ascent that could, in many cases, be the high point of a lifetime. And as they did so, the PA system blasted out a deafening version of Cyndi Lauper's "Girls Just Wanna Have Fun."

"Kyoto?" a member of Bruce Springsteen's band had pronounced in *Newsweek* the day I arrived in the ancient capital. "It was just like New Jersey." As it happened, I thought, he was righter than he knew. For the Stars and Stripes was everywhere in Japan: waved by children at baseball games, fluttering from tables in restaurants, haloed by neon in the streets. As I ate my enormous American-style buffet breakfast in an enormous American-style coffee shop, the room was flooded with a piped-in rendition of "Home on the Range." And when I rang up a hotel a little later, I was put on hold, and once again there floated over the line the anesthetic strains of the same All-American tune.

The deer and the antelope played here, all right, and seldom was heard a discouraging word. But even so, Japan did not really feel like home to me. Not just because the Mister Donut outlets offered powdered green tea shakes. Nor even because "Radio City" was a disco here, and "The Village Voice" a bar (while "Manhattan St. NYC Coffee" carried a message inviting one to "taste the happiness of New York . . . where the streets speak to you, something good will probably happen"). But mostly because the Japanese seemed to have erected all the postcard-perfect props of American Suburbia, even as they continued, behind them, to enact their own unfathomable rites. Waseda University had painstakingly re-created an entire Shakespearean theater, I read, and then turned it into a Kabuki museum.

And if the first familiar truism about Japan was its conspicuous consumption of all things Western, the second was its inability ever to make those things fully its own. "There are few who would seriously object to exposure to foreign habits and customs through copying," wrote an eighteen-year-old local high school student, Raymond Wong, in a magazine called *Tokyo*, "but when absorbed only at face value—and without understanding —the purpose is lost and the original intention devalued." Certainly, the culture often appeared to be perversely determined to forswear the matchless refinement that seemed its birthright in favor of an imported crudity that suited it not at all. The best examples of this, I often thought, were the chic young ladies who marched in battalions through the Tokyo streets in Western styles of elegant blandness. Dressed all alike in clothes that deviated not an inch from the textbook norm, they invariably had Givenchy sewn on their skirts and Gucci on their bags (no trace of Issey Miyake here!). But in their eyes was still a shyness, and in their bearing a reticence, that was only and inalienably Japanese. And it was a revelation to me, on the Night of a Thousand Lanterns in Kyoto, to see the same girls who looked so awkward in their cutoff pants and off-the-shoulder provocations sloughing off their imported styles and suddenly returned to inarguable grace in kimonos that moved with the motions of their flowing bodies.

Yet most of these skin-deep anomalies turned on nothing deeper than the funniness of brand names and fashion statements mistranslated. In Japanese baseball, however, I felt that something more complex must be going on. For in baseball,

Japan had taken over not just an American prop but an American rite, a living drama, a healthy slice of the All-American Pie. More than designer jeans or Burger Kings or the Beach Boys, baseball occupied a special place in the American imagination. It was, in a sense, the story that America told itself about what it could be, its rose-tinted image of an unfallen garden where all races worked together and heroes walked tall on sunlit patches of green, while families watched the rites of innocence over hot dogs and Cokes on a never-ending summer's afternoon. Baseball was in many ways a repository for certain cherished aspects of the American Daydream.

What, I wondered, could Japan hope to make of this?

AT SEVEN O'CLOCK on a Sunday morning, while the broad streets of Tokyo were eerily desolate, armies of pitchers warmed up on mounds throughout the sleeping city.

And late at night, in the narrow-waisted back streets of Asakusa, I saw a woman pitching a shuttlecock at a shaven-headed boy who met it with a sweet baseball swing, over and over and over again, while two men crouched in the dark to watch his form. A snatch of a folk song was caught on the breeze. A full moon rose above the nearby temple.

II

When Japan's favorite team, the Yomiuri Giants, came to Osaka to play their traditional rivals, the Hanshin Tigers, I took a Hanshin Express from the Hanshin department store and arrived at the Hanshin Tigers' Koshien Stadium ninety minutes early—only to learn that I was late. Because of the capacity crowds expected for this regular midseason contest, the gates had been opened six hours before gametime; many fans had actually camped out overnight in order to be sure of tickets. And already, there issued forth from within the stadium a steady, relentless, deafening chant. Da da da, da-da da da.

In the forest of shops that encircled the stadium, it was not hard to find pledges of allegiance. Souvenir booths were selling Tiger towels, Tiger pens, Tiger pins, Tiger fans; they had Tiger rings, Tiger opera glasses, Tiger hats, Tiger alarm clocks; they offered Tiger lighters, Tiger radios, Tiger drums, even Tiger telephones. The huge central gift shop also displayed Tiger purses, Tiger postcards, Tiger pillboxes and Tiger pillows on which was inscribed: "50th Anniversary established. We must win a VICTORY this year. HOLD OUT." All these items were being snapped up in huge numbers by fans in flowing black-and-golden Tiger kimonos, gold-and-black happi coats and Tiger caps (complete with tails), many of whom had doubtless given prayers at the Tiger shrine. And all around, from every corner, came the solemn martial strains of the Tiger fight song.

Inside, more than an hour before the first ball, the right-field bleachers were already a swelling sea of black and gold. Flags of the Rising Sun snapped in the breeze, and around them fluttered as many as twenty other banners—Tiger flags, numbered pennants, and even the Stars and Stripes. At the front of each row, white-gloved cheerleaders with megaphones were telling the audience when to clap; in the aisles, men in black coats and golden headbands banged heartily on drums to intensify the noise. Most of the time, the fans sat obediently, without a word, in their uniform rows; as soon as they were given their cue, however, they thrust their yellow bullhorns into the air, in perfect unison, and joined together in a thunderous chant. Da da da, da-da da da.

The fans seemed never to tire of their single, monotonous battle cry, and they raised it, and raised it, and raised it again, whenever instructed to do so. Da da da, da-da da da. And by the time the game was ready to begin, the chorus had turned into a deafening roar. Caught up in the sound and the fury, I felt myself irresistibly stirred. I also felt part of a single huge, and single-minded, body. All of us were one, I thought; teenagers and kindly-looking grandmas and self-possessed young mothers and businessmen, all of us were united in our single common cry. Da da da, da-da da da.

Thus the chanting continued, always on time, always in synch, as regular as the tick-tock of a metronome. Whenever a Tiger came up to the plate, the cheerleaders leaped on top of the dugout, the men pounded their drums and the entire army of black and gold rose to its collective feet, waving its bullhorns and rending the air with a special chant devised for every player. As soon as the Giants came up, the crowd fell absolutely silent. The next inning, up again would rise the surging chants. Then silence again. The regularity of this push-button rhythm was disrupted only when a Tiger pitcher had two strikes on a Giant; then, the fans would rouse themselves from stillness to let out a low, owl-like hoot that rose like a wave and crashed with a roar to throw off the unfortunate batter.

Not once in the game, though, did a single fan shout out of turn, or give way to a sudden yell or solitary jeer. Nobody screamed at the umpire. Nobody cheered on a favorite player. Nobody threw curses, let alone beer cans, at an enemy player. Never once was there an undignified scramble—or any scramble at all—after a foul ball that landed in the stands (instead, it was calmly picked up and ceremonially handed back to a bowing attendant). Everyone cheered only when everyone else cheered, at the prescribed time in the prescribed way. The roars were followed by silence; the silence was followed by a roar. Here was passion by remote control.

Inevitably, the great tribalism of the occasion—the ritual incantation of the massed chant, the black-and-golden regalia, the thronged partisanship—took me back to the crowds I had seen at British soccer matches. But these fans were as wholesome as their British counterparts were not. Soccer fans were all too often nothing more than unemployed layabouts with knives in their shoes and switchblades in their eyes, scrounging for a fight; the Tiger supporters, by contrast, were uniformly well dressed and well behaved; they would rather, I imagined, switch than fight. Indeed, they presented a virtual model of an ideal social order. For even in the bleachers, there were no bums, no drunkards, no necking couples or unruly kids. Four children in front of me tidily poked at four tidily boxed meals of noodles and rice, while their mother anxiously snapped photos of them. Pairs of teenage girls whispered to one another and giggled. Senior citizens looked on with serenity. When the Tigers scored, everyone turned around and shook hands with everyone else, decorous as parishioners at an Easter service. And when their moment came, everyone joined together, on time and on cue, again and again and again, in their single compact chant. Da da da, da-da da da.

As I traveled to other games around the country, I managed to register a few regional differences. At Meiji-Jingu Stadium in Tokyo, the stalls sold "Hot Man Dogs" and "Guten Burgers" (no pun, I think, intended); ivy-covered, double-decker Korakuen, home of the mighty Giants, was ringed by an amusement park, complete with batting cages, baseball video games and a sock-hop pop group in pink-Cadillac suits singing "Route 66." The Giants had two pom-pom girls in every row, and a scoreboard that told the fans when to clap by flashing an image of mechanically clapping hands. Supporters of the Taiyo Whales struck up the Notre Dame fight song, greeted a Hispanic star with a jaunty rendition of "La Cucaracha" and serenaded another favorite—almost too perfectly, I thought—with the Mouseketeer chant. Fans of the Seibu Lions traveled to every home game en masse, in a specially decorated train (a show of unity encouraged by the stadium's policy of providing no parking places). Whenever an opposing pitcher was yanked from the game, Tiger fanatics cried out *"Sayonara, sayonara,"* and then launched into a remorselessly poignant version of "Auld Lang Syne."

Yet for all the minor variations, the ritual was effectively everywhere the same: the same chants at the same time, begun before the game and continued for ten minutes after the final out. (Equally punctual, television broadcasts of Japanese games traditionally lasted for exactly one hour and twenty-six minutes. No more. No less. No matter the context or the occasion: one hour and twenty-six minutes.) Every now and then, I was told, all the feeling that was so scrupulously contained would suddenly erupt, and the fans would go berserk, in what the Japanese call a fit of "temporary insanity," storming the field or pummeling an umpire. But that was only the exception that proved the rule. Generally, the control at the games was as regular, as rhythmic, as relentless as the chanting. Da da da, da-da da da.

And every time I saw ten thousand fans filling the air in unison with black-and-yellow bullhorns, I found myself shuddering a little at the militarism of the display—and at its beauty. For the rites of Japanese baseball, however orchestrated, were lovely in their lyricism. When the fans scattered pieces of colored paper or rice into the night air, it looked as if fireflies were lighting up the darkness. In the middle of the seventh inning, the crowd chose not to sing "Take Me Out to the Ball Game," but let off flares, scarlet and mysterious, into the sky. And after the final out, spectators sent rainbowed streamers fluttering out onto the field that streaked the air with their brightness. The teams in the Japanese leagues were not called Dodgers or Expos or Astros; they were Dragons, Swallows and Carp. And the song the Tiger fans were singing was called, quite beautifully, "When the Wind Blows Down from Mount Rokko."

IN ORDER TO get closer to the heart of the sport, however, I decided one day to pick up the English-language autobiography of Sadaharu Oh, the Babe Ruth of Japan and the country's unquestioned king (in symbol-perfect Japan, even his name meant "king"). The classic works of American baseball reminiscence—Jim Bouton's *Ball Four,* for example, or Sparky Lyle's *The Bronx Zoo*—are, famously, gossip columns crossed with jokebooks that throw open the doors on a madcap whirl of cokeheads, birdbrains, rakes, flakes and lovable bumpkins; Oh's book, by comparison, ushers his reader into a world as hushed and solemn as a monastery.

The story of the star's ascent unfolds, in fact, like nothing so much as a Japanese *Pilgrim's Progress,* with its author a kind of earnest Zen Everyman bumbling along an archetypal obstacle course of pitfalls and temptations. Instead of accounts of key games or late-inning heroics, Oh devotes most of his space to chronicling his "fatheaded clumsiness" as a youth, his typical off-field errors in the entertainment districts of the Ginza, his sense of obligation to the fans. "Outside the world of baseball," he matter-of-factly reports, "I was a fairly boring fellow." And instead of dwelling on his greatest hits, he concentrates on the stages of his often painful quest for spiritual maturity. The stars of this morality play are Providence and Time; its protagonists a strange, half-magical group of spirits and forces and guardian angels that seem to govern Oh's destiny much more than the man himself.

Thus everything in the player's life takes on an almost mystical glow. When the fledgling star was still in his teens, he records, he consulted a soothsayer for advice. Keep always the image of a dragon in your mind, said the sage, and change your name for a year. Oh did so, and became a star. When the schoolboy pitcher developed a blister on his finger before a crucial game in the High School Championship, while far from home in a dingy boardinghouse, a man suddenly appeared at his door. It was his father, there to proffer an ancient medicinal cure of ginseng root mixed with Chinese wine, before vanishing again into the night. Many years later, when he was struggling to beat Hank Aaron's world record of 755 home runs, Oh was in desperate need of help. The more he pressed, the less he achieved. The less he achieved, the more he pressed. Days passed, the record remained unbroken, camera crews and police escorts dogged his every move. The star tried everything he knew to break the slump. He stood on his head, he held his breath while swinging, he practiced *kiai*, a special Zen method of shouting. All to no avail. Then, one day, as he sat in the clubhouse before a game, his mother abruptly materialized, as from a mist, before him. In her hand she carried a bag full of apples and a box full of crickets. The apples, she explained, were for Sada's teammates, the crickets for his daughters. With that sibylline utterance, she disappeared again. Mysteriously strengthened by her appearance, Oh went out and broke the record.

As befits such an unearthly history, Oh's story, subtitled *A Zen Way of Baseball*, was not only shot through with poetry; it was also steadied by a temple of oracular aphorisms ("In combat, I learned to give up combat. An opponent was someone whose strength joined to yours created a certain result. Let someone call you enemy and attack you, and in that moment they lost the contest"). Whenever he was asked for an autograph, the slugger copied down, next to his name, the characters for "patience," "spirit" or "effort." He never once asked for a salary raise. And the glossary at the back of his volume does not explain such terms as "goof off," "gopher ball," "beaver shooter" or "bonus baby," but Japanese phrases that connote "the path of an echo," "tender feeling" and "internal or spiritual balance."

Remarkably too, everyone else in Oh's world seemed to move within this same high realm of rarefied abstraction. A member of the star's fan club used to express his devotion to his hero by visiting the grave of Oh's sister whenever Oh could not make the trip himself. The Giant manager prepared for the season by purifying himself at a Buddhist retreat, and after disappointing showings, he delivered public apologies to the fans. The man who made the slugger's bat wandered through a forest in search of a tree whose soul would match the soul of the hitter. And perhaps the closest thing to a hero in the story was Oh's *sensei*, Hiroshi Arakawa, the batting coach who trains him in aikido,

Zen, Kabuki and, ultimately, the traditional arts of swordsmanship, teaching him how to hit by showing him how to wait.

Ghostwritten, so it seemed, by a samurai monk-poet, Oh's book was in many parts movingly beautiful. Closer in spirit—and "spirit" was the word that tolled through the book like a prayer bell—to *Walden* than *The Mick*, it transported one from the beer-stained bleachers of the American game to a shrine in the mist at the top of a mountain. Suddenly, baseball was seen from a great and cloudless height, *sub specie aeternitatis*. Indeed, the game seemed only to interest Oh as a model of man's larger universal striving. The diamond was just a reflection of the diamond path, the base path just a narrow road to the deep north within. The game was taken seriously only because it was not in itself taken seriously. Baseball, I thought, was back in proportion.

Or was it? The single great problem with the Japanese game, I was told by Robert Whiting, the longtime American expat who has become the foremost Western expert on Japanese baseball, was that, in truth, everything—absolutely everything—was deadly serious. Everything was pitched at the exalted, almost dizzying heights inhabited by Oh. Poker-faced committee men thrashed out the implications of the game's minutiae. Managers and fans pored over statistical breakdowns of every single pitch thrown by every single pitcher. Editorials in the *Japan Times* solemnly deliberated over the pros and cons of aluminum bats (which increase the potential for home runs, but break all too easily: progress has its price). Teams, above all, were managed like Marine camps, in which players had to run endless, mindless exercises in order to toughen their "fighting spirit." Some managers determined the marriages of their players; one had recently slapped his shortstop and kicked his catcher. "It's almost a military-type discipline," Dennis Barfield, a U.S. import, said on TV, explaining how the teams had to perform their wind sprints together, chanting the same slogans and running in formation like a squadron. Players had to be as relentlessly well drilled as their fans.

In America, the special charm of baseball had always seemed to lie in its casualness, each game and season drifting past with the rhythm of a lazy daydream. Baseball was full of spaces, interstices, silences for Memory or Fancy to fill. And since every team played 162 games in a year, very few individual contests greatly mattered; a trip to the stadium was really a leisurely outing on a spring afternoon, a prolonged seventh-inning stretch, a languorous distraction. The game offered none of the jazzed-up jive and nighttime ghetto fire of pro basketball, nor the power-politicking head games of football. It flowed instead like a family picnic. Basketball was about drugs, football about sex. Baseball was good clean fun.

So too, the whole mythos of American baseball had to do with summertime flights of whimsy and wackiness, red herrings and gentle amusements. The game was the domain of screwballs who came out of left field. Its most cherished figures were not such superstar exemplars of decency and hard work as Dale Murphy, Steve Garvey or Rod Carew, but Characters—Tommy Lasorda, for example, the pasta-eating Italian with a joke for every occasion, or "Spaceman" Lee, the dope-smoking free spirit beloved of rock stars, or Gaylord Perry, gray-haired master of the illegal spitball. The Marvelous Mets, slapsticking their way to last place season after season, had gained much more attention than the routinely successful Orioles; the oral history of the game lay not with Lou Gehrig or Ted Williams, but with salty curmudgeons and masters of the malapropism like Casey Stengel and Leo Durocher. *Baseball Is a Funny Game* was the title of Joe Garagiola's first book, while Jay Johnstone's autobiography reveled in precisely the element that the Japanese generally preferred to forget: *Temporary Insanity*. True, Bill Freehan's seminal book of memoirs, *Behind the Mask*, did enjoy the perfect title for a study of Japan—and one that had, in fact, been used for a book on Japanese subculture—but the Detroit catcher had meant the phrase in only the most literal of senses.

In Japan, however, baseball was not a funny game. Oh rarely cracked a smile in his book, and the fans I saw never guffawed. There was no time—or room—for folly in the Japanese game. Watching the high school contests on TV, I told Whiting, I was much impressed by how expertly the teenagers mimicked all the moves and mannerisms of the pros—were it not for the scoreboard, I would not have been able to tell whether I was watching a major-league game or a high school one. That, said Whiting, was no surprise. Many high schools were in fact nothing more than baseball factories, set up for the assembly-line production of pros. The boys had to practice 350 days a year, and often through the night. Each of them had to shave his head as a sign of devotion to the team, and each was likely to get slapped if he did not chant in harmony with the team. In the stict *kohai senpai* hierarchy that governed these squads, every freshman had to dance attention on his seniors. The bullying that resulted could make even the fagging of British boarding schools sound benign by comparison; recently, said Whiting, a freshman had died at the hands of a senior.

In the professional ranks, of course, the regimen was even more tyrannical. Before every single game of the season, whether in midwinter or 100-degree heat, the players had to practice for four hours and run three miles. One team did a daily "Death Climb" that included twenty sprints up and down the 275 steps of a Shinto shrine; others did "1,000 ground ball" drills, performed 500 "shadow swings" daily, or ran sprints with weights tied to their backs and tires attached to their legs. A laggard player was routinely humbled by having balls hit directly at his body for hours on end. In the United States, star pitchers are handled like precious objects who need at least three days of rest between appearances; in Japan, a successful pitcher is made to appear day after day after enervating day, until he virtually collapses into retirement in his mid-twenties. "American players start spring training on March 1, Japanese on January 15," Whiting explained succinctly in a television interview. "American players spend an average of three hours a day on the field, the Japanese spend eight. Americans run one mile a day on average in camp, Japanese run ten." In 1987, even Lou Gehrig's seemingly unbreakable record of playing in 2,138 consecutive games had been shattered by Sachio Kinugasa of the Hiroshima Carp, who had appeared in every game for 12 years.

Japanese baseball, in fact, was driven by the same unbending will to succeed, the same single-minded determination, the same almost inhuman commitment to industry that had made the entire country a world leader in industry. Hard work, and more hard work, and then still more. Practice, practice, practice. Practice made perfect, and perfection made for supremacy. If the country could lower its birthrate, increase its average height by four inches in four decades and solve what had been the worst pollution problem in the world, why could it not also conquer a game? Mind, it was felt, could always master matter; greatness could be achieved through willpower alone. Even the dignified Oh, for all his emphasis on toughening the spirit, acknowledged that one of the keys to his accomplishments was simple repetition. "I have always believed," he said, "that success in this life owes to a strong will."

Thus the coaches in Japan worked on the assumption that there was nothing that a man could not be trained—or forced—to do. "If your mental attitude is right," said Giant pitcher Tsuneo Horiuchi, "you can make your body work." Absolute efficiency was the highest goal. "The fewer mistakes you make," said Shigeo Nagashima, once Oh's only rival as the greatest player in the land, and later a coach, "the more games you will win." The logic was as relentless as calculus: do not try to manufacture felicities, just eliminate all mistakes. Do not make good, just make perfect. The Japanese were already working on such technological innovations as a system to warn outfielders of the proximity of the fence, and a batter's helmet equipped with electronic buttons for the relaying of instructions. But the greatest of all the creations they envisaged was a man, or a group of men, who could be made to operate as flawlessly as a car. Nothing could defeat an error-free machine.

A purification of the spirit and a series of soulless exercises, a way of elevating men into monks and of reducing them into machines: from head to toe, the Japanese game seemed thoroughly Japanese, and not much of a game.

III

As I spent longer in Japan, I increasingly came to feel that the "empire of signs" was, as I had half expected, the most complex society I had ever seen, and to that extent, the most impossible to crack. If nothing else, its assumptions were so different from those of the West that to understand it seemed scarcely easier than eating a sirloin steak with chopsticks. The Japanese might drink the same coffee as their American counterparts, and their magazines might boast English titles. But how could one begin to penetrate a land where shame was more important than guilt, and where public and private were interlocked in so foreign a way that the same businessman who unabashedly sat on the subway reading a hard-core porno mag would go into paroxysms of embarrassment if unable to produce the right kind of coffee for a visitor? Japan defied the analysis it constantly provoked; Japan was the world's great Significant Other.

By the same token, I also found that discussions among foreigners about the true nature of Japan continued endlessly, and fascinatingly, yet never seemed to come to anything new. Every foreign "explanation" of the country seemed finally to revolve around exactly the same features—a reflection of the place's homogeneity, perhaps, but also of its impenetrability. How, every foreigner wondered (in unison), could a culture promiscuously import everything Western, yet still seem impenetrably Eastern? How did the place remain so devoted to its traditions even as it was addicted to modernity and change? What to make of a people with an exquisite gift for purity as well as an unrivaled capacity for perversity? And how on earth could a land of ineffable aesthetic refinement decorate its homes with the forms of cartoon kitties?

Japan, for the foreigner, was all easy dichotomies: samurai and monk, Chrysanthemum and Sword, a land, as Koestler wrote, of "stoic hedonists." If the test of a first-rate mind, as Fitzgerald once wrote, is the ability to hold two opposed ideas at the same time and still keep going, Japan had the most first-rate mind imaginable.

To me, however, all these familiar contradictions seemed finally to resolve themselves into a single, fundamental division: between the Japan of noisy, flashy, shiny surfaces and the Japan of silence and depth. The first—the face of modern Japan—afforded a glimpse into a high-tech, low-risk future, a passage into the clean, well-lit corridors of a user-friendly utopia, where men glided on conveyor belts into technocentric cells that were climate-controlled, sweetly scented and euphoniously organized by a PA system. Here was society as microchip, a tiny network of linked energies. Commuters functioned like computers, workmen like Walkmen. Every morning, armies upon armies of workers—men all in jackets and ties, women all in look-alike skirts and blouses—surged through the subways of Tokyo, undifferentiated, unerring, and undeflected.

This was the Japan of no fuss and no static, the Japan where everything was accurate to umpteen significant places. In parking lots, all the nearly identical cars were lined up in perfectly symmetrical rows, shiny and well organized as compact, economical little boxes (and, in Japan, I saw no big cars, no old cars, no dirty cars, or showy cars). In the bullet trains, every passenger placed his suitcase, just so, on the overhead rack, then sat down bolt-upright, and in silence. Taxi drivers here wore the spotless white gloves of a queen's lady-in-waiting. Everyone, in fact, seemed to have been provided with the same well-packaged contentment kit. Art, wrote Pater, should approximate to the condition of music; Life, the Japanese seemed to believe, should approximate to the condition of its ever-present Muzak.

And though such formal perfection could be cloying at times, and antiseptic at others, it was also undeniably comforting. I always relished flying with Japan Air Lines, for example, because I always knew—could be 100 percent certain—that the flight would proceed without slip-ups, disturbances or arguments. In demonstrating the safety maneuvers, each of the hostesses performed a harmonious miniaturized ballet in which every act of mock desperation was suggested by one tiny gesture as slight as it was beautiful. And throughout the flight, the cabin attendants themselves seemed to work on automatic pilot, cruise-controlling the aisles without wasted motion, tending to every need with clockwork grace and a smile. Japan had brought class to economy by making an art form of convenience.

In Japan, in fact, everything had been made level and uniform—even humanity. By one official count, 90 percent of the population regarded themselves as middle-class; in schools, it was not the outcasts who beat up the conformists, but vice versa. Every Japanese individual seemed to have the same goal as every other—to become like every other Japanese individual. The word for "different," I was told, was the same as the word for "wrong." And again and again in Japan, in contexts varying from the baseball stadium to the watercolor canvas, I heard the same unswerving, even maxim: "The nail that sticks out must be hammered down."

One paradigm of this sense of flawless conformity was the perfect being: the robot. When I picked up a copy of *The Student Times*, a bilingual newspaper designed to assist the study of

English, I found its longest article entitled "Robot Walks at Almost Human Speed." Its Tom and Jerry cartoon featured B3-Ze, a robotized mouse. Two months later, I read that the country's latest toy was a $14,000 kimono-clad female robot that served as the Perfect Receptionist, welcoming visitors with a smile, ushering them into the office and seeing them off with a courteous farewell. Naturally, the robot never complained, never grew tired, never fouled up (though a malfunctioning robot on an automobile assembly line *had*, it was true, recently claimed its first human victim). In Japan, where there are almost twice as many television sets as people, one company had even started having robots manufacture other robots.

But an even more eloquent microcosm of modern Japan, I thought, was Tokyo Disneyland. A vision of an ideal order—sanitized, homogenized, unsmudged by human hand—it was a perfect toy replica of the tinkling, sugarcoated society around it, a perfect box within a box. Immaculate in its conception, it was flawless in its execution. American Disneylands are impeccably clean; Tokyo Disneyland was more so. American Disneylands are absurdly efficient; the Tokyo branch put them to shame. Within its sparkling, fairy-tale portals, everything—and everyone—worked, and worked perfectly.

In Tokyo Disneyland, everything had been thought of, and nothing was left to chance. Suddenly discover that you need extra money? No problem: around the corner is a Mitsui Bank. Torn by a wish to get rid of a loved one? Never fear: there is a Baby Center not far away, as well as a Pet Club. Subject to unusual needs? Relax: there are thirteen rest rooms for the handicapped here and (since dining, according to the official program, "will be an important part of your visit to Tokyo Disneyland") more than forty restaurants. Outside the main pavilions were parking spaces for baby strollers; and along the dustless malls stood a Signature Shop, in which every one of your souvenirs could be "personalized." Not only was there a "Parade of Dreams Come True," but the miracle took place every day, and promptly on the hour.

To me, however, the particular, the preeminent charm of the Disneylands at home—what gave them their life and narrative tension—had always been the unending friction between the seamless perfection of the place and the irredeemable, intractable, sometimes intolerable, humanity of its visitors. Technologically, Disneyland was a monument to all that was great in man, his ability to manufacture perfection and to make even the most cartoonish of conceits grand and moving through sheer mechanical wizardry. Yet in the midst of all these glittering conceptions were fat women in shorts and slobbering bikers, stringy blondes on the make and screeching brats with ice cream dribbling down their cheeks.

Tokyo Disneyland, however, had no such enlivening contrasts. Indeed, there was no disjunction at all between the perfect rides and their human occupants. Each was as synchronized, as punctual, as clean as the other. Little girls in pretty bonnets, their eyes wide with wonder, stood in lines, as impassive as dolls, while their flawless mothers posed like mannequins under their umbrellas. Mass-producing couples and 1.7-children families waited uncomplainingly for a sweet-voiced machine to break the silence and permit them to enter the pavilion—in regimented squads. All the while, another mechanical voice offered tips to ensure that the human element would be just as well planned as the man-made: Do not leave your shopping to the end, and try to leave the park before rush hour, and eat at a sensible hour and do not, on any account, fail to have a good time.

In a recent poll, a group of Japanese had been asked what had given them the most happiness in life. More than half of them had answered, "Disneyland."

THE BEAUTY OF the Zen temples was, of course, quite the opposite. There were no signposts along their paths, and no signs. Every visitor had to make his own way, fill the emptiness with something from within. There was nothing for him to see or do, nothing to find save what he had brought himself. And that, very often, was the greatest find of all.

I loved the quiet places in Kyoto, the places that held the world within a windless moment. Inside the temples, Nature held her breath. All longing was put to sleep in the stillness, and all was distilled into a clean simplicity. The smell of woodsmoke, the drift of incense; a procession of monks in black-and-gold robes, one of them giggling in a voice yet unbroken; a touch of autumn in the air, a sense of gathering rain. Bells tolling through the dusk, calling the faithful to prayer.

In Kamakura, at the end of a bright afternoon, everything was mute. An old man sat on a wooden bench, motionless, lost in contemplation. Light fell through the hushed, unpeopled groves. Nothing stirred. The mind absorbed the calmness, the calmness absorbed the mind. Thoughts fell away, or were gentled into something purer. And the air was filled with something more than wonder: peace, and the drift of meditation.

And all about the lantern-lit passageways of Kyoto in the twilight hung the same enraptured stillness. A little boy threw a pitch, and a littler boy missed, missed, missed the luminous yellow ball, and a girl looked on from the curb. Behind every tidy vertical white sign was a blond-wood door, and through the door, red lanterns led the way to tiny rock gardens. The silence was quickened by the sound of falling water.

After nightfall, the cobbled streets grew secret, almost silent, but for an occasional footstep in the distance, the sound of a faraway piano. I saw a shiver of light beneath a bamboo screen. I glimpsed a pair of slippers twinned outside a tatami room. I heard the rustle of a kimono swishing upstairs. Now and then, I caught a snatch of laughter from an upper room.

The same Japanese who relished Tokyo Disneyland seemed also to enjoy a remarkable gift for stillness, for furnishing their lives with absolutes. Clean lines, empty spaces. Silence and space. Water and air. In the ringing, silver purity of the streets, the abstract was brought close and given warmth. It was given further plangency by the country's sense of exquisite agony, its appreciation of the way in which all the floating world is shadowed by mortality, so that loveliness is sad, and sadness lovely. Thus the bare rooms and sparse trees of the gardens were designed to register all the inflections of the passing seasons, and the gardens themselves became elegiac odes, haikus that arrest all the fugitive sensations that catch at the Japanese heart: longing and parting, the passage of time, the ache of recollection.

A less thoughtful people might be maddened by the seething buzz-saw noise of cicadas in August. But the Japanese reminded themselves that the insects came up from underground only on the final day of their lives, and so found in even the cacophony a lovely, haunting symbol. "It is the sound of summer," a Japanese girl explained to me, "and it makes us sad. Because it makes us think of their dying. And then we realize that we too must die."

Deepest of all the autumnal beauties of the Zen gardens, though, was their simple rightness. Some blessings, I knew, came from Nature, unbidden and unplanned: the play of moonlight on the water, or mountains at daybreak; the woods at dusk. But the Zen gardens were images of a perfection that came not from the heavens, but from men. The lantern, the wooden bridge, the stream had been placed just so, not by accident but design. The gardens showed how perfection could be fashioned out of nothing. They revealed how, through attention and deliberation alone, men could be brought into harmony with the ideal. They sang, in effect, of how much humanity could achieve.

AND IT WAS here, I felt, that the two sides of Japan, the lyrical and the mechanical, the frenzy of the video revolution and what Kawabata called "the deep quiet of the Japanese spirit," came together. The mechanical smoothness that I saw all around me was, in its way, just the secular equivalent of the garden, a profane counterpart to that exact geometry of the spirit. The items laid out in the department-store racks were no less perfect in their man-made arrangement than the rocks in the raked gravel of the temples; the rides in Disneyland were no less precise than the empty spaces of Kyoto. Both worlds were governed by the same aesthetic clarity, the same delicacy of suggestion, the same will for harmony. Both, in fact, arose from the same perfectionist ideal: not life, liberty and the pursuit of happiness, but unity, discipline and the pursuit of purity.

Thus the one thing that seemed to run like an electrical current through every aspect of Japan, linking its computers to its temples to its ballparks to its offices, was an impatience with all limitation. The Japanese did not see why everything should not be made perfect. Whatever can be, they seemed to say, shall be. And the people had not only the vision to see what was wrong but the discipline to correct it. Thus everything was made flawless, and no draft was rough. Between the idea and the reality, between the construction and the creation, there fell no shadow. Everything, in fact, approximated to its Platonic image: every

Zen garden was a picture-perfect image of what a Zen garden should be; the Emperor disappeared within the idealized role of an Emperor; and every geisha corresponded exactly to the prototypical model of a geisha (a Tokyo rose was a Tokyo rose was a Tokyo rose). Everything not only conformed, but conformed to the ideal (and I often wondered whether this in part explained the much-remarked Japanese fondness for photography, the art of suspended animation which composes the chaotic world into tidy pieces, reduces 3-D mess to 2-D order, and not only transfixes the evanescent, but also domesticates life into still life). Calligraphers in Japan would devote themselves to making just a single stroke, and making it perfect; gardeners would cultivate one flawless chrysanthemum a year. In Japan, I had little sense of wasted hope or rusted ambition: everything—including the future—could be programmed; everything—including humanity—could be perfected.

One of my favorite examples of pidgin English (though in Japan it might more fittingly, perhaps, be called "dove English") was the helpful sign put up in every tiny room in my humble Kyoto inn to explain the workings of the shower. "You are adjust able to likely temperature," it advised gnomically. Only after a while did I realize that "likely" in fact meant "likable." And only after a longer while did I recognize that the slip—like everything else in Japan—was absolutely perfect. For in Japan, so it seemed, the "likely" and the "likable," the probable and the desirable, were one and the same. Everything was the way it was supposed to be.

These images of perfection were often wonderfully inspiring. But I also found them a little suffocating. Where, I wondered, was the room for change, the opportunity for improvement? Where were the country's ragged edges, and where its loose ends? Where, above all, was the life in this perfection? The bonsai tree was lovely, but it knew no natural exuberance, no element of caprice or surprise. So much in Japan was exquisite, agreed a longtime American resident, "but it is always hard to feel passion here, or fire." Whenever I listened to a Japanese speaking English, I could not tell whether he was saying "order" or "ardor."

And if their remarkable sense of refinement had made the Japanese, in many respects, the most aesthetically sophisticated people in the world, that same high pitch of sensitivity when applied to matters of the heart, resulted often in perversity. And if the people's enlightened gift for bringing silence and harmony to perfection gave Japan a transcendental loveliness more exalting than anything I had ever seen, the country's determination to impose that same perfection on all that was meant to be changing and breathing and imperfect—emotions, relations, people themselves—made for its coldest horrors.

IV

This strain of chill perfectionism was most alarming to foreigners, of course, when it came to their social relations with the Japanese. For it is almost axiomatic that the Japanese are absolutely peerless in their equanimity, unerring in their courtesy. Through the dutiful performance of ritual, they present a face to the world that is always flawless and always idealized. They are always polite. They are always hospitable. They always smile. They always have their act very much together.

But an act it always seems to be. And their unfailing correctness seems often to be a way of keeping the world at a distance. Just as the chic young girls of Tokyo seem to decorate their porcelain faces with the conscientious, impersonal precision that they might otherwise bring to folding paper or arranging flowers, many of their compatriots display themselves with the impeccable polish and impossible finish of a lovely lacquered screen. The surface is as exquisite as it is opaque.

One sign placed in my Kyoto inn begged of its guests: "Please have friendly relations with foreign people at meals." That, I thought, was a peculiarly Japanese request: friendliness was something to be planned and fashioned in advance. And that is exactly the impression that disconcerts many a foreigner in Japan: every gesture of hospitality seems rehearsed, every kindness studied. A sign outside the Tootsie Men's Club in Roppongi, Tokyo's foreigners' ghetto, announced that a table cost 1,000 yen. "Service charge" was another 400 yen. "Charm" cost another 400 yen.

Japanese hospitality was so innate, the tourist brochures maintained, that the word for "customer" was the same as the word for "guest." But did that not also mean that guests were no better than customers? Perfect hosts in every way, the Japanese were always perfect strangers.

However much they gave away, they seemed to surrender nothing. And the regularity of the kindness was made the more unsettling by the sense that one could hardly be perfectly polite to someone one genuinely liked or trusted. It was no coincidence, I thought, that T-shirts and discos and magazines in Japan habitually took on the names of clubs; the Japanese seemed to love these free-masonic units, which served at once to band the elect together and to keep out the rest of the world. The biggest, and most exclusive, club of all was Japan itself.

And so, for all the familiarity of many of its surfaces, I had to admit that I found Japan quite the most alien society I had ever visited. And though the standards of convenience and smoothness and efficiency were higher here than in any other place I knew, I often felt lost and bewildered in Japan. I made contact with none of the expressionless eyes I saw in the street, I never managed to orient myself in its maze of electric possibilities. I could find few signs in English, and still fewer Japanese willing to speak a less than perfect English. Yes, I could skate along the culture's bright surfaces, but Japan, at heart, seemed a secret society.

Many of the foreign residents I met in Japan seemed equally shut out. They had found there all the purity and stillness they sought, they said, but still they had never really made their peace with the contemporary culture, or with its people. For that matter, the Japanese seemed decidedly pleased that the majority of foreigners, or *gaijin* (the word itself means "outside person"), could live in their country for years without ever mastering its intricate code of nuances and resonances—as oblique and precise as in some Nō drama. The French, a shrewd Australian once told me, despise anyone who cannot speak their language; the Japanese suspect anyone who can.

"There is nothing more dangerous," an American who had recently begun working in Japan announced one morning at breakfast in my *ryokan*, "than a Japanese who visits America for one year, maybe two. Instantly he thinks he knows everything. But actually"—and here he whooped most heartily—"he doesn't know a goddam thing." The irony of this assessment was, I think, quite lost on its speaker.

FOR ALL ITS famous aloofness toward the outside world, however, Japan could not shut it out altogether. Indeed, the Japanese seemed often to be training an uneasy eye over their shoulders in the direction of the West. Even the lordly Oh, who protests again and again that he never tried to compete with his American counterpart Hank Aaron, admits to being driven by the thought of eclipsing Babe Ruth; at the end of his English-language autobiography, a lofty testament to humility, he cannot resist including two appendices. The first consists entirely of testimonials to his skill offered by Americans (to the effect that he would have been a superstar even in America); the second pointedly lines up his statistics, on a year-by-year basis, against those of Aaron and Ruth. Anything you can do, we can do too, the Japanese seemed to imply. And better.

In a sense, then, Japan reminded me of a nervous beauty, who constantly needs reassurances from something other than the mirror. Thus foreigners were welcomed in Japan, up to a point, but mostly so that they could give external confirmation of the glory of Japan. Like many *gaijin*, I soon discovered that the Japanese I met almost never asked me about England or America or India, as other Asians might; but invariably, and anxiously, they asked me how I found Japan.

The Japanese, in fact, seemed touchingly eager to introduce a foreigner to their national treasures, willing to go to any length to give him a better picture of their land ("We must work harder to educate the world about ourselves and our way of life," ran the stern admonition in a TV ad for the Japanese Overseas Telephone System). In the same way, the Japanese preserved their own traditions with a care and deliberation one did not find among the Egyptians, say, or the Indians or the Greeks, not least perhaps because the Japanese romanticized their past as much as did any wistful admirer from abroad. When I told the owner of my Tokyo *minshuku* that I was off to Kyoto, he begged me, with much more sincerity than the occasion seemed to demand, not, please, on any account, to miss Nara; by the same token, when I told him, upon returning from Mount Fuji, that it resembled the paintings of Hokusai and Hiroshige, he was so delighted that he rewarded me with the ultimate compliment—calling me "half Japanese."

Another evening, I enjoyed an even more endearing example of this eagerness to please. A California friend and I had gone to the Mariachi Mexican restaurant in Kyoto. We were sitting in our booth, minding our *tostadas*, when, without a warning, our waitress, a typically demure and decorous matron in her early forties, suddenly began racing around the room, yanking castanets and tambourines down from the wall, and handing them out to us, and to the three diners at the next table. As she did so, a mariachi singer, bearing a guitar, casually strolled in. Instantly, the ever-surprising waitress whizzed back across the room, dragged out a pair of congas and began thumpin' out a beat, with considerable conviction, while the mariachi man began strumming. Before we knew it, our neighbors—a trio of amiable, and decidedly sozzled, department-store workers—were belting out "La Bamba," "La Cucaracha" and a host of other South of the Border favorites, and we were joining in, jumping up at intervals to fling castanets to them across the table, receiving extended tambourines in return. And by the time the revelry had subsided, the five of us had become bound together in an unlikely fraternity.

The minute the singer retreated, therefore, our bleary partners diligently set about trying to show the visitors from America a Japanese good time. They offered us beers. They wished us many, many fantastic times with Japanese girls. Apologizing profusely, they insisted on taking us to a Japanese bar, and introducing us to some local delicacies. And they concluded with a brief seminar on how to bewitch Japanese womankind. After delegating one of his cohorts to make a peace offensive call to his waiting wife ("a Superwoman," he gloomily reported), a salesman with the soft face of a fourteen-year-old coached us in reciting a line of indeterminate obscenity. Then the ringleader of the group, a cheerily rumpled fellow with the round red face of a Japanese Jackie Gleason, solemnly gave us the ultimate open sesame: "Say, 'I am from California,' " he suggested, "and Japanese girl will say, 'I love you.' " (And the other way around? "Ah," he sighed with infinite glumness. "We are shy. To Japanese men, every California girl look like Hollywood model. We are too afraid to speak.")

I was treated to the same kind of slightly worried hospitality, to more sorrowful effect, when I went to a ball game between the Taiyo Whales and the Yakult Swallows, both among the Central League's least accomplished teams. For the first six innings, I sat in complete isolation. Then, in the middle of the seventh, an affable middle-aged worker in spectacles left his seat and came over to me. "Have you ever seen no-hit, no-run game?" he asked, pointing to the scoreboard with undisguised pride. I had not. He beamed. "I am glad you can see this pitcher at his best condition." I forbore from asking whether the pitcher's best condition was assisted in part by an opposition that was sixth in a league of six, and able to win barely 30 percent of its games. We returned to watching the game.

In the eighth inning, the first batter fouled out. The next one came up to the plate and, with scant respect for posterity, smashed a clean single down the line. My disappointment was keen; my neighbor's, I feared, was almost terminal. I was sorry to have narrowly missed a moment of history; he was clearly devastated, not that he had missed a moment of history, but that I had—and, with it, a show of Japanese perfection. Nonetheless, he took the loss philosophically. "Is difficult"—he shrugged after a long silence—"to complete no-hit, no-run game."

In all my travels, I had never encountered a race so desperately keen to make its sights available to the foreigner (while at the same time so determined to keep its real features concealed). In other Asian countries, national pride seemed to take the form of smiling at all compliments from foreigners, affirming a fervent loyalty to the motherland and then proclaiming an equally fervent desire to leave it. In safe and spotless Japan, however, the locals had no desire to hustle susceptible foreigners. Nor did they betray any keenness to migrate. Their ulterior motives lay further back. They were not interested in selling postcards or antiques or local girls; they simply wanted to sell Japan.

ONE WEEK BEFORE I arrived in Tokyo, the New York *Times* had chanced to run a front-page story on Japan's National Intercity Amateur Baseball Tournament, in which fifty of the country's leading companies annually field teams to fight it out for baseball supremacy. The corporations, said the article, take these games very seriously: they sign up the finest amateur players in the country and subject them to eighty games a season and eleven months a year of practice. This year, the finals of the competition were to be held before a sellout crowd at Korakuen Stadium on August 2, only four days after my arrival. Clearly, this was something altogether different from the intramural softball leagues that bring Manhattan professionals out to Central Park on lazy summer afternoons for halfhearted swings and barrels full of beer. Clearly, this was something I had to see.

On August 2, therefore, I made my way to the stadium. As soon as I arrived, at four o'clock, my heart quickened. Brown boxes were lying along the walkways, piled high with Toshiba cowboy hats. Regulation businessmen, in ties and glasses, were marching around in platoons, jackets slung over their shoulders and, in their hands, matching bullhorns through which they could shout out the verses of their company song. In one spot, twenty-five Nissan cheerleaders had gathered in a circle, and were dancing, dervishing and chanting in a whirlwind show of team spirit. Players were being tossed into the air by their fellows. All about, there was shouting, singing, pep-rally frenzy. The tension was palpable, the excitement mounting. Both teams were clearly ready to go.

And so indeed they were. As I stood around the Nissan circle, scribbling frantically, a man stepped over to ask what I was doing. Auditing the pre-game excitement, I replied. He looked a little embarrassed, and I went back to writing. After a few more moments, we exchanged more pleasantries, and then our business cards. Miyaoka-san, I discovered, was a Special Planning Division Manager of the stadium. But when I asked him to explain the niceties of the pre-match routine, he looked almost inconsolable. Well, he began reluctantly, to begin with, the game had finished. The final had started at one o'clock, Nissan had won by a score of 4–3 and they were now in the process of celebrating their victory. The stadium was empty. The tournament was over.

I felt a little like Wordsworth, in Book 6 of *The Prelude*, when he learns that the crossing of the Alps, the highlight of his trip to Europe, has come and gone without his noticing.

Yet my new friend seemed ready to do almost anything to assuage my disappointment. Abandoning the boss who was waiting to take him home—a breach of duty that could, I imagined, lead to ritual suicide—he led me briskly into the stadium. We passed through Gate Number 1, the Oh Gate (in which Oh's achievements are inscribed in English, and only in English: 868 home runs! Not just a Japanese, but a worldwide record! Take that, America!). Then he led me onto the hallowed turf itself, the most sacred ground in Japanese baseball. He urged me to join the stadium workers enjoying a picnic on the tarpaulin. He offered me a glass, and poured out some beer. He offered me some more beer, and then some more (half Japanese, perhaps, I did not have the heart to tell him that I didn't drink). Then he hurried off to get a schedule. Please, he said, would I tell him which team I would like to see the Giants play? Naturally, all the games were sold out months in advance, but I could have tickets to any one of them I chose. He himself would be away next week (inspecting stadia in America), Miyaoka-san explained, but he would organize a free tour, a VIP seat, anything I wanted to make up for my loss today (caused, after all, by nothing except my own inefficiency). With that, he bundled off to tend to his (doubtless furious) boss.

It was, I thought, a typical show of Japanese kindness beyond the call of duty, a routine extension of hospitality the likes of which I had never found anywhere else. But at the same time, I was sure, the charity was prompted by another conviction—that this bewildered *gaijin* should not on any account leave Japan without seeing the Giants, Japan's team, in action. Foreigners must see Japan in its best condition.

V

At the heart of Japan's relations with the outside world, then, stood a paradox as large and implacable as the Sphinx. The Japanese might study and imitate all things Western, but they did not really like Westerners (in much the same way, perhaps, as they had liberally borrowed from the Chinese during the Heian period without ever acknowledging much fondness for the Chinese people). In answer to a 1980 poll, 64 percent of all Japanese had claimed that they did not wish to have anything to do with foreigners. In ancient times, people who committed the crime of being foreign were beheaded; nowadays, they were simply placed before the diminishing eye of the TV camera (entire shows were devoted to portraying the stupidities of *gaijin*). In the Japanese context, imitation was the insincerest form of flattery.

For all that, however, the Japanese were still determined to impress *gaijin*, and they still coveted the foreigners' lifestyles. In the flesh, *gaijin* might strike many Japanese as freakish, foul-smelling and crude; but as symbols—of prosperity and progress —they possessed a glamour to which few Japanese were immune. Thus blue-eyed blondes were still much sought after for commercials and regarded almost as trophies—walking advertisements for the Good Life—to be shown off to the neighbors, even as they were giggled at by schoolgirls and inspected by toddlers with fearful fascination.

When it came to baseball, of course, this already vexing double standard grew even more vexed. For the Americans, as the creators of the sport, were generally assumed to be its masters; yet the Japanese could not, would not, be content with being number two—they were determined to try harder and try harder and try still harder until they were the best. Unlike, say, the Filipinos, who play basketball, or the Latin Americans, who have taken up baseball, the Japanese refused to accede to Americans the home-team advantage.

This insistent desire to escape the shadow of Big Brother had begun to haunt every aspect of the game. During my visit, I heard much lamentation about the eclipse of the traditional *obento* box lunches at baseball games by American fast-food imports—Korakuen, the National Shrine of Baseball, was appointed with a Kentucky Fried Chicken outlet, a Mister Donut store and, of course, the Golden Arches. I read a column in the *Japan Times* that grimly debated whether foreigners should be admitted to the *meikyukai* club, the country's unofficial Hall of Fame, reserved for players with 200 wins or 2,000 hits. The anxiety had even, by now, seeped into the trade war: Washington had persuaded the Japanese to accept U.S.-made aluminum bats, and Japan had accepted, but then had quickly modified its rules so as to make the bats effectively illegal.

Yet in typically contradictory fashion, the Japanese had also sought to reverse the supremacy of the American leagues by importing American players. And as I followed the major leagues at home, I noticed, every now and then, that a onetime star, now in his early thirties perhaps, and three or four years away from his last All-Star appearance, would suddenly vanish; he was reborn, I gathered, across the Pacific. By now, Don Newcombe, Frank Howard, Clete Boyer, Joe Pepitone and a hundred other stars had jumped to Japan. And when I attended my first Giants game, I was startled to see a familiar form standing in front of me in center field. I looked a little closer, and saw that it was Warren Cromartie, who, when last I looked, had been leading the Montreal Expos to one near-pennant after another. Old players didn't die; they just went to Japan.

American baseball, of course, takes great pride in its role as a model of the melting pot, a happy community of integration. Black-dominated basketball is often shadowed by the prospect of racism, inverted or otherwise; football coaches still tend to give the most cerebral positions to whites, the most athletic to blacks. But baseball ideally presents a rainbow coalition of Hispanics, blacks and All-American boys, integrated as slaphappily as a prime-time platoon. Willie Mays has become as much a part of the pantheon as Mickey Mantle, while the Minnesota Twins boast a pitcher who last went to bat for Anastasio Somoza's National Guard. A single small town in the Dominican Republic, San Pedro de Macorís, is the birthplace of fourteen current major-league players.

In Japan, however, the incorporation of foreign players was an altogether trickier proposition. For one thing, Japanese baseball turned all the values of the American game on their head, imposing on every alien an entirely new set of values. Thus the recently arrived American had to learn to be as obedient and well disciplined as a child. He had to agree not to show off his talent, not to seek out flashy statistics, not, in short, to become a star. He had to recall that unity came from unanimity, that his identity lay only with the team. When one player made an error, all his colleagues hit one another so as to share the responsibility. And strategic decisions were reached, not by the pitcher and catcher alone, but by huge consensus (in the first two innings of a 1–0 game, I saw seven different board meetings on the mound, many of them attended by a full quorum of nine). In Japan, players were nothing more than verses in a single poem.

In a system in which everyone was everyone else's peer, moreover, peer pressures were unavoidably intense. Thus *gaijin* had to submit to fifteen-hour days and backbreaking workouts. Sometimes, they had to live with their fellows in a collective dorm and observe an unyielding 10 p.m. curfew. In the off-season, they had to accompany the team as it toured remote areas to play exhibition games for those who would not otherwise be able to see professionals; almost immediately thereafter, they had to report back to training camp in time for the next season. "In my country," writes Oh, "it is impossible to play just for oneself. You play for the team, the country, for others."

The transplant had also to pledge lifelong loyalty to his squad. In Japan, a baseball team does not represent a city, but a company; team spirit is thus indistinguishable from corporate loyalty. Players in Japan, moreover, are good company men; they do not, as a rule, offer their talents to the highest bidder, or negotiate with owners; their reward is simply the support of the corporate clan (while a World Series winner in 1984 received $50,000, a Japan Series winner made only $2,500). Comfort, in fact, is almost regarded as a handicap. ("He has big salary, he has good family," a Japanese colleague of mine once complained about a star. "He has no fighting spirit.") And as with any other Japanese company, the team becomes for its employee family, home and religion (if marriages in Japan often seem like corporate mergers, jobs often resemble surrogate spouses). "I guess [my colleagues] have girlfriends," said Dennis Barfield, the first American to live in a team dorm, "but I don't see them."

Many onetime American stars were little disposed, however, to check in their individualism at customs. They were accustomed to arguing and bartering and basking in the limelight. They talked back to managers and haggled with owners. They led their own lives and battled with their teammates. They even—and this was heresy in the Japanese game—showed emotion. In Japan, a player smiles when he strikes out and does not try to break up double plays. After every one of his home runs, Oh had circled the bases without a trace of emotion, lest, in exulting, he humiliate his opposition. What, then, could the fans of the Yomiuri Giants be expected to make of such imported stars as Clyde Wright, a fallen California Angel? On being taken out of a 1–1 game one day, as Robert Whiting tells it, Wright did not calmly hand the ball to the Giant manager, the revered Nagashima. Instead, he flung it into the stands, stalked into the dugout, tore up his uniform, threw it into the team bath, kicked over a trash can and threatened to leave Japan—all before 25-million stunned citizens on national television! In panic, the Giant front office instantly laid down a formal series of 10 Commandments which every *gaijin* was expected to obey. The list made specific the need for obedience, discretion, tidiness and teamwork. ("Do not severely tease your teammates." "Do not return home during the season." "Take good care of your uniform." "Do not scream or yell in the dugout or destroy objects in the clubhouse.") The only thing the elaborate battery of rules did not address, however, was the most basic problem of all—the reluctance of American players to adhere to rules in the first place.

Sometimes, Japanese teams tried to solve the problem by simply jettisoning American players who would not play by Japanese rules, while keeping those who would (the Chunichi Dragons recently got rid of the American who was their leading home-run hitter, while hanging on to a less troublesome *gaijin* who was hitting .190). Yet even that did not get around the most difficult problem of all: that many American imports, however accommodating and acclimatized, were simply too good for the league. Cromartie, for example, had won over many Japanese by graciously giving his newborn child the middle name of "Oh"; yet still the fact remained that every time he came up to the plate, it looked as if he could hit the ball into the next prefecture, almost at will. The first three times I saw him hit, he smashed three solid singles without even appearing to exert himself; over the previous six games, he had hit five home runs. Another American, Boomer Wells, had been virtually pushed out of the Minnesota Twins organization and forced against his will to move to Japan. A failure at home, he had won the Triple Crown in his second season in Japan.

In 1985, in embarrassing fact, the list of statistical league leaders was a virtual roll call of American names. Randy Bass, who had distinguished himself with all of seven home runs in his first five years in the United States, made mincemeat of the pitchers in Japan's Central League, hitting a remarkable 54 home runs in a 130-game season, and coasting to the Triple Crown (a feat he repeated the next season too). In the Japan Series, Bass helped the Hanshin Tigers to victory by belting homers in each of the first three games; inevitably, he was voted the Series' Most Valuable Player. The winning pitcher in two of the three Tiger victories was Rich Gale, in his first season away from the Kansas City Royals. And the star of the Tigers' opponents, the Seibu Lions, was a former Chicago Cub by the name of Steve Ontiveros. By 1987, the crisis was becoming even more acute, as Bob Horner, a superstar still in his prime, came over and clouted four home runs in his first two games.

That the league's few *gaijin* so effortlessly dominated the game was a source of abiding unease for the Japanese. The imported stars could, to be sure, be shown off as adornments of the Japanese game; but they were also unpleasant reminders of the apparent superiority of the American game. Thus the Japanese found themselves painfully divided. On the one hand, they did not like *gaijin*; on the other, they did not like losers (incredibly, almost one fan in every two across the country supports the Yomiuri Giants, the powerhouse that once won nine pennants in a row).

In the end, then, the Japanese had tried to unriddle the knot with still more regulations, many of them unwritten. The Giants had long made a point of fielding no foreigners at all. For years, no foreigner appeared on the cover of *Baseball* magazine. And to this day, only two *gaijin* are allowed on every team (even in the All-Star Game, where, by rights, five or six probably deserve to qualify). Sometimes, however, even rules cannot bend Nature, and the Japanese were driven to acts of quiet desperation. At the end of the '85 season, Bass came into Tokyo needing only one more home run to tie the all-time single-season record, set by the legendary Oh in his miracle season of 1964. The American's opponents were the Giants, managed by Oh. The first time Bass came up to the plate, he was intentionally walked. The second time, he was walked again. And the third time too. And yet again the fourth. And four times the next game too. No matter that the play was foul; by taking the bat out of Bass's hands, the Giants successfully ensured that the record remained safely in Oh's thoroughly Japanese hands (that Oh was in fact half-Chinese was a fact usually overlooked). "It's a funny situation when a foreigner is the ace pitcher of the team or the home-run leader," Whiting quotes the League Commissioner as declaring. "Foreigners, at best, should be by-players to bolster Japanese teams."

Foreign players, then, were simultaneously given the red carpet and the cold shoulder. The Japanese flocked to see Bass hit, and he was once rewarded for his skills with a year's supply of rice; yet nobody wanted him to beat Oh's record. Within a few days of his arrival, Horner had become a kind of folk hero, and as three TV stations organized "Horner Corner" updates, while a soft drink company asked him to endorse a vegetable drink called "Toughman," many Japanese spoke fretfully of a dangerous "Horner Syndrome." Yet as I looked down on Cromartie doffing his cap in center field, as the Korakuen crowd cheered his every move ("Cro mar tei! Cro mar tei!"), and raising his glove to acknowledge their applause after his catching of a routine fly ball, he struck me as a slightly lonely and bewildered figure.

Off the field, many *gaijin* found themselves in even more of a gilded cage. Horner, for example, was paid $1.3 million for one year, more than 20 Japanese players might hope to earn, in addition to a $500,000 bonus just for signing; all his living expenses were paid for him, and he and his family were set up in a three-bedroom "mansion" apartment. Many others were given personal interpreters, and chauffeurs to drive them to each game. But there they had to practice—often for six hours each day—with teammates who could not speak their language and did not share their interests. And though they might be feted— waiters at restaurants would often give them free meals, for example—they were also fated never to be accepted as part of Japan. "You read a lot of books," said Bass in describing his life in Japan. "You can't talk to anyone. You've got nothing to do but sit here and think." In coming to Japan, the typical American had traded in a cozy mediocrity for the most alienating kind of success.

THE CONTRADICTIONS that haunted Japan's uneasy importing of baseball were very similar, I thought, to those that shadowed all the goods and techniques that it had brought over from the West. For even as the Japanese omnivorously cannibalized the world outside, they never appeared to defer to it, or to worry that Japanese integrity might be compromised by the feverish importation. Their willy-nilly consumption of foreign goods seemed less, in fact, an act of homage than a way of making their own land a composite of all that was best in the world. Again, the logic was flawless: if Japan had everything good from the West, together with all its own homegrown virtues, how could anyone surpass it?

And again, I thought, Tokyo Disneyland was eloquent. For though it was based, down to the last detail, upon its American counterpart, its effect was to serve as a shrine to Japan's self-validating beliefs, a monument to the motherland. Thus it fed off borrowed images from the Wild West, but domesticated them with its own urban cowboys. It took what is known in American Disneylands as Main Street, and turned it into the World Bazaar, where all the products and all the possibilities of all the continents in the world are brought together in one synthetic complex that was wholly Japanese. In the Meet the World pavilion—a ride not to be found in American Disney-lands—a sagacious crane guides a little boy and his kid sister around what is not only a history of Japan but also a defense of the Japanese way. The bird points out a group of cavemen seated around a campfire. "They have learned," pronounces the Feath-ered One, "the importance of banding together to survive." Then it goes on to introduce the children to a samurai. "At least," boasts the warrior, "we never became a colony." And in the Magic Journeys ride—again peculiar to Tokyo Disneyland —a whirlwind trip across all five continents culminates, dra-matically, in a return to "our beloved Japan, where our heart always remains."

Some of that same spirit could be found among Japanese in the United States. When Chinese or Indian or Korean or Vietnamese immigrants move to the Promised Land, they generally lose no time at all in assimilating themselves; they set up shops and see about working, often very hard, in the confident hope that if they work hard enough, they can create a new life for themselves in the land of opportunity, fashion a fresh American destiny. Many Japanese in America, however, were much less conspicu-ous, and much less American. One third of the Japanese in New York, according to a poll, never read an American periodical; around a half admitted (or boasted?) that they had no American friends at all.

The Japanese abroad, indeed, whether tourist or expat, often reminded one less of sightseers than of undercover spies, assiduously observing, and even mastering, the ways of an alien land, in order to bring home new assets to the motherland. Instead of mingling with the locals, the Japanese famously traveled in groups (confirming many a Western stereotype, in part perhaps because a stereotype is what they aspire to) and sequestered themselves in specifically Japanese base camps: in Manhattan, they generally forswore the Rainbow Room or the roadside hot-dog stand in favor of transplanted Japanese piano bars, and on their sex tours, salarymen did not hit the streets along with German or Australian or American males, but stayed in special Japanese hotels appointed with Japanese waiters and Japanese-seeming girls. Even their furious clicking away with cameras could sometimes seem a way of capturing a foreign place only in order to take it back home. The Japanese, as John David Morley notes, are unrivaled in their collection of *omiyage*, or souvenirs. Yet as a Japanese friend explains to Morley, "We take something back home less as a reminder of the place where it was bought than as proof we'd been thinking of home at the place we bought it."

In its relations to the world at large, then, Japan reminded me, in the end, of a tribal conqueror who dons the armor, or even eats the heart, of a defeated opponent, so that his enemy's strength will become his own. Oh's spiritual breakthrough had come, I recalled, when his teacher took him to another *sensei* for an explanation of the central Kabuki principle of *ma*, "the space and/or time in between." "Make the opponent yours," declared the sage. "Absorb and incorporate his thinking as your own. Become one with him so you know him perfectly and can be one step ahead of his every movement." The central notion of *ki*, or "spirit power," like the guiding principle of judo, was similarly angled: "Make use of an opponent's strength and yours will be doubled."

IN RECENT YEARS of course, this strategy had met with astonishing success; Japan had made good, to a remarkable degree, on its determination to beat the West at its own game, be it baseball or technology or trade. While mastering nearly every Western technique, the Japanese had overtaken nearly every Western nation. On the day that I left New York for Tokyo, the cover story of *The New York Times Magazine* was a long article by

Theodore H. White describing the Japanese surrender in 1945, and discussing the country's almost militaristic drive for success in the intervening forty years. Japan, White implied, had exacted revenge for its defeat in the war by trouncing the West in the trade war. Though America had invented the radio and the black-and-white TV, he noted, it now imported both products from Japan, together with nearly all its VCRs, calculators, watches and even pianos. "Perhaps we did not win the war," he wrote, with some rancor. "Perhaps the Japanese, unknown even to them, were the winners."

A former baseball reporter from Minneapolis made the same point to me, more casually, after attending a game in Koshien. "Jesus!" he marveled. "They've out-Americaned America."

Yet still the Japanese seemed as unready to accept victory as defeat, as anxious as ever, and as serene. This came home to me most hauntingly when I went to Hiroshima on the fortieth anniversary of the day the American bomb had dropped from the heavens. I arrived at the Peace Park expecting to find the historic occasion marked by huge crowds, lobby groups, placards and policemen. There was none of that. The moment was observed with quintessential Japanese delicacy: it was a day of resounding quietness.

In the great open space of the park, little girls in bonnets were bending down to feed pigeons. Old men in T-shirts that said "Peace" staggered, foot by twisted foot, toward the shrine. In the shade, a schoolgirl sat under her mother's parasol, sketching the outline of the famous dome whose skeleton was all that remained after the bombing. Off to one side, in a quiet grove, an old lady who had survived the attack stood before a circle of hushed listeners, describing all that she had experienced. And everywhere, heaped on the Children's Peace Monument, gathered in boxes, fluttering across the grass, were hundreds upon hundreds of rainbowed banners plaited together in the shape of a many-colored crane. Anyone who tied 1,000 of these streamers together, the Japanese believed, was assured of a long life. The paper that now blanketed the park recalled a little girl who had survived the bombing and managed to tie together 960 colored banners, and then had died.

As the day wore on, all the soft moments began to gather weight, and their pathos started to build. Six old women held up sticks of incense before a Buddhist cenotaph, to be joined by a pudgy teenage monk in a steady, mournful keening. And in a golden glade at twilight, in a circle of trees spangled by the sun, thirty anti-nuclear protesters put their arms around each other's shoulders and sang, slowly and with feeling, "We Shall Overcome."

That night, hundreds upon hundreds of candlelit paper lanterns—golden and red and green and white—were sent down the Honkawa River, in memory of the departed. Along the riverbank, the faces of children, lit up by the flickering candles, looked hollow and unearthly. Nothing was said as the lanterns continued their silent, leisurely flow. For more than an hour they drifted downriver, with the gentleness of time or reminiscence. Then, in silence, they sailed under a bridge and away into the dark.

Like much else I had seen in Japan, the occasion was graced, almost transfigured, by a beauty that left the heart quite still.

Yet the surfaces that surrounded me were as busy and incongruous as ever. Inside the Peace Museum, rows of stark black-and-white photos chronicled, unblinkingly, the inexpressible horror of the bomb: long, terrible processions of the lame and dying through gutted streets, whole neighborhoods wiped from the earth, ghastly disfigurements tearing skins apart, bodies twisted in the last convulsions of protracted deaths. The Japanese who inspected these harrowing documents wore T-shirts that said "No. 1 American Beer," "Carolina Western Express" and "Cherry ice-cube steak." Others were emblazoned with "Billy Club" and "Carrot Club" and "Baseball Club." One advertised "U.S.A. Soul: Nostalgic Train."

By then, I had grown familiar with the willful brightness of Japanese surfaces, the mass-produced optimism of a culture awash in sugary tunes that sold "Sunny California" cars and "Sunshine Heart" coolers, consumed "Sweet Kiss" candies and tuned TV sets to *The Nice Morning Show.* By then too, I knew that the Japanese had followed, to perfection, Arnold's famous maxim that "the pursuit of perfection is the pursuit of sweetness and light." But still I could not reconcile the memory of 200,000 lives destroyed in an instant with T-shirts that said "Fine Day" and "Good Time." The Japanese were not just putting the best face on things, they were putting an ideal face on them, as if to deny themselves, even in the face of their deepest sorrow, a human response, which could only be a flawed response. "Have a nice day," they seemed to sing in unison as they trotted toward Apocalypse.

Modern Japan had in a sense been created by the most advanced of all scientific achievements, the Bomb, that monster marvel that revealed, in a terrible flash, how far progress can push us backwards and how much technology may outstrip vision. In that single nightmare moment, the full breadth of human possibility had been suddenly lit up, and it was a prospect that brought as much horror as awe. Begotten in that double-edged instant, modern Japan had now become almost a model of that uplifting and unsettling ambiguity. It had revealed, exhilaratingly, how much humanity can achieve—but it had done so, perhaps, at the expense of humanity. It had shown how close perfection could be, but also how terribly costly. It had extended sophistication to the limit, but also to the breaking point. And whenever I looked at Japan, I could not help but think of the haiku of the Zen poet Issa: "Closer, closer to paradise. How cold!" And I could not help but wonder whether the sticking-out nails that were being so efficiently hammered down were, in fact, being driven into perfect, look-alike coffins.

Yet who but a churl would argue with success?

In 1985, for the first time ever, not a single American team qualified for the final of baseball's Little League World Series, and, for the fifteenth time in eighteen years, the competition was won by a team from Asia.

And at the Los Angeles Olympics in 1984, where the United States, as host, chose to introduce baseball to the world as an exhibition sport, the home team fielded what was said to be the strongest amateur team in history. "The gold is ours," said one American pitcher, speaking for the entire country. "They'll need an army to take it away from us." In the final, however, before 55,235 fans, one of the largest crowds ever to witness a game at Dodger Stadium, the Japanese decisively trounced the Americans at the American national sport, by a score of 6–3.

The Empire Strikes Back

The West asks for clear conclusions, final
judgments. A philosophy must be correct or incorrect,
a man good or bad. But in the wayang, no such
final conclusions are ever drawn. The struggle of
the Right and the Left never ends, because neither
side is wholly good or bad.

— *C.J. Koch*, The Year of Living Dangerously

I HAD THOUGHT,
when first I visited the Orient, that I would find myself witnessing the West in conquest of the East, armies of its invaders bearing their cultural artifacts across the barren plains of Asia. Yet the discovery I made most consistently throughout my travels was that every one of my discoveries had to be rejected or, at best, refined. And as I got ready to leave the East, I began to suspect that none of the countries I had seen, except perhaps the long-colonized Philippines, would ever, or could ever, be fully transformed by the West. Madonna and Rambo might rule the streets, and hearts might be occupied with secondhand dreams of Cadillacs and Californians; but every Asian culture I had visited seemed, in its way, too deep, too canny or too self-possessed to be turned by passing trade winds from the west.

Bali, for example, drew its strength, its magic and its eerie purity from the ancestral currents that pulsed through its soil, currents that Westerners could sense, perhaps, but never touch; just so, the moving yet unwavering faith of Tibet would withstand the ravages of tourists, I hoped, as surely as it had withstood the vicious assaults of the Chinese. Burma had calmly closed its door to the world, and China had opened it up just enough, so it planned, to take what it wanted, and nothing more. Prodigal, hydra-headed India cheerfully welcomed every new influence from the West, absorbing them all into a crazy-quilt mix that was Indian and nothing but Indian; Japan had taken in the West only, so it seemed, to take it over. As for Nepal, and Thailand even more, both gauged Western tastes so cleverly and adapted Western trends so craftily that both, I felt, could satisfy foreigners' whims without ever becoming their slaves. Even Hong Kong, the last pillar of the Western Empire, was now getting ready to return to Asian hands.

On other fronts too, the East had clearly outmaneuvered its self-styled saviors from the West. Vietnam, for example, had added a political victory to its military triumph, according to William Shawcross, by fabricating an entire famine in order to win funds from a West made gullible by its guilt. Gradually, the overfamiliar lines from Kipling began to seem less specious than once I had supposed:

> And the end of the fight is a tombstone white
> with the name of the late deceased,
> And the epitaph drear: "A Fool lies here
> who tried to hustle the East."

As I made my way home, in fact, I began to suspect that my original formulation should, if anything, be reversed: the East was increasingly moving in on the West. "The wheel has come full circle," as Norman Lear once observed, "and now the Marco Polos and Francis Xaviers of the Orient set out for the Hangchow of the West, Manhattan Island."

En route from Bombay to L.A., I happened to stop off for three days in London. There I found West Indian sitcoms crowding the airwaves and *samosas* filling the sandwich bars. Culturally, the talk of the town was a new movie written by a twenty-nine-year-old Pakistani, *My Beautiful Laundrette*. The film had shocked English audiences with its unblinking portrayal of an alliance between a soft-faced Pakistani boy and his skinhead neo-Fascist chum. More startling to me, however, was the deeper social conquest it revealed: in *Laundrette*, every white is on the dole, and every black on the rise. The movie draws back the curtains on a Britain so tossed about by a new sense of meritocracy that the imperialists now lording it over the natives are the chic and silk-shirted Pakistanis: it is the Pakistanis who hire unemployed Englishmen, the Pakistanis who command white mistresses, the Pakistanis who turn people in and turf them out of their apartments. The picture might almost have been an undeveloped negative of some portrait of the Raj, so precisely does it transpose the familiar positions of black and white.

Much the same point had been made by Timothy Mo in *Sour Sweet*, in which a Hong Kong Chinese family settles down in a London so cantonized—and Cantonized—that throughout the novel's 278 pages of English life, not a single Englishman is named. And in *Oxford Blood*, the princess of the status quo, Lady Antonia Fraser, had slyly introduced her readers to the ultimate upstanding Englishwoman, who just happens to be Chinese, and the proverbial Scottish nurse, who turns out to be West Indian.

Thus the colonials were effectively staging their own takeover, erecting tandoori palaces in their former rulers' home, introducing their own pungent terms into the mainstream, even seizing control of much of the nation's culture (during the '80s, the highest literary trophy in Britain, the Booker Prize, had been won by an Indian, an Australian, a New Zealander and a South African). The empire had struck back.

When I got back to the United States, I felt more than ever like some Rip Van Winkle awakening to the lineaments of a new order. My featureless neighborhood in Manhattan had now, I gathered, become Koreatown, with Little India just around the corner: in the building next to mine, Miss Kim—one of the Koreans who had taken over more than half the grocery stores on the island—was energetically dishing out sushi, gelati, moussaka and salad twenty-four hours a day, 365 days a year. In L.A., fifty Thai restaurants had sprouted up along Sunset Boulevard almost overnight, and my first night back in town I was taken to a sing-along Japanese country-and-western joint. The Great California Novel, I was told, had been written by Vikram Seth, a British-educated Indian. And before the month was through, I was greeting the New Year in downtown San Francisco, in a

Cambodian restaurant just down the street from Bangkok Massage, Thailand Massage and a mess of Vietnamese cafés.

On a broader level too, the Asians seemed sovereign. For as the world had been turned on its axis, all the old trade routes were being reversed. These days, in fact, David was giving Goliath a hand-up. Thus the Sandhurst-educated Sultan of Brunei, a British puppet just one year before, now was pumping several billion dollars into sterling in order to boost the economy of his former white rajah rulers (and also, it later turned out, helping Washington in its covert arms dealings). Japan was so dominating the markets of its onetime American conquerors that it now sat uncertainly on a $50-billion trade surplus. And in Australia, it was said, local whites were pulling rich Japanese tourists along in the modern equivalent to the rickshaw, the pedicab!

Deeper than all the surface imports from the East, though, and deeper in its way than anything in the Western penetration of the East, was a more fundamental trend: the Asians had begun to take over the American Way of Life itself. Masters of adaptation and design, they had so faithfully reproduced the models they took from America that they were, in effect, producing forms more American than the American. A decade ago, as Gita Mehta has shown, lines of communication were so crossed that the East looked to the West to bring it the wisdom of the East; now, the process was reversed. For what the Asians brought over to the West were often not so much fragments of the East as new and improved versions of the West: the Japanese provided Tokyo-made Plymouths; the Thais filled L.A. with Bangkok-style American bars; the Chinese served up sweet-and-sour pork (a dish created expressly for Western palates). Japanese country-and-western bars, Korean grocery stores, Vietnamese French restaurants, Indian-run motels—all suggested that the Asians had absorbed the West, and mastered it, more fully and more subtly than anything that could be imagined in reverse (were there American-owned *bhel puri* stands on the streets of Bombay, or English-made temples in the hills around Chiangmai?). Turn over any American product or practice these days, and you would likely find the telltale stamp: "Made in Japan," "Made in Hong Kong."

That mark was even on the country's founding principles. For the greatest of all the Asian immigrants' products were simple All-American success stories. In reviving the country's economy, the Asians had resuscitated many of its hallowed myths; they had brought new life, new meaning to the Puritan ideal of a clean-living, family-based community, to Franklin's belief in hard work and thrift, to Whitman's affirmation of a collective identity larger than the self and, most of all, to Horatio Alger tales about turning rags to riches. Not only were almost half the Phi Beta Kappas at Harvard in 1985 of Asian extraction; not only did Asians, who represented less than 2 percent of the population, account for 30 percent of the places at Juilliard and 30 percent of the winners of the Westinghouse Talent Search; but the most moving monument in the capital, a testament to the country's losses in the East, was the work of a twenty-year-old Chinese girl from Yale. The Asians devoutly believed that America was the land of freedom and boundless opportunity. And by acting on that belief, they had made it true.

THE ORIENT, THEN, was taking over the future, a realm that had long seemed an exclusively Western dominion. More and more, indeed, the West was looking to the East not just for its spiritual but also for its material and technological needs. Thus the influence of Japan was everywhere in the United States— but not so much in its traditional forms of white-heron lyrics and snow-soft woodblocks as in its ready provision of all the latest in post-post-Modernist chic: Miyake gowns and sushi carrings, New Wave designs and Laurie Anderson motifs. Japan was now the source of rock videos as much as rock gardens and Japan was fast becoming the Paris of the '80s, the place where the young went to be young: as Fitzgerald and Hemingway and Miller had once gone to the banks of the Seine to steep themselves in both the old and the new, so such contemporary descendants as Jay McInerney, Brad Leithauser and John David Morley—to pick but three—sought the same cultural currency in the Land of the Rising Yen.

In part, of course, this latest development betrayed nothing more than the universal fascination with the foreign: it was hardly surprising that Americans who defined their status in terms of Ferraris, Rolexes and Harris Tweeds (or even such ersatz exotica as Le Bag and Häagen-Dazs) would fill the air of East Village clubs with clove-scented cigarettes, Nam June Paik videos and cuts from Lucia Hwong. Even artificial grass was greener on the other side, and as surely as the trendies of Roppongi wore their Gucci watches to the local burger joint, so their counterparts in Soho and West Hollywood inevitably wore Yamamotos to the sushi bar.

But beyond the fads of the moment, Asia seemed the place to which everyone was headed. Asia was now the state of the art. "The whole world is looking east," gushed Diana Vreeland, arbiter of taste, in *Vanity Fair*, anthology of trends, "to the Orient—to the future." When the West fashioned blueprints of its destiny—in the movie *Blade Runner*, for example, or in the picture of a future London on the cover of *The Economist*—the result looked suspiciously like the back streets of Shinjuku today. When pundits talked of geopolitical prospects, their favorite new buzzword was the "Pacific Rim." Already, the two fastest-growing regions in the world were the Far West and the Far East. And before very long, there seemed little doubt, the world would be read from right to left, if not from bottom to top.

Ten years ago, the shrewdest and most seasoned of modern travelers, Jan Morris, had looked at Singapore and Hong Kong and seen "a new energy of the East . . . a sort of mystic materialism, a compelling marriage between principle and technique which neither capitalism nor Soviet Communism seems to me to have achieved." By now, that formidable channeling of Communist forces and Confucian values into capitalist systems had sent many bright, high-rising Asian societies into overdrive; using American principles of free enterprise, they had begun to eclipse the Americans themselves. Indeed, perhaps the greatest surprise of all my travels was to find many Asian cities—Singapore, Tokyo, Hong Kong, even Bangkok—so highly developed and technologized, through industry both human and mechanical, that they actually made the West seem backward and inefficient by comparison. "Nobody looks to the West," chirped a Singapore pop singer called Don Lee, "nobody wants second best."

As it was, when one flew across the International Date Line, one already felt oneself, in mind as well as in fact, to be winging one's way into tomorrow. And as the influence of laser blips and microchips expanded, so too, no doubt, would that of their Eastern masters. If the nineteenth century was generally regarded as the European century and the twentieth as the American, the twenty-first, I thought, would surely be the Asian.

ON A MORE personal level, though, the transaction was, as ever, more complex and more equivocal. For myself, I found that the East had staked a much deeper claim than ever I would have expected. It was only when I returned home that I felt homesick —not just for the gentleness and grace that I had found in many parts of Asia, but also, and more deeply, for the gentler self it had found in me. It was not corruption that stayed with me from my travels, but purity—the absolute stillness of mornings in the high monasteries of Tibet; chill winter sunshine above the villages of Nepal; the dazzle of blue afternoons in Burma; and lanterned nights in Kyoto so lovely that I almost held my breath for fear I might shatter the spell. Surrounded by conveniences at home, I began to long for the luxuries to which I had grown accustomed—open hearts and quiet mornings and smiles that asked for nothing but smiles in return.

Once back in New York, I tried very hard to keep something of that spirit alive. I took long walks by the river at dawn and listened in the darkening afternoons to the unearthly strains of the gamelan. I read deeply in the Zen poets by the light of a single candle and I fasted and burned incense when the moon was full. I joined local groups of Tibetans in their seasonal festivities, and I haunted Thai cafés on East Coast and West. Mostly, though, I spent my hours flipping through photographs and reading old diaries, trying to revisit, in memory and imagination, the places and friends I had known.

Some of these characters, as the months went on, did indeed manage to draw closer to their American dreams. Jain, for example, my constant guide in Burma, informed me that he had befriended a girl from Seattle on her first seven-day trip around his closed country; he had traveled with her, chastely, when she returned for another visit, and had listened, in surprise, as she told him on the eve of her departure that she loved him; and, after she had turned around in Bangkok and flown back for a third seven-day stay, he had taken her to be his wife in the drafty old Anglican church in Rangoon. They had enjoyed a six-day honeymoon around Burma; then she had returned to Washington, and he to working outside the Strand Hotel in order to save up for his ticket—though she had offered to pay, he said, he did not wish her to feel used. And though his mother was grieving that she might never see him again, he had tried to convince her that his was truly an affair of the heart. "My wife is not beautiful," he said quietly, "but I can really say I love her. And look at me. I have no job. I am not handsome. I have no degree. I am just a driver. I think she must love me for myself."

A little later, however, a California friend of mine came back from Rangoon with the news that Jain had been arrested for unofficial tour guiding, and was now condemned to two years in jail.

More cheering news came from Didien, a nineteen-year-old Indonesian girl with whom I had chatted for a couple of hours one morning as we waited for different trains in a small station in eastern Java. At the time, she was on her way to Jakarta to apply for an Australian residency visa. On her first trip ever to the capital, she had not even managed to leave the station before she was robbed of the $100 it had taken her months to save. Now, having saved up again, she was off for another try. If she passed her interview at the embassy, she told me, she would be free to join her sister and her Australian brother-in-law Down Under. Only four months later, I received a birthday card from Canberra: it came from Didien, who was now, she reported happily, studying English at a local college. In the months that followed, she greeted me often with photos of her cat and cheery postcards of Australian cities, bright in the winter sun.

Most remarkable of all, perhaps, was the story of Joe, the friendly entrepreneur of Guangzhou. Just before leaving China, I had given him 25 U.S. dollars to pay for the TOEFL (Test of English as a Foreign Language) exam demanded of foreign applicants by American universities. Our transaction had made me wistful, as the encouragement of pipe dreams always does; if trips to America were hard to imagine in most parts of the world, they seemed next to impossible in Communist China.

Six months later, I was sleeping in my apartment at six o'clock one Sunday morning when I was jolted into wakefulness by the insistent ringing of my phone. Groggily, I picked it up—to be assaulted by a relentless torrent of words. "Hullo, Pico! This is Joe from Guangzhou! You can call me John now! I am here in Manhattan! It is like a dream to me, it is so exciting. I walked down Broadway last night and saw many black men. It is very strange for me. One man, a strong man, came up and asked me for money. That was more exciting to me than the Empire State Building. Also, I saw many, many beggars. As you know, we do not have beggars in Guangzhou."

On and on the breathless narrative raced. "It is so exciting here. Everything here is so old. The buildings are old. Even the cars are old. The streets are very dirty. Many fat women call out to me in the streets, 'Come here, baby.' Today, I wake up at three o'clock to write to Wu about all I have seen in New York. You know, it is like a dream to me."

The world had indeed come full circle: here was a visitor from an impoverished peasant nation savoring New York, not for its skyscrapers and limousines—he had seen all that at home—but for its unimagined supply of beggars, prostitutes, filth and Third World anarchy!

Then I heard an ominous click: our three minutes were almost up. Then I heard another click, and the voice started irresistibly up again. "Here I can find a telephone and put in coins and talk to you! I talked to an operator, and she said, 'Please put in twenty-five cents.' Then I put in fifty cents and the phone rings and she tells me to collect my change! Now I can pay more money and talk to you again! For as long as I like! In Guangzhou, as you know, we have no public telephones!"

Before hanging up, Joe smartly invited himself to stay, and I soon reacquainted myself with his curious blend of innocent energy and quick-witted acquisitiveness. (Not, it seems, a unique blend. A couple of months earlier, his friend Wu had written me a reproving letter: "I am always looking forward to your letter after your departure, but I have got no news from you ... I here write to you for your help ... Thank you in advance for your kindness to send the magazines as you promised ... Awaiting your answer ..." As soon as I sent him a cache of old *Cosmos*, he fired back an extravagantly grateful reply: "Thank you very much indeed for your kind letter . . . It made me really very happy to hear from you . . . I felt quite lucky to have the chance to know you, a man of so considerable culture and so kind . . . Thank you again . . . I don't know how to express my thanks for your kindness, what I can do for thanking you . . .") For his part, Joe, within a few minutes of entering the flat, began ransacking my bookcases for "gifts," and showering me with names of Chinese sources who would, he said, be invaluable to me in my work.

He had managed to get out of China, he explained, by befriending an American patron, and then by treating the two local officials in charge of his visa application to a 100-yuan dinner; he would be spending the next four years studying theology in North Carolina. He anticipated no trouble in financing his studies, Joe went on: he would simply travel around churches in the Bible Belt, denouncing the Communist system and affirming his faith in Jesus. He would also explain to his fellow Christians the value of investing in his future. If they gave him $1,000, he would point out, he could win fifty new converts at home. That came to only $20 per Chinese Christian. And if each of his converts made another fifty converts, his American donors would, in effect, be spending only 40 cents for each saved soul! Quite a bargain.

On his second night in New York, this latter-day Charlie Soong eagerly headed off to his first XXX movie. Later, he reported that the experience had been of great sociological interest: he had not been very taken by the business on screen, but he had, from the balcony, enjoyed an excellent view of solitary men in the audience sidling up to one another, conferring in whispers and then leaving in pairs. His observation had been cut short, however, when an old man sidled up to him and began conferring with him in whispers.

Making his way home, Joe had gone into a deli and paid $10 for a cup of coffee. Just as he was leaving, though, a waiter rushed after him to give him $9 in change. "He was an Italian immigrant," Joe told me. "I had read *The Godfather* and I had a bad impression of them. But he was very honest." Noting the recurrent theme of his New York experiences, I took care to warn him about the three-card monte sharks on Broadway. "No problem," he shot back after I had finished my long explanation. "We have same trick in Guangzhou."

A few hours later, in the middle of the night, Joe suddenly leapt up from the floor where he was sleeping and threw himself into an eloquent sermon on the works of Christ and the horrors of totalitarianism. By now, the full-circle ironies were beginning to strain credulity: here was a student from Communist China visiting New York to convert an employee of Henry Luce to Christianity and democracy!

In the months that followed, I received many spirited updates from Joe—now wind-surfing on a Carolina beach, now devouring sociology textbooks, now dashing off articles for the Chinese dissident press. Three months into his stay, he declared, with great solemnity, "I have fallen in love with America."

OTHERS OF THE friends I made in Asia were not so fortunate. Sarah, the virginal waitress I came to know in Manila, wrote to me more faithfully than anyone else I knew. She always sustained what seemed a characteristically Filipino blend of evergreen optimism and unguarded warmth. And she always wished me well. But her plaintive and affectionate letters, poignant at the best of times, became even more heartrending as they became more open:

> Dear Pico,
>
> I received your letter last June 2, 19/86, and thanks a lot. A simple gift you have giving me, a white lady watch. I'm so happy it's because you cannot forget me as your best friend. I hope you will not change your attitude. By the way, Pico, please help me again. Enrollment is coming. I have money but it is lack to continue my studies. The lack is 450.00 pesos. Please, I know you arc my friend who concern me and nobody else.
>
> Pico, I know your boaring to help me but please don't issitate because who knows someday I reach your country and that's the beggining you know me better. My attitude is forever. I recover all the crisis I have done and thanks to the Lord Jesus Christ that he have given me a strength to do everything. Yes, I always remember the

days when you are here in Manila going to Calle 5. We're changing conversation that is full of jokes and etc.

Pico, don't get marriage yet. Just wait for me—okey?

Love forever,
Sarah

Maung-Maung, the trishaw driver I had met in Mandalay, was equally loyal. Ours was not by any means an easy correspondence to maintain: I had to send his letters care of a trishaw stand, registering every envelope lest the government confiscate it. He in turn had to smuggle his letters out through tourists who could post them for him from Bangkok. Once, he begged me not to ask him about politics because "sometimes the police come ask me questions about it and may be put me in jail." And sometimes I received nothing but empty envelopes from Maung-Maung, their seals cut open and their contents removed.

For all the hazards, though, my friend managed regularly to get through long and thoughtful letters.

Trishaw Stand,
Mandalay,
Burma

My dearest Pico Iyer—

Hello, how are you? I hope you are fine. As for me, I am fine. Thank you very much for your letter and thank you for your kindness to me while you stayed in Mandalay. I enjoyed very much. I keep your photo with trishaw to remember you.

I could not reply to your letter at once because I am very busy at the trishaw. Sadly, I am always thinking and worrying about losing this trishaw out of my hand because the trishaw owner will sell to other the end of this month. Has only given me one month to buy it but I don't have enough. Now I try to search for my new job. But it is not easy. So now as usual I am on my trishaw. My ambition is to become a teacher of Mathematics in Middle School.

If you send to me your friends, they can see me at the trishaw strand. Some people will tell them that I go back to Shan State or something. They will lie to your friends.

Don't be carried away by their speech. If your friends don't see me first day, they can see me the next day because I never move to everywhere. When they come to Mandalay I will do my very best according to their plans as much as I can—no need to worry for everything. Because from my point of view, though we are far away, our friendship is the bridge that closes the distance between us. I don't have enough money but I am always ready to help others.

May I stop here because I will now go to bed. I must never forget you. I wish you all the best and I hope everything is going well with you in America. By the grace of God, shall we meet again in the future.

Your loving friend,
Maung-Maung
(B.-Sc.Mathematics)

Month after month, in beautifully curled English that must have taken him hours—and constant trips to his dictionary—to complete, Maung-Maung sent me increasingly fluent reports of his own life and solicitous best wishes for mine. When it was hot, in midsummer, he wrote that "sometimes I don't even get one kyat for a day. Anyhow, I will try to improve for my living and I will support to my old parents. I have to try for success, then happiness. But I don't want to wish for what is impossible. For example, I don't want to get a star from the sky. Some people ride the car and live in the brick house, I can't own a trishaw. But I like to do the right things, whether rich or not."

When I sent him a small gift, he thanked me warmly, but added, "I don't want to take too much advantage of your kindness. Let me say that I am not a man for the money. Because money cannot buy happiness." When I apologized for being slow to reply, explaining that work had been all-consuming, he wrote, "Don't feel deject if you cannot succeed. You will know that industry is the keynote to success. Also please be patient in everything." Another time, he took pains to remind me that "you are indeed fortunate because you were born from America, and America is the riches and improve city in the world."

And once, when I commended Maung-Maung on his English, he wrote back to say that "my English is not better than the

English of most Americans as you tell, because I am a simple Burmese trishaw-man in Mandalay as you know. But I shall learn by experience."

THE ONE OTHER friend with whom I tried to keep up was Ead, the small and serious Thai girl I had met in the flashy neon bar strip of Soi Cowboy, who did not seem to have the heart for her ambiguous profession. Before I left Bangkok, I had spent one long day with Ead, hearing about her life as we wandered through the city one still and brilliant Sunday. Early in the morning, we had met at Wat Sraket, the golden temple that stands on a hill above the city, and together we had climbed to the top and looked out across the gilded pagodas in the cloudless morning calm. Ead had gone off to pray at a shrine, put in a coin for a kind of Buddhist lottery and then returned with a smile: for the first time ever, she explained, she had received the number 1, the highest token of good fortune. Afterwards, we had joined the city's families in the zoo, watching the bears and tapirs in the bright holiday sunshine; and that evening, we had gone together to a program of classical Thai dance. Next day, Ead came to my hotel to accompany me to the "well-wisher's lounge" at the airport.

A few weeks later, back in New York, I sent Ead a pair of jeans for her birthday, then rang up the Friends Bar to see if the parcel had arrived. "Hello," called out a girl at the other end. "Hello. Hello?" But all I could hear was the thump of disco music in the background, and the raucous squeals and beery cacophony of a Bangkok bar in full swing. I blurted out a message, and quickly hung up.

A month or so later, though, a letter arrived from Ead, thanking me for my gift, and asking me to excuse her for missing my call—she had been in the hospital, she wrote. Now, she reported, she was healthy again and "my daughter stay with my mama in upcountry."

Later that same year, I happened to be passing through Bangkok again, and, on my first free day, I went out from my five-star hotel in search of my friend. It did not take me long to track down the winking neon bars and video pubs of Soi 21—Soi Cowboy—and even on a gray afternoon the place was as loud and brazen as I had remembered. Its air of noisy glamour was just the same as ever. But as I began to look more closely at the bars, I noticed that all their details had changed. The Friends Bar was gone now, and most of the young girls in the area were new, and all the sites I recalled seemed to have vanished, as if in a dream.

I still had Ead's home address, though, copied out by her on a small scrap of paper: 193 Soi 22 (Room 404). This, I guessed, must be just down the street from Soi 21—a modest flat, I assumed, in one of the area's leafy residential streets. I made my way across the main road just as the first fat drops of the daily monsoon started to come down.

As I turned into Soi 22, the pounding of the bars began to subside behind me, and within a few yards the fancy drugstores and air-conditioned cafés also began to fall away. By the time I got to Number 180, the rain was coming down more heavily, and I could only with difficulty make out the number on the next dilapidated building: 210. Between the two ran a muddy alleyway, bordered by two ditches that were quickly filling up with rainwater. Number 193, I assumed, must lie down here.

Wobbling my way down two creaking planks that had been placed across the sludge, strands of wet hair flopping across my face, I followed the path down a few yards and around a corner. In front of me was a jumble of broken tin shacks. Their flimsy walls were shaking under the pounding of the rain. A few naked children waded about in the filthy puddles. Half-naked women stared at me from the openings of darkened doorways, babies at their breasts. Everywhere was sewage.

I could hardly believe that this was the right place, and I looked again at my crumpled piece of paper. The writing was growing smudged in the downpour, but I could still just make out "193." A little boy scampered past me on the planks, head bowed, and I stopped him and showed him my paper. He shook his head, and raced along. A fat woman came edging her way carefully along the boards, a cloth over her head. "Ead?" I asked. "Ead?" She stopped and squinted at me through the rain. I pointed again to the blurred "193," and she motioned vaguely toward a nearby shack. I sloshed my way over to a wooden fence, and knocked. No answer. Finally, a haggard, wild-eyed woman appeared above me on the second floor. "Ead?" I called up. "Do you know Ead?" She shouted something out, then hurried back into her shelter. Clearly, it was useless. I turned and made my soggy way back to my luxury hotel.

Before I left Bangkok, I sent Ead a note telling her about my visit. A few weeks later, to my surprise, I received a reply. She was very sorry to have missed me, Ead wrote, but she had briefly returned home to help her Mamá on the farm: she had not been able to reply sooner, because nobody in her village could write English. Next time I came, she wrote, please could I tell her my flight number, and she would meet me at the airport. Inside, she included a photo of herself, seated on a swing in some sunny northern village with a pixie's shy smile—scarcely older, so it seemed, than her seven-year-old daughter. And at the end of the letter, she wrote, simply, "I hope you can remember that girl name Ead."

More than a year passed before I was back in Bangkok, on what I suspected would be my last visit for some time. On my way there, I sent Ead several letters telling her how to get in touch with me. But when I got to town, there were no messages for me at my small hotel, and none at the *Time* bureau, and none at the local American Express office.

I was still determined, though, to make one last attempt to track her down, and, one bright day, I retraced my steps down the noisy main strip, past the Pizza Hut parlors and the shiny boutiques, past the bars and the sparkling department stores, down to Soi 22. It did not take me long to find the narrow alleyway, and I made my way quickly to the mess of broken shacks. As a little boy skipped past, I showed him the number 193. He pointed to a gate, and I walked hesitantly through. Five or six doors were arranged around a small, dusty courtyard. On one of them, in the corner, I found the number 404. I knocked, and there was a long silence. Then at last a slight teenage girl opened up. Behind her was a tiny, barren room scarcely big enough for the three mattresses on its floor. On the wall a few *Playboy* pinups flapped idly. Two other frightened-looking girls —one of them nursing a baby—looked up at me from where they were sitting on their beds.

"Ead?" I asked. "Do you know Ead?" They looked at each other in bemusement, then chattered something in Thai. I tried again, and one of them said something I couldn't follow. Then the girl at the door motioned me to remain where I was and hurried off into the courtyard. "Ead?" I asked again, and the two others nodded and smiled. One, I was sure, was Ead's little sister.

A couple of minutes later, I heard footsteps behind me. Heart pounding, I turned around. It was not Ead, though, but some other small teenager dressed in a pink Mickey Mouse T-shirt that came hardly lower than her waist. She knew a little English —learned, I assumed, in the nearby bars.

"Hello."

"Hullo."

"Can you tell me, please, where Ead is?"

"She gone."

The finality of the reply sent a chill through me. Then I began to catch her drift. "You mean she's gone back to her village?"

She nodded.

"For long time?"

"Yes."

"Will she be coming back here, do you think?"

"No."

"Never?"

"No."

There was a silence, and no easy words to fill it. "Well," I said, fairly sure she could not follow me, "if you see Ead, could you please tell her that I came to say hello?"

She nodded vaguely, and the girls smiled back at me. Smiling back my thanks, I headed off toward the clatter of the noisy tourist strip. Though sorry to have missed Ead, I was happy too, and relieved, to know that she had freed herself from the gaudy bars and from her nightly commute to the dirty shacks. She had always seemed too thoughtful to remain for long in Soi Cowboy, and in a way, I thought, she had indeed found the great good fortune that the Buddha had promised at the temple.

But as I continued on to my hotel, I began to wonder how much she could ever really go back to her village. It could not be easy, I thought, to be back with her daughter and her Mamá, in the world that she knew, yet set apart by her memories of another world, of the bright lights she had seen and the grand hotels, of the Aussie who had promised to take her away and the stories of a good life in the West. And it must be strange for her to be back inside the family hut, yet alone with her thoughts, and alone with the English she had taught herself.

I often thought of Ead in the months that followed, by herself in her northern village with her jeans, her "Hello Kitty" handbag and her dime-store photo album with a bee on the cover. And I realized, when I did, that I had never left Asia at all; while she, like all the others, could never quite go back.

Acknowledgments

My warmest thanks are due, first of all, to my editors at *Time*, an institution that richly deserves its reputation for civility and hospitality. I know few other companies that would allow a young employee, on the job for less than a year, to take three long vacations in Asia in the space of a year and then to take off six more months to pursue his Eastern interests still further. In the course of that leave, the *Time* family was again as godfatherly as ever: in many a faraway place, colleagues I had never met guarded my mail, lent me their facilities, and gallantly rescued me, with fine meals and local intelligence, from the style to which I was growing accustomed.

I owe a different kind of thanks to all the friends who shared and shaped a few of these adventures, especially Louis Greig, my schoolfriend, doctor, driver, guide, and sidekick, everywhere from Rome to Rangoon, Vegas to Gstaad, and Istanbul to Marrakesh; and Kristin McCloy, a whirling dervish with a pilgrim soul. Thanks are due no less to all those other kind beings who put up with me and put me up in Asia, especially Georges Holzberger in Hong Kong, Lawrence Macdonald in Beijing, my relatives in India, and the many others, named and unnamed, who grace these pages.

In writing up my experiences, I am also, as ever, deeply grateful to all my friends in Santa Barbara, whose generosity and idealism have long indulged, as much as they have humbled, me. In this context, I owe particular thanks to Joe and Donna Woodruff, who sustained me with wonderful food and warm companionship all the time I was writing; and to Elton Hall and Kilian Coster, who frequently dropped whatever they were doing in order to rescue a sorcerer's apprentice from life-and-death struggles with computers, printers, and other modern beasts. I could not hope to find better readers, more discriminating and yet understanding, than Mark Muro and Steve Carlson, who made honesty and sympathy seem good friends after all.

Finally, I would like to thank the people at Knopf, who were gracious enough to reply to an anonymous proposal sent through the mail in a brown envelope, and trusting enough to give this unknown quantity their support. Through the patience and care of his editing, Charles Elliott has taught me a great deal about writing.

My first debt is recorded in the dedication; so too is my last.

Pico Iyer was born in Oxford, England, and educated at Eton, Oxford, and Harvard. For four years he wrote on World Affairs for *Time*, and he continues to contribute essays and reviews to the magazine. His literary pieces have appeared in *Partisan Review*, *Smithsonian*, *The Village Voice*, the *Times Literary Supplement*, and many other publications.

A NOTE ON THE TYPE

The text of this book was composed in Trump
Mediæval. Designed by Professor Georg Trump in the
mid-1950s, Trump Mediæval was cut and cast by the
C. E. Weber Type Foundry of Stuttgart, West Germany.
The roman letter forms are based on classical proto-
types, but Professor Trump has imbued them with his
own unmistakable style. The italic letter forms,
unlike those of so many other type faces, are closely
related to their roman counterparts. The result is a
truly contemporary type, notable for both its legibility
and its versatility.

Composed by New England Typographic Service, Inc.,
Bloomfield, Connecticut
Printed and bound by R. R. Donnelley & Sons,
Harrisonburg, Virginia
Designed by Julie Duquet